IN BEAUTY I WALK

In Beauty I Walk

THE LITERARY ROOTS OF NATIVE AMERICAN WRITING

Edited by Jarold Ramsey
and Lori Burlingame

UNIVERSITY OF NEW MEXICO PRESS

ALBUQUERQUE

Library of Congress Cataloging-in-Publication Data
In beauty I walk : the literary roots of Native American writing /
    edited by Jarold Ramsey and Lori Burlingame.
        p. cm.
Includes bibliographical references (p.   ) and index.
ISBN 978-0-8263-4369-7 (PBK. : ALK. PAPER)
1. American literature—Indian authors.
2. American literature—19th century.
3. American literature—20th century.
4. Indians of North America—Literary collections.
I. Ramsey, Jarold, 1937– II. Burlingame, Lori, 1966–
PS508.I5I53 2008
810.8'0897—dc22

                        2008032104

Book design and type composition
    by Kathleen Sparkes
This book was composed using
    Adobe Warnock OTF PRO 10.5/13.5, 26P.
    Display type is also Warnock.

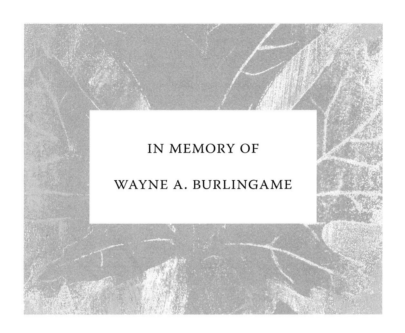

IN MEMORY OF

WAYNE A. BURLINGAME

CONTENTS

PART TWO: Early Modern Native American Literature

PREFACE

When N. Scott Momaday won the Pulitzer Prize in 1969 for his first novel, *House Made of Dawn*, the news of the award caught many Americans by surprise. Few had heard of Momaday, and the notion that an American Indian writer writing about modern Indian life had been awarded the nation's most prestigious literary prize was puzzling, even disconcerting. Readers and scholars were initially at a loss to provide an interpretive context for understanding Momaday's powerful novel—where was it coming from, out of what sources and traditions?

Reviewers did note with satisfaction that the style and narrative strategy of *House Made of Dawn* owed something to the work of William Faulkner—but the implications of the book's title for an understanding of its literary heritage were mostly unnoticed at first. "House made of dawn" is a key refrain in the great Navajo ceremony of healing, the *Night Chant*, and in weaving it into his story (his hero, Abel, is singing it at the story's conclusion), Momaday was self-consciously engaging for his own purposes a masterpiece of traditional Native literature.

In this and other ways, *House Made of Dawn* is rooted in the rich and still too-little-known oral/literary traditions of the American Indians—as are the writings of most of the Native novelists who soon followed his dramatic "breakthrough" with books of their own. Leslie Silko, James Welch, Simon Ortiz, Gerald Vizenor, Linda Hogan, Louise Erdrich, Sherman Alexie, to name just a few, are firmly grounded in the traditional narrative, poetic, and ceremonial traditions of their tribal groups. What might have seemed in 1969 to be an isolated achievement in the case of Momaday's novel can now be understood as part of a fruitful imaginative continuity in American literature, extending from the anonymous Indian stories and songs of pre-Columbian times to the work of Momaday and his successors, on into the twenty-first century. It is, in fact, the oldest such continuity in our collective literary heritage as Americans.

Today's gifted Native writers are also building on and continuing a more recent line of influence and precedent—that of earlier Native *writers*, going back into the eighteenth century. The flourishing over the past fifty years of what has been aptly called "the American Indian Renaissance" has drawn attention—long overdue—to important but little-known predecessors of Momaday, Silko, and their "breakthrough" generation. Before them, there were pioneering novelists, poets, and essayists, striving to use English imaginatively to come to terms with the perplexities of being Native in white America.

The achievements of such trail-blazing figures as John Rollin Ridge, Sarah Winnemucca, Francis La Flesche, Charles Eastman, E. Pauline Johnson, and "Mourning Dove" are all the more remarkable because in their time, there was no lack of Anglo writers eager to write about Native subjects, generally with more enthusiasm than knowledge or insight. But, sometimes with scanty education and little encouragement, these early Native writers persisted because they knew they had their own stories to tell, and they were not willing to let others speak for them. Historically, this line of Native writers culminates around the years of World War II with the powerful novels and short stories of D'Arcy McNickle, who thus stands as the immediate forebear of Momaday and his contemporaries.

This anthology of oral traditional verbal art and early Native writing has grown out of many years of teaching "Indian Literature" and helping our students (from freshmen to graduate students) understand and appreciate the diverse and complicated American Indian literary continuum outlined above. In our experience, it makes no sense to introduce our students to contemporary Native writing without first providing them with some experience of what has come before these brilliant works, literarily speaking. And we would argue that the reverse of this proposition is also true—that to teach and study "classical" traditional Native texts without engaging their remarkable transformations in today's poetry and fiction by Native American writers is short-sighted and misleading.

Today's Native writing is, of course, one manifestation of something much larger: the dramatic emergence of American ethnic writing in the years since World War II. Bold works by African Americans and authors of Hispanic, Latino, and Asian descent have irrevocably expanded and enriched the scope of what Walt Whitman called our singing strength as a nation. "American Lit," once essentially the domain of Anglo writers, will never be the same, a drastic cultural change that is surely good news for us all! Each emergent ethnic literary movement has brought with it features that are distinctively its own, yet authentically American. What is unique about modern Native American writing in these terms is that its cultural and imaginative roots run so deep, so far back, in the American land itself.

Hence the content and format of this anthology. For readers who have already begun their exploration of the challenging territory of Native writing, it will, we hope, provide some useful historical guidance through the terrain. And for those readers (perhaps in introductory "Native Lit" or "Indian Studies" courses) who are just coming into the territory, these readings should make the journey more expeditious and more rewarding, by suggesting what in Native traditions and early writing has led on to the creation of American masterpieces like *House Made of Dawn, Ceremony, Tracks,* and *Fools Crow.*

ACKNOWLEDGMENTS

In compiling and editing this anthology, we are beholden to many—but first and foremost, we feel a debt of gratitude to the traditional Native storytellers and singers and to the early poets and writers whose works we have gathered together here. None of these artists is living today for us to thank (or in many cases even to identify), but because we believe in the literary heritage of Native America as a vital continuum, a futurity as well as a past, we are assigning one-half of our royalties from *In Beauty I Walk* to the American Indian College Fund, for the encouragement of young writers.

Many scholars and editors in the field of Native American studies have helped us in our search for texts and authors. In particular, we want to express our gratitude to A. LaVonne Ruoff, Karl Kroeber, Ken Roemer, the late Howard Horsford, Rob Evans, Karen Kilcup, Dexter Fisher, Jim Ruppert, John Purdy, George Aguilar, and Dell and Virginia Hymes.

We are grateful to the University of Rochester and Eastern Michigan University for institutional support of our endeavors. And to our colleagues and students, we want to say thanks for the indispensable gift of their attention, both assenting and dissenting! Thanks, too, to our editors at University of New Mexico Press, for their understanding of and patience with this long-drawn-out project: to Beth Hadas, who welcomed our initial ideas for the book and kept us going through a mid-course shift of focus; and to Lisa Pacheco, Ben Reed, and Frances Purifoy, who have ably seen us through into print.

To our families—to Lori Burlingame's parents, Wayne and Dorothy Burlingame, and her special friend Spooky, and to Jarold Ramsey's wife, Dorothy, and their children, Kate, Sophia, and John, and their families— we inscribe here the words of gratitude for all your loving support, but what we feel on that score runs deeper than words.

Jarold Ramsey

Madras, Oregon

Lori Burlingame

Ypsilanti, Michigan

Grateful acknowledgment is made to the following for permission to reprint material copyrighted or controlled by them:

American Ethnological Society, for "Lullaby for a Little Girl," by Marius Barbeau, in *The Tsimshian: Their Arts and Music*, ed. Viola Garfield and Paul Wengert. Publications of the America Ethnological Society, 1951.

American Folklore Society, for "The Garden of Eden," "Coyote the Eye-juggler," and "The True Beginning of This Earth," in Isabel Kelly, "Northern Paiute Tales," *Journal of American Folklore* 51 (1938); "Red Horse" in Elsie Clews Parsons, *Kiowa Tales*, Memoirs of the American Folklore Society, Vol. 22 (1921).

Columbia University Press, for "Coyote and the Shadow People," in Archie Phinney, *Nez Perce Texts*, Columbia University Contributions to Anthropology 25 (1934); "Omaha Song for Releasing the Spirit," in Reo Fortune, *Omaha Secret Societies*, Vol. 14 (1932).

Dakota Press, for "She-Who-Dwells-in-the-Rocks," "The Sacred Arrow," and "Iktomi Conquers the Iya," in Ella Deloria, ed. *Dakota Texts*, 1978.

Doubleday and Co./Random House, for "Santo Domingo Corn Dance," "Moon," "Shadow on Snow," "Spring Morning—Santa Fe," "The Hollow," and "Footprints," in Lynn Riggs, *The Iron Dish*, 1930.

"Hard Riding" from *The Hawk Is Hungry and Other Stories*. Edited by Birgit C. Hans. We acknowledge Ms. Antoinette McNickle Vogel and the estate of D'Arcy McNickle.

Barbara Hogenson Agency, for "Scene Seven" of *The Cherokee Night*, by Lynn Riggs, 2003, 1936.

Michigan State University Press for "Resignation," "By an *Ojibwa Female* Pen / To Sisters on a Walk in the Garden, After a Shower," "Lines Written Under Severe Pain and Sickness," "Otagamiad," and "Invocation To My Maternal Grandfather On Hearing His Descent From Chippewa Ancestors Misrepresented," by Jane Johnson Schoolcraft, in *The Literary Voyager, or Muzzeniegun*, by Henry Rowe Schoolcraft, ed. Philip P. Mason, East Lansing.

Newberry Library, for D'Arcy McNickle, "Train Time," published in *The Hawk is Hungry*, ed. Birgit Hans, University of Arizona Press, 1992.

Random House, for "Pima Oriole Songs," from Donald Bahr and Vincent Joseph, "Pima Oriole Songs," in Brian Swann, *Coming to Light: Contemporary Translations of the Native Literatures of North America*, 1994.

The Smithsonian Institution, for Francis La Flesche, "The Song of Flying Crow," "The Old Man Who Weeps," and "Ne-Ma-Ha," in National Anthropological Archives, Fletcher/La Flesche Papers, #4558/48.

Theodore Stern, for "Lulu'laidi," first published in Suzi Jones and Jarold Ramsey, eds., *The Stories We Tell: An Anthology of Oregon Folk Literature*, Oregon State University Press, 1994.

Texas Christian University Press, for "Kiowa Lullaby," "Kiowa Wind Song," "Kiowa Peyote Song," and "Saynday and Smallpox," in Maurice Boyd, *Kiowa Voices*, Vol. 1: *Ceremonial Dances, Rituals, and Songs*; Vol. 2: *Myths, Legends, and Folktales*, 1983.

Thomson Learning and Schocken Books, for Episodes 4, 5, 12, 13, 14, 31, from Paul Radin, *The Trickster*, 1972.

University of Arizona Press, for "Yaqui Song about Bats," in *Yaqui Deer Songs/Maso Bwikan: A Native American Poetry*, by Larry Evers and Felipe Molina © 1987 Arizona Board of Regents; for E. Pauline Johnson, "A Red Girl's Reasoning," in *The Moccasin Maker*, introduction, annotations, and bibliography by A. LaVonne Ruoff, 1987, 1913; and John Oskison, "The Problem of Old Harjo," *The Singing Spirit: Early Short Stories by North American Indians*, ed. Bernd C. Peyer, 1989.

University of California Press, for "Songs to Pull Down the Rain," "Papago Corn Song," and "Papago Animal Songs," in Ruth Underhill, *Singing for Power*, 1938.

University of Chicago Press, for "Apache Courting Song," in
   Morris Opler, *Apache Life Way*, Publications in Anthropology,
   Ethnographic Series, 1969.
University of Nebraska Press, for "Blackfoot Genesis," "The Ghost Wife,"
   and "The Origins of the Beaver Medicine," in George Bird Grinnell,
   Blackfoot Lodge Tales, 1962; "The Stone Boy," from James R. Walker,
   Lakota Myths, ed. Elaine Jahner, 1983; "The Bear Man," from George
   Bird Grinnell, *Pawnee Hero Stories and Folktales*, 1961; J. Barre
   Toelken and Tacheeni Scott, "Coyote and the Prairie Dogs," in Karl
   Kroeber, ed., *Traditional Literatures of the American Indians: Texts
   and Interpretations*, 1984, 1997; "High Horse's Courting," from
   John Neihardt, *Black Elk Speaks*, 1979; "Scar-face and the Origin of
   the Sweat-lodge," from Clark Wissler and D. C. Duvall, *Mythology
   of the Blackfoot Indians*, 1995; "William Sherman," in Francis
   La Flesche, *The Middle Five: Indian Schoolboys of the Omaha
   Tribe*, 1900, 1978; Charles Eastman, "An Indian Boy's Training"
   and "First Impressions of Civilization," in *Indian Boyhood*, 1991,
   1902; for "Going East," in Luther Standing Bear, *My People the
   Sioux*, 1975, 1928; for Letters 61–63, headnotes and footnotes in
   Alexander Posey, *The Fus Fixico Letters*, ed. Daniel F. Littlefield Jr.
   and Carol A. Petty Hunter, Foreword by A. LaVonne Ruoff, 1993; for
   Zitkala-Ša, "The School Days of an Indian Girl," in *American Indian
   Stories*, Foreword by Dexter Fisher, 1979, 1921; for Chapter 7: "The
   'Ladies' and the 'Squaw' Race," in Mourning Dove (Humi-shu-ma),
   *Cogewea, the Half-Blood: A Depiction of the Great Montana Cattle
   Range*, Notes and Biographical Sketch by Lucullus McWhorter,
   Introduction by Dexter Fisher, 1981, 1927.
University of Nevada Press, for excerpts from Sarah Winnemucca,
   Life Among the Piutes: Their Wrongs and Claims, ed. Mrs. Horace
   Mann (1883), Foreword by Catharine S. Fowler, 1994.
University of Oklahoma Press, for excerpt of *The Life and Adventures of
   Joaquín Murieta, the Celebrated California Bandit* (1854), 1977.
University of Pennsylvania Press and Dell Hymes, for "Seal and Her
   Younger Brother," "Chinook Jargon Song," and "Workingman's
   Song for His Firstborn Son," in Dell Hymes, *'In Vain I Tried to
   Tell You': Essays in Native American Ethnopoetics*, 1981.
University of Toronto Press, for "A Cry from an Indian Wife,"
   "As Red Men Die," "The Song My Paddle Sings," "Penseroso,"

"Ojistoh," "The Songster," "The Corn Husker," "The Quill Worker,"
"Rondeau: Morrow-Land," "To C.H.W.," "Heidleburgh," and
"A Red Girl's Reasoning," in E. Pauline Johnson (Tekahionwake),
Collected Poems and Selected Prose, ed. Carole Gerson and
Veronica Strong-Boag, 2002.

University of Washington Press, University of Washington Publications
in Anthropology, for "Chinook Jargon Song" in Melville Jacobs,
"Texts in Chinook Jargon," 7, 1, (1926); "Wishram Naming
Ceremonies," from Leslie Spier and Edward Sapir, *Wishram
Ethnography*, 3, 1 (1930).

University Press of New England and Judith A. Ranta, for "Indian
Pledge," in *The Life and Writings of Betsey Chamberlain: Native
American Mill Worker*, 2003.

U.S. Bureau of American Ethnology, *Bulletin of American Ethnology*,
for "Papago Vision Song" and "Papago Running Song," in Frances
Densmore, *Papago Music*, Vol. 90 (1929).

Washington Academy of Sciences, for J. W. B. Hewitt, "The
Re-quickening Address of the Iroquois Condolence Council," in
Journal of the Washington Academy of Sciences, March 15, 1944.

Wadsworth for "Papago Vision Song" and "How the Papago Got Corn,"
in Ruth Underhill, *Papago Woman*, 1979.

Wenner-Gren Foundation, for "Badger and Coyote Were Neighbors," in
Melville Jacobs, *The Content and Style of an Oral Literature*, 1959.

PART ONE

Native American Oral Traditional Literature

INTRODUCTION

[handwritten marginalia: Good god. What a wrong white dude.]

[handwritten marginalia, left margin: very unfortunate]

In "The Gift Outright," Robert Frost's celebrated poem about the serial occupation of the American land by foreigners who became, in the process, "Americans," he imagines "the land vaguely realizing westward, / But still unstoried, artless, unenhanced. . . ." (Frost 1979, 348). It's an unforgettable image and true to history from a Eurocentric point of view. But from a Native American perspective, Frost's lines convey a basic falsehood about the human history of this nation. By now surely (if not in Frost's time), we do have some awareness that our landscapes *were* storied, enhanced by thousands of years of verbal, pictorial, and musical art, region by region, before the Europeans arrived with the "enhancements" of their cultures. It's taken us a long time to begin to appreciate this Native legacy of story, song, and image, and lamentably much of it has been lost through neglect and the disruption of Indian cultures. But what survives and carries forward—specifically in the form of stories, songs, and ceremonies—is a great (if still-neglected) treasury of the imagination for all Americans. What follows, in part 1 of *In Beauty I Walk*, is a modest sampling of that treasury.

As well as carrying on in the collective memories of tribal groups, oral/traditional stories, songs, and other materials have been recorded by anthropologists, folklorists, and linguists according to their professional purposes since the nineteenth century. Most of this recorded material has languished unexamined in libraries, archives, and academic journals, but at least it *was* preserved, for which we can be grateful. The appearance of new Indian writers and poets in the 1960s and the ensuing surge of critical interest in their work has had the effect of drawing the attention of scholars, editors, and anthologists to the traditional Native literatures—so that the "American Indian Renaissance" of the last fifty years has been a true literary renaissance, not only yielding a wonderful array of new writings by Native Americans from every region of America and Canada, but also inspiring a rebirth of interest in the traditional literatures as well. The happy point here is that the two movements are complementary, each vitally encouraging and energizing the other.

The relatively new academic field of Native American literary studies embraces both the new and the old, and part of its endeavor is to study the lines of continuity between the two. Another focus on the part of critics and theorists (and for that matter translators and editors) has been on the formal differences between the conventional premises of our print-based Western literature and the premises of the traditional Native repertories. Where in earlier times Native American songs and stories were generally presented to readers according to Western conventions (stories being formatted as "fiction," for example), now there is a concerted effort to understand the literary assumptions that shaped the old stories and songs and present them on the page accordingly. Such work defines the critical methodology known as "ethnopoetics."

Consider for a moment how different the assumptions and "rules" of print-based literary works and those in Native and other orally based literatures really are. Given what readers generally assume about how imaginative writing "works," a myth narrative from, say, the Lakota Sioux seems to come to a printed format from three removes.

1. In its origins and throughout its original life in tribal culture, its existence was *oral*—that is, it lived solely in dramatic performances by storytellers and in the memories of tribespeople who heard it told. One way of defining the essence of oral literature is to note that if for some reason portions of it stop being performed, and the people forget them, they vanish utterly—the tragic fate of much of the Native repertories because of cultural disruption. It's no exaggeration to say that the orality of traditional literature conditions everything about it.

2. Not only did our Lakota story once exist orally; it was essentially *traditional* in the sense that it existed not as the self-expressive and datable creation of an author (as in the print-literature scheme of things), but

rather as the shared, cherished, anonymous property of the people who knew it, who learned from and were entertained by it, and who passed it on to succeeding generations. It should be obvious, given these circumstances, that such works would not exist in fixed, "authoritative" forms but rather would evolve in retellings over many years into different versions, both within one cultural group and among cultural groups. There are probably several recorded versions of our hypothetical Lakota narrative—and also probably analogs to it in the traditions of other Sioux communities and those of their allies.

3. A third point of fundamental difference between "book literature" and the oral repertories of the Indians is perhaps the most problematic— namely, differences of *culture*. If *culture* is definable as the sum of all the tacit assumptions a community of people make about who they are, what they have distinctively in common, what are the "right" (that is, the customary) ways of doing things, and so on, then the importance of cultural considerations in attempting to understand, say, our myth narrative from the Lakota people becomes very clear.

First of all, there is the central cultural fact that the story had its whole existence in the Lakota language: how to translate it into a radically different language, English, with as little loss and distortion of meaning as possible? Further, as a myth, how did the story fit into the Lakota mythological and religious order? If its protagonist strikes today's readers as being a "culture hero," in thinking this are we perhaps imposing our own cultural notions of the heroic onto the Indian story, thereby distorting it? If the story seems to have humorous moments, how can we be sure that what seems amusing in it would have amused traditional Lakota audiences? Furthermore, in terms of literary conventions relating to such important matters as characterization, point of view, plot, and narrative method (and in the case of a Lakota song text, such poetic issues as meter and rhythm, rhyme, and poetic form), what can readers do to understand the work as much as possible on its own Indian terms, without reinventing it according to their own assumptions about how literary entities work?

These are challenging theoretical and critical questions, not only for scholars and translators (and editors of anthologies!), but for anyone who wants to read and understand works from Native traditions. The best that can be said is that much has been learned in recent years—in large part because of ethnopoetic theory—to the effect that such questions

must be asked relentlessly. And if all the answers are not in hand (not by any means!), there at least some practical guidelines to follow. On the issue of English translations of Native-language originals, for example, texts translated directly from Native performances or from linguistically sound transcripts are the accepted ideal. Conversely, English "versions" in the forms of retellings, paraphrases, and summaries remote from and unaccountable to the Native originals are not to be trusted. In the selections making up the "traditional" part of this anthology, we have tried to avoid the latter and include the former as much as possible.

On matters of cultural difference, the best guideline is the obvious one—to inform oneself as much as possible about the traditional culture of the people whose stories and songs are being read. This is the province of *ethnography*—"writing about culture"—and if older Native Americans still joke about how many ethnographers it takes to make a reservation, the fact is that sound ethnographic commentary is available for nearly every American Indian group, and it can be indispensable for literary purposes. In the case of our Lakota myth text, consulting ethnographic work on the Lakotas should turn up illuminating details about their religious beliefs, about their ceremonies (which might be alluded to in the myth), about when and how they formally recited their myth repertory, and so on. And there is often interpretive profit in simply reading other texts from a tribe's oral literature: as in any literary investigation, related imaginative works have a way of shedding light on one another.

Again, a major challenge in fairly understanding Native verbal art is that we incline to read it in conformity with our own familiar literary expectations. What follows is full of rather sweeping generalizations that need to be tested and qualified on individual cases, but maybe these propositions will be helpful along the way through part 1 of *In Beauty I Walk*, and beyond. They are in part adapted from Jarold Ramsey's "A Note on Reading Indian Stories" (Jones and Ramsey 1994, xxiv–xxv).

1. Indian stories are not to be approached as children's stories, as nineteenth-century and early-twentieth-century editors and readers often did, although they do often appeal to children's imaginations. In their original performances, they were enjoyed by all ages together.

2. Many traditional narratives are myths, unfolding the beginnings of the world, and are thus set in a "myth age" when reality was still unfixed and important elements of reality, both good and bad, were being established for the real People yet to come by transforming figures like Coyote

as they traveled around. Often, mythic events occur under very earthy, even obscene circumstances, especially, of course, when tricksters like Coyote are involved. The separation of "sacred" and "profane" in Judeo-Christian culture is absent in traditional Native cultures: their devotion to the sacred is no less strong than with Anglos, but what is sacred to them is closely connected to earthly life and the here and now.

3. If modern works of literature tend to concentrate on individuals, very often heroically at odds with their societies, in traditional Native literatures the doings of individual actors are almost always meant to be judged and understood in terms of their relations with their societies. A trickster's self-seeking mischief may be amusing, scene by scene, but in the final analysis it usually registers as a threat to the collective good; in the case of a healing ritual like the Navajo *Night Chant*, the recovery of the ritual's individual subject implicates the welfare of his/her whole community and requires everybody's sympathetic participation in the healing process—"one for all, all for one." Individuals are fundamentally bound to their human communities, and also to the natural and spiritual realms as well, comprising what Paula Gunn Allen (1992) has aptly called "the sacred hoop" of life, in which human existence finds its ultimate meaning (54–75).

4. As with all oral literature, Indian storytelling and song rely considerably on *repetition*. In stories, crucial events happen in sequences of repeated actions, usually in fours or fives depending on tribal convention, building to the "last one," which is decisive. In songs and poetry (and ceremonial texts as well), the lyrics are often structured by repetition with variations, so that meaning seems to accumulate by increments—as in the great Navajo *Night Chant*. Repetition is generally a negative in Western literary schemes, but editors of Native texts who excise repeated elements in the interest of brevity are falsifying the Indianness of the texts in doing so.

5. The style of traditional Indian stories (and, for that matter, songs) tends to be terse, unelaborated, more dramatic than discursive in presentation (in stories, this means emphasis on dialogue), and less overtly descriptive than in Western literature. And due to the traditional, anonymous basis of Native verbal art, interior monologues and first-person meditations by the author or his/her persona are rare.

6. In both storytelling and song, there is likely to be a reliance on conventional phrases and verbal formulae, which are of course the stock-in-trade of all oral literatures, "there" for the using by skillful recitalists and singers.

7. Likewise, characterization tends to be conventional rather than individualized or innovative. Stock figures like Coyote (trickster/transformer), Eagle (exemplary hero and leader), Bear (dangerously unpredictable), and Raccoon (spoiled brat) run all through a given tribe's repertory of stories. Given that most of these personages have the names of animals, how should they be visualized? It's a tricky question: the best answer is probably to assume that figures like Coyote or Eagle have human form most of the time but that their salient characteristics are those of their animal namesakes.

8. Apart from what they do and say, the emotions of characters generally must be inferred from the situation at hand. Motivation is usually left undefined; action is more important than motive. American Indians in traditional times who knew their tribe's entire "mythbody" (as the Nez Perce scholar Archie Phinney called it) undoubtedly had a richer and more nuanced understanding of characters in the stories than we can have, knowing only a few of their adventures. But knowing, say, even a few Navajo stories about Ma'i (Coyote) will help to illuminate what goes on in any one of them.

9. The basis in orality and performance of all these works means that in their original forms they were calculated, so to speak, *for performance* by skilled storytellers and singers, who knew how to make the most of dramatic and performative possibilities inherent in the works at hand. For us as readers, even in translation, even in the medium of printed pages, something of their oral/dramatic qualities can be appreciated by reading the texts aloud.

But whether they are read aloud or silently, traditional Native works like the following can be accessible and enjoyable today if they are read carefully and imaginatively with an informed awareness that their origins are in cultures and languages very different from what we customarily assume to be in effect when we pick up a short story or a poem. That despite these differences they can speak to us in the here and now testifies to the verbal and imaginative artistry of the tribal storytellers, ritualists, and singers of long ago, whose direct inheritors are the Indian writers featured in part 2 of this collection, and their modern successors.

Creation Myths

The word "myth" has acquired so much loose baggage that it is tempting to abandon it to the junkyard of corrupted words and start afresh. But properly understood and used, it is still the right word to use to describe sacred narratives that tell the people who know them who they are, why they inhabit their homeland, and how to live there. Considered in this light, Native creation myths are, in their very different ways, like imaginative charters, laying down in story form the original whys and wherefores of a given tribal group's collective life in their particular world.

Comparisons between Native creation stories (or cosmogonies) and the episodes of the biblical book of Genesis are probably inevitable, and potentially illuminating, being expressive of profound differences between Judeo-Christian conceptions of reality and Indian beliefs. When the Klamath story of creation begins, for example, the basic stuff of the world is already at hand; what matters is the creation of the Klamath world, centered on Klamath Lake (in southern Oregon). The work of creation is performed not by a single all-knowing, omnipotent Creator but rather as the result of a genial competition between two myth figures, Kamukampts (who is also the Klamath trickster) and Pocket Gopher. And the majestic prioritized order of creation in Genesis, building up to the making of humankind, is replaced in the Indian story with a much more casual, improvised-seeming sequence of steps. The invention of games and amusements, for example, comes prior to the creation of game animals before, at last, almost as an afterthought, the appearance of people in the Klamath country is noted. *What is not an afterthought here, or in any other Indian creation myth, is the story's emphasis on the essential goodness and bounty of the life the first people have been called into. The two creators "listened, and heard the sound of people talking, and of children laughing and playing. The people increased very rapidly, and the animals and plants in the mountain multiplied" (Curtis 1970c, 210).*

Not that the world is mythically established in such Indian stories as this one (or the Seneca and Keresan equivalents given below) as necessarily perfect, or finished. *Reality in Indian myth narratives is, on the contrary, understood as plastic, unfinished, often requiring the services of a transformer, who like Old Man in the Blackfoot cosmogony, or Kamukampts in subsequent Klamath episodes, travels around, fixing things up and setting precedents on an improvisational basis—even, regrettably, the precedent for death! Still, as narrative charters, setting forth how it all came about for the People, these stories eloquently convey a conviction that "ever since," life has been beneficent and good, if not perfect; richly supplied and worthwhile, if not necessarily carefree and painless.*

[margin handwriting: Reality unfinished]

Creation of the Klamaths (Klamath)

There was no land, only a great lake. Kamukamts came from the north in a canoe. It floated along. It stopped. He shook it, but could not move it. He looked down, and in the water he saw the roof of a house. It was the house of Pocket Gopher. Gopher looked up. Then Kamukamts went down into the house, and they talked.

Kamukamts said, "You had better be thinking of what is the best thing to do."

"Yes, I am thinking of that now," replied Gopher.

"If you can plan anything better than I can do, you shall be the older brother," promised Kamukamts. "What kind of food are we going to have?"

Gopher opened his mouth to yawn, and fish, roots, and berries came forth.

"It seems that you will be the elder brother," said Kamukamts.

That night Gopher caused his companion to sleep, and he burrowed under the bottom of the lake and made it bulge up into hills and mountains, which raised their tops above the surface. In the morning

[margin handwriting: Food land]

he said, "You had better go and look around!" When Kamukamts went out he was astonished. Gopher asked what should become of his house, and Kamukamts replied, "It will always remain as the oldest mountain [Modoc Point]."

"What will our children have for amusement?" asked Kamukamts. They played the game of throwing spears at a mark. They threw them, and their targets were hills. Kamukamts's spear knocked off the top of Bare Island, and so it is today. Then they invented all the other games. *games*

Gopher asked, "What will live on the mountains?"

"Mountain lions, bears, elk, deer." Kamukamts named all the animals, both beasts and birds. *animals*

"What will grow in the mountains?"

"I will walk over the earth and see what I can do," replied Kamukamts. So he went about and selected homes for the different tribes, and in each *plants* territory he placed something which was to characterize that particular tribe, such as obsidian in the Paiute country, marble in the Shasta country, and tules in the Klamath country. Then he looked about and saw smoke.

Kamukamts said, "What is the matter, I wonder? I see smoke here and there."

And Gopher replied, "You have beaten me. You are the eldest brother." *people created by* For he knew that the smoke was from the fires of people brought into being by Kamukamts. They listened, and heard the sound of people talking, and of children laughing and playing. The people increased very rapidly, and the animals and plants on the mountains multiplied.

Trickster

—Edward S. Curtis (1970c, 210)

The Blackfoot Genesis (Blackfoot)

See allusions to this myth in James Welch's novel of nineteenth-century Blackfoot life, Fools Crow, *notably to the myth's emphasis on the moral significance of human mortality as something that binds people together: "People must die, that they may always be sorry for one another."*

All animals of the Plains at one time heard and knew him, and all birds of the air heard and knew him. All things that he had made understood him, when he spoke to them—the birds, the animals, and the people.

Old Man was traveling about, south of here, making the people. He came from the south, traveling north, making animals and birds as he passed along. He made the mountains, prairies, timber, and brush first. So he went along, traveling northward, making things as he went, putting rivers here and there, and falls on them, putting red paint here and there in the ground—fixing up the world as we see it today.

He made the Milk River [the Teton] and crossed it, and, being tired, went up a little hill and lay down to rest. As he lay on his back, stretched out on the ground, with arms extended, he marked himself out with stones—the shape of his body, head, legs, arms, and everything. There you can see those rocks today. After he had rested, he went on northward, and stumbled over a knoll and fell down on his knees. Then he said, "You are a bad thing to be stumbling against," so he raised up two large buttes there, and named them the Knees, and they are called so to this day. He went further north, and with some of the rocks he carried with him he built the Sweet Grass Hills.

Old Man covered the plains with grass for the animals to feed on. He marked off a piece of ground, and in it he made to grow all kinds of roots and berries—camas, wild carrots, wild turnips, sweet-root, bitterroot, sarvis berries, bull berries, cherries, plums, and rosebuds. He put trees in the ground. He put all kinds of animals on the ground. When he made the bighorn with its big head and horns, he made it out in the prairie. It did not seem to travel easily on the prairie; it was awkward and could not go fast. So he took it by one of its horns, and led it up into the mountains, and turned it loose; and it skipped about among the rocks, and went up fearful places with ease. So he said, "This is the place that suits you; this is what you are fitted for, the rocks and the mountains."

While he was in the mountains, he made the antelope out of dirt, and turned it loose, to see how it would go. It ran so fast that it fell over some rocks and hurt itself. He saw that this would not do, and took the antelope down on the prairie, and turned it loose, and it ran away fast and gracefully, and he said, "This is what you are suited to."

One day Old Man determined that he would make a woman and a child; so he formed them both—the woman and the child, her son—of clay. After he had moulded the clay in human shape, he said to the clay, "You must be people," and then he covered it up and left it, and went away. The next morning he went to the place and took the covering off, and saw that the clay shapes had changed a little. The second morning there was still more change, and the third still more. The fourth morning he went to the place, took the covering off, looked at the images, and told them to rise and walk; and they did so. They walked down to the river with their Maker, and then he told them that his name was *Na'pi*, Old Man.

As they were standing by the river, the woman said to him, "How is it? Will we always live here, will there be no end to it?" He said, "I have never thought of that. We will have to decide it. I will take this buffalo chip and throw it in the river. If it floats, when people die, in four days they will become alive again; they will die for only four days. But if it sinks, there will be an end to them."

He threw the chip into the river, and it floated. The woman turned and picked up a stone and said, "No, I will throw this stone in the river; if it floats we will always live, if it sinks people must die, that they may always be sorry for each other." The woman threw the stone into the water, and it sank. "There," said Old Man, "you have chosen. There will be an end to them."

It was not many nights after, that the woman's child died, and she cried a great deal for it. She said to Old Man, "Let us change this. The law that you first made, let that be a law." He said, "Not so. What is made law must be law. We will undo nothing that we have done. The child is dead, but it cannot be changed. People will have to die."

That is how we came to be people. It is he who made us.

—George Bird Grinnell (1962, 137–39)

you belong hair
to a certain place.

The Woman Who Fell from the Sky (Seneca)

The conflict in this narrative between the good twin and the evil twin is expressive of an Iroquoian viewpoint, that reality is to be understood as a dynamic interplay of good and bad elements. Each twin can modify the other's innovations, but neither can nullify what the other has brought into reality. Thus it would have been very nice to have "two-way" rivers to navigate, according to Little Sprout's benevolent plan, but although Flint makes the rivers all flow just one way, at least some of the time canoeists can "go with the flow"! The point is that reality is a mixture of good and bad, difficult and easy.

A long time ago human beings lived high up in what is now called heaven. They had a great and illustrious chief.

It so happened that this chief's daughter was taken very ill. [. . .] All the people were very anxious as to the outcome of her illness. Every known remedy was tried in an attempt to cure her, but none had any effect.

Near the lodge of this chief stood a great tree, which every year bore corn used for food. One of the friends of the chief had a dream, in which he was advised to tell the chief that in order to cure his daughter he must lay her beside this tree, and that he must have the tree dug up. This advice was carried out to the letter. While the people were at work and the young woman lay there, a young man came along. He was very angry and said, "It is not at all right to destroy this tree. Its fruit is all that we have to live on." With this remark he gave the young woman who lay there ill a shove with his foot, causing her to fall into the hole that had been dug.

Now, that hole opened into this world, which was then all water, on which floated waterfowl of many kinds. There was no land at this time. It came to pass that as these waterfowl saw this young woman falling they shouted, "Let us receive her," whereupon they, at least some of them, joined their bodies together, and the young woman fell on this platform of their bodies. When they were wearied they asked, "Who will volunteer to care for this woman?" The great Turtle then took her, and when he got tired of holding her, he in turn asked who would take his place.

At last the question arose as to what they should do to provide her with a permanent resting place in this world. Finally it was decided to prepare the earth, on which she would live in the future. To do this it was determined that soil from the bottom of the sea should be brought up and placed on the broad, firm [shell] of the turtle, where it would increase in size to such an extent that it would accommodate all the creatures that would be produced thereafter. After much discussion the toad was finally persuaded to dive to the bottom of the waters in search of soil. Bravely making the attempt, he succeeded in bringing up soil from the depths of the sea. This was carefully spread over the [shell] of the Turtle, and at once both began to grow in size and depth.

After the young woman recovered from her illness from which she suffered when she was cast down from the upper world, she built herself a shelter, in which she lived quite contentedly. In the course of time she brought forth a girl baby, who grew rapidly in size and intelligence.

When the daughter had grown to young womanhood, the mother and she were accustomed to dig wild potatoes. Her mother had said to her that in doing this she must face the west at all times. Before long the young daughter gave signs that she was about to become a mother. Her mother reproved her, saying that she had violated the injunction not to face the east, as her condition showed that she had faced the wrong way while digging potatoes. It is said that the breath of the West Wind had entered her person, causing conception.

When the days of her delivery were at hand, she overheard twins within her body in a hot debate as to which should be born first and as to the proper place of exit, one declaring that he was going to emerge through the armpit of his mother, the other saying that he would emerge in the natural way. The first one born, who was of a reddish color, was called Othagwenda; that is, Flint. The other, who was light in color, was called Djuskaha; that is, the Little Sprout.

The grandmother of the twins liked Djuskaha and hated the other; so they cast Othagwenda into a hollow tree some distance from the lodge.

The boy that remained in the lodge grew very rapidly, and soon was able to make himself bows and arrows and to go out to hunt in the vicinity. Finally, for several days he returned home without his bows and arrows. At last he was asked why he had to have a new bow and arrows every morning. He replied that there was a young boy in a hollow tree in the neighborhood who used them. The grandmother inquired where the tree stood, and he told her; whereupon then they went there and brought the other boy home with them.

When the boys had grown to man's estate, they decided that it was necessary for them to increase the size of their island, so they agreed to start out together, afterward separating to create forests and lakes and other things. They parted as agreed, Othagwenda going westward and Djuskaha eastward. In the course of time, on returning they met in their lodge at night, then agreeing to go the next day to see what they each had made.

First they went west to see what Othagwenda had made. It was found that he had made the country all rocks and full of ledges, and also a mosquito which was very large. Djuskaha asked the mosquito to run, in order that he might see whether the insect could fight. The mosquito ran, and sticking his bill through a sapling, made it fall, at which Djuskaha said, "That will not be right, for you would kill the people who are about to come." So, seizing him, he rubbed him down in his hands, causing him to become very small; then he blew on the mosquito, whereupon he flew away. He also modified some of the other animals which his brother had made.

After returning to their lodge, they agreed to go the next day to see what Djuskaha had fashioned. On visiting the east the next day, they found that Djuskaha had made a large number of animals which were so fat that they could hardly move; that he had made the sugar-maple trees to drop syrup; that he had made the sycamore tree to bear fine fruit; that the rivers were so formed that half the water flowed upstream and the other half downstream.

Then the reddish-colored brother, Othagwenda, was greatly displeased with what his brother had made, saying that the people who were about to come would live too easily and be too happy. So he shook violently the various animals—the bears, deer, and turkeys—causing them to become small at once, a characteristic which attached itself to their descendants. He also caused the sugar maple to drop sweetened water only, and the fruit of the sycamore to become small and useless; and lastly, he caused the water of the rivers to flow in only one direction, because the original plan would make it too easy for the human beings who were about to come to navigate the streams.

The inspection of each other's work resulted in a deadly disagreement between the brothers, who finally came to grips and blows, and Othagwenda was killed in the fierce struggle.

—Jeremiah Curtin and
J. N. B. Hewitt (1918, 460 ff.)

Saynday Brings the People Out (Kiowa)

In his The Way to Rainy Mountain, *the Kiowa writer N. Scott Momaday retells this myth and reflects on its implications for Kiowa history.*

Saynday was coming along in darkness upon the face of the sunless earth. He was both lonely and curious as he wandered in a world without people and animals. Stumbling along, he stretched out his arms and felt something. Carefully probing with his hands and fingers, he recognized the rough surface of a cottonwood tree. Tired and discouraged, Saynday stopped to rest.

As Saynday rested he heard strange sounds coming from beneath the hollow cottonwood tree. Rapping on it, he called out, "Who is there? Who are you?"

"We are people. We want to come out into your world. Help us," came the answer.

Surprised and excited, Saynday reached through an opening of the hollow tree into the underground darkness. Holding out his hand, he clasped the hand of the person nearest him and instructed everyone else to do the same, thus forming a chain of people.

Saynday pulled the first person through a hole in the trunk made by a Sawpole (Owl), and he watched in amazement as the people poured out like ants. After some had emerged, a pregnant female became stuck in the opening of the hole and could move neither forward nor backward. She blocked the way for those behind her and no more came out.

Those who had crawled outside gathered together and looked up at Saynday. Bending down and smiling at them, he said, "My name is Saynday. I am happy to see you! As your friend *say-gei-do*, I will teach you how to live in this world, how to find food to eat, and how to be happy. I will be your Uncle Saynday and you will be my people."

Those who came from the hollow cottonwood tree became the Principal People known as the Kiowas. And because the pregnant female prevented all of the people from coming out into the world, the Kiowas have always been a small tribe.

—Maurice Boyd (1983b, 14)

The Keresan Emergence Story (Keresan/Pueblo)

In her great novel Ceremony, *the Laguna Pueblo writer Leslie Silko re-creates this narrative, versions of which are common to all the Keresan-speaking Pueblo communities of New Mexico. In effect, Silko's retelling of this and other traditions establishes an intricate subtext for her fictional narrative about the recovery of Tayo from his World War II traumas: the mythic subtext point-for-point prefigures and shapes the main text.*

A long time ago there in the north at the place of emergence, below there our mother, corn mother, worked miracles. Everything that has names developed, the sun and moon, and the stars and rain storms and spirits and katsinas and the shamans and game and the people were completed, then our mother Nau'ts'ity'i and our father I'tcts'ity'i said, "How is it," said our mother Nau'ts'ity'i, "Is it not yet done? Shall we not put out our children?" The our father I'tcts'ity'i spoke thus, "No," said he. "First I shall divide water and land." Then spoke our mother Nau'ts'ity'i, "Go ahead," said she. Then our father I'tcts'ity'i said, "Let me try to see," said I'tcts'ity'i.

Then to the mountain top went our father I'tcts'ity'i. Then there below he looked around. Then he divided water and land. He shook it. There it was shaking. Then he looked at it. Then he said, "Earth and water have become good," thus he said. Then he also said, "Only the earth will be ripe," said I'tcts'ity'i, our father. Then again the earth he turned inwards (towards himself). When he turned it there was a light breeze. Then next he turned water and sky, both. Then again there was a light breeze.

Then said our father, "Let me look at the earth and at the sky," said he. Then was sitting on top of the clouds in his turn our father I'tcts'ity'i. Then he said, "Enough," said he, "now it is good," said he. Then he made writing on something like a stone. There below it was rounded on one side, on the lower side it was square. Then there in the middle he wrote down numbers, seven numbers. As far as six he wrote them down. Then spoke our father I'tcts'ity'i. Then he rested from his work.

Then in his turn he went to tell our mother Nau'ts'ity'i. Then went down our father. Then there below he arrived at the place of emergence. Then, "Here I come, Gaau'na," said our father. "It is good," said our mother Nau'ts'ity'i. Then she spoke to him. She asked him, "How is this? What did you see?" said our mother Nau'ts'ity'i. Then spoke our father I'tcts'ity'i, "Good has become the earth and the sky," said he. "Only the earth will be dry. Then it will be ready for the people and the cattle and the game to go out to the top from below."

Then next spoke our father I'tcts'ity'i. He questioned her, "How is it?" said he, "Gaau'na, did you finish?" Then spoke our mother Nau'ts'ity'i, "Yes," said she. Then said our father I'tcts'ity'i, "Then go on! Hand me the seeds. First you will hand me the grass seeds and everything with which the mountains and the earth will be beautiful." Then she gave him the seeds. Our father went up out again with the clouds. Then already his body was transparent. First when (up) he went out, to the right-hand side he went. To the northwest and southwest and southeast and northeast and also to the middle north. When he reached the north he went up to the middle west and next to the middle east. When he had gone there he finished. Then again our father I'tcts'ity'i took a rest.

Then again he went there to the north. At the place of emergence he arrived. Then he spoke, "I came here, Gaau'na," said our father I'tcts'ity'i. "How is it?" said our mother Nau'ts'ity'i. "Did you finish everything?"— "Yes," said I'tcts'ity'i. Then spoke again our father, "I shall try this first and I shall see on which side the sun will be fitting," thus said our father I'tcts'ity'i. "Go ahead then," said our mother Nau'ts'ity'i. Then she opened it. There the sun was inside. At that time everything was dark. Then was spoken to the sun by our father I'tcts'ity'i, "Come, my child, come out. Go ahead. Try it. See how large the earth is." Then he put it up there. Then he spoke, "Here you will fit," said our father I'tcts'ity'i. Then he turned the sky and the earth, both inward (towards himself). Then it was as though that way in the north the sun came out.

Then our father I'tcts'ity'i spoke, "It is not fitting that the sun is in the north. Go ahead, next time from the west," said our father I'tcts'ity'i. Again he put it up. Then again he turned the earth and the sky. Then spoke again our father I'tcts'ity'i, "It is not yet fitting," said he. Then he put up the sun from the south. Again he turned earth and sky. Then he said, "It is not yet fitting." Next up from the east put up the sun our father I'tcts'ity'i. He put it up there and again he turned the earth and the sky. Then indeed it was good and fitting. Then again I'tcts'ity'i took a rest.

Then he went to the north again. Then our mother Nau'ts'ity'i he met her. Then he told her to put out the people and the cattle and the game and the katsinas and everything he had made. Then said Nau'ts'ity'i, "It is good," said our mother Nau'ts'ity'i. Then first the crops, the fruits and grasses, and all kinds of plants; next our father I'tcts'ity'i, "It is good," said he. "Now with this the people and the cattle and the game and the katsinas will not starve," said our mother Nau'ts'ity'i.

Next our father I'tcts'ity'i said, "It is good," said he. "First the crops will be well ripe and also the plants will be well ripe," said our father I'tcts'ity'i. "It is good," said our mother Nau'ts'ity'i. "Now let us wait four days. Then it will be ready."—"Then after four days," said our father I'tcts'ity'i, "first I shall put out the moon and stars and the rain-storms and the game."—"It is good," said our mother Nau'ts'ity'i. "Go ahead," said she.

Then they were ready and he put them out. "First to the northeast up for a good while there they will go," said our father I'tcts'ity'i. Then they went. Then up there in the east came out the stars and the moon. Then it was really good. Then again our father I'tcts'ity'i took a rest. He was sitting on the clouds above. He was on top of a mountain. From there he saw below the earth and the plants. Then he said, "Enough," said he. Then he went down to the east. Then again from the east he looked. Again he said, "It is good," said our father I'tcts'ity'i. Again early next he looked from the south and again spoke our father I'tcts'ity'i, "It is good," said he. Again early next he looked from the west. Then he said, "Enough," said he, "it is good," said he.

Then next early in the morning there above from the middle of the sky he saw everything all around below. There earth and sky lay in touch (the horizon). "Enough, it is good. Now they can all go out," said our father I'tcts'ity'i. Then he went down there. Again he went to tell our mother Nau'ts'ity'i.

He arrived there. Then our father I'tcts'ity'i said, "Gaau'na," said he, "now everything is good," said he. "Now you can bring out the children."

Then spoke our mother, Nau'ts'ity'i, "It is good," said she, "let me put them out," said she. "I shall put them out with this," said she, "with rain-storms and with the katsinas and with songs and with prayers and with shamanistic power and carrying prayer sticks and carrying in their arms corn and carrying in their arms altars and grinding stones and carrying in their arms mullers and having tied in their hair eagle feathers." "My children will be thus," said our mother Nau'ts'ity'i. "Next the katsinas and the spirits will be in the world from now on, our means of life. I shall put them out also. Some of them, when I put them out, will go this way; to the northeast will go the spirits. Next this way to the northwest and southwest will go the katsinas," said our mother Nau'ts'ity'i. "When I first put the people then first from now on they will increase. Then, when we see that people are not good, then you yourself, Gaau'na I'tcts'ity'i will know with what to punish our children," said our mother Nau'ts'ity'i.

Then said our father I'tcts'ity'i, "Let them go. It is good," said he. "Well then, you I'tcts'ity'i, you will watch every day our children, the people," said our mother Nau'ts'ity'i. "It is good," said our father I'tcts'ity'i. "Now you yourself, every day you shall take care of all the work that we have done," said our mother Nau'ts'ity'i. "It shall be thus," said to her our father I'tcts'ity'i. Then our mother Nau'ts'ity'i said, "Well then, here below I shall help you always every day. Well, then, with this the earth will be good always every day. Good the plants will be and all the crops will be good. I, with my power, and father I'tcts'ity'i with your power, everything will be good. Thus it will be, I'tcts'ity'i," said our mother Nau'ts'ity'i.

Then said our father I'tcts'ity'i, "It is good," said he. "Let them go. From now on every day, it will be good. You, mother, with your power, you mother Nau'ts'ity'i, you also will help them thus every day that our children may be good. With this the earth will always be ripe, mother, with your power. With my power also will be good everything, every day what we have made," said our father I'tcts'ity'i.

"It is good," said our mother Nau'ts'ity'i. "Then, enough, everything has come to be good and is completed. Now probably there will be daylight for a long time. Therefore the people will live well and therefore the earth will be good and therefore the people will be well always. It is well," said she.

"Now everything has become good. Our children, the people and the cattle and the game are nicely placed in the world (where the sun shines) above and on the earth above. They will sit and they will always walk nicely every day. Therefore, the people on this world will always be every day happy and always every day here below I shall give them instructions and I shall take care of them and I shall look upon them, and I shall help the people and their works; and also when they desire animals and also when they desire anything for their own use, I shall help them." Thus spoke our father I'tcts'ity'i.

Then our mother Nau'ts'ity'i also spoke, "I shall also help my people. I love them very much, and therefore I shall help them. They shall never starve with this, that every spring when everything arrives, the different kinds of crops will increase when the people plant," said our mother Nau'ts'ity'i. "Then the father goes down there and it will rain and with that he will make good the different kinds of crops," said our mother Nau'ts'ity'i. Then our father spoke, "It is well. Now it is enough. Thus we shall watch for a while the world and for a while the people will live, as long as we take care of them," thus said our father I'tcts'ity'i. Then said our mother Nau'ts'ity'i, "It is well," said she.

—Franz Boas (1928, pt. 1, 1–5)

Origin Myths

Origin myths are continuous with creation myths, and are in effect sequels to the main episodes of creation—setting forth particular innovations or precedents in the evolving, unfinished world—notably the acquisition of fire, the invention of important rituals and customs, the consolidation of the present-day tribal landscape, and so on. It would be a mistake to understand such narratives as merely "explanatory," in the vein of Kipling's "Just So" stories; more than just explanations, they typically convey important moral and spiritual values—the importance of cooperation, for example, in the Shasta "Theft of Fire," and the value of tribal kinship with animal species in the Blackfoot "Beaver Medicine" tale.

The Theft of Fire (Shasta)

Long ago, in the beginning, people had only stones for fire. In the beginning everyone had only that sort of fire-stone. "Do you hear? There is fire over there. Where Pain lives, there is fire." So Coyote went, and came to the house where Pain lived. The children were at home, but all the old people were away, driving game with fire. They had told their children, "If any one comes, it will be Coyote." So they went to drive game by setting fires.

Coyote went into the house. "Oh you poor children! Are you all alone here?" said he. "Yes, we are all alone. They told us they were all going hunting. If anyone comes, it will be Coyote. I think you are Coyote," they said. "I am not Coyote," he said. "Look, way back there, far off in the mountains, is Coyote's country. There are none near here." Coyote stretched his feet out toward the fire, with his long blanket in which he had run away. "No, you smell like Coyote," said the children. "No, there are none about here," he said. Now, his blanket began to burn, he was ready to run. He called to Chicken Hawk, "You stand there! I will run there with the fire. I will give it to you and then you will run on. Eagle, do you stand there! Grouse, do you stand there! Quail, do you stand there!" Turtle alone did not know about it. He was walking along by the river.

Now, Coyote ran out of the house; he stole Pain's fire. He seized it, and ran with it. Pain's children ran after him. Coyote gave the fire to Chicken Hawk, and he ran on. Now Chicken Hawk gave it to Eagle, and he ran on. Eagle gave it to Grouse, and he ran on. He gave it to Quail, and he ran far away with it. Turtle was there walking about. The Pains were following, crying, "Coyote has stolen fire!" Now, Turtle was walking about; he knew nothing, he was singing. "I'll give you the fire," cried Quail. "Here! Take it!" Just then the Pains got there. Turtle put the fire under his armpit, and jumped into the water. Pain shot at him, shot him in the rear. "Oh, oh, oh! That is going to be a tail," said Turtle, and dove deep down into the River.

All the Pains stood together. By and by they gave it up, and went away. Coyote came up, and asked, "Where is the fire?"—"Turtle dove with it," they said. "Curse it! Why did you dive with it?" Coyote said. He was very angry.

After a while Turtle crawled out of the water on the other side. Coyote saw him. "Where is the fire?" he called out. Turtle did not answer. "I say to you, where did you put the fire?" said Coyote. "Curse it! Why did you jump in the water?" After a while Turtle threw the fire all about. "You keep quiet! I will throw the fire all about," said Turtle. "Oh children, poor children," said Coyote; he said all kinds of things, he was glad. Now, everyone came and got fire. Now we have got fire. Coyote was the first to get it, at Pain's that way. That is all. That is one story.

—Roland Dixon (1911, 13–14)

Red Horse (Kiowa)

Another Kiowa myth retold in N. Scott Momaday's The Way to Rainy Mountain *and used by him to emphasize the primary importance of words and language in Kiowa culture.*

There was a camp. They began to make a horse out of clay. They made it in the shape of a horse, they blew their breath through its nostrils, they stuffed it with wind. They killed a snake and used the skin for its hide.

When they had finished, they heard it move. They had to hold it. They could not hold it, it got away from them in a whirlwind, up into the sky.

After it went up they prayed to it and asked it not to run over the Indians, and if it came along to remember them because they had made it. That was Red Horse (*Tsaigul*), or Cyclone. When they speak to Cyclone, the Kiowas believe, it will go some other way, because they made it.

—Elsie Clews Parsons (1929, 15–16)

The Theft of Light (Tsimshian)

Giant flew inland (towards the east). He went on for a long time, and finally he was very tired, so he dropped down on the sea the round little stone which his father had given to him. It became a large rock way out at sea. Giant rested on it and refreshed himself, and took off his raven skin.

At that time there was always darkness. There was no daylight then. Again Giant put on the raven skin and flew toward the east. Now, Giant reached the mainland and arrived at the mouth of Skeena River. There he stopped and scattered the salmon roe and trout roe. He said while he was scattering them, "Let every river and creek have all kinds of fish!" Then he took the dried sea-lion bladder and scattered the fruits all over the land, saying, "Let every mountain, hill, valley, plain, the whole land, be full of fruits!"

The whole world was still covered with darkness. When the sky was clear, the people would have a little light from the stars; and when clouds were in the sky, it was very dark all over the land. The people were distressed by this. Then Giant thought that it would be hard for him to obtain his food if it were always dark. He remembered that there was light in heaven, whence he had come. Then he made up his mind to bring down the light to our world. On the following day Giant put on his raven skin, which his father the chief had given to him, and flew upward. Finally he found the hole in the sky, and he flew through it. Giant reached the inside of the sky. He took off the raven skin and put it down near the hole of the sky. He went on, and came to a spring near the house of the chief of heaven. There he sat down and waited.

Then the chief's daughter came out, carrying a small bucket in which she was about to fetch water. She went down to the big spring in front of her father's house. When Giant saw her coming along, he transformed himself into the leaf of a cedar and floated on the water. The chief's daughter dipped it up in her bucket and drank it. Then she returned to her father's house and entered.

After a short time she was with child, and not long after she gave birth to a boy. Then the chief and the chieftainess were very glad. They washed the boy regularly. He began to grow up. Now he was begin-ning to creep about. They washed him often, and the chief smoothed and cleaned the floor of the house. Now the child was strong and crept about every day. He began to cry, "*Hama, hama!*" He was crying all the time, and the great chief was troubled, and called in some of his slaves to carry about the boy. The slaves did so, but he would not sleep for several nights. He kept on crying, "*Hama, hama!*" Therefore the chief invited all his wise men, and said to them, that he did not know what the boy wanted and why he was crying. He wanted the box that was hanging in the chief's house.

This box, in which the daylight was kept, was hanging in one corner of the house. Its name was *Ma*. Giant had known it before he descended to our world. The child cried for it. The chief was annoyed, and the wise men listened to what the chief told them. When the wise men heard the child crying aloud, they did not know what he was saying. He was crying all the time, "*Hama, hama, hama, hama!*"

One of the wise men, who understood him, said to the chief, "He is crying for the *ma*." Therefore the chief ordered it to be taken down. The man put it down. They put it down near the fire, and the boy sat down near it and ceased crying. He stopped crying, for he was glad. Then he rolled the *ma* about inside the house. He did so for four days. Sometimes he would carry it to the door. Now the great chief did not think of it. He had quite forgotten it.

Then the boy really took up the *ma*, put it on his shoulders, and ran out with it. While he was running, someone said, "Giant is running away with the *ma*!" He ran away, and the hosts of heaven pursued him. They shouted that Giant was running away with the *ma*. He came to the hole of the sky, put on the skin of the raven, and flew down, carrying the *ma*. Then the hosts of heaven returned to their houses, and he flew down with it to our world.

At that time the world was still dark. He arrived farther up the river, and went down river. Giant had come down near the mouth of Nass River. He went to the mouth of Nass River. It was always dark, and he carried the *ma* about with him. He went on, and went up the river in the dark. A little farther up he heard the noise of the people, who were catching *olachen* [candlefish], in bag nets in their canoes. There was much noise out on the river, because they were working hard.

Giant, who was sitting on the shore, said, "Throw ashore one of the things you are catching, my dear people!" After awhile, Giant said again, "Throw ashore one of the things you are catching!" Then those on the water scolded him. "Where did you come from, great liar, whom they call [Giant]?" The people knew it was Giant. Therefore they made fun of him. Then Giant said again, "Throw ashore one of the things that you are catching, or I shall break the *ma*!" and all those who were on the water answered, "Where did you get what you are talking about, you liar?" Giant said once more, "Throw ashore one of the things you are catching, my dear people, or I shall break the *ma* for you!" One person replied, scolding him.

Giant had repeated his request four times, but those on the water refused what he had asked for. Therefore Giant broke the *ma*. It broke, and it was daylight. The north wind began to blow hard; and all the fishermen, the Frogs, were driven away by the north wind. All the Frogs who had made fun of Giant were driven away down river until they arrived at one of the large mountainous islands. Here the Frogs tried to climb up the rock; but they stuck to the rock, being frozen by the north wind, and became stone. They are still on the rock. The fishing Frogs named him [Chemsem], and all the world had the daylight.

—Franz Boas and
Henry Tate (1916, 60 ff.)

How the Papago Got Corn (Papago)

In the summer everyone came home to our village and we planted corn. The corn was once a man and he lured a woman away to sleep with him. She stayed a long time, and when she came home, she knew the songs that made the corn grow. So when the men all went to their meeting, this man did not go but he stayed at home hearing his wife sing. The men from the meeting came to speak to him. "Why are you absent?"—"Because I am listening to my wife."—"How can it be that a man can learn more from a woman than from talking with us? Let us hear her, too."

So she came to the men's meeting and she sat between the chief and her husband. "Sing." And she sang the corn songs.

At the first song those men began to sing. At the second, they danced. At the third, the women came out of the houses, creeping to the council house to listen to the singing. At the fourth, they were all dancing, inside the council house and outside, to the woman's singing.

We sang those songs as we put the corn into the earth, but it was the men who sang, for women do not do those things now. We stood ready with the corn kernels while the men sang, then we went down the field together, each woman behind a man. The man dropped his stick into the soft earth, thud! As deep as my hand is long. The woman dropped in four corn kernels and scraped her bare toes over that red earth to cover them.

Then the corn came up. The fair stalks, the thick root, the broad leaves.

> I saw the tassels waving in the wind
> And I whistled softly for joy.

My father used to sing that at night while the corn was growing.

I used to like it in the summertime when all our friends and relatives were around us. The houses were scattered all over the flatland—round brush houses like ours. In every house there were women grinding corn, and down by the wash there were men bending over the fields where the corn and beans and squash were growing.

> In the furrow
> At the corner
> The corn is growing green
> Growing green.

I used to hear those songs coming from the houses, because we were so happy in summertime. We had rain. Every morning the sky was bright and every afternoon the little white cloud stood over the mountains to the east. [...]

—Ruth Underhill (1979, 52–53)

Origin of the Beaver Medicine (Blackfoot)

Readers of James Welch's novel Fools Crow *will recognize that a retelling of this myth figures prominently in the novel. Like Leslie Silko in* Ceremony, *Welch makes his people's mythic traditions a foundation for the historical-fictional narrative of Fools Crow and his people, the Pikuni Blackfeet.*

. . . Then there was peace among all the tribes. They met, and did not kill each other. They had no guns and they had no horses. When two tribes met, the head chiefs would take each a stick and touch each other. Each had counted a coup on the other, and they then went back to their camps. It was more a friendly than a hostile ceremony.

Oftentimes, when a party of young men had gone to a strange camp, and had done this to those whom they had visited, they would come back to their homes and would tell the girls whom they loved that they had counted a coup on this certain tribe of people. After the return of such a party, the young women would have a dance. Each one would wear clothing like that of the man she loved, and as she danced, she would count a coup, saying that she herself had done the deed which her young lover had really done. Such was the custom of the people.

There was a chief in a camp who had three wives, all very pretty women. He used to say to these women, whenever a dance was called, "Why do not you go out and dance too? Perhaps you have some one in the camp that you love, and for whom you would like to count a coup?" Then the women would say, "No, we do not wish to join the dance; we have no lovers."

There was in the camp a poor young man, whose name was Api-kunni. He had no relations, and no one to tan robes or furs for him, and he was always badly clad and in rags. Whenever he got some clothing, he wore it as long as it would hold together. This young man loved the youngest wife of the chief, and she loved him. But her parents were not rich, and they could not give her to Api-kunni, and when the chief wanted her for a wife, they gave her to him. Sometimes Api-kunni and this girl used to meet and talk together, and he used to caution her, saying, "Now be careful that you do not tell any one that you see me." She would say, "No, there is no danger; I will not let it be known."

One evening, a dance was called for the young women to dance, and the chief said to his wives, "Now, women, you had better go to this dance. If any of you have persons whom you love, you might as well go dance for them." Two of them said, "No, we will not go. There is no one we love." But the third said, "Well, I think I will go and dance." The chief said to her, "Well, go then; your lover will surely dress you up for the dance."

The girl went to where Api-kunni was living in an old woman's lodge, very poorly furnished, and told him what she was going to do, and asked him to dress her for the dance. He said to her, "Oh, you have wronged me by coming here, and by going to the dance. I told you to keep it a secret." The girl said, "Well, never mind; no one will know your dress. Fix me up, and I will go and join the dance anyway."

"Why," said Api-kunni, "I never have been to war. I have never counted any coups. You will go and dance and will have nothing to say. The people will laugh at you." But when he found that the girl wanted to go, he painted her forehead with red clay, and tied a goose skin, which he had, around her head, and lent her his badly tanned robe, which in spots was hard like a parfleche. He said to her, "If you will go to the dance, say, when it comes your turn to speak, that when the water in the creeks gets warm, you are going to war, and are going to count a coup on some people."

The woman went to the dance, and joined in it. All the people were laughing at her on account of her strange dress—a goose skin around her head, and a badly tanned robe about her. The people in the dance asked her, "Well, what are you dancing for? What can you tell?" The woman said, "I am dancing here today, and when the water in the streams gets warm next spring, I am going to war; and then I will tell you what I have done to any people." The chief was standing present, and when he learned who it was that his young wife loved, he was much ashamed and went to his lodge.

When the dance was over, this young woman went to the lodge of the poor young man to give back his dress to him. Now, while she had been gone, Api-kunni had been thinking over all these things, and he was much ashamed. He took his robe and his goose skin and went away. He was so ashamed that he went away at once, traveling off over the prairie, not caring where he went, and crying all the time. As he wandered away, he came to a lake, and at the foot of this lake was a beaver dam, and by the dam a beaver house. He walked out on the dam and on to the beaver house. There he stopped and sat down, and in his shame cried the rest of the day, and at last he fell asleep on the beaver house.

While he slept, he dreamed that a beaver came to him—a very large beaver—and said, "My poor young man, come into my house. I pity you, and will give you something that will help you." So Api-kunni got up, and followed the beaver into the house. When he was in the house, he awoke, and saw sitting opposite him a large white beaver, almost as big as a man. He thought to himself, "This must be the chief of all beavers, white because very old."

The beaver was singing a song. It was a very strange song, and he sang it a long time. Then he said to Api-kunni, "My son, why are you mourning?" and the young man told him everything that had happened, and how he had been shamed. Then the beaver said, "My son, stay here this winter with me. I will provide for you. When the time comes, and you have learned our songs and our ways, I will let you go. For a time make this your home." So Api-kunni stayed there with the beaver, and the beaver taught him many strange things. All this happened in the fall.

Now the chief in the camp missed this poor young man, and he asked the people where he had gone. No one knew. They said that the last that had been seen of him he was traveling toward the lake where the beaver dam was.

Api-kunni had a friend, another poor young man named Wolf Tail, and after a while, Wolf Tail started out to look for his friend. He went toward the lake, looking everywhere, and calling out his name. When he came to the beaver house, he kicked on the top and called, "Oh, my brother, are you here?" Api-kunni answered him, and said, "Yes, I am here. I was brought in while I was asleep, and I cannot give you the secret of the door, for I do not know it myself."

Wolf Tail said to him, "Brother, when the weather gets warm a party is going to start from camp to war." Api-kunni said, "Go home and try to get together all the moccasins you can, but do not tell them that I am here. I am ashamed to go back to the camp. When the party starts, come this way with the moccasins, and we two will start from here." He also said, "I am very thin. The beaver food does not agree with me. We are living on the bark of willows." Wolf Tail went back to the camp and gathered together all the moccasins that he could find, as he had been asked to do.

When the spring came, and the grass began to start, the war party set out. At this time the old beaver talked to Api-kunni a long time, and told him many things. He dived down into the water, and brought up a long stick of aspen wood, cut off from it a piece as long as a man's arm, trimmed the twigs off it, and gave it to the young man. "Keep this," the beaver said, "and when you go to war take it with you." The beaver also gave him a little sack of medicine, and told him what he must do.

When the party started out, Wolf Tail came to the beaver house, bringing the moccasins, and his friend came out of the house. They started in the direction the party had taken and traveled with them, but off to one side. When they stopped at night, the two young men camped by themselves.

They traveled for many days, until they came to Bow River, and found that it was very high. On the other side of the river, they saw the lodges of a camp. In this camp a man was making a speech, and Api-kunni said to his friend, "Oh, my brother, I am going to kill that man today, so that my sweetheart may count coup on him." These two were at a little distance from the main party, above them on the river.

The people in the camp had seen the Blackfeet, and some had come down to the river. When Api-kunni had said this to Wolf Tail, he took his clothes off and began to sing the song the beaver had taught him. This was the song:

> I am like an island,
> For on an island I got my power.
> In battle I live
> While people fall away from me.

While he sang this, he had in his hand the stick which the beaver had given him. This was his only weapon.

He ran to the bank, jumped in and dived, and came up in the middle of the river, and started to swim across. The rest of the Blackfeet saw one of their number swimming across the river, and they said to each other, "Who is that? Why did not someone stop him?" While he was swimming across, the man who had been making the speech saw him and went down to meet him. He said, "Who can this man be, swimming across the river? He is a stranger. I will go down and meet him, and kill him."

As the boy was getting close to the shore, the man waded out in the stream up to his waist, and raised his knife to stab the swimmer. When Api-kunni got near him, he dived under the water and came up close to the man, and thrust the beaver stick through his body, and the man fell down in the water and died. Api-kunni caught the body, and dived under the water with it, and came up on the other side where he had left his friend. Then all the Blackfeet set up the war whoop, for they were glad, and they could hear a great crying in the camp. The people there were sorry for the man who was killed.

People in those days never killed one another, and this was the first man ever killed in war.

They dragged the man up on the bank, and Api-kunni said to his brother, "Cut off those long hairs on the head." The young man did as he was told. He scalped him and counted coup on him; and from that time forth, people, when they went to war, killed one another and scalped the dead enemy, as this poor young man had done. Two others of the main party came to the place, and counted coup on the dead body, making four who had counted coup. From there, the whole party turned about and went back to the village whence they had come.

When they came in sight of the lodges, they sat down in a row facing the camp. The man who had killed the enemy was sitting far in front of the others. Behind him sat his friend, and behind Wolf Tail, sat the two who had counted coup on the body. So these four were strung out in front of the others. The chief of the camp was told that some people were sitting on a hill nearby, and when he had gone out and looked, he said, "There is someone sitting way in front. Let somebody go out and see about it." A young man ran out to where he could see, and when he had looked, he ran back and said to the chief, "Why, that man in front is the poor young man!"

The old chief looked around, and said, "Where is that young woman, my wife? Go and find her." They went to look for her, and found her out gathering rosebuds, for while the young man whom she loved was away, she used to go out and gather rosebuds and dry them for him. When they found her, she had her bosom full of them. When she came to the lodge, the chief told her, "There is the young man whom you love, who has come. Go and meet him." She made ready quickly and ran out and met him. He said, "Give her that hair of the dead man. Here is his knife. This is the coat he had on, when I killed him. Take these things back to the camp, and tell the people who made fun of you that this was what you promised them at the time of that dance."

The whole party then got up and walked to the camp. The woman took the scalp, knife, and coat back to the lodge, and gave them to her husband. The chief invited Api-kunni to come to his lodge to visit him. He said, "I see that you have been to war, and that you have done more than any of us have ever done. Now take my lodge and this woman, and live here. Take my place and rule these people. My two wives will be your servants." When Api-kunni heard this, and saw the young woman sitting there in the lodge, he could not speak. Something seemed to rise up in his throat and choke him.

So this young man lived in the camp and was known as their chief.

After a time, he called his people together in council and told them of the strange things the beaver had taught him, and the power that the beaver had given him. He said, "This will be a benefit to us while we are a people now, and afterward it will be handed down to our children, and if we follow the words of the beaver we will be lucky. This seed the beaver gave me, and told me to plant it every year. When we ask help from the beaver, we will smoke this plant."

This plant was the Indian tobacco, and it is from the beaver that the Blackfeet got it. Many strange things were taught this man by the beaver, which were handed down and followed until today.

—George Bird Grinnell (1962, 114–25)

Origin of Bear Lodge and the Big Dipper (Kiowa)

The story is widespread among Plains Indians; N. Scott Momaday in The Way to Rainy Mountain *retells this Kiowa version in the course of narrating his people's legendary migration from the Rocky Mountains onto the Great Plains. The Anglo name for "Bear Lodge" is Devil's Tower.*

Once long ago several Kiowa girls were taking turns at imitating a bear and chasing the others. One girl, whose family lived under a bear taboo, reluctantly agreed to play the bear after she warned her sister to flee at the first sign of danger.

Then suddenly something took possession of the bear girl's spirit. She shook all over and dropped to her hands and feet. As she chased the girls on all fours, her hands and feet grew claws and her body sprouted fur; a bear had replaced the girl.

It chased, caught, and devoured the others, while the sister escaped down a trail where she encountered six other Kiowas. As the bear approached, they fled terrified over hills and across rivers. Finally the girls came to a stone, and it spoke to them. It told them to climb on it, and as they did so it rapidly grew to an enormous height in the sky.

The bear raced up the sky to kill them, but the girls were beyond its reach. The animal tried four times to leap up to the pinnacle of the rock; each time it left deep claw marks which are still visible today on the face of the rock. Eventually the seven girls were safely lifted into the sky, where they remain today as the seven stars of the Big Dipper.

—Maurice Boyd (1983b, 10–11)

Scar-Face and the Origin of the Sweatlodge (Blackfoot)

James Welch's adaptation of this story in the "visionary" next-to-last section of Fools Crow *is a remarkable instance of how modern Native American writers have continued and built on the storytelling traditions of their people.*

Once there was a very poor young man who lived with his sister. He had a chum. In the camp was a very fine girl, the daughter of a chief, with whom all the young men were in love. Now the poor young man was in love with her also, but he had a long, ugly scar on his cheek. One day he asked his sister to go over to the chief's lodge to persuade the girl to marry him. Accordingly, the sister went over; but when the girl found out what she wanted, she said she was willing to marry Scar-Face whenever that ugly scar disappeared. She made all manner of fun of Scar-Face.

Now the sister returned and told Scar-Face what the girl had said. He was very much hurt, and decided to go away to seek someone who could aid him in removing the scar. Yet, though he traveled far, no one could aid him in removing the scar. At last, he decided to go to the Sun. So he traveled on and on, and the farther he went, the blacker the people became. As he went along, he inquired for the Sun's house. Always he was told to go on until he came to a very high ridge where some people lived who could tell him the whereabouts of the Sun's house.

At last Scar-Face came to this ridge. There he saw a nude man with very black skin and curly hair. Scar-Face called to him, "Where is the Sun's lodge?"—"It is at the end of this ridge," said the black man. "But go back, go back! You will be burned very badly!" Scar-Face said, "Well, I shall go on anyway; it is better to die than go back."—"Look at me!" said the black man. "You can see how I have been burned black. You had best take my advice and go no farther."—"Where do you live?" asked Scar-Face.

"I have a cave to live in," replied the black man. "I stay in this cave when the sun is hot, otherwise I should be burned up." (It was just about sundown that Scar-Face met the black man.) The black man advised him to travel only by night.

Now Scar-Face went on towards the place where the Sun lived. Presently he saw a young man standing alone. The young man called to Scar-Face. "Where are you going?" "I am going to the Sun," said Scar-Face. "Oh!" said the young man. "Sun is my father, this is his house." (This young man was Morning Star.) "My father is not a [kind] man. He is not at home now, but when he comes in the morning he will surely kill you. However, I will talk with my mother, who is a good woman and will treat you kindly."

Then Morning Star took Scar-Face up to his father's lodge, and addressed his mother, saying, "Mother, I have brought home a strange young man here. I wish him for a companion. He has come a long way to find us, and I wish you would take pity on him, that I may enjoy his company."—"Well," said the mother, "bring him in. We will talk to your father when he returns; but I fear we shall not be able to keep the young man."

When Scar-Face was taken into the lodge, he saw on the ground a kind of earthen square, some cedar brush, and buffalo-chips. This was the Sun's smudge-place. After a time the old woman, who was Moon, said to Scar-Face, "Is there anything that you especially care for?" "Yes," answered Scar-Face, "I want this scar taken from my face." "Well," replied Moon, "it is about time for my husband to come in. If he takes pity on you—well, we shall see."

In a little while Moon said, "Now he is coming." The she took Scar-Face to one side of the lodge and covered him up with cedar. Now Scar-Face began to feel very warm, because Sun was approaching. He began to shift about under the cedar, but Moon whispered that he must be quiet. So he lay very still, but became very hot as Sun came up. Finally Moon said to Scar-Face, "Now Sun is at the door." Sun looked into the lodge and said, "Oh, my, this lodge smells bad!" "Yes," Moon replied. "Morning Star has a chum here."—"Well," said Sun, "make a smudge with cedar."

After this had been done, Sun entered the lodge. Now Scar-Face was very hot. Finally Sun said, "Where is that young man?" "We covered him up," said Moon. "Come," said Sun, "get up." Then Scar-Face came out from under the cedar. He could not look Sun in the face. As Sun looked upon him, he knew that this was a poor unfortunate boy, and took pity on him. The heat then gradually grew less.

Now it seems that Morning Star was out on one of his journeys, and Sun waited for his return. When Morning Star came into the lodge and sat down in his usual place, Sun addressed him, saying, "My son, do you wish this young man for a companion?" Then Morning Star said he did very much, as he wished for a companion to go with him. He was lonesome on his journeys. "Well," said Sun, "you must make a sweat-house."

Then Morning Star went out and prepared a sweat-house. When all was ready, Sun went out. He had a disk of metal at the back of his head. This disk looked like brass. The Sun went into the sweat-house and began to wipe off the metal disk. Then he brought Morning Star and Scar-Face into the sweat-house. When they were in, the covers were closed down. At last, when all was ready, the covers were raised and the light let in. The two boys now looked alike.

Now, Moon came out, and Sun said to her, "Which is Morning Star?" Moon looked at them for a moment, then pointed at one; but she made a mistake, for she pointed at Scar-Face. "Oh!" said Sun, "you are a foolish woman! This is the star you mistook for Morning Star. After this, his name shall be, 'The-one-you-took-for Morning Star.'"

Now Scar-Face stayed with his new companions at Sun's house. Sun told him that he could go anywhere in the sky-land except straight west or straight down; he could go in any other direction. One morning, when Morning Star and Scar-Face were out together, Scar-Face said, "Let us go that way," pointing to the west. "No," replied Morning Star. "It is dangerous. My father said we must not go there." "Oh," said Scar-Face, "let us go anyway." Morning Star refused, but at the fourth request he said, "All right, let's go."

So the two boys went in the forbidden direction, and presently they came to a place where there were seven large white geese. At once the birds attacked them. Morning Star ran, calling out, "Now you see." Scar-Face did not run, but killed the seven geese with his club, and ran home. Before he reached home, he overtook Morning Star, and said to him, "There is no danger now. I killed all those birds."

When they reached home, Morning Star told his mother what Scar-Face had done, but she said to Scar-Face, "I will not believe you until you get their heads." So the boys returned and took the heads of the seven birds. (This is supposed to be the origin of scalping, and no one will believe that an enemy is killed until his scalp is produced.)

Some time after this, Scar-Face and Morning Star went out together as before, and Scar-Face said, "Let us go that way again."—"No," said Morning Star. "It will be more dangerous than before." Scar-Face insisted, and at the fourth request, Morning Star consented. As they were going along, they saw seven cranes. When the cranes saw the boys, they took after them. Morning Star ran as fast as he could. These cranes were terrible looking birds, and Scar-Face was badly frightened; but he took off his robe and held it in front of him. As the cranes came up, they began to peck at the robe, whereupon Scar-Face struck them one by one with his club.

Now when Scar-Face reached home, Sun was there and asked where he had been. Scar-Face said that he was walking along, when some large cranes took after him, and that he had killed them all with his club. "Oh!" said Sun, "I will not believe you until you have shown me their heads." So Scar-Face returned to the scene of his conflict, and brought away the heads of the cranes.

When Sun saw the heads, he believed him. Sun was greatly pleased at the courage of Scar-Face, and brought out a bundle. "Here," said he, "are some clothes for you—a shirt and leggings. These I give you because you have killed some very dangerous and troublesome birds." Then Sun took up the leggings, and painted seven black stripes on them, saying, "I make these here as a sign that you killed enemies. All your people shall wear black stripes on their leggings when they kill enemies." Then Sun sang some songs which were to go with the clothes.

After a time, Scar-Face said to Sun, "Now I should like to return to my people. I have been here long enough."—"All right," said Sun, "You may go." Then Sun took Scar-Face out, put a hoop or ring of cedar around his head, and as soon as the hoop was on, Scar-Face found that he could see down to his people. "Now," said Sun, "shut your eyes." Scar-Face shut his eyes. When he opened them, he found himself down by the camp of his people.

Now in the camp at that time there were some Indians who were playing at the wheel-and-arrow game; and one of the players, looking up, saw a black object coming down from the sky. He called out, "Oh, look at that black thing!" Then all stopped to look. They saw the object coming closer and closer. At last it reached the ground, some distance from them. It appeared to be a person. Then the old chum of Scar-Face, who was among the young men playing at the wheel-game, recognized Scar-Face, and rushed up to him; but as he approached, Scar-Face said, "Go back! You must get some willows, and make a sweat-house out here from the camp."

Then the chum went back to the people of the camp and explained to them. A sweat-house was prepared. When all was ready, Scar-Face went into the sweat-house with the bundle containing the suit of clothes given him by the Sun. When the bath had been taken, Scar-Face came out, carrying the bundle in his arms. He said to his chum, "My friend Sun gave me a suit of clothes: now I will give them to you."

Now this is why our people say that the sweat-house came from the sun. The medicine-lodge we make at the sun-dance is the lodge of the sun where Scar-Face had been. The weasel-tail suit which Scar-Face brought to his chum was just like those you see today. There was a disk on the back and one on the front. There were seven black stripes on the sleeves. These were for one group of seven birds that Scar-Face had killed. Sometimes the feet of the birds are painted on the shirt. The seven bands on the leggings are for the seven other birds that Scar-Face killed. Scar-Face directed that only such persons as performed great deeds were to be allowed to wear such a suit. After a time Scar-Face went back and became a star.

—Clark Wissler and
D. C. Duvall (1995, 61–65)

The Origin of Trouble, and Hummingbird's Quest (Keresan/Pueblo)

Leslie Silko's dramatization of "witchery" and evil in modern-day Pueblo life in her novel Ceremony *is mythically grounded, so to speak, on this account of how "trouble" first came into the world through the recklessness of some shamans. As in the myth, so in the novel: once evil is loose in the world, undoing it is a very slow, painstaking process, a difficult quest. When her battle-fatigued hero Tayo recalls a pre-war memory of seeing Hummingbird, Fly, and other figures in this myth at a sacred spring, his eventual recovery is mythically prefigured.*

Long ago—Eh.—Long ago at White-House they lived. Then the shamans took each their means of working their art, and on top of their house they danced. Then our mother Nau'ts'ity'i hid from them entirely the food for seven years.

Then it happened that they called a meeting. They discussed where they might find again our mother. Then in the middle of the south wall above, Hummingbird Boy stayed at night. Then they asked him, "Where from, behold, do you eat? Always you have enough to eat."—"Do you wish [to know]?"—

"Yes," said all the shamans and chiefs and war chiefs, and all the others.

Then spoke thus Hummingbird, "There, in the fourth place in the earth, there is our mother."—"Then how will she look to us again, and her food, and her body?"—"Find a chief's daughter. From her knee take dirt. Then you will bring it here to me; then also a jar and a new buckskin. Then down you will put it into it."

Then down they put it into it. After some time Fly became alive. It arrived in one place after another. "For what am I needed here?"— "Hummingbird and you will go to the fourth earth below. Then take these beads and prayer sticks and pollen."—"Give these to us," they said. Then all blew on them (on the beads, the prayer sticks and pollen). "Now let us go," said the two.

Then the two went, that way down there to the fourth world below. When they arrived, there was another daylight. There eastward they went. How beautiful everything—corn stalks and wheat and watermelons—everything they saw. The Fly was going to eat. He was stopping in places and honey he was sucking. Then spoke Hummingbird, "Don't, but first let us meet our mother."—"All right," said [Fly].

Then they met our mother. Then they [conferred] with her. "Here are pollen and beads and prayer sticks. We brought them here."—"I suppose you want something."—"Yes, we want food and your body and storm clouds."— "Well," she said, "first up above on the east wall Old Turkey Buzzard you will meet. First he will purify above towards the south down and above towards the east down and above towards the north down and above towards the west, he will purify."—"All right," they said, "let us go ahead."

Then the two went. There up they went. Then, when they arrived there, they said, "How are things?"—"It is good. Did you come here?"— "Yes," they said. "What did you find out?"—"Oh, first above on the east wall meet Old Turkey Buzzard that he may purify the town."—"Indeed?" they said, "go ahead."

Then they took pollen and beads and prayersticks and there up they went. There they arrived and inside he [Buzzard] was. Then the two said, "You, inside, how are things?"—"It is well. Who is this? Nobody has ever been walking here."—"We are Hummingbird and Fly."—"Indeed, what do you want?"—"We want you to purify the people and the earth and thunder clouds."—"Indeed? Wait a while. Your offering is not complete. There is no tobacco."—"Is that so? Let us go."

They went down. "Let us go," they said. "Go along," they were told. Then down they went. When they arrived there they were asked, "Did you meet Old Turkey Buzzard?"—"Yes," they said, "it was not complete what we took there."—"And what more was needed?"—"Tobacco."—"That is it."—"Then where shall we find it?"—"To our mother go again."—"Let us go." Then they went.

Down there they arrived in the fourth world. There was another daylight. They met our mother. "We have come back here."—"Maybe you want something."—"Yes," they said, "for tobacco asked us Turkey Buzzard. Where are we going to find it?"—"There in the southwest above, there on a hill, there right in the middle is a doorway. There Caterpillar lives. Him you will ask for tobacco."—"Permit us to go, let us go."—"Go ahead," she said to them.

Then there west they went. There in the west they arrived. When they came to the edge they said, "You downstairs, how are things?"—"It is well. Come down."—"Indeed, we will go down."—"Indeed, now sit down. Maybe you want something?"—"Yes," they said, "it is tobacco we want."—"Then I will give it to you." Then down he spread corn husks. There on them he wiped off his hands. Then tobacco came off from them. Then he gave it to them. After they had taken it they said, "Let us go."—"Go ahead," he said to them.

Then up they went. They came out above, and they entered the kiva. "Did you find it?"—"Yes," they said. "Indeed, it is well." Then they divided it and one-half they took to Old Turkey Buzzard. There above they arrived. "We have come again."—"Indeed?"—"We have found tobacco."—"Indeed, it is well. Now I shall purify the town."

Then he smoked to the north, to the west, to the south, and to the east. He smoked to his mothers, the chiefs. Then, "Let us go," they said. "Go ahead," said he to them. "Now I shall purify the town."—"That is it," they said. "Thus tell the shamans and the chiefs and the war chiefs."

Then there down they went. Then they arrived. "Have you come?"

they said. "Yes," they said. "Did you do it?"—"Yes, the town will be purified."—"Indeed, it is well." Then he purified first from the south down; afterwards from the east down; afterwards from the north down; and afterwards from the west down.

Then everything could become clear all around; storm clouds, crops, and happiness there around was spread. Then was renewed the food. They saw it again. Then our mother said, "Do not from now on in the future make trouble." Thus our mother gave instructions in olden times long ago.

—Franz Boas (1928, pt. 1, 1–5)

Trickster Stories

Narratives about trickster figures—wily animals like Coyote and Raven, humanoid beings like the Sioux Iktomi and the Winnebago Wakdjunkaga—are probably the most popular Indian stories today—both in traditional versions and in "updated" tales about Coyote's misadventures with anthropologists, government officials, and tourists.

Tricksters represent a folk figure of truly global distribution. African, Asian, European, and Indian tricksters are all different from one another in important ways (notably in how they engage their particular homelands), but at bottom they all seem to share what might be called the trickster essence—enormous, apparently unkillable vitality, voracious appetite for food and sex, cleverness and shiftiness, but also (most of the time) a lack of perseverance and focus; inability to accept social restraints and roles, but also (paradoxically) on occasion a desire to "shine" socially and to play the Big Man.

Paul Radin has argued that the trickster embodies a very ancient, primordial mode of human consciousness and thus serves as a sort of mental mirror, showing us the primitive urges and attitudes that survive in us, despite social conditioning, and perhaps underlie our survival as a species. Another function, especially prominent in Indian trickster stories, is that of mediation—between things that tend to be in opposition in a given society—Nature and Culture, male and female, hunting and agriculture, the Way of the Individual and the Way of the Community. Although "outsiders," tricksters always manage to be in the middle of trouble, often of course as its instigator; their amoral escapades seem well-calculated to provide vicarious relief from the burdens of tribal morality and good *citizenship and thus serve to mediate between what people should do and what in fact they'd like to do.*

In this way, the very freedom of tricksters from conventional morality makes them (paradoxically) important elements of the moral systems they flaunt. As the Navajo storyteller Yellowman said of Ma'i (Coyote), "If he did not do all those things, then those things would not be possible in the world" (Toelken and Scott 1999, 80–81). What this means is that by being capable of trying every kind of action, no matter how reprehensible or irresponsible, Coyote makes the morality of the Navajo world accessible to the imagination. Putting it crudely, he tries things out for our edification.

The fact that such a rascally figure is also sometimes a mythic creator and transformer, with god-like powers of changing and fixing reality, is disconcerting to most readers—until they realize that in the Native scheme of things, there is really no contradiction between the two roles. Contrary to the Judeo-Christian concept of the world's original divine perfection, in Native terms the mythic world was raw and unfinished, needing a sort of humanly intelligible "handyman" to fix things up—as they are now, not to perfection, certainly, but in humanly understandable terms. When Coyote in the Nez Perce Orpheus story blunders, out of impatience, and loses both his wife and the opportunity to make death revocable, we regret his blunder and its mortal consequences, but we are also given to understand the basis of both in human nature.

It says something about the serious moral and philosophical importance of trickster stories in Indian societies, and also something about their seductive appeal, that many tribes prohibited telling them formally except during the winter, when extended religious and spirit-power celebrations were held. In warm weather, there was serious work to be done, mostly outdoors; telling trickster tales then was to misuse their special power and thus to risk serious misfortune according to tribal taboos.

Coyote the Eye-juggler (Northern Paiute)

Coyote was walking along. He heard someone laughing. "Come in," they said. Wild Cat and some others were sitting there. I think Skunk was there too. Coyote asked them, "What shall I do?"—"Take out your eyes. Throw them in the air. Then hold your head back, and they will fall in again."

Coyote tried hard to take out his eyes. He took them both out and threw them up, but not very far. He held back his head, and the eyes fell right in the sockets. Everybody laughed.

Then Wild Cat tried it again. He threw his eyes way up in the air, and they came back. Everybody laughed and told Coyote to try it again. "Throw them way up in the air this time," they said. He did it. One had a stick in his hand. When Coyote's eyes were coming down, he knocked them to one side. Then everybody ran away. They took Coyote's eyes with them.

Coyote couldn't see a thing. He was all alone. He tried to follow but he couldn't find the way. He ran into the Sagebrushes, and he scolded them. They said, "We never move. You come right over us." Then he ran into the Rocks. "You're in my way all the time!" he told them. But the Rocks said, "We never move. You just run over us."

Coyote heard some Birds singing. He went over there and called them. The Birds came to him. "Will you give me your little eye so that I can see?" They gave him a little one so that he could see where he was going.

Coyote traveled until he came to a camp. An old woman was there and Coyote asked her, "Where is everybody?" She told him, "I have three daughters. They're out there dancing over Coyote's eyes."—"What do you do when the girls come back?"—"I tell them to get me water. That's the first thing I say," the old lady told him. Then Coyote said, "How do you cook for them?"—"I cook *wa'da* for them."

Then Coyote took a rock. He hit the old woman on the head and hid her away. He took off her clothes and put them on. Then he lay down where she had been. The girls came back, and Coyote asked them for water the first thing. One ran to get water. Soon the girls said to him, "Everybody wants you over there, grandmother. They're going to dance over Coyote's eyes."—"How am I to go?"—"We can pack you on the back."

One picked up Coyote and packed him. When she was tired, another packed him. The girls were pretty tired. Then Coyote said, "Let me go. I'll go myself." And then he went on alone. The girls were over a hill, and Coyote ran to save time. When anyone was looking, he leaned on his stick and walked like an old woman.

Then he reached the place where they were dancing. "Let me have that Coyote's eyes for a while. I want to dance with [them]," he said. They gave the eyes to him. He held them in his hand and danced. "I feel like flying away," he said. Then he ran, taking the eyes with him.

They all ran after him, but nobody could catch him. Fox tried to take the eyes from him. Coyote told him, "These are my own eyes," so Fox let him go.

Coyote put his eyes in a spring to soak. They were pretty dry. He soaked them and put them in their sockets. Then Coyote was all right again.

—Isabel Kelly (1938, 418–19)

Old Man Coyote's Visit to the Crow Indians (Crow)

When the Crow camp had increased to a considerable size, Old Man Coyote paid his first visit there. The women were busy getting bark from the cottonwoods and were drinking the sap. Old Man Coyote said, "I'll visit the Crow Indians, whom I made."

A mountain-goat was eating before him. He made a white horse out of it and painted it so that it appeared as a pinto with red ears; it was a pretty horse with a yellow rump. He rode it, bidding it prance in lively fashion. He put his legs up tight. The horse said, "What do you want me to do?"—"Paw the ground and neigh aloud."

After a while he made the horse stand quiet. He took the bark used by women and from it made feather trappings for his horse. He fashioned a fancy bridle out of bark; he took the biggest leaves to be found and stretched them together for a mountain-lion skin saddle-cloth. He made red and green flannel out of leaves for his horse, also some fancy breast ornaments.

He stood a little ways from his horse and thought its decoration was fine. Then he took dirt and painted himself. He made a switch decorated with porcupine work. He looked at himself in a glass and thought he looked fine. His leggings and other garments were fine. He had pretty beaded moccasins. He had braids down to his waist, with bells on them. He saw his outfit was complete. He took an old buffalo shoulder-blade and made an eagle-tail fan out of it.

When the sun was low, he said, "I'll go into camp." He was so fully decorated that he could hardly move. "I'll have the Crows imitate me." He went a little ways, then tightened his hold on the horse, which would then paw and neigh.

The Crows were playing the hoop game. Old Man Coyote approached. He appeared, not noticing anyone. All stopped and looked. "Who is this

Crow? There's no one like him." The women ran out to look at this handsome man. The women were having a plum-seed game. He would watch them, then he would tighten his hold on the horse, which acted according to his instructions. He was also holding a coup-stick.

He went to where they could all watch him. All gathered around to see his dress. He would make his horse paw and neigh. The horse was shy. When he came up and they cheered the winner in the [hoop] game, the noise frightened the horse. It shied and Old Man Coyote tumbled off with his finery. All shouted. His horse ran away and turned back into a [mountain goat] again, and escaped to the brush.

All recognized him then. They cried, "Catch him!" All tried to hold him in order to get his advice. All ran for him. His finery fell off. He turned into a wolf, and ran off barking. His decorations were strung out along the road. They looked at all his finery, but when they picked it up, it was nothing but bark. Hereafter all adopted the kind of dress seen on Old Man Coyote.

—Robert Lowie (1918, 304)
Narrator: Medicine Crow

Coyote Frees the Fish (Wasco Chinook)

This story and those immediately following it are from a loose cycle of Wasco Chinookan stories in which Coyote goes up the Columbia River, performing as both a trickster and a transformer, making some mischief but in general doing more good than bad for the people to come. At the end of this first story, Coyote's transformation of the selfish women into swallows is still remembered by Wasco and other Indian fishermen on the Columbia: when the swallows return to the river, the salmon can be expected soon.

Coyote heard about two women who had fish preserved in a pond. Then he went to them as they were collecting driftwood from the river. He turned himself into a piece of wood (trying to get them to pick him up). He drifted along. But they did not get hold of him. He went ashore, ran off way yonder up river, and transformed himself into a boy. He put himself into a cradle, threw himself into the river, and again drifted along.

The two women caught sight of him wailing. They thought, "Some people have capsized, and this child is drifting towards us." The younger one thought, "Let us get hold of it." But the older woman did not want to have the child. Now it was drifting along. The older one thought, "That is Coyote." Nevertheless the younger woman took the child and put it in a canoe.

The two women started home towards their house. The child was wailing, and they arrived home with it. They took off the cradle from it and looked closely at it. As it turned out, the child was a boy. The younger one said, "A boy is better than driftwood." And then she went and cut an eel and put its tail in his mouth. Then straightaway he sucked at it and ate it all up. She gave him another eel, and again he sucked at it, eating only half. Then he fell asleep, and half the eel was lying in his mouth. The two women said, "He is asleep now; let us go for some more wood."

And then they went far away. Coyote arose and saw them going far off. Then he made himself loose and seized their food. He roasted the fish on a spit; they were done and he ate. He caught sight of the fish, which were their food, in a lake. Then he examined the lake carefully, and discovered a spot where it would be easy to make an outlet from it to the river. "Here I shall make the fish break out, and then they shall go to the Great River" [wi'mahl—the Columbia].

He made five digging-sticks, made them out of young oak. And then he put them down in that place. He started back home towards their house. Again, just as before, he put himself into the cradle. Again, there in his mouth lay the eel's tail. Again he fell asleep.

Now the two women arrived. "The boy is sleeping." They said, "Very good is the boy, being a great sleeper." And then they retired for the night. Daylight came, the boy went on sleeping. Again they went for wood. Again he saw them going far away. Then he got up and took their food. He roasted it on a spit and ate it all up. Then straightaway he went to where his digging-sticks were.

He took hold of one of the digging-sticks. Then he stuck it into the ground; he pulled it out, and the earth was all loosened up; his digging-stick broke. He took hold of another one and again stuck it into the ground. Then he loosened up the earth, and his digger was all broken to pieces. He took hold of another one of his digging-sticks. Again, he stuck it into the ground; he loosened the earth all up, and his third digger was all broken to pieces. He took hold of the fourth one; again his digger broke. Now at last he took hold of the fifth, and stuck it into the ground; he loosened the earth all up. And then the fish slid over into the Great River.

Now then the older woman bethought herself. She said to her companion, "You said, 'The child is good.' I myself thought, 'That is Coyote.' Now this day Coyote has treated us two badly. I told you, 'Let us not take the child, that is Coyote.' Now we have become poor. Coyote has made us so." Then they went to their house, and Coyote met them there.

He said to them, "Now by what right, perchance, would you two keep the fish to yourselves? You two are birds, and I shall tell you something. Soon now people will come into this land. Listen!" And the people could be heard, *du'lulululu*, like thunder rumbling afar. "Now they will come into this land; those fish will be the people's food. Whenever a fish will be caught, you two will come. Your name will be Swallows. Now this day I have done with you; thus I shall call you 'Swallows.' When the people will come, they will catch fish; and then you two will come, and it will be said of you, 'The swallows have come, Coyote called them so.' Thus will the people say: 'From these two did Coyote take away their fish preserved in a pond; now they have come.'" Thus did Coyote call those two.

—Jeremiah Curtin (1909, 18–20)

Coyote and the Mouthless Man (Wasco Chinook)

Again Coyote traveled up the river. In the winter he saw the canoe of a certain person, a man. He saw how the man dived into the water. He came up out of the water, his hands holding one sturgeon on that side and one sturgeon on this; he put the sturgeons down in the canoe. Then Coyote saw him count them with his finger, pointing about in the canoe. He thought, "When he dives, I shall take hold of and steal from him one of his sturgeons; let us see what he'll do."

The person dived under water. And then Coyote swam towards his canoe. He seized one of his sturgeons. He went and took the person's sturgeon with him, and hid it in the bushes. And then that Coyote seated himself there and hid. Then the person came up out of the water into his canoe; he put his sturgeons down in the canoe, again one and one. And then he counted them; again he counted them. Quite silently he counted them [one sturgeon was missing].

And then the person pointed his finger out, first up high, then a little lower, again a little lower, again a little lower still, finally lower still, on the ground. There he pointed, where Coyote was sitting! Silently he held his finger there. Coyote tried to move to one side, there again was the finger. No matter which way Coyote moved, there was that finger pointing at him, Coyote. Now when his finger was pointed, that person went straight up to Coyote. Straightaway he went to meet Coyote. . . . He kept pointing at him; Coyote kept dodging from side to side; the person kept him well in eye.

Coyote looked at the person [as he came up]; he was strange in appearance. As it turned out, he had no mouth; he had only a nose and eyes and ears. He spoke to Coyote with his nose; but he could not hear him; just deep down in his nose could he be heard: "*Dnn Dnn Dnn Dnn*." In fact he was scolding Coyote in this way. Thus he said to him with his nose, "You are not good." Thus the person kept telling him; his heart was dark within him. Coyote thought, "Perhaps now this man desires his sturgeon; perhaps he is going to kill me. [. . .]"

And then the person went back to his canoe. Coyote made a fire when he had gone. He gathered some stones and heated them in the fire. And they all became hot. He cut the sturgeon in two, cut it all up, and carefully made ready the stones. He laid the sturgeon out on the stones and steamed it; it was entirely done. And then he removed it and laid it down. Then the man who had no mouth came back; he met Coyote as he was eating.

And then [the person] took hold of that good well-done sturgeon. Then thought Coyote as he was eating, "Wonder what he'll do with it?" [Coyote] looked at him; he took the good sturgeon. [The person] just sniffed at the sturgeon, then threw it away. And then Coyote thought, "It is not well." He went and brought the sturgeon back and brushed it clean. Now Coyote was thinking, "What is he going to do with it?" Once again the person took hold of it and did with it as before.

[Coyote] went up to him and looked at him closely. And then he thought, "I don't know what I shall do to make him a mouth." Secretly he took a flint and chipped it on one side; it became just like a sharp knife. And then he went up to the person with the flint secretly in hand and looked at him closely. In vain the man tried to dodge from side to side. Now Coyote put the flint down over his mouth. He sliced it open, and the person's blood flowed out. He breathed "Haaa! Haaa!" Coyote said to him, "Go to the river and wash yourself."

When the person had come out of the water, he stopped and spoke to Coyote. "You do not seem to have steamed a large sturgeon." And then Coyote said, "Well, you would have killed me; you wanted the sturgeon for yourself. You got after me for the sturgeon."

Now the people [of the mouthless man's village] told one another: "There is a man whose mouth has been made for him." In truth, all the people of that same village had no mouths. And then they betook themselves to [Coyote]. He made mouths for all the people of that village. He called that village *Nimishxa'ya* (located below Castle Rock on the Columbia]. They said to him, "We will give you a woman." He said, "No! I shouldn't care for a woman; I'll not take one."

—Jeremiah Curtin (1909, 19–24)

Coyote and the First Pregnancy (Wishram Chinook)

So Coyote left *Nimishxa'ya*, and a little above that place he saw a man turning somersaults, landing on his head, and yelling loudly, as if it hurt him. Coyote was curious, and going to see what it all meant, he found that the man had his ankles tied, and between his legs was a bundle of firewood.

"What is the matter, friend?" he asked. "My wife is about to have a child," the man answered, "and I am carrying wood for the house."—"But that is no way to carry wood," said Coyote. He untied the man's legs, cut some hazel-brush, and began to twist it into a rope, which he attached to the bundle as a pack-string. He swung the faggot on his back, passing the loop of the rope across his forehead.

"Take the lead, and I will carry this for you," he said. So the man went ahead, and Coyote followed, bearing the bundle of fuel. "Here is my home," said the man after a while. Coyote threw down the load, and said, "That is the way to carry wood. Where is this woman who is to have a child?"

The man showed him a woman lying on a bed with a pile of robes wrapped around her hand. She did not seem to be pregnant, and Coyote unwrapped the hand, in a finger of which he saw a sliver embedded in a mass of pus. "Is this what is the matter?" he asked. "Yes," was the answer. "That is nothing; let me show you," said Coyote. He took a small sharp flake of bone, pricked the finger open, and pressed out the sliver.

"Now I will show you how to make a child," he said. He then did so.

Coyote remained a few days in that house, and the woman said that she was soon to be a mother. In a short time the child was born. "That is your child," Coyote said to the man. "I give it to you."

—Edward S. Curtis (1970a, 112–13)

Coyote and the Prairie Dogs (Navajo)

Barre Toelken and Tacheeni Scott's elaborate rendering of this well-known Navajo Coyote story is a masterpiece of ethnopoetic translation and textual presentation. It is based on a scrupulously careful and linguistically and culturally well-informed transcription of a performance of the Ma'i story by Toelken's late friend Yellowman. Reading the text carefully, paying attention to the textual notations, conveys about as much as can be conveyed in print of a sense of the story as it might actually be experienced in performance, in a Native setting. The numbers between sections indicate the narrator's pauses in seconds; [!!!] indicates special emphasis by him.

Ma'i was trotting along [having always done so].
-4-
At a place I'm not familiar with called "Where the Wood
Floats Out," he was walking along, it is said.
-4-
Then, also in an open area, it is said [!!!],
He was walking along in the midst of many prairie dogs. [!!!]
-1-
The prairie dogs were cursing him, it is said [!!!].
All crowded together, yelling.
-1-
He went further into their midst.
-1-
Then he walked further.
-3-
[!!!] He got angry and soon began to feel hostile.
-2-
After awhile it was noon.
-1-

He wanted [implied: looking upward] a cloud   [*slower, nasal*]
        to appear
(His reason was that he started hating the prairie dogs),
        so he asked for rain.
        -2-   [*smiles, quiet laughter*]
Then a cloud appeared, it is said.
"If it would only rain on me," he said.   [*smiles, heavy breathing*]
And that's what happened, it is said.
        -2-
"If only there could be rain in my footprints."
And that's what happened, it is said.
"If only water would ooze up between my toes
        as I walk along," he said
        -3-   [*open amusement*]
Then everything happened as he said, it is said.
        -4-   [*clears throat*]
"If only the water would come up to my knees," he said.
And that's what happened.
        -2-
"If only the water would be up to my back
        so that only my ears would be out of the water."   [*nasal*]
        -13-   [*heavy breathing*]
"If I could only float," he said.   [*nasal*]
Then, starting to float,
"Where the prairie dogs are,
if I could only land there," he said.
        -3-   [*quiet laughter*]
He came to rest in the midst of the prairie dog town, it is said.
        -3-
Someplace in the *diz*—   [*smiles, quiet laughter*]
        (*diz* is the name of a plant that grows in clumps)—
        he landed [implied: along with other debris] hung up
        in the clump, it is said.
        -4-   [*quiet laughter*]
And there he was lying after the rain.
And then Golizhi [Skunk] was running by to fetch water   [*slower*]
        (Ma'i was pretending to be dead)   [*smiles exchanged*]
Then he [Golizhi] was running.   [*Glances*]

He (Ma'i) called out to him, it is said.
"Come here," he said, and Golizhi came to him,   [*very nasal*]
        it is said.
      -6-   [*suppressed giggling*]
"Shilna'ash [comrade]," he said   [*very seriously*]
      -2-   [*quiet laughter, expelling air*]
"'The hated one has died, and has washed up
       where the prairie dogs are,' tell them that, shilna'ash."
      -3-
"'He's already got maggots,' you tell them," he said.   [*nasal*]
      -2-
"Slendergrass, it is called—shake that slendergrass
       so the seeds fall off.
In my crotch, in my nose, in the back part of my mouth,
       scatter some around, then put some inside my ears,"
        he said.
"'He's got maggots,' you tell them.   [*quiet laughter*]
'The hated one has been washed out.' Make four clubs and
       put them under me.
      -3-   [*quiet laughter*]
'We'll dance over him.
We're all going to meet over there,'
       You tell them," he said.
      -1-
"This is how," he said.
. . . [wording indistinct] . . .
. . . "dancing around" . . .
[implied: Golizhi is to join in these actions]
. . . "'Hit Ma'i in the ribs'" . . .   [*breathing*]
      -1-
"Be careful not to hit me too hard!
'Slowly, gently, like this,'
       you tell them," he said.
      -5-   [*clears throat*]
This happened.   [*normal tone*]
He ran home, and gave out the word to the prairie dogs, it is said.
"The hated one is washed out."
      -2-

There were rabbits and other animals [there],
>   and even groundsquirrels.
(Those animals which are food for him were gathered [!!!].)
[!!!] Now the people were dancing, it is said, at the meeting.
>   -3-
First, he [Golizhi] said, "It's true! It's true!   *[tones exaggerated]*
Let's have one of you who runs fast run over there to find out."
>   -1-
Then Jackrabbit ran and "It's true!" he said,   *[quiet giggling]*
>   running back, it is said.
>   -1-
Then Cottontail ran and "It's true!" he said,
>   running back, it is said.
>   -1-
Then Prairie Dog ran and, they said, "It's true!" he said,
>   running back, it is said.
>   -1-
At that time there was a big gathering [!!!].
They were dancing [implied: couples periodically stepping
>   into a circle], it is said.
Whatever they were singing, I don't know.
>   -2-
"The hated one is dead," they were saying [!!!].
>   The club is beside him; they were hitting
>   him in the ribs, it is said.   *[delivered in one long breath]*
>   —REST—   *[expelling of air]*
—*[narrator rests for about five minutes, drinks coffee]*—
Then they continued with what they were doing,
>   And more and more people came.
Then Golizhi-y-ne said (remembering Ma'i's plan)
"You are all dancing;
>   while you are looking up, while you are saying,
>   you say 'Dance in that manner,' you tell them [!!!]
>   'While you're in charge there, shilna'ash,'" he said.
>   -2-
Then they were dancing.
Then, "Waay, waay up there a *t'aadzilgai* is running through
>   the air," he said,

Golizhi said.   [*one girl: hn!*]
        -1-
Then, when they were all looking up,
        He urinated upward
so that it fell in their eyes, the urine.
        -3-   [*open laughter*]
His urine the animals were rubbing from their eyes [!!!].
"'The one who is hated is dead?'" he [Ma'i] said, jumping up [!!!].
        -1-   [*laughter, giggling*]
He grabbed the clubs from under him [!!!].

                                                      [*laughter, giggling*]
        -3-
He used the clubs on them [all in a row, in one circular swing].
They were all clubbed to death   [*laughter*]
                                                      [*laughter*]

        -8-
Then
"Let us cook by burying, shilna'ash," he said
"Dig right here," he said [!!!].
And he dug a trench, Golizhi did.
        -2-
After he dug a ditch, he built a fire.
He put the food into the pit.
Then he [Ma'i] thought of something new.
        -1-
"Let's have a foot race, shilna'ash.
Whoever comes back first,
        this will be his," he said   [*light laughter*]
"No," he [Golizhi] said, but he [Ma'i] won the argument.
"I can't run fast," he [Golizhi] said.
"While I stay here, you start loping," he [Ma'i] said.
        -1-
. . . [indistinct] . . . while Ma'i pretended to do something
to his ankles, he [Golizhi] started to run.
Then, over the hill he ran,
        And ran into an abandoned hole.
        -2-
In a little while, he [Ma'i] suddenly spurted away.

-3-
A torch he tied to his tail
and the smoke was pouring out behind him
   as he ran.   *[laughter]*
   -17-   *[laughter]*
While he was running over there,
Golizhi ran back, it is said,
   there where he had buried the food [!!!].
He dug them up and took them up into the rocks,
   it is said.   *[amusement]*
Four little prairie dogs he reburied,
then he was sitting back up there, it is said.
[!!!] Ma'i ran back, it is said,   *[light laughter]*
   back to the place where the prairie dogs were buried.
He leaped over it.
   -4-   *[increased laughter]*
"Hwah!" he said.   *[laughter]*
   -8-
"Shilna'ash—I wonder how far back he's plodding,
   Mr. His-Urine," he said.
   -6-
[!!!] Sighing, he lay down,
   pretended to lie down, in the shade.
He jumped up and leaped over to the pit.   *[laughter]*
   -1-   *[laughter]*
He thrust a pointed object into the ground
and grabbed the tail of the prairie dog first, it is said.
Only the tail came loose.   *[chuckle]*
   -1-   *[light laughter]*
"Oh no! The fire has gotten to the tail," he said.

             [loud laughter]
So he grabbed the stick and thrust it into the ground again;
   a little prairie dog he dug up, it is said.
   "I'm not going to eat this [meat]," he said,
     and he flung it away toward the east.
   -2-   *[light laughter]*
He thrust it into the ground again;
   a little prairie dog he dug up.

"I'm not going to eat this," he said,
>   and he flung it away toward the south.
>   -2-   *[light laughter]*
He thrust it into the ground again;   *[slower]*
>   a little prairie dog he dug up.
"I'm not going to eat this," he said,
>   and he flung it away toward the west.
>   -2-   *[breathing]*
He thrust it into the ground again;   *[sleepily]*
>   a little prairie dog he dug up.
"I'm not going to eat this," he said,
>   and he flung it away toward the north.
>   -1-   *[breathing]*
He thrust repeatedly in many places, it is said,
>   and couldn't find any.
Nothing, it is said.
There weren't any, it is said.
>   -2-   *[expelling breath]*
He couldn't, he walked [frustrated] around in circles.
He went around and he picked up those little prairie dogs he
had thrown away.
Then he picked up every little bit
>   and ate it all.
>   -2-   *[quiet laughter]*
Then he started to follow [Golizhi's] tracks,   *[amusement]*
>   it is said, but he couldn't pick up the trail.
He kept following the tracks, back and forth,
>   to where the rock meets the sand.   *[boy: hn!]*
(He didn't bother to look up.)
>   -1-
He [Golizhi] dropped a bone and he [Ma'i] looked up, it is said.
>   It dropped at his feet.
>   -1-   *[quiet laughter]*
"Shilna'ash, share with me again
[implied: what I shared with your previously]."   *[brief laughter]*
>   -5-   *[brief laughter]*
"Certainly not," he said to him, it is said.   *[slowly, seriously]*
He was begging, to no avail, it is said.

Golizhi kept dropping bones down to him.
He chewed the bones, it is said.

        -4-   *[small burst of quiet laughter]*

That's how it happened, it is said.

—J. Barre Toelken and
Tacheeni Scott (1997, 116–22)

Iktomi Conquers the Iya (Dakota Sioux)

Compare the depiction of an evil Iya figure in this Dakota Sioux story with the representation of a much more fearsome Dakota Iya monster in "The Stone Boy," p. 104.

Iktomi was wandering off in a certain direction, walking along at random. Just as he reached the hilltop, Iya the eater also reached it, coming up from the other side; so Ikto was much frightened and, "Ah, so it is on a day like this that I am to die, is it?" he thought suddenly.

He took some earth and polished his thigh vigorously and said, "Well, well, well! My younger brother,—or is he my elder brother?—*Ha's!*—which of us is the elder anyway?" But each time Iya took in his breath he jerked Ikto towards him, with such force that he staggered; he therefore was very much frightened and said, "Now, now, my younger brother,—or my elder,—stand farther off, can't you? I too have something I can do; I can pull you towards me if I care to!" he said.

But Iya did not reply; so then, once more, "Come now, my younger brother,—or is he my elder brother?—*Ha's!*—Which of us is the elder, anyway? . . . Well, when were you born?" Ikto asked. Iya answered, "Why, I was born when this earth and this sky were created." Ikto clamped his palm over his mouth, surprised. "So? Well, you fool, I made the earth and the sky myself! Oh, of course, now, as I recall it, there was a bit of leavings, after I had finished making the earth and sky, which I didn't know what to do with; I therefore rolled it into a wad and tossed it aside. And you grew from that! There isn't any doubt now. I am the elder!" he said. "Now then, little brother, what errand are you on?"

And Iya said, "Over in this direction there is a tribal camp, and I am going there. I shall eat the people, for they are mine."—"Well of all things! Funny, isn't it? Yet what else can you expect, with brothers? Why, little brother, that is just the people I am going to; and we shall travel together!" Ikto told Iya.

They were now traveling, but Iya could not manage his weight, and they were obliged, therefore, to stop often; but they were now stopping for the night near the encampment. When Iya slept, Ikto ventured to look into his body through his mouth, and saw there all the tribes that Iya had eaten in the past, living on in contentment in their respective tribal circles. Inside Iya, they were living and having their being in exactly the same fashion as when they lived on earth. Races and games were in progress. Yonder, on the other hand, a game of Dakota ball was being played with great skill; while, in the other direction could be seen a group of *Miwatani* Society dancers performing their dance around the circle.

Meanwhile, successful hunters were returning with game; and also the White-Pack Strap group were going along, dancing. Another thing else was that women were taking food to the council tipis, and there the old men of the tribe foregathered, with much feasting and the recounting of past glories. Taken all in all, the sight presented a picture of the good old days when the people lived; such Ikto saw inside the Iya's body.

Very much frightened, Ikto tried to think out a way to capture the Iya. And when he woke, this is what Ikto said to him, "All appearances to the contrary notwithstanding, there must be something that you fear?"— "Yes; the sound of rattles, and drums, the hooting of owls, and the shouts of men—all these I fear," Iya admitted. So then, "Well of all things! Just what you would expect, though, of brothers! Why, little brother, those are exactly what I too fear!" Ikto said. He added, "I'd suggest you stay here, little brother, while I go ahead. I will select the center tipi, and mark it with a cross, and then I shall return. Then we two can go together, and, starting at either end, we shall progress towards the center tipi, eating the people as we go. And he who arrives first at that center tipi shall have the right to eat his opponent, as his reward for winning." And Iya thought that was a good idea.

So Ikto ran hard and soon he arrived, shouting, at the tribal camp. "Hear ye, everybody! I have something to tell you, so listen! I have just deceived a very supernaturally powerful Iya, and I have come. And when I questioned him, he admitted that he feared certain things: rattles, and drums, and the hooting of owls, and the shouting of men. So make haste!" he said. "Moreover, while he slept, I looked into his mouth, and inside his body there actually live great tribes of people. Tipis with tops painted blue, and some painted black,—many painted tipis I saw," he said.

So immediately the people prepared in frantic haste, and followed Ikto out. At a little distance away, hidden by a hill, they stopped, and allowed Ikto to proceed alone, and after he had disappeared downhill, and it seemed time that he had reached Iya, they charged forth, making all those noises that Iya feared. Iya jumped up and sat with his head turning nervously from side to side, as if someone pulled it about; but they soon surrounded and clubbed him to death. They tore open his body; and then, for one entire day, great tribes of people crawled out of Iya, moving their camps, and settled by groups in the many pleasant bends of the river; and soon they built their fires for cooking the evening meal, and no matter being where one looked, one could see the campfires, sparkling like stars, and it was a beautiful sight.

Now, if Iya had not been destroyed in just that way, he would undoubtedly still be eating people up, White people and all. Iya was killed and that is why the entire country is now so full of people that it is impossible to find any open spaces anymore. From that time on, the expansion of peoples began in earnest, they say. Now, that was one time at least that Ikto must be given credit; he did do a great service to people and merits thanks for it. And from then on, who knows where Ikto went next? That is all.

—Ella Deloria (1978, 3–5)

Episodes from the Winnebago Trickster Cycle (Winnebago)

Paul Radin's study of the adventures of the Winnebago trickster Wakdjunkaga is the fullest, most detailed account we have of an American Indian trickster cycle, and is an essential starting point for anyone wanting to follow the trickster figure through his many variations in Indian cultures. What is unusual in Radin's presentation of Wakdjunkaga's adventures is that they begin with him wholly socialized, a chief in fact, and then follow him as he leaves his people and regresses into a tricky, ridiculous, primitive being, perhaps (as Radin suggests) a refracted image of our primitive forebears—and more to the point an image of the survival of primitive, pre-social instincts in us. Later in the cycle, Wakdjunkaga seems to return to a semblance of social identity.

4

As he, Trickster, walked along, suddenly, he came in sight of a knoll. As he approached it, he saw, to his surprise, an old buffalo near it. "My, my, what a pity! If I only hadn't thrown away that arrowbundle, I would now be able to kill and eat this animal," he exclaimed. Thereupon he took a knife, cut down the hay and fashioned it into figures of men. These he placed in a circle, leaving an opening at one end. The place was very muddy.

Having constructed this enclosure, he went back to where he had seen the buffalo and shouted, "Oho! My younger brother, here he is! Here he is indeed eating without having anything to worry about. Indeed let nothing prey on his mind! I will keep watch for him against intruders." Thus he spoke to the buffalo who was feeding to his heart's content. Then he continued, "Listen, younger brother, this place is completely surrounded by people! Over there, however, is an opening through which you might escape." Just then the buffalo raised his head unsuspiciously and, to his surprise, he seemed really to be completely surrounded by people. Only at the place Trickster had designated did an opening appear.

In that direction, therefore, the buffalo ran. Soon he sank in the mire and Trickster was immediately upon him with his knife and killed him. Then he dragged him over to a cluster of wood and skinned him. Throughout all these operations he used his right arm only.

5

In the midst of these operations suddenly his left arm grabbed the buffalo. "Give that back to me, it is mine! Stop that or I will use my knife on you." So spoke the right arm. "I will cut you to pieces, that is what I will do to you," continued the right arm. Thereupon the left arm released its hold. But shortly after, the left arm grabbed hold of the right arm. This time it grabbed hold of his wrist just at the moment that the right arm had commenced to skin the buffalo.

Again and again this was repeated. In this manner did Trickster make both his arms quarrel. That quarrel soon turned into a vicious fight and the left arm was badly cut up. "Oh, oh! Why did I do this? Why have I done this? I have made myself suffer!" The left arm was indeed bleeding profusely.

Then he dressed the buffalo. When he was finished he started off again. As he walked along the birds would exclaim, "Look, look! There is Trickster!" Thus they would cry and fly away. "Ah, you naughty little birds! I wonder what they are saying?" This continued right along. Every bird he met would call out, "Look, look! There is Trickster! There he is walking about!"...

11

Again he wandered aimlessly about the world. On one occasion he came in sight of a shore of a lake. To his surprise, he noticed that, right near the edge of the lake, a person was standing. So he walked rapidly in that direction to see who it was. It was someone with a black shirt on. When Trickster came nearer to the lake, he saw that this individual was on the other side of the lake and that he was pointing at him. He called to him, "Say, my younger brother, what are you pointing at?" But he received no answer.

Then, for the second time, he called, "Say, my younger brother, what is it you are pointing at?" Again he received no answer. Then for the third time, he addressed him, again receiving no answer. There across the lake the man still stood, pointing. "Well, if that's the way it's going to be, I, too, shall do that. I, too, can stand pointing just as long as he does. I, too, can put a black shirt on." Thus Trickster spoke.

Then he put on his black shirt and stepped quickly in the direction of this individual and pointed his finger at him just as the other one was doing. A long time he stood there. After a while Trickster's arm got tired so he addressed the other person and said, "My younger brother, let us stop this." Still there was no answer. Then, for the second time, when he was hardly able to endure it any longer, he spoke, "Younger brother, I am hungry! Let us eat now and then we can begin again afterward, I will kill a fine animal for you, the very kind you like best, that kind I will kill for you. So let us stop." But still he received no answer.

"Well, why am I saying all this? That man has no heart at all. I am just doing what he is doing." Then he walked away and when he looked around, to his astonishment he saw a tree-stump from which a branch was protruding. This was what he had taken for a man pointing to him. "Indeed, it is on this account that the people call me the Foolish One. They are right." Then he walked away.

12

As he was walking long suddenly he came to a lake, and there in the lake he saw numerous ducks. Immediately he ran back quietly before they could see him and sought out a spot where there was a swamp. From it he gathered a large quantity of reed-grass and made himself a big pack. This he put on his back and carried it to the lake. He walked along the shore of the lake carrying it ostentatiously.

Soon the ducks saw him and said, "Look, that is Trickster walking over there. I wonder what he is doing? Let us call and ask him." So they called to him, "Trickster, what are you carrying?" Thus they shouted to him, but he did not answer. Then, again they called to him. But it was only after the fourth call that he replied and said, "Well, are you calling me?"—"What are you carrying on your back?" they asked.

"My younger brothers, surely you do not know what it is you are asking. What am I carrying? Why, I am carrying songs. My stomach is full of bad songs. Some of these my stomach could not hold and that is why I am carrying them on my back. It is a long time since I sang any of them. Just now there are a large number in me. I have met no people on my journey who would dance for me and let me sing some for them. And I have, in consequence, not sung any for a long time."

Then the ducks spoke to each other and said, "Come, if we ask him to sing? Then we could dance, couldn't we?" So one of them called out, "Well, let it be so. I enjoy dancing very much and it has been a very long time since I last danced."

So they spoke to Trickster, "Older Brother, yes, if you will sing to us we will dance. We have been yearning to dance for some time but could not do so because we had no songs." Thus spoke the ducks. "My younger brothers," replied Trickster, "you have spoken well and you shall have your desire granted. First, however, I will erect a dancing-lodge." In this they helped him and soon they had put up a dancing-lodge, a grass-lodge. Then they made a drum. When this was finished he invited them all to come in and they did so.

When he was ready to sing he said, "My younger brothers, this is the way in which you must act. When I sing, when I have people dance for me, the dancers must, from the very beginning, never open their eyes."—"Good," they answered. Then when he began to sing he said, "Now remember, younger brothers, you are not to open your eyes. If you do, they will become red." So, as soon as he began to sing, the ducks closed their eyes and danced.

After a while one of the ducks was heard to flap his wings as he came back to the entrance of the lodge, and cry "Quack!" Again and again this happened. Sometimes it sounded as if the particular duck had somehow tightened its throat. Whenever any of the ducks cried out then Trickster would tell the other ducks to dance faster and faster.

Finally a duck whose name was Little-Red-Eyed-Duck secretly opened its eyes, just the least little bit it opened them. To its surprise, Trickster was wringing the necks of his fellow ducks! He would also bite them as he twisted their necks. It was while he was doing this that the noise which sounded like the tightening of the throat was heard. In this fashion Trickster killed as many as he could reach.

Little-Red-Eyed-Duck shouted, "Alas! He is killing us! Let those who can save themselves." He himself flew out quickly through the opening above. They struck Trickster with their wings and scratched him with their feet. He went among them with his eyes closed and stuck out his hands to grab them. He grabbed one in each hand and choked them to death. His eyes were closed tightly. Then suddenly all of them escaped except the two he had in his grasp.

When he looked at these, to his annoyance, he was holding in each hand a scabby-mouthed duck. In no way perturbed, however, he shouted, "Ha, ha, this is the way a man acts! Indeed these ducks will make fine soup to drink!" Then he made a fire and cut some sharp-pointed sticks with which to roast them. Some he roasted in this manner, while others he roasted by covering them with ashes. "I will wait for them to be cooked," he said to himself. "I had, however, better go to sleep now. By the time I awake they will unquestionably be thoroughly done. Now, you, my younger brother, must keep watch for me while I go to sleep. If you notice any people, drive them off." He was talking to his anus. Then, turning his anus to the fire, he went to sleep.

13

When he was sleeping some small foxes approached and, as they ran along, they scented something that seemed like fire. "Well. There must be something around here," they said, and, after a while, truly enough, they saw the smoke of a fire. So they peered around carefully and soon noticed many sharp-pointed sticks arranged around the fire with meat on them. Stealthily they approached nearer and nearer and, scrutinizing everything carefully, they noticed someone asleep there. "It is Trickster and he is asleep! Let us eat this meat. But we must be very careful not to wake him up. Come, let us eat," they said to one another.

When they came close, much to their surprise, however, gas was expelled from somewhere. "Pooh!" such was the sound made. "Be careful! He must be awake." So they ran back. After a while one of them said, "Well, I guess he is asleep now. That was only a bluff. He is always up to some tricks." So again they approached the fire. Again gas was expelled, and again they ran back. Three times this happened. When they approached the fourth time gas was again expelled. However, they did not run away. So Trickster's anus, in rapid succession, began to expel more and more gas. Still they did not run away. Once, twice, three times it expelled gas in rapid succession. "Pooh! Pooh! Pooh!"

Yet they did not run away. On the contrary, they now began to eat the roasted pieces of duck. As they were eating, the Trickster's anus continued its "Pooh!" incessantly. There the foxes stayed until they had eaten up all the pieces of duck roasted on sticks. Then they came to those pieces that were being roasted under ashes and, in spite of the fact that the anus was expelling gas, "Pooh! Pooh! Pooh!" continuously, they ate these all up too. Then they replaced the pieces with the meat eaten off, nicely under the ashes. Only after that did they go away.

14

After a while Trickster awoke. "My, O my!" he exclaimed joyfully, "the things I have put on to roast must be cooked crisp by now." So he went over, felt around, and pulled out a leg. To his dismay it was but a bare bone, completely devoid of meat. "How terrible! But this is the way they generally are when they are cooked too much!" So he felt around again and pulled out another one. But this leg also had nothing on it. "How terrible! These, likewise, must have been roasted too much! However, I told my younger brother, Anus, to watch the meat roasting. He is a good cook indeed!" He pulled out one piece after the other. They were all the same.

Finally he sat up and looked around. To his astonishment, the pieces of meat on the roasting sticks were gone! "Ah, ha! Now I understand! It must have been those covetous friends of mine who have done me this injury!" he exclaimed. Then he poked around the fire again and again but found only bones. "Alas! Alas! They have caused my appetite to be disappointed, those covetous fellows! And you, too, you despicable object, what about your behavior? Did I not tell you to watch this fire? You shall remember this! As a punishment for your remissness, I will burn your mouth so that you will not be able to use it!"

Thereupon he took a burning piece of wood and burnt the mouth of his anus. He was, of course, burning himself, and, as he applied the fire, he exclaimed, "Ouch! Ouch! This is too much! I have made my skin smart. It is not for such things that they call me Trickster! They have indeed talked me into doing this just as if I had been doing something wrong!"

Trickster had burnt his anus. He had applied a burning piece of wood to it. Then he went away.

As he walked along the road he felt certain that someone must have passed along it before for he was on what appeared to be a trail. Indeed, suddenly, he came upon a piece of fat that must have come from someone's body. "Someone has been packing an animal he had killed," he thought to himself. Then he picked up a piece of fat and ate it. It had a delicious taste. "My, my, how delicious it is to eat this!" As he proceeded, however, much to his surprise, he discovered that it was a part of himself, part of his own intestines, that he was eating. After burning his anus, his intestines had contracted and fallen off, piece by piece, and these pieces were the things he was picking up.

"My, my! Correctly, indeed, am I named Foolish One, Trickster! By their calling me thus, they have at last actually turned me into a Foolish One, a Trickster!" Then he tied his intestines together. A large part, however, had been lost. In tying it, he pulled it together so that wrinkles and ridges were formed. That is the reason why the anus of human beings has its present shape.

31

As he was running along, he came to a valley. There he heard someone beating a drum, the drumming followed by many war whoops. Someone there was making a great noise. So loud was this noise that it seemed to reach the skies. "Well, I wonder what these people are up to? I guess I will go over and see for I have not had any fun for a long time. Whatever they are doing, I will join them. If they are going to dance, why I will dance too. I used to be a fine dancer." Thus Trickster spoke. Then, as he walked across the valley, again and again he heard that noise. Everyone was shouting for joy. It was wonderful!

"Ah! There must be many people over there," he was thinking to himself. Again he heard them shout and, once again, when the drum was beaten, it seemed as if the heavens would burst asunder. Then again the people gave a tremendous shout. Now he became so anxious to join them that he began to run. The shouting was now quite close to him. Yet he could see no one anywhere. Again he heard the shouting. It was very loud. It sounded as if the sky would burst asunder.

To him it seemed as if, even at that moment, he was walking in the midst of people shouting. Yet he did not see anything. Not far away, however, he saw, lying around, the bones of an animal and, farther still, he saw an object that turned out, on closer inspection, to be an elk's skull. It had many horns branching in every direction. He watched this head quite carefully and then he saw where the noise had come from and where the celebration was taking place. It was in the elk's skull. The head was filled with many flies. They would go inside and then, when they rushed out, they made the noise that he had heard and which he had taken to be shouting. He looked at the flies and he saw that they were enjoying themselves greatly and he envied them.

"Well, I said that I would join in whatever they were doing and I am going to. I wonder what I would have to do in order to join them?" Thus pondered Trickster. Then he said, "Younger brothers, you are certainly having a lot of fun. You surely are doing an important thing. I would very much like to be like one of you. How can I do it? Do show me how I can do it so that I, too, can join you." Thus he spoke.

Then they answered him, "Well, there is no difficulty involved. We enter through the neck as you must have seen by this time." Thus they spoke. Then Trickster tried to enter but failed. He wanted very much to enter but he was unable. "How do you manage to get in, my younger brothers?" he asked. Great man that he was, he could not accomplish it, much as he wished to! Then they said to him, "If you wish to come in just say, 'Neck, become large!' and it will become large. In that way you can enter. That is the way we do it." Thus they told him.

So he sat down and said, "Neck, become large!" and the hole in the neck became large. Then he put his head in and entered. He put his head in up to his neck. All the flies ran away and the opening into which he had thrust his head became small again. Thus he was held fast. He tried to free himself, exerting all his power but it was of no avail. He could do absolutely nothing. He was unable to free his head from the skull of the elk. When he realized that nothing could be done, he went down to the stream wearing the skull. He had long branching antlers, for he was wearing an elk's skull.

When he came to the river he walked along the edge, and as he went along he came to a place inhabited by human beings. There he waited until night. The next morning he did the following. As soon as the people came to get water from the river, he stretched himself out and lay there with his racoon-skin blanket, quite a fear-inspiring object to look upon. His whole body was covered with the racoon-skin blanket and he had long branching horns on his head.

Early in the morning a woman came for water and saw him. She started to run back but he said to her, "Turn back; I will bless you." So she turned back and when she got there, he said to her, "Now, go home. Get an axe and bring it over here. Then use all the offerings that are customary, of which your relations will tell you. If you strike the top of my head with the axe, you will be able to use what you find therein as medicine and obtain anything that you wish. I am an elk-spirit. I am blessing this village." Thus he spoke to her. Then he continued, "I am one of the great spirits living in these waters."

So the woman went home and when she got there she told all the people what had happened. "There is a water spirit at the place where we dip for water, who blessed me. He told me that he had a 'medicine-chest' in the box that he carried and that if we brought an axe and suitable offerings, placed them there and then split his head open, what we found within his skull we could use for making various medicines." Thus she spoke.

Thereupon the people went to the river with their various offerings, and, sure enough, there they found him, quite fear-inspiring to look upon. The offerings—red feathers, white deer skin, and red-yarn belts—they brought in great quantities. After they had placed all these things before him, they selected a man who was to take the axe. He struck the skull and split it open and behold! There they found Trickster laughing at them.

He arose and said, "A nice head-dress I have been wearing but now you have spoiled it!" Then he laughed uproariously. When he got up the people said, "It is Trickster!" However he spoke to them and said, "Inasmuch as you have made these offerings to me they will not be lost. For whatsoever be the purpose for which you use this head, that purpose will be accomplished." So then they made themselves various medicinal instruments and afterwards found that they were efficacious. Then Trickster left and continued wandering. [. . .]

—Paul Radin (1972, 7–8, 13–14,
16–18, 32–34 ff.)

Coyote Forgets the Song (Zuni)

Long, long ago lived Coyote. Not far away at Wempo lived the locusts. They would climb up the pinon-tree, and there all day they sang:

> Locust, locust, flute.
> Locust, locust, flute.
> They climb up the pinon-tree.
> Flute, flute.

Coyote said to his wife, "I am going hunting." His wife said, "Go hunting. Maybe you will kill a rabbit. When you come, we will eat." He went hunting. He went to various places, until he finally went to the place where the locusts were. He heard a sound. The locusts were singing,

> Locust, locust, flute.
> Locust, locust, flute.
> They climb up the pinon-tree.
> Flute, flute.

He stopped. He said, "What is that? What a pretty song to put the children asleep!" They sang again.

> Locust, locust, flute.
> Locust, locust, flute.
> They climb up the pinon-tree.
> Flute, flute.

Coyote looked up into the tree. There were the locusts. He said, "Grandmothers, Grandfathers, are you playing?" The locusts said, "Yes." Coyote said, "May I play too?" "Yes." Coyote said, "How can I get up?" The locusts said, "Sit on that branch. When we sing, you must sing too." Coyote jumped on the branch. They sang,

> Locust, locust, flute.
> Locust, locust, flute.
> They climb up the pinon-tree.
> Flute, flute.

Then Coyote repeated the song ponderously on a lower scale.

At sunset Coyote said, "I must go home. I am going." The locusts answered, "Go!" Coyote said, "I will come again tomorrow." The locusts said, "Come!" At mid-day the locusts went up into the pinon-tree and sang their song. Coyote came. The locusts said, "Grandfather, are you coming?" Coyote said, "Yes." The locusts said, "Jump on the branch, and we will sing." He jumped on the branch. They sang,

> Locust, locust, flute.
> Locust, locust, flute.
> They climb up the pinon-tree.
> Flute, flute.

The sun went down. Coyote said, "I must go home." He went home, and he tried to sing the song to put his children asleep. He sang,

> Locust, locust. . . .

The rest of the song he forgot. His wife said, "Did you get the song?" He said, "No, I forgot it." He kept on saying,

> Locust, locust. . . .

The next morning Coyote returned to Wempo. He said to the locusts, "I don't want to stay all day with you, but I want to take the song to my house." They sang for him. He left them. On his way back he fell into a mole-hole. He lost his song. He went back again to the locusts. He said, "I fell into a mole-hole and I forgot my song. You must sing it to me again." So they sang,

> Locust, locust, flute.
> Locust, locust, flute.
> They climb up the pinon-tree.
> Flute, flute.

He went off. He stepped on a brittle branch, and he hurt his foot and forgot his song. So he went back again. He said, "I stepped on a brittle branch, and I hurt my foot and I forgot the song. You must sing it for me again." They did. He went off once more. On his way he stepped on a cactus-plant. He fell down and hurt his foot and forgot the song. He returned to the locusts and said, "I stepped on a cactus-plant and fell and hurt my foot and forgot the song. You must sing it for me again." They sang it again. He went off still another time. This time he fell in another mole-hole and lost his song. He started back to the locusts.

They said, "We have sung for him four times. Let's not sing it for him again!" So they went into their holes. They took off their masks, filled them with pebbles, and set them on the pinon-tree. They saw Coyote approaching, and they went into their tree.

Coyote came and said to the locusts' masks, "Sing for me again. I fell into a mole-hole, and I forgot the song." They did not answer. Coyote said, "Sing to me, or I'll come up on the tree and eat you." They did not answer. "I shall ask you four times," said Coyote. "Once, will you sing for me?" They did not answer. "Twice, will you sing for me?" They did not answer. "Three times, will you sing for me?" They did not answer. "I shall give you one more chance. Will you sing the song you sang to me?" Nobody answered. He said, "They want to be eaten up."

He jumped up and seized the masks. He knocked out his teeth as they closed on the pebbles in the masks. His mouth was full of blood. He went to his house. His wife said, "Why is your mouth full of blood?" Coyote said, "I asked the locusts to sing me a song. I asked them four times. Then I jumped at them and knocked my teeth out on their masks." Coyote said, "We must not live here. We must live where we can live all the time." So they went to Kosenakwi.

This is why at Kosenakwi you can always see coyotes, just as at Wempo you always see locusts. Thus it was long ago.

—Elsie Clews Parsons (1918, 77–79)

Orpheus Stories

The haunting Greek myth about Orpheus's quest to bring his wife Eurydice back from the underworld provides a generic title for a kind of story found around the world, in nearly every culture—we call them "Orpheus" or "Orphic" stories.

In typical form, they belong in the category of origin myths; what they originate and set a binding precedent for is the permanency of death. In mythic terms, an Orphic story invites us to imagine that once upon a time, it might have been possible under certain very strict conditions to bring a loved one back from death, but as it happens, the Orphic hero's failure to do so usually means that he has lost not just his loved one but also the opportunity to set a precedent for posterity. Death's permanence in our world is surely something we already know about and accept (except in our dreams), but perhaps such sad stories have the power to console us by showing how deeply mortality is ingrained in our human frailty—the Orphic hero's "fatal mistake" just at the moment of success is, as we say, "all too human."

Native American Orpheus stories are numerous and widely distributed, testifying to their importance to the groups who knew them, and also indicating, perhaps, that they are very old. Their heroes range from bereaved husbands and parents to tricksters like Coyote, whose all-too-human waywardness foreshadows that their heroic quest will fail at the end. Sometimes, as in the Nez Perce and Klamath versions given here, the Orphic hero loses his loved one back to death, and then tries again, on his own. It is indicative both of the inherent power of the Orpheus theme and of deep feelings on the part of Native storytellers for it that stories like the Nez Perce "Coyote and the Shadow People" are among the most beautiful of traditional Indian narratives.

Coyote and Eagle Go to the Land of the Dead (Wishram Chinook)

Coyote had a wife and two children, and so had Eagle. Both families lived together. Eagle's wife and children died, and a few days later Coyote experienced the same misfortune. As Coyote wept, Eagle said, "Do not mourn; that will not bring your wife back. Make ready your moccasins, and we will go somewhere." So the two prepared for a long journey, and set out westward.

After four days they were close to the ocean; on the one side of a body of water they saw houses. Coyote called across, "Come with a boat!"— "Never mind, stop calling," said Eagle. He produced an elderberry stalk, made a flute, put the end into the water, and whistled. Soon they saw two persons come out of a house, walk to the water's edge, and enter a canoe. Said Eagle, "Do not look at those people when they land." The boat drew near, but a few yards from shore it stopped, and Eagle told Coyote to close his eyes. He then took Coyote by the arm and leaped to the boat. The two persons paddled back, and when they stopped a short distance from the other side, Eagle again cautioned Coyote to close his eyes, and then leaped ashore with him.

They went to the village, where there were many houses, but no people were in sight. Everything was as still as death. There was a very large underground house, into which they went. In it was an old woman [Frog] sitting with her face to the wall, and lying on the floor on the other side of the room was the moon. They sat down near the wall.

"Coyote," whispered Eagle, "watch that woman and see what she does when the sun goes down!" Just before the sun set they heard a voice outside calling, "Get up! Hurry! The sun is going down, and it will soon be night. Hurry! Hurry!" Coyote and Eagle still sat in a corner of the chamber watching the old woman.

People began to enter, many hundreds of them, men, women, and children. Coyote, as he watched, saw Eagle's wife and two daughters among them, and soon afterward his own family. When the room was filled, Nikshia'mchash, the old woman, cried, "Are all in?" Then she turned about, and from a squatting posture she jumped forward, then again and again, five times in all, until she alighted in a small pit beside the moon. This she raised and swallowed, and at once it was pitch dark. The people wandered about, hither and thither, crowding and jostling, unable to see. About daylight a voice from outside said, "Nikshia'mchash, all get through!" The old woman then disgorged the moon, and laid it back in its place on the floor; all the people filed out, and the woman, Eagle, and Coyote were once more alone.

"Now, Coyote," said Eagle, "could you do that?"—"Yes, I can do that," he said. They went out, and Coyote at Eagle's direction made a box of boards, as large as he could carry, and put into it leaves from every kind of tree and blades from every kind of grass. "Well," said Eagle, "if you are sure you remember just how she did this, let us go in and kill her."

So they entered the house and killed her, and buried the body. Her dress they took off and put on Coyote, so that he looked just like her, and he sat down in her place. Eagle then told him to practice what he had seen, by turning around and jumping as the old woman had done. So Coyote turned about and jumped five times, but the last leap was a little short, yet he managed to slide into the hole. He put the moon into his mouth, but, try as he would, a thin edge of the moon still showed, and he covered it with his hands. Then he laid the moon back in its place and resumed his seat by the wall, waiting for sunset and the voice of the chief outside.

The day passed, the voice called, and the people entered. Coyote turned about and began to jump. Some [of the people] thought there was something strange about the manner of jumping, but others said it was really the old woman. When he came to the last jump and slipped into the pit, many cried out that this was not the old woman, but Coyote quickly lifted the moon and put it in his mouth, covering the edge with his hands.

When it was completely dark, Eagle placed the box in the doorway. Throughout the long night Coyote retained the moon in his mouth, until he was almost choking, but at last the voice of the chief was heard from the outside, and the dead began to file out. Everyone walked into the box, and Eagle quickly threw the cover over and tied it. The sound was like that of a great swarm of flies.

"Now, my brother, we are through," said Eagle. Coyote removed the dress and laid it down beside the moon, and Eagle threw the moon into the sky, where it remained. The two entered the canoe with the box, and paddled towards the east.

When they landed, Eagle carried the box. Near the end of the third night, Coyote heard someone talking; there seemed to be many voices. He awakened his companion, and said, "There are many people coming."— "Do not worry," said Eagle, "it is all right." The following night Coyote heard the talking again, and, looking about, he discovered that the voices came from the box which Eagle had been carrying. He placed his ear against it, and after a while distinguished the voice of his wife. He smiled, and broke into laughter, but he said nothing to Eagle.

At the end of the fifth night and the beginning of their last day of traveling, Coyote said to his friend, "I will carry the box now; you have carried it a long way."—"No," replied Eagle, "I will take it; I am strong."— "Let me carry it," insisted Coyote; "suppose we come to where people live, and they should see the chief carrying the load. How would that look?" Still Eagle retained his hold on the box, but as they went along Coyote kept begging, and about noon, wearying of the subject, Eagle gave him the box.

So Coyote had the load, and every time he heard the voice of his wife he would laugh. After a while he contrived to fall behind, and while Eagle was out of sight around a hill, he began to open the box, in order to release his wife. But no sooner was the cover lifted than it was thrown back violently, and the dead people rushed out into the air with such force that Coyote was thrown to the ground. They quickly disappeared in the west. Eagle saw the cloud of dead people rising in the air, and came hurrying back. He found one man left there, a cripple who had been unable to rise; he threw him into the air, and the dead man floated away swiftly.

"You see what you have done, with your curiosity and haste!" said Eagle. "If we had brought these dead all the way back, people would not die forever, but only for a season, like these plants, whose leaves we have brought. Hereafter trees and grasses will die only in the winter, but in the spring will be green again. So it would have been with the people."—"Let us go back and catch them again," proposed Coyote; but Eagle objected: "They will not go to the same place, and we would not know how to find them; they will be where the moon is, up in the sky."

—Edward S. Curtis (1970a, 127–29)

The Ghost Wife (Pawnee)

One time there were living together, a man and his wife. They had a young child. The woman died. The man was very sad, and mourned for his wife.

One night he took the child in his arms, and went out from the village to the place where his wife was buried, and stood over the grave, and mourned for his wife. The little child was helpless, and cried all the time. The man's heart was sick with grief and loneliness. Late in the night he fell asleep, fainting and worn out with sorrow.

After a while he awoke, and when he looked up, there was a form standing by him. The form standing there was the one who had died. She spoke to her husband, and said, "You are very unhappy here. There is a place to go where we would not be unhappy. Where I have been nothing bad happens to one. Here, you never know what evil will come to you. You and the child had better come to me."

The man did not want to die. He said to her, "No, it will be better if you can come back to us. We love you. If you were with us we would be unhappy no longer."

For a long time they discussed this, to decide which one should go to the other. At length the man by his persuasions overcame her, and the woman agreed to come back. She said to the man, "If I am to come back you must do exactly as I tell you for four nights. For four days the curtain must remain let down before my sleeping place; it must not be raised; no one must look back behind it."

The man did as he had been told, and after four days had passed, the curtain was lifted, and the woman came out from behind it. Then they all saw her, first her relations, and afterward the whole tribe. Her husband and her child were very glad, and they lived happily together.

A long time after this, the man took another wife. The first wife was always pleasant and good-natured, but the new one was bad-tempered, and after some time she grew jealous of the first woman, and quarreled with her. At length, one day the last married became angry with the other, and called her bad names, and finally said to her, "You ought not to be here. You are nothing but a ghost, anyway."

That night when the man went to bed, he lay down, as was his custom, by the side of his first wife. During the night he awoke, and found that his wife had disappeared. She was seen no more. The next night after this happened, the man and the child both died in sleep. The wife had called them to her. They had gone to that place where there is a living.

This convinced everyone that there is a hereafter.

—George Bird Grinnell (1961, 129–31)

Lulu'laidi (Klamath)

This remarkable variation on the Orpheus format (which shares with the Nez Perce story the Orphic hero's second *attempt to recover his wife) was told by a Klamath woman named Lulu Lang to the anthropologist and folklorist Theodore Stern, who rendered it in Lang's own "reservation English." Editorially correcting her grammar, syntax, and so forth would surely diminish the effectiveness and authority of Mrs. Lang's narration; Stern's editorial approach to the story anticipates the approach taken by modern ethnopoetic scholars like Dell Hymes and Dennis Tedlock.*

Once there was a lot of people living at the mouth of the Williamson River. So, this Lulu'laidi, she was grea-a-a-t singer. And she had husband. Whenever people would get together and when they sing songs and she would be the loudest singer all the time; and she was pretty woman, too. And so, she took sick, and finally after quite a while, somehow she died. And her spirit-soul went toward West, toward nolis gaeni [the spirit place].

And so, her man started to get ready, and he followed her. Whenever night came, he would camp, and his wife's spirit would be taking pity on him and would be setting up on limb there all night, waiting for him. She didn't like to leave him behind. And so, next morning he got up early and started again. And he traveled *all* day, tired, never eating anything, all scratched up, looking pitiful. Then night would come up on him again. Then there he would camp again, and this spirit-wife would be *same* way, would be up there someplace, taking pity on him, don't want to leave him behind. Then he would start up *early* in the morning again. Then he would be going *all* day. Then night would come up on him again. And again he would stop overnight, pretty tired and worried about his wife's leaving him.

Then he would get up early next morning again. Then he would start out again next morning to follow her. And so, this woman in spirit, she was taking *awful* pity on him because he was looking so pitiful, tired, and worn-out traveling. So that night came over on him again. Then again he stop overnight and his spirit-wife, Lulu'laidi, would be sitting up in tree above him. She didn't like to leave him. And so, next morning, again he got up, *early*, weary, tired, and worn-out. He struck out again, he traveled a . . . . ll day. And so, then night would come on him again. And there he stop overnight again, take rest—he was pretty badly worn-out. Then he started out again, *early* morning, and finally in evening he got to *nolis gaeni*.

And so, when he got there, Lulu'laidi, his wife, was there already. And so, he stayed there, and those people, daytime they was all quiet, them *skoks* [ghosts]. And so, that evening, all these dead people come back to just like live people, they going to have [a] time. Then start to singing. And he could hear her voice just like he hear her voice when she was living on earth. Oh, and he recognize her voice. And so, he said to himself, "Oh, that's her!"—Lulu'laidi, his wife. And so, next morning they was all just like sleep again.

And he figured around, he don't know what to do, and he study about it pretty nearly all day, thinking what to do and what can he do, and what he's going to try to do. And so, evening come, and he was there, and when darkness come, people began to walking around this way and that way, just like they were waking up. So they got together again that night. Then they start their songs up again. And he would hear her voice just the same as he would hear her voice on earth. Singing *loud*, loud above *all* of them. And he said [*narrator: gentle voice*], "Well, there she is. She's there."

And next morning come, and sometime that day he happened to come across this Kemuk'amps's daughter—she was living over there in *nolis gaeni*. And he went to her and he started to talk to her. And he told her about what had happened. And so, he said to her, "Can you get that soul back for me some way? Can you do something for me?" (It was great loss to him that Lulu'laidi, great singer and all, it was a great loss to him.) And Kemuk'amps's daughter said [*narrator: reflective voice*], "Well, I'll see, I see if I can get close enough to her." (Spirits, you can't touch it, you can't get close to it.)

And so, that night again they got together. And this Kemuk'amps's daughter, she got one of these *'nai* [winnowing basket] and a seed gatherer. Those dead people start to singing. And this Kemuk'amps's daughter, she heard Lulu'laidi's voice among them, and so does her husband. And this Kemuk'amps's daughter, she tried to get close to her, and she couldn't make it. She couldn't make it.

So next night again, she's going to try it again. And she come li . . . . ttle bit close to her when they were singing. So she didn't get chance to get her. (Kemuk'amps's daughter wasn't spirit, she just happened to be living there, *nolis gaeni.*

And so, the next night again they get together again, they come to be people—daytime there was nobody to be seen. And now, they start up their meeting again, and so old Kemuk'amps's daughter, [she] got this *'nai* and seed gatherer, and she went clo . . . . ser to her. She was singing lou . . . . d and had g . o . o . d voice, Lulu'laidi. And [she] come close to her—and she couldn't make it.

And so, next morning come and everyone disappear—gone. All go back to ghosts. And then, that night again, this man, this Lulu'laidi's husband, commenced to see people walking around again, going this way and that way—all directions. Then a . . . . ll at once, they got together again. And they start to sing again. And this Lulu'laidi's husband, he hear her voice singing, and he feel glad just to hear her singing, although he was almost worried to death about losing her. And so, this Kemuk'amps's daughter, [she] got his *'nai* again and that seed fanner. So, [she] went around to them again and [she] got li . . . . ttle bit closer, by ca . . . . reful movements. And so, [she] come pretty close to getting her, that time.

And so, daylight come. And everybody's gone—nobody to be seen. So that man, Lulu'laidi's husband, he just wandered around, almost worry himself to death. And so, then night come again, And he was glad, because he could hear her voice. And so, darkness come again and he could see them walking as persons in all directions. Then, pretty soon, they a . . . . ll get together in crowd. And so, they start to sing, and he could hear her voice as she was singing above all of them. And this Lulu'laidi's husband heard, "She's there. That's her voice."

And so, now this Kemuk'amps's daughter, she worked around so that now [she's] going to do something. Then [she] got his *'nai* and that seed fanner. Then she come in right close to them and by quick action she did the trick. She took the seed fanner and she whipped that soul into that *'nai.* And she covered the *'nai* up, quick as she can—she sealed it up tight. And now he got her back.

And then next day, Kamuk'amps's daughter, she told this man, "Now," [she] said, "when you take this *'nai* and this soul sealed tight, when you sleep overnight on the way, if she try to talk to you, do . . . . n't answer when she try to talk to you." And he said, "All right!" She said to him, "She'll bother you e . . . . very night when you stop. She'll try to talk to you, try to make you speak and answer her, but do . . . n't answer. Don't speak."

And so, he started out, started to come back home with his wife's spirit in that *'nai* sealed up tight. So he come a . . . . ll day. Night overtook him. So he took off the pack off his back—that *'nai*—and set it down on the ground. So, after he went to bed, Lulu'laidi, she said, "My husband!" She started to talk to her husband. And so, he pretty nearly speak. But a thought came into him not to answer, because Kemuk'amps's daughter advise him to no . . . . t say anything to her and not answer her.

So, next morning again he got up early, almost worn out, tired. And put the pack on his back and he started out again. Traveled a . . . ll day, walk. And he walked, tired and worn-out. Then night came on him again. And he stop overnight right there, took his pack off and set it down and went to lay down. Then again that night, she told him, "My husband, my husband!" He didn't answer. Then she talk to him, try to make him speak, try to get him to answer when she called him. And she kept *after* him, *after* him. But he never answered. He never say anything.

So, he woke up early, in the morning, ragged and tired. So, he got ready and he pick up that *'nai*, put it on his back and he started out again. And so, he walked a . . . . ll day. He tried to come as *fast* as he could so that he could get home. And so, night come on him again. And so, he start to camp again. He took his pack off and set it down on ground. Then he start to lay down alongside it, go to bed. And when it got so dark, she commenced to talk to him. And she talked, kept up talking to him, asking him questions, he never answered, he *never* answer.

So, next morning he got up early and he strike out again and he come as fast as he could, even [though] he was all worn out, tired. So, night overtook him again. And he took his pack off and he set it on ground. And he lay down alongside of it. That's where he go to bed. And so, as soon as darkness come, she said, Lulu'laidi said, "My husband!" She said, "My husband!" She spoke suddenly, so that he might answer. But he didn't answer. Then she commenced to talk to him *everything* that they were talking when they were both living together. She ask him questions, call upon him and tell him things. Try to make him say something. But he *never* speak, *never* answer her.

So, next morning he struck out. He started early. So, he come just as fast as he could come, even though he was *a . . . ll* worn out, tired. And night overtook him. So, he set his pack down on ground and started camping again. And this man, he lay there and listened by that pack. He was listening. So, she commenced to call on him, tried to tell him something. Tried to make him answer. But she couldn't. That man stick to the advice of that Kemuk'amps's daughter. And Lulu'laidi coul . . . dn't make him speak and coul . . . . dn't make him answer all those nights they were on the road traveling.

And so, he struck out a little bit earlier in the morning. So, he started fast, and he got back across the lake [Klamath Lake], towards Pelican Bay. He got back there and he hollered for someone to come and get him. And that he had got back and that [he] was Lulu'laidi's husband. And so, people hear of it. They begin to get excited, because she dies and her soul went to *nolis gaeni*. Somehow, they guessed that something happened. And there was one or two canoes got ready. And there was people stirring around, getting ready to get into canoe to come over to get him. And this man saw them moving around like that and he hollered over, he said, "No, just one person! One canoe got to come after me—not too many!" And he kept hollering over for them not to come—only one, and one canoe.

So the people didn't mind him. There was two, three canoes and two or three in each canoe started to come over after him. And still he hollered over, "No, no! only one, only one person, one canoe!" So these people didn't mind him; they kept coming.

And so, they got over there, close to shore, and this Lulu'laidi, she start to flew out of that *'nai* and went back. Went back. And that man, he pretty near drop over and fainted. He told them [*narrator: calm, reproachful tone*], "Now, you people ought to know and listen to me, what I told you to do." And he said it then [*same tone*], "You see what you people done to me?"

And so, he got ready again, going to follow his wife again. He struck out to the west to that *nolis gaeni*. And he stop overnight. So, his spirit-wife sat up in the tree, took pity on her husband, saw him tired, broken-down, almost a goner.

And next morning he started out again. She didn't leave him. So, night come on him again. And he lay down, stop overnight again—tired, worried, almost a goner.

Then next morning he struck out again. Then she stayed close to him in the air, taking pity on him that he was looking so pitiful, tired, broken-down, worn-out. And he was going, still going, *and*, somehow, when he stopped to camp that night, he died—worried, tired, worn-out. He died.

And then, his spirit-soul went right up to his wife, and they both strike out for West, *nolis gaeni*, going both in spirit now. And when they got to *nolis gaeni*, they started to settle down and live there with the rest of the people.

At gadani hak. [And that ends the story.]

—Told by Lulu Lang,
transcribed by Theodore Stern,
in Jones and Ramsey (1994, 220–24)

Badger and Coyote Were Neighbors (Clackamas Chinook)

The story ends with a moment of truth for Coyote: having let his grief and guilt run away with him, having attempted suicide in various ways, he ultimately comes to understand that in social as well as psychological terms there must be an end to mourning, and in his transformer role he lays down the law that after a prescribed term of formal mourning, the bereaved person must take up his or her place in society again.

Coyote and his five children lived there, four males, one female. Badger was a neighbor there, he had five children, all males. Each day they (all ten children) would go here and there. They came back in the evening. And then next day they would go out again. Now that is the way they were doing. They would go all over, they traveled about.

Now they reached a village, they stayed up above there, they looked down below at it, they saw where they (the villagers) were playing ball. And as they stayed there and watched, the people (of the village beneath) saw them now. They went to the place where they played ball. Now they (the villagers) played. When they threw the ball it was just like the sun. Now they stayed (above) there, they watched them playing. Sometimes it (the ball) would drop close by the ten children. Now the villagers quit (playing). Then they (the ten children) went back home, they went to their houses.

The next day then they did not go anywhere. All day long they chatted about that ball (and schemed about stealing it). They discussed it. Now their father Badger heard them. He said to his sons, "What is it that you are discussing?" So they told their father. "Yes," they said to him, "we got to a village, and they were playing ball. When the ball went it was just like the sun. We thought we would go get it."

Now then he said to his children, "What do you think (about talking this over with Coyote, too)?" So then they said to Coyote, "What do you think?" He said, "My children should be the first ones (to run with the ball), if they bring the ball." Badger said, "No. My children should be the first ones to do it." Coyote said, "No. My children have long bodies, their legs are long. They can run (faster than your children). Your children have short legs." So then Badger replied to him (Coyote), "Very well then."

Now the next day they got ready, and they went. They reached there. At that place one of them (the oldest son of Coyote) went immediately to the spot where the ball might drop. He covered (buried) himself at that place on the playing field. Then another (the next eldest son) buried himself further on, and another one (the third in age) still farther away. All four (sons of Coyote) covered themselves (with soil on the field). The last one farther on at the end (was) their younger sister. Now the (five) children of Badger merely remained (on the hill above the field), they watched.

Soon afterwards then the people (of that village) came there, they came to play ball. Now they threw the ball to where it fell close by him (Coyote's eldest son). He seized it. They looked for it, they said . . . "Coyote's son is hiding it!" He let it go, and they took it, and they played more. Now it dropped close by him there once again. So then he took it, and he ran. The people turned and looked, they saw him running, he was taking the ball. Now they ran in pursuit, they got close to him, he got close to his younger brother (the second in age), he threw the ball to him. He said, "We are dying (going to be killed) because of the ball. Give a large chunk of it to our father." (His pursuers now caught up to him, and killed him.)

Then the other (the second) one took it, and he ran too. The people pursued him, he got close to his younger brother (Coyote's third son). Now they seized him (the second son), and he threw the ball to his younger brother. So they killed all four of them. Now only their younger sister held the ball, she ran, she ran and ran, she left them quite a distance behind (because she was the fastest runner of all). She got close to the Badgers. Now as they seized her she threw the ball to them (the five Badger children), she said to them, "Give the biggest portion to our father (to Coyote). We have died because of the ball."

The Badgers took the ball. He (the first and oldest Badger child) dropped it when he picked it up. Another (the next-to-oldest) took it, he also dropped it when he picked it up. They (the pursuers) got to there, and stood there (watching the Badger children fumbling the ball). They said, they told them, "So those are the ones that would be taking away the ball!" They laughed at them. . . . They said, "Let it be a little later before we kill them!" Soon now they (the Badgers) kicked at the ground, and wind blew and dust and darkness stood there. Dust covered (everything), and the wind blew. Now the Badgers ran, they ran away with the ball. And those people pursued them. They got tired, they got thirsty (from dust and wind), they turned back to their home.

On the other hand those others (the Badgers) lay down (from exhaustion) right there when they had gotten close (to their home). And there they sat (and rested). Now they hallooed, they said to their father, "Badger! We left you children far back there!" Now they hallooed again, they went and told Coyote, "Back yonder we left your children." That is the way they did to them (they first deceived Badger and Coyote).

Now Badger went outside, he said to his children, "Now really why did you do like that? You have been teasing and paining him (Coyote)." Then they (the Badger children) went downhill (and entered the village), it was only Badger's children (who returned). They brought the ball with them.

Now Coyote tried in vain to drown himself. He did not die. Then he built a fire, he made a big fire, he leaped into it there. He did not burn, he did not die. He took a rope, he tied it, tied it on his throat, he pulled himself up, once more he did not die. He took a knife, he cut his throat, (again) he did not die. He did every sort of thing that he intended for killing himself. He gave up. I do not know how many days he was doing like that. . . . Now he quit it, and he merely wept all the day long. (After a while) he gave that up (too).

Then Badger said to his children, "He has quit (mourning) now. So then cut up the ball for him. Give him half." And they did that for him, they gave him half. He took it, and he went here and there at the place where his children used to play. There he now mashed (into many pieces) that ball, at the place where they used to play. That was where he took it, he mashed it up, the ball was entirely gone (now).

Then they continued to live there, and Coyote was all alone. Now he went to work, he made a big loose pack basket. Then it was getting to be springtime, and when the leaves were coming out, now he got ready, and he went to the place where they had killed his children. He got to the (grave of the) first one (his eldest son). He picked ferns, he lined his pack basket with them. He got to the place where they had killed the first of his sons, he collected his bones, he put them into it (the basket), he laid them into it neatly. Then he got more ferns, he picked the leaves, he covered (the bones of) his son. Now he went a little farther, and he again got to the bones (of his second son). Then he also put them into the basket, and that is the way he did again. He collected the bones of all five of his children.

Now he went on, he proceeded very slowly, he only went a short distance. Then he camped overnight. The next day he proceeded again, also very slowly like that. On the third day, then, he heard them (talking to one another in the basket). They said, "You are lying upon me. Move a little." Then he went along all the more slowly. Now he kept going, he went just a short distance, and then he picked more leaves, he covered it all (with utmost care and constantly replenishing with fresh leaves). And that is the way he did as he went along.

She (perhaps a centipede) would run across his path, she would say to him, "Sniff sniff sniff! . . . Coyote is taking dead persons along!" He paid no heed to her. Now she ran repeatedly and all the more in front of him, again she would speak like that to him, "Sniff! Coyote is carrying dead persons along!" He laid his basket down very very slowly . . . he got a stick, he ran after her. I do not know where she went and hid.

Then he was packing his carrying basket on his back again, and now he went very, very slowly, and he heard his children. Now they were chatting, they were saying, "Move around slowly and carefully! We are making our father tired." Then he was glad, and he went along even more slowly and cautiously. He walked so very slowly that he saw his (previous night's) campfire, and then he again camped overnight.

He went right on the next morning, and then that thing (the bug) ran back and forth across his path right there by his feet. Now he became angry. He placed the basket down, and again he chased it. I do not know where it hid.

On the fifth day then he heard them laughing. So he went along even more painstakingly. Now that thing went still more back and forth in front of him by his feet. He forgot [. . .], he (much too abruptly) loosened and let go his pack basket. "Oh, oh, oh," his children sounded (and at once died from the shock of the sudden movement of the basket). All done, he finished, and he again put his basket on himself. When he went along now he did not hear them talking at all. He went along then. They were dead now when he uncovered his basket. Only bones were inside it. He reached his house. The following day he buried them. He finished [. . .], he wept for five days.

Then he said, "Indeed I myself did like that (and lost my children because of my doing). The people (who will populate this country) are coming and are close by now. Only in that one manner shall it be, when persons die. In that one way had I brought my children back, then the people would be like that (in later eras). When they died in summertime, wintertime, or toward springtime, after the leaves (came on the trees), they (all the dead) would have come back to life, and such persons would have revived on the fifth day (following a ritual like the one I attempted). But now his (any mourner's) sorrow departs from him after ten days (of formal mourning). Then he can go to anywhere where something (entertaining) is happening or they are gambling, and he may (then shed his mourning and) watch it."

—Told by Victoria Howard,
in Jacobs (1959, 95–98)

Coyote and the Shadow People (Nez Perce)

Coyote and his wife were dwelling there. His wife became ill. She died. Then Coyote became very, very lonely. He did nothing but weep for his wife.

There the death spirit came to him and said, "Coyote, do you pine for your wife?"—"Yes, friend, I long for her [. . .]" replied Coyote. "I could take you to the place where your wife has gone, but, I tell you, you must do everything just exactly as I say; not once are you to disregard my commands and do something else."—"Yes," replied Coyote, "yes, friend, and what else could I do? I will do everything you say." Then the ghost said to him, "Yes. Now let us go." Coyote added, "Yes, let it be so that we are going."

They went. There he said to Coyote again, "You must do whatever I say. Do not disobey."—"Yes, yes, friend, I have been pining so deeply, and why should I not heed you?" Coyote could not see the spirit clearly. He appeared to be only a shadow. They started and went along over a plain. "Oh, there are many horses; it looks like a round-up," exclaimed the ghost. "Yes," replied Coyote, though he really saw none, "yes, there are many horses."

They had arrived now near the place of the dead. The ghost knew that Coyote could see nothing but he said, "Oh look, such quantities of service berries! Let us pick some to eat. Now when you see me reach up you too will reach up and when I bend the limb down you too will pull your hands down."—"Yes," Coyote said to him, "so be it, thus I will do." The ghost reached up and bent the branch down and Coyote did the same. Although he could see no berries he imitated the ghost in putting his hand to and from his mouth in the manner of eating. Thus they picked and ate berries. Coyote watched him carefully and imitated every action. When the ghost would put his hand into his mouth, Coyote would do the same. "Such good service berries these are," commented the ghost. "Yes, friend, it is good that we have found them," agreed Coyote. "Now let us go on." And they went on.

"We are about to arrive," the ghost told him. "There is a long, very, very long lodge. Your wife is in there somewhere. Just wait and let me ask someone." In a little while the ghost returned and said to Coyote, "Yes, they have told me where your wife is. We are coming to a door through which we will enter. You will do in every way exactly what you see me do. I will take hold of the door flap, raise it up, and bending low, will enter. Then you too will take hold of the door flap and do the same." They proceeded now in this manner to enter.

It happened that Coyote's wife was sitting right near the entrance. The ghost said to Coyote, "Sit here beside your wife." They both sat. The ghost added, "Your wife is now going to prepare food for us." Coyote could see nothing, except that he was sitting there on an open prairie where nothing was in sight; yet he could feel the presence of the shadow. "Now she has prepared our food. Let us eat." The ghost reached down and then brought up his hand to his mouth. Coyote could see nothing but the prairie dust. They ate. Coyote imitated all the movements of his companion. When they had finished and the woman had apparently put the food away, the ghost said to Coyote, "You stay here. I must go around to see some people."

He went out but returned soon. "Here we have conditions different from those you have in the land of the living. When it gets dark here it has dawned in your land and when it dawns for us it is growing dark for you." And now it began to grow dark and Coyote seemed to hear people whispering, talking in faint tones, all around him. Then darkness set in. Oh, Coyote saw many fires in a longhouse. He saw that he was in a very, very large lodge and there were many fires burning. He saw the various people. They seemed to have shadow-like forms but he was able to recognize different persons. He saw his wife sitting by his side.

He was overjoyed, and he joyfully greeted all his old friends who had died long ago. How happy he was! He would march down the aisles between the fires, going here and there, and talk with the people. He did this throughout the night. Now he could see the doorway through which he and his friend had entered. At last it began to dawn and his friend came to him and said, "Coyote, our night is falling and in a little while you will not see us. Stay right here and then in the evening you will see all these people again."—"Yes, friend. Where could I possibly go? I will spend the day here."

The dawn came and Coyote found himself alone sitting there in the middle of the prairie. He spent the day there, just dying from the heat, parching from the heat, thirsting from the heat. Coyote stayed here several days. He would suffer through the day, but always at night he would make merry in the great lodge.

One day his ghost friend came to him and said, "Tomorrow you will go home. You will take your wife with you."—"Yes, friend, but I like it here so much, I am having a good time and I should like to remain here."— "Yes," the ghost replied, "nevertheless you will go tomorrow, and you must guard against your inclination to do foolish things. Do not yield to any queer notions. I will advise you now what you are to do. There are five mountains. You will travel for five days. Your wife will be with you but you must never, never touch her. Do not let any strange impulses possess you. You may talk to her but never touch her. Only after you have crossed and descended from the fifth mountain you may do whatever you like."— "Yes, friend," replied Coyote.

When dawn came again, Coyote and his wife started. At first it seemed to him as if he were going alone, yet he was dimly aware of his wife's presence as she walked along behind. They crossed one mountain, and now, Coyote could feel more definitely the presence of his wife; like a shadow she seemed. They went on and crossed the second mountain. They camped at night at the foot of each mountain. They had a little conical lodge which they would set up each time. Coyote's wife would sit on one side of the fire and he on the other. Her form appeared clearer and clearer.

The death spirit, who had sent them, now began to count the days and to figure the distance Coyote and his wife had covered. "I hope that he will do everything right and take his wife through to the world beyond," he kept saying to himself.

Here Coyote and his wife were spending their last night, their fourth camping, and on the morrow she would again assume fully the character of a living person. They were camping for the last time and Coyote could see her very clearly as if she were a real person who sat opposite him. He could see her face and body very clearly, but only looked and dared not touch her.

But suddenly a joyous impulse seized him; the joy of having his wife again overwhelmed him. He jumped to his feet, and rushed over to embrace her. His wife cried out, "Stop! Stop! Coyote! Do not touch me. Stop!" Her warning had no effect. Coyote rushed over to his wife and just as he touched her body she vanished. She disappeared—returned to the shadow land.

When the death-spirit learned of Coyote's folly he became deeply angry. "You inveterate doer of this kind of thing! I told you not to do anything foolish. You, Coyote, were about to establish the practice of returning from death. Only a short time away the human race is coming, but you have spoiled everything, and established for them death as it is."

Here Coyote wept and wept. He decided, "Tomorrow I shall return to see them again." He started back the following morning and as he went along he began to recognize the places where he and his spirit friend had passed before. He found the place where the ghost had seen the herd of horses, and now he began to do the same things they had done on their way to the shadow-land. "Oh, look at the horses; it looks like a round-up." He went on until he came to the place where the ghost had found the service berries. "Oh, such choice service berries! Let us pick and eat some." He went through the motions of picking and eating berries.

He went on and finally came to the place where the lodge had stood. He said to himself, "Now when I take hold of the door flap and raise it up you must do the same." Coyote remembered all the little things his friend had done. He saw the spot where he had sat before. He went there, sat down, and said, "Now, your wife has brought us food, let us eat." He went through the motions of eating again. Darkness fell, and now Coyote listened for the voices, and he looked all around. He looked here and there, but nothing appeared. Coyote sat there in the middle of the prairie. He sat there all night but the lodge didn't appear again nor did the ghost ever return to him.

—Told by Wayilatpu,
in Phinney (1934, 283–85)

Stories for Learning
How to Live in This World

For many readers, "Native American story" denotes creation and origin myths and perhaps trickster tales. But in fact every tribal repertory included a preponderance of stories of a more realistic bent, engaging human life as it has to be negotiated and lived, challenge by challenge, decision by decision. Many of these stories do contain mythic and supernatural characters and situations, but their primary focus is rather like most fiction—addressing how to live in a complex, unpredictable world, where moral directions are often ambiguous or lacking altogether.

In the words of the Dakota story about the boy who thoughtlessly borrows and then loses his brother's sacred arrow, "Hakela . . . was scared; how he ought to act was not plain." As it turns out, Hakela's choice of brave and resourceful actions succeeds heroically; but in the Wasco Chinookan story of the young elk-hunter, his decision to obey his worthless father rather than his spiritual guide leads to calamity. The point is that narratives like these, whether heroic or tragic, are "learning stories," not in any simplistic or didactic way but rather in dramatizing the actions of young men and women trying to cope with the difficult circumstances that life inevitably brings.

Dirty-Boy (Okanagan)

The people of a certain region were living together in a very large camp. Their chief had two beautiful daughters of marriageable age. Many young men had proposed to them, but all had been refused.

The chief said, "Whom do my daughters wish to marry? They have refused all the men." Sun and Star, who were brother and sister, lived in the sky, and had seen all that had happened. Sun said to his sister, "The chief's daughters have rejected the suits of our friends. Let us go down and arrange the matter! Let us try these girls!" They made clothes, and at night they descended to earth.

During the darkness they erected a lodge on the outskirts of the camp. It had the appearance of being very old, and belonging to poor people. The poles were old and badly selected. The covering was tattered and patched, and made of tule mats. The floors were strewn with old dried brush and grass, and the beds were of the same material. Their blankets consisted of old mats and pieces of robes; and their kettles and cups were of bark, poorly made. Star had assumed the form of a decrepit old woman dressed in rags; and Sun, that of a dirty boy with sore eyes.

On the following morning the women of the camp saw the lodge, and peered in. When they returned, they reported, "Some very poor people arrived during the night, and are camped in an old man's mat lodge. We saw two persons inside—a dirty, sore-eyed boy; and his grandmother, a very old woman in ragged clothes."

Now, the chief resolved to find husbands for his daughters. He sent out his speaker to announce that in four days there would be a shooting-contest open to all the men, and the best marksman would get his daughters for wives. The young men could not sleep for eagerness. On the third day the chief's speaker announced, "Tomorrow morning everyone shall shoot. Each one will have two shots. An eagle will perch on the tall tree yonder; and whoever kills it shall have the chief's daughters."

Coyote was there and felt happy. He thought he would win the prize. On the following morning an eagle was seen soaring in the air, and there was much excitement as it began to descend. It alighted on a tree which grew near one end of the camp. Then the young men tried to shoot it. Each man had two arrows. The previous evening Sun had said to Star, "Grandmother, make a bow and arrow for me." She said, "What is the use? You cannot shoot. You never used bow and arrows." He replied, "I am going to try. I shall take part in the contest tomorrow. I heard what the chief said." She took pity on him, and went to a red willow-bush, cut a branch for a bow, and some twigs for arrows. She strung the bow with a poor string, and did not feather the arrows.

Coyote, who was afraid someone else might hit the bird, shouted,

"I will shoot first. Watch me hit the eagle." His arrow struck the lowest branch of the tree and fell down, and the people laughed. He said, "I made a mistake. That was a bad arrow. This one will kill the eagle." He shot, and the arrow fell short of the first one. He became angry, and pulled other arrows from his quiver. He wanted to shoot them all.

The people seized him, and took away his arrows, saying, "You are allowed to shoot twice only."

All the people shot and missed. When the last had shot, Sun said, "Grandmother, lift the door of the lodge a little, so that I can shoot." She said, "First get out of bed." She pulled the lodge mat aside a little, and he shot. The arrow hit the tail of the eagle. The people saw and heard the arrow coming from Dirty-Boy's lodge, but saw no one shooting it. They wondered. He shot the second arrow, and pierced the eagle's heart.

Now, Wolf and others were standing near Dirty-Boy's lodge, and Wolf desired much to claim the prize. He shouted, "I shot the bird from the lodge-door!" and ran to pick it up; but the old woman Star ran faster than he, picked up the bird, and carried it to the chief. She claimed his daughters for her grandson. All the people gathered around, and made fun of Dirty-Boy. They said, "He is bed-ridden. He is lousy, sore-eyed, and scabby-faced." The chief was loath to give his daughters to such a person. He knew that Dirty-Boy could not walk. Therefore he said, "Tomorrow there shall be another contest. This will be the last one, I cannot break my word. Whoever wins this time shall have my daughters."

He announced that on the morrow each man would set two traps for fishers, an animal very scarce at the place where the camp was located. If anyone should catch a fisher one night, then he was to stay in the mountains another day to catch a second one. After that he had to come back. Those who caught nothing the first night had to come home at once. Only two traps were allowed to each man; and two fishers had to be caught—one a light one, and one a dark one—and both prime skins. When all the men had gone to the mountains, Sun said to his sister, "Grandmother, make two traps for me." She answered, "First get out of bed!" However, she had pity on him, and made two deadfalls of willow sticks. She asked him where she should set them; and he said, "One on each side of the lodge-door."

On the following morning all the men returned by noon; not one of them had caught a fisher. When Star went out, she found two fine fishers in the traps. Now the chief assembled the men to see if any had caught the fishers. He was glad, because he knew that Dirty-Boy could not walk; and unless he went to the mountains, he had no chance to kill fishers. Just then the old grandmother appeared, dragging the fishers. She said, "I hear you asked for fishers; here are two that my grandson caught." She handed them over to him, and then left.

Coyote had boasted that he would certainly catch the fishers. When he went up the mountain, he carried ten traps instead of two. He said, "Whoever heard of setting only two traps! I shall set ten." He set them all, remained out two nights, but got nothing.

The chief said to his daughters, "You must become the wives of Dirty-Boy. I tried to save you by having two contests; but since I am a great chief I cannot break my word. Go now, and take up your abode with your husband." They put on their best clothes and went. On the way they had to pass Raven's house, and heard the Ravens laughing inside, because the girls had to marry Dirty-Boy. The elder sister said, "Let us go in and see what they are laughing about!" The younger one said, "No, our father told us to go straight to our husband." The elder one went in, and sat down beside Raven's eldest son. She became his wife. Like all the other Ravens, he was ugly, and had a big head; but she thought it better to marry him than to become the wife of a dirty, sickly boy.

The younger one went on, entered Dirty-Boy's lodge, and sat down by his side. The old woman asked her who she was, and why she had come. When the old woman had been told, she said, "Your husband is sick, and soon he will die. He stinks too much. You must not sleep with him. Go back to your father's lodge every evening; but come here in the daytime, and watch him and attend him."

Now, the Raven family that lived close by laughed much at the younger daughter of the chief. They were angry because she had not entered their house and married there, as her elder sister had done. To hurt her feelings, they dressed their new daughter-in-law in the finest clothes they had. Her dress was covered with beads, shells, elk's teeth, and quill work. They gave her necklaces, and her mother-in-law gave her a finely polished celt of [jade] to hang at her belt. The younger sister paid no attention to this, but returned every morning to help her grandmother-in-law to gather fire-wood, and to attend to her sick husband.

For three days matters remained this way. In the evening of the third day Sun said to his sister. "We will resume our true forms tonight, so that people may see us tomorrow." That night they transformed themselves.

The old mat lodge became a fine new skin lodge, surpassing those of the Blackfeet and other tribes, richly decorated with ornaments, and with streamers tied to the top and painted. The old bark kettle became a bright copper kettle, and new pretty woven baskets and embroidered and painted bags, were in the house. The old woman became a fine-looking person of tall figure, with clothes covered with shining stars. Dirty-Boy became a young, handsome man of light complexion. His clothes were covered with shining copper. His hair reached to the ground and shone like the rays of the sun. In the morning the people saw the new lodge, and said, "Some rich chief has arrived, and has camped where the poor people were. He has thrown them out."

When the girl arrived, she was much surprised to see the transformation. She saw a woman in the door, wearing a long skin dress covered with star pendants, with bright stars in her hair. She addressed her in a familiar voice, saying, "Come in and sit with your husband!" The girl knew then who she was. When she entered, she saw a handsome man reclining, with his head on a beautiful parfleche. His garments and hair were decorated with bright suns. The girl did not recognize him, and looked around. The woman said, "That is your husband; go and sit beside him." Then she was glad.

Sun took his wife to the copper kettle which stood at the door. It contained a shining liquid. He pushed her head into it, and when the liquid ran down over her hair and body, lines of sparkling small stars formed on her. He told her to empty the kettle. When she did so, the liquid ran to the chief's lodge, forming a path, as of gold-dust. He said, "This will be your trail when you go to see your father."

—James Teit (1917, 65 ff.)

The Hunter Who Had an Elk for a Guardian Spirit (Wasco Chinook)

In this very short but powerful story, Chinookan young people along the Columbia River would have learned from the young hunter's tragic experience about the importance of maintaining a respectful, modest attitude toward the natural order; and they would also have seen how the hunter's obedience to his worthless father, instead of keeping his vow to his spirit-guardian, brings calamity to himself and by implication to his people. The justice of his end is undeniably harsh—after all, he does not know what we know, that the father is lying to and exploiting him—but he does violate his vow to the Elk, and as we are learning today in environmental disasters like Love's Canal, Nature doesn't give us warnings that we are going too far and had better stop before it is too late.

There was a man at Dog River [Hood River] in days gone by, whose wife was with child. Pretty soon she gave birth to a boy. While she was sick, the man carried wood, and one day a piece of bark fell on his forehead and cut him. When the boy was large enough to shoot, he killed birds and squirrels; he was a good shot. One day, however, his father said to him, "You don't do as I used to. I am ashamed to own you. When I was of your age, I used to catch young elks. One day when I killed a young elk, the old one attacked me and made this scar you see on my forehead."

Then the boy had a visit from an elk, and the Elk said, "If you will serve me and hear what I say, I will be your master and will help you in every necessity. You must not be proud. You must not kill too many of any animal. I will be your guardian spirit."

So the young man became a great hunter, knew where every animal was—elk, bear, deer. He killed what he needed for himself, and no more. The old man, his father, said to him, "You are not doing enough. At your age I used to do much more." The young man was grieved at his father's scolding. The Elk, the young man's helper, was very angry at the old man. At last [he] helped the young man to kill five whole herds of elk. He killed all except his own spirit elk, though he tried without knowing it to kill even [that one.] This elk went to a lake and pretended to be dead; the young man went into the water to draw the elk out, but as soon as he touched it, both sank.

After touching bottom, the young man woke as from a sleep, and saw bears, deer, and elk without number, and they were all persons. Those that he killed were there too, and they groaned. A voice called, "Draw him in." Each time the voice was heard, he was drawn nearer his master, the Elk, until he was by his side. Then the great Elk said, "Why did you go beyond what I commanded? Your father required more of you than he himself ever did. Do you see our people on both sides? These are they whom you have killed. You have inflicted many needless wounds on our people. Your father lied to you. He never saw my father, as he falsely told you, saying that my father had met him. He also told you that my father gave him a scar. That is not true; he was carrying firewood when you were born, and a piece of bark fell on him and cut him. Now I shall leave you, and never be your guardian spirit again."

When the Elk had finished, a voice was heard saying five times, "Cast him out." The young man went home. The old man was talking, feeling well. The young man told his two wives to fix a bed for him. They did so. He lay there five days and nights, and then he told his wives, "Heat water to wash me, also call my friends so that I may talk to them. Bring five elk skins." All this was done. The people came together, and he told them, "My father was dissatisfied because, as he said, I did not do as he had done. What my father wanted grieved the guardian spirit which visited and aided me. My father deceived me. He said that he had been scarred on the head by a great elk while taking the young elk away. He said I was a disgrace to him. He wanted me to kill more than was needed. He lied. The guardian spirit has left me, and I die."

—Told by Donald McKay or Charlie Pitt,
in Curtin (1909, 257–59)

She-Who-Dwells-in-the-Rocks (Dakota Sioux)

As in so many other Native stories, the heroine of this one enters into an intimate and spiritually empowering relationship with another species—compare the Blackfoot story, "Origin of the Beaver Medicine" (pp. 28 and others.

That one they call the Rock-dweller was [. . .] married to an Oglala man, after he had long been buying her. But he was always very cruel, and kept guard over her always; whenever he was going away he blackened the soles of her moccasins, and when he returned, he examined them for indications that she had been away from home; and when he found such indications by an erasure of the black, he whipped her, so that her lot was a sad one. Because she wept so often, her eyes were swollen and hidden by the swelling.

Once again the man was away, when the mother of the man's mother (his maternal grandmother) who lived behind the camp-circle said to her daughter-in-law (i.e., the wife of her grandson). "Daughter-in-law, try to be brave, you shall go home," she said. "No matter how badly my grandson treats you, say nothing; but meantime, get ready some moccasins and food. When you complete this, you shall go."

From that time, the woman's courage rose; so, they lived on, and one day, her husband's grandmother came to her again and said, "Now daughter-in-law, you shall start; beware about looking back." Her husband was walking across the camp, as they stood watching him, and soon he entered a big tent where they were playing a gambling game. "There, daughter-in-law, he is going to gamble; when he is so occupied he stays away long, as you know. Go, over here, along the short branch of the creek, I have hung your rawhide bag on that oak tree."

So the woman went indoors, and took some little things she wished to keep, and went outside, and glanced a few final times towards the gambling tipi across the camp-circle; assuring herself that her husband was there for at least some time, she started running away from camp, toward the place the old woman had suggested, and there she found her, already waiting. "Now, daughter-in-law, keep generally towards that constellation known as Man-Being-Carried [the Big Dipper; Ursa Major], hide during the day and travel only by night; in three or four days you should be home," she said. Then she embraced the young woman, over and over again, and, "My daughter-in-law, how much I love her, alas!" she said and wept. Then she went towards her tipi; so the young woman started northward.

After traveling some time, she began to think of and pity herself, and then she wept. "I who was always so timid: can this be I, suffering so?" she thought, and ran and cried at the same time; and now it was dawn, so she settled down to hide in the thick woods. She changed to dry moccasins, and ate her pounded dried meat; and then she slept. When night came on, she traveled again. For three days that was her program. Again it was night, very dark, as she was coming to a deep creek. She was groping along and feeling her way with her feet.

At last she entered into the creek bed, down the steep banks. But her feet were so wet that she stopped in a clump of bushes, and, sitting under them, she was taking off her moccasins to change to others, when she heard some kind of voice, echoing down the entire creek. *"Hi! Hi! Hi!"* it said; and she thought, "Even if it should kill me, what of that? I barely live on, anyway!" and she sat with her blanket pulled up over her head when that being arrived, and went around her and said, "Young woman, how does it happen that you travel alone like this?" So she replied, telling him all things. "A man with whom I lived treated me very cruelly; I am therefore going to my own people," she said. "Very well; of course, I am not what I used to be, anymore, but so that when you get home you may be useful to us, it shall be thus until you get home, that nobody shall be able to see you," he said. "Thank you," the young woman answered.

Somehow, from that time on, she felt braver; so that she ventured to travel during the day, too. But from then on, something came over her, and she lost her eagerness to reach her people. She climbed to the top of a hill, and finding many flat rocks about, she sat down on one of them, and looked about over the pleasant country. Just then one drop of water, and now another, came down; so she entered a cave in the rocks, for shelter; and very soon, it was raining very hard. It was dark in the room. The cave seemed like a room, with perpendicular walls of rock, so she carried in sage-brush, and spread it for a bed, and there she lay down to sleep. Her old mother-in-law had given her a small ax, so she used it to cut the sage.

She stayed there all day, and then when the sun set, a wolf entered, and sprang lightly over her legs as she slept, and went farther into the cave. Her young cubs were in there, the woman inferred, by the whining of cubs which came forth. She stayed where she was, regardless of it, and when morning came the wolf came back out, once again jumping over her legs. But the strange thing was that it didn't so much as growl at her. The sun was high now, so she sat outdoors, looking down on the valley, where there appeared black spots here and there. She guessed those might be where butchering had been done; so she went to investigate and found that she was right; some buffalo hoofs lay about, so she carried them on her back and came home. She cut them apart and ate the fat that lay between the bones of the feet; and broke the long bones, and ate the marrow.

And then she saw a pack of wolves surrounding and driving a herd of buffalo along, by hiding around and then suddenly appearing, causing the buffalo to run. Then, of a sudden, as one might snap a twig in two, they all charged the herd and killed one calf, and soon, another; and only calves they picked out and killed; all this, while she sat watching. She came to them, and they stopped and scattered, so she butchered one of the calves and put the meat on her back and took it home; as it was now warm summer time, she cut the meat into thin layers for preserving and spread it over the flat rocks to dry,

At first she would take the dried meat and pound it, uncooked, into her rawhide container, mixing marrow-fat with it; and this she ate. But once the notion came to her that she could have fire, and then she worked on that. She took redgrass, and the downy part of *nape'-oi'le-kiyi* ("they-cause-it-to-burn-in-their-hands," a kind of plant); this latter she rolled into a ball, and placed it with some very fine twigs; and then she held two transparent stones which she struck against each other until she made a spark; then she carefully and hurriedly blew on it and caused it to ignite. From then on she had fire; so she cooked and ate her meat like a human being.

Things were so much improved that she guarded her fire always to keep it alive; but one day a rain came and extinguished it, so from then on she was without fire again. The cubs were now large so whenever she sat outdoors, they would come out and sit around her. When she ate, she cut up pieces of meat for them and they ate. The mother returned, every so often, but her coming did not frighten the woman at all; rather she lived with the wolf as she might live with a dog.

The *ti'psila* were now ripe, and grew thick on the hillside, so she sharpened a digging stick and was out getting them when the wolf came to her and said, "Grandmother, tomorrow you will see some human beings." And the thought came to her, "How contentedly I have lived here, alas!" and it saddened her. Next morning the wolf spoke again, "Grandmother, I must leave before they arrive. So remember, when you get home, hurry matters on my account."

By afternoon, she saw two men come into sight, over on the second hill from hers. "Even though they should be enemies, and should kill me, what of that?" she thought as she walked along finding *ti'psila*; and then, they must have been coming nearer in an effort to recognize her, for they shouted, "Are you a Dakota?" So she would answer them, but the words stuck in her throat and she could not utter them; this happened unexpectedly, so they came on close, and on recognizing her, they waited over her. They wished to take her with them, but she refused. So, "The people will arrive tomorrow," they said, and went away without her.

The next day, the people came by, and her aunt was in the company, so she took her and returned with her. Thus it was one complete time (half-year), that she lived alone, and now she had returned to be among people again. But this was a fragment of her own band, so the man she was hiding from was not here. The people now had a buffalo hunt so she said to her aunt, "Aunt, I want a collection made of all the fat that the people can spare"; so, when her aunt reported it, two young men took a hair-less buffalo-robe, and walked about the circle for contributions; and they took the resulting pile of fat to the young woman, so she asked them to empty it all at a place away from, but in sight of, the camp.

Then she went out and stood by the pile, and gave a peculiar call, and then, in the Dakota tongue, "All right, now; where have you gone?" And all the wolves in the world sprang up from somewhere as though they had been sitting there waiting for the signal; and promptly ate everything up. "She dreams the wolf-dream," they said of her. Soon after, she asked that a tipi be erected for her; it was done, and there she impersonated that being with the transparent eyes which first came to her [when she ran away], right in the sight of all the people; so they decided that her supernatural powers were limitless.

And, they say, that being which first came to her was what is known as Double-Face. In the mystery act, they would bind her tightly into a buffalo fur hide, and place a mirror outside, but corresponding to her forehead, and then, lying inside the bundle, she would be able to look about outside without the slightest difficulty; so whenever anything was lost she would use this device for her eyes, and find it easily, they say. And whenever she doctored the sick, she was always successful, but, they say, in time she abandoned this practice. She was pregnant when she left, so now she gave birth to a baby, a girl; she was the child of the man who had maltreated her so.

When this girl was now a very old woman, she once came to our home, and spent the night there. She occupied the space on the left side of the fireplace [place of honor], and when we were all in bed for the night, she told this story, so I myself heard it from her lips.

—Ella Deloria (1978, 118–21)

The Bear Man (Pawnee)

There was once a young boy, who, when he was playing with his fellows, used often to imitate the ways of a bear, and to pretend that he was one. The boys did not know much about bears. They only knew that there were such animals.

Now, it happened that before this boy was born his mother had been left alone at home, for his father had gone on the warpath toward the enemy, and this was about five or six months before the boy would be born. As the man was going on the warpath, he came upon a little bear cub, very small, whose mother had gone away, and he caught it. He did not want to kill it because it was so young and helpless. It seemed to him like a little child. It looked up to him, and cried after him, because it knew no better; and he hated to kill it or to leave it there.

After he had thought about this for a while, he put a string around its neck and tied some medicine smoking stuff, Indian tobacco, to it, and said, "*Pi-rau'*—child, you are a *Nahu'rac; Ti-ra'-wa* will take care of you. He will look after you, but I put these things about your neck to show that I have good feelings toward you. I hope that when my child is born, the *Nahu'rac* will take care of him, and see that he grows up to be a good man, and I hope that *Ti-ra'-wa* will take care of you and of mine." He looked at the little bear for quite a long time, and talked to it, and then he went on his way.

When he returned to the village from his warpath, he told his wife about the little bear, and how he had looked at it and talked to it.

When his child was born, it had all the ways of a bear. So it is among the Pawnees. A woman, before her child is born, must not look hard at any animal, for the child may be like it. There was a woman in the Kit-ke-hahk'-i band, who caught a rabbit, and because it was gentle and soft, she took it up in her hands and held it before her face and petted it, and when her child was born it had a split nose, like a rabbit. This man is still alive.

This boy, who was like a bear, as he grew up, had still more the ways of a bear. Often he would go off by himself, and try to pray to the bear, because he felt like a bear. He used to say, in a joking way, to the other young men, that he could make himself a bear.

After he had come to be a man, he started out once on the warpath with a party of about thirty-five others. He was the leader of the party. They went away up on the Running Water, and before they had come to any village, they were discovered by Sioux. The enemy pursued them, and surrounded them, and fought with them. The Pawnees were overpowered, their enemies were so many, and all were killed.

The country where this took place is rocky, and much cedar grows there. Many bears lived there.

The battle was fought in the morning; and the Pawnees were all killed in a hollow. Right after the fight, in the afternoon, two bears came traveling along by this place. When they came to the spot where the Pawnees had been killed, they found one of the bodies, and the she bear recognized it as that of the boy who was like a bear. She called to the he bear, and said, "Here is the man that was very good to us. He often sacrificed smokes to us, and every time he ate he always used to take a piece of food and give it to us, saying, 'Here is something for you to eat. Eat this.' Here is the one that always imitated us, and sang about us, and talked about us. Can you do anything for him?"

The he bear said, "I fear I cannot do it. I have not the power, but I will try. I can do anything if the sun is shining. I seem to have more power when the sun is shining on me." That day it was cloudy and cold and snowing. Every now and then the clouds would pass, and the sun came out for a little while, and then the clouds would cover it up again.

The man was all cut up, pretty nearly hacked in small pieces, for he was the bravest of all. The two bears gathered up the pieces of the man, and put them together, and then the he bear lay down and took the man on his breast, and the she bear lay on top to warm the body. They worked over it with their medicine, and every now and then the he bear would cry out, and say, "*A-ti'-us*—Father, help me. I wish the sun was shining." It was still all cut up, but it began to have life. Pretty soon the man began to move, and to come to life, and then he became conscious and had life.

When he came to himself and opened his eyes, he was in the presence of two bears. The he bear spoke to him, and said, "It is not through me that you are living. It was the she bear who asked for help for you, and had you brought back to life. Now, you are not yet whole and well. You must come away with us, and live with us for a time, until all your wounds are healed."

The bears took him away with them. But the man was very weak, and every now and then, as they were going along, he would faint and fall down; but still they would help him up and support him; and they took him along with them, until they came to a cave in the rocks among the cedars, which was their home. When he entered the cave, he found there their young ones that they had left behind when they started out.

The man was all cut up and gashed. He had also been scalped, and had no hair on his head. He lived with the bears until he was quite healed of his wounds, and also had come to understand all their ways. The two old bears taught him everything that they knew.

The he bear said to him, "None of all the beings and animals that roam over the country are as great and as wise as the bears. No animal is equal to us. When we get hungry, we go out and kill something and eat it.

I did not make the wisdom that I have. I am an animal, and I look to one above. He made me, and he made me to be great. I am made to live here and to be great, but still there will be an end to my days, just as with all of us that *Ti-ra'-wa* has created upon this earth. I am going to make you a great man; but you must not deceive yourself. You must not think that I am great, or can do great things of myself. You must always look up for the giver of all power. You shall be great in war and great in wealth.

"Now you are well, and I shall take you back to your home, and after this I want you to imitate us. This shall be a part of your greatness. I shall look after you. I shall give to you a part of myself. If I am killed, you shall be killed. If I grow old, you will grow old.

"I want you to look at one of the trees that *Ti-ra'-wa* made in this earth, and place your dependence on it. *Ti-ra'-wa* made this tree (pointing to a cedar). It never gets old. It is always green and young. Take notice of this tree, and always have it with you; and when you are in the lodge and it thunders and lightens, throw some of it on the fire and let the smoke rise. Hold that fast."

The he bear took the skin of a bear, and made a cap for him, to hide his naked skull. His wounds were now all healed, and he was well and strong. The man's people had nearly forgotten him, it had been so long ago, and they had supposed that the whole party had been killed.

Soon after this the he bear said, "Now we will take that journey." They started, and went to the village, and waited near it until night. Then the bear said to him, "Go into the village, and tell your father that you are here. Then get for me a piece of buffalo meat, and a blue bead, and some Indian tobacco, and some sweet smelling clay."

The man went to the village, and his father was very much surprised, and very glad to see him. He got the presents and brought them to the bear, and gave them to him, and the bear talked to him.

When they were about to part, the bear came up to him, and put his [paws] about him, and hugged him, and put his mouth against the man's mouth, and said, "As the fur that I am in has touched you it will make you great, and this will be a blessing to you." His paws were around the man's shoulders, and he drew them down his arms, until they came to his hands, and he held them, and said, "As my hands have touched your hands, they are made great, not to fear anything. I have rubbed my hands down over you, so that you will be as tough as I am. Because my mouth has touched your mouth you shall be made wise." Then he left him, and went away.

So that man was the greatest of all warriors, and was brave. He was like a bear. He originated the bear dance which still exists among the tribe of Pawnees. He came to be an old man, and at last died of old age. I suspect the old bear died at the same time.

—George Bird Grinnell (1961, 121–28)

The Stone Boy (Lakota Sioux)

Sometimes in Lakota and Dakota stories, "Iya" figures are simple-minded monsters, but here, in the Lakota storyteller Bad Wound's elaboration, Iya is evil incarnate, such a formidably fiendish enemy of humanity that even when he is finally vanquished by Stone Boy, one is left wondering whether "the evil one" will return to afflict the people. The "duet" of songs sung by Iya and Stone Boy near the climax of the story illustrates the way songs are often incorporated in Native narratives at dramatic moments, rather like Shakespeare's use of songs in his romantic comedies. For an illuminating discussion of this story as an example of the artistry of traditional Indian storytelling, see Karl Kroeber's Artistry in Native American Myths *(1998, 255–84).*

The Four Brothers lived together, with no woman, so they did the woman's work.

As the oldest was gathering wood, after night, something ran into his big toe. This pained him but little, and he soon forgot it, but his toe began to swell and was soon as big as his head. Then he cut it open and found something in it. He did not know what this was, but his brothers washed it clean and found that it was a little baby girl.

The Four Brothers kept this baby and gave it good food and fine clothes so that it grew to be a beautiful young woman. She could do all of woman's work well and quickly and never allowed anyone to leave their tipi cold or hungry. She could dress skins so that they were white and soft and make good clothing from them, upon which she put beautiful ornaments and each ornament meant something.

Many young men tried to get her to live with them but she would not leave the Four Brothers. So they told her that they would keep her always as their sister and they did everything so as to please her.

The oldest brother said, "I will go and hunt deer so that our sister may have skins to make herself clothing."

He went away and did not return.

Then the next oldest brother said, "I will go and hunt buffalo so that our sister may have skins to make robes for herself."

He went away and did not return.

Then the next to youngest brother said, "I will go and hunt elk so that our sister may have meat for herself."

He went away and did not return.

Then the youngest brother said, "Sister, our brothers have gone away and have not returned. I will go and find them."

So he went away and did not return.

When the youngest brother had been gone one moon, the young woman went to the top of a high hill to mourn and to seek a vision. While she was mourning, she saw a pebble. She looked at this pebble for a long time for it was very smooth and very white so she put it in her mouth to keep herself from being thirsty.

She fell asleep with this pebble in her mouth and swallowed it and while she slept the vision came to her in the form of the Great Beast which said that the Four Brothers were kept by a stone and that a stone would find them and bring them back to her.

She told this vision to a shaman and asked him to tell her what it meant. The shaman told her that she should marry and name her son The Stone.

But she would not live with any man for she remembered the Four Brothers, how they were good and kind to her and she wished to live for them only.

Soon she grew big with child and gave birth to a boy baby. The flesh of this baby was as hard as stone and she knew that it was mysterious [*wakan*] and came from the pebble which she had swallowed.

She went far away and lived with her son alone. She taught him all the games and songs and all about roots and plants and animals and birds so that he was cunning and wise.

She gave him fine clothes and good food so that he grew up strong and brave but his flesh was hard as stone.

She would not allow him to hunt or go in a war party for she was afraid he would go away and never return like the Four Brothers.

Each moon she would go to the top of the hill and mourn.

When her son had grown to be a man, he asked her why she went to mourn each moon and she said to him, "My son, you are now a man and I will tell you why I mourn."

So she told him the story of the Four Brothers, of her coming to them, of how they went away and did not return, of his own birth and the vision of the Great Beast.

She sang him this song:

> I am a mysterious woman.
> I am [not] like other women.
> You are a mysterious man.
> Your flesh is like a stone.
> You are the Stone Boy.
> You are the one the Great Beast told of.

Then he sang to her this song:

> I am the Stone Boy.
> I am the stone that will aid you.
> I will bring back your brothers.
> My mother, I will make you happy.

He then said to her, "Mother, I will go and find your brothers. I will bring them to you."

She said, "I am afraid you too will go away and never come back."

He said to her, "What did the Great Beast tell you? I am the stone."

So she made a great feast and invited a wise shaman, a wise old woman, a great hunter and four maidens as the chief guests and all the people as common guests.

She placed the people according to the bands and her son among the chief guests, and when all were satisfied with eating, she stood before all the people and told the story of the Four Brothers, of her coming to them, of their going, of her vision, of the birth and life of her son.

She then told them to examine her son that they might know that he was mysterious [*wakan*]. The people all examined the young man and when they found that his flesh was hard like stone they said he was indeed mysterious and that he was the Stone Boy.

She then told them that her son was to go in quest of the Four Brothers and she had made this feast so that the people might have a good heart towards him and she invited the chief guests so that they would help her prepare her son for this quest with magic.

The chief guests agreed to do what she should ask of them.

The shaman gave him a charm [*pejuta wakan rca*] that would keep all harm from him.

The old woman gave him a robe on which she had painted a dream. This dream made the robe magical so that it hid one who wore it from the sight of everything.

The warrior gave him a magical spear that would pierce anything, a magical shield that would ward off anything and a magical club that would break anything.

The hunter showed him how to find anything.

His mother made his clothes of good deer skins and the young women put ornaments on them. While ornamenting his clothes they sang love songs and the shaman conjured the ornaments [*ca hina wakan kaga*] so that they were magical.

On the sides of his moccasins they put mountains so that he could step from hill to hill without touching the valleys. On the tops they put dragonflies so that he could escape all danger. On his leggings they put wolf tracks so that he would never grow weary.

On his shirt they put the tipi circle so that he could find shelter everywhere.

He stood before the people clothed in his magical garments, his shield on his back and his spear in his hands. His face was toward the rising sun. Before him was his mother, and on one side, the shaman, warrior, and hunter; on the other, the old woman and the four young women.

He said to his mother, "I will bring the Four Brothers back to you." And to the young women, "When I return I will take you four as my women." And to the men, "What you have taught me I will use to release the Four Brothers." And then turning his face toward the setting sun, he said to the old woman, "I go."

Then the old woman threw the robe about him and he was seen no more; but there was a wind as if the Thunderbird flew toward the setting sun and his mother fell on her face as one dead. But the people heard a voice high in the air, clear and loud like the voices of the cranes when they fly toward the region of the pines and this is what it said, "A stone shall free the Four Brothers."

When the Stone Boy went from the people he stepped from hill to hill more swiftly than the stars fall at night [falling meteors].

From each hill he looked carefully into each valley so that he saw all there was in every valley but he found nothing of the Four Brothers until he came to the high hills toward the setting sun.

In the valleys here there was much game of every kind and in one of them he found a stone knife that he knew belonged to the oldest brother. In another valley he found a stone arrowhead that he knew belonged to the next oldest brother. In another he found a stone axe that he knew belonged to the next youngest brother and in another he found a stone bone-breaker that he knew belonged to the youngest brother.

So he knew he was on the right way to find the brothers and looked carefully into each valley.

Beyond this, toward the setting sun, the hills became higher and higher until they were mountains.

Near the mountains he saw a valley that was barren with nothing in it but a stone, a tree, and a little old brown hill. He saw smoke coming from the little brown hill so he took off his robe and sat down to watch this, and soon a huge coyote, larger than a buffalo, came out of the hill and began to jump up very high and yelp very loud; then the stone began to roll and bump about and the tree began to move from place to place.

The Stone Boy took off his robe and sat down to watch these things and soon a growl like thunder came from the hills beyond. When this growl sounded, the coyote jumped very high and fast and yelped and yelled and the stone moved about and bumped the ground and the tree moved from place to place.

Then the coyote sniffed toward him and then trotted a little way and sniffed again, then yelped and howled and jumped up and down.

Then a bear came towards the hill he was on, running very fast and growling like thunder.

The Stone Boy quickly put his robe on and when the bear was almost at him he stepped to another hill and the bear stopped and looked very foolish and said, "That must have been a Thunderbird passed by me."

Then the coyote sniffed toward him again and jumped up and down, and the bear ran toward the hill he was on, but when he got there the Stone Boy stepped to another hill and the bear looked very foolish and said, "I think that is a Thunderbird going by."

Then the coyote sniffed again towards the hill the Stone Boy was on and again jumped up and down and the tree walked that way and the stone also. And the bear growled like very heavy thunder and came creeping towards the hill watching everything very closely. But when he got near, the Stone Boy stepped to another hill. Then the bear was afraid and ran back to the little hill whining and whimpering for he thought it was a Thunderbird.

Then a little old woman ran out of the hill and the coyote yelped and jumped up and down and ran around and around and the branches of the tree squirmed and licked their tongues out and hissed like a great wind.

And the stone jumped up and down and every time it would come down it would shake the earth.

Then the Stone Boy stood up and took off his robe and jeered at them and mocked at them and they saw him and the old woman screamed at him and the coyote yelped louder than ever and jumped up and down and the tree walked towards him, every snake hissing loud and the stone rolled and tumbled towards him and the bear came very fast towards him growling like a thunder cloud.

When the bear was very close he raised his paw to strike him and the Stone Boy shot one of the arrows through his heart and killed him.

Then the coyote came jumping up and down and every time he jumped up he went higher and higher and when he was near, he jumped up so as to come down on the Stone Boy, but the Stone Boy set his spear on the ground and when the coyote came down, the spear ran through his heart and killed him.

Then the stone came rolling and tumbling and smashing everything in its path and when it was near it was about to roll on the Stone Boy and smash him also, but he raised the war club and struck it a mighty blow and broke it into pieces.

The tree could not walk up the hill so Stone Boy went down into the valley and when he came near the tree, the branches began to strike at him, but he held up the shield the warrior had given him and when one of the branch snakes would strike it, its teeth would break off and its head would be smashed. And so the Stone Boy danced about the tree and sang and shouted until every branch had smashed itself to death on his shield.

The little old woman then went into the little hill and the Stone Boy came near it and cried, "Ho, old woman, come out!"

But the old woman said, "My friend, I am a weak old woman. Have pity on me and come into my tipi."

So the Stone Boy found that the little hill was a strange kind of a tipi and he found the door open and went in when the woman said, "My friend, I am a weak old woman, but you are welcome to my tipi. I will get you something to eat and drink."

But the Stone Boy noticed that her tongue was forked so he was wary and watched her closely.

She said, "My friend, you must be tired. Lie down and rest while I get food for you."

So the Stone Boy lay down and the old woman passed close to him saying, "The meat is behind you." And as she leaned over him, she stabbed him over the heart but her stone knife broke off when it struck him.

She said, "My friend, I stumbled and fell on you."

The Stone Boy said, "I will sit up so that you will not stumble over me."

So she said, "My friend, sit near the center of the tipi so I can go about you without stumbling on you."

So the Stone Boy sat near the center of the lodge and the old woman went about him and as she passed behind him, she struck him on the head with a war club, but it only bounced up without hurting him so she said, "My friend, that was a stone that fell from the top of the tipi."

So the Stone Boy said, "I will sit by the door of the tipi so that stones will not fall on me," and he sat outside the door.

The old woman said, "My friend, you must be hungry, and I will make soup for you to drink," so she made soup with bad medicine in it and gave it to Stone Boy, who drank it.

Then the old woman said, "Ho, you are the one whom I hate. I am *Iya* the evil spirit. I hate all Indians. I destroy all Indians. I have given you that which will destroy you. You have swallowed poison. It will kill you. I am *Iya* the evil one. I know whom you seek. You were hunting for your mother's brothers. They are there in that tipi. They are like tanned skins. You will soon die and I will make a tanned skin of you. But I must have a living stone to flatten you out. But there is only one other living stone and I must find it. The living stone was my master. He is the only one I feared. He is the only one who could hurt me. No one else can do me any harm. His only relation is a living stone. He is now my master and none other. But you will die from the poison I have given you and I will sing your death song."

So she sang:

A young man would be wise.
A young man would be brave.
He left the place he knew.

He came to strange places.
He came to death's valley.
He came to *Iya's* tipi.
He slew *Iya's* son the coyote.
He slew *Iya's* daughter the snake tree.
He broke the living stone.
He broke *Iya's* only master.
Iya will be revenged on him.
Iya will see him die.
He slew my friend the bear.
Iya will laugh and see him die.

Then the Stone Boy said, "May I also sing a song?"

And *Iya* said, "Ho, sing what you will. It is your death song and it is music that will make my heart glad."

Then the Stone Boy sang:

The living stone was *Iya's* master.
The living stone had but one relation.
He had a son that was little.
A pebble white as the snow.
Iya feared this pebble and stole it.
Feared it because it was white.
You will not laugh and see me die.
For this is not my death song.
I am the pebble you threw away.
I am the Stone Boy, your master.

Then *Iya* said, "How shall I know you to be my master?"

The Stone Boy said, "Do my bidding or I will punish you."

Then *Iya* said, "I am a weak old woman. Have pity on me and do not punish me."

The Stone Boy said, "Your tongue is forked and you do not tell the truth. You are not a woman. But you are an evil old man. You have pity on no one but do evil to everyone. Tell me. Where are my mother's brothers?"

Iya said, "I do not know."

Then the Stone Boy seized him by the foot and placed his foot on the ground and trod on it and he howled in pain. But the Stone Boy demanded of him to tell where his mother's brothers were and *Iya* declared that he did not know. Then the Stone Boy flattened his other foot in the same way and *Iya* sobbed and cried with pain and said he would tell the Stone Boy if he would not punish him any farther for he recognized that he was truly his master.

Iya said, "In ancient times I found game plentiful in the valleys about here and good hunters and brave men came here to hunt it. These good men could not be made to do evil so I could not do them mischief. So I made a bargain with your father, the living stone and with the Great Bear and brought my son and daughter with me and we all lived here in this valley.

"The bargain was that the bear would go out among the game and when a good man came to hunt them, the bear would show himself and being so big, the hunters would chase him until they came near here where they could see my son who would jump up and down and scare them so that they would fall down with no strength. Then the bear would take them in his arms and bring them to my daughter who would sting them so that they would be paralyzed. Then the living stone would roll on them and flatten them out like skins and I would heap them up on my tipi poles. And as they were alive, this would always be a torment to them. In this way I could do mischief to good men.

"We often heard of the four men who lived alone and did a woman's work and who never did evil to anyone, so that I could not torment them but they would not hunt or go on the war path and we thought they would never come within our power.

"So I determined to get a woman into their tipi that they might do some evil but I could not get an ordinary woman among them. Then I tried to break off a branch from my daughter, the snake tree, and put it into their tipi but the branches would not break and the only way I could get a part of my daughter was by digging out a part of the heart of the tree. This I did and placed it near the tipi of the four men so that when one of them went to get wood he would step on it and stick it into his toe.

"But these men were so good that when they cared for this child it grew up to be a good woman such as they were men but I waited patiently for I knew they would not live as they had when she grew up to be a woman.

"So when she was a woman, they came to hunt for her and the bear enticed them and they were caught and flattened and are now tormented on my tipi poles.

"When I threw the white pebble away, I knew that no ordinary woman could nourish it into life and growth, and when your mother grew up to be a woman I did not think of her as being a mysterious woman who could give life and growth to the pebble.

"So my own evil has brought the punishment on me for I know that you are my master and that you will not let me do evil anymore. But those who now lie on my tipi poles will still be tormented."

Then the Stone Boy said, "Tell me, how can these people that are on your tipi poles be restored to their natural conditions?"

And *Iya* said, "I will not."

The Stone Boy said, "I am your master. Tell me or I will punish you."

Then *Iya* said, "Remember I am your grandfather and do not punish me."

The Stone Boy said, "I broke my own father in pieces because he was evil. Do you think I would spare you because you are my grandfather?"

Iya said, "I will not tell you."

Then the Stone Boy said, "Give me your hand," and he took *Iya's* hand and trod on it and it was flattened like a dried skin, and *Iya* howled with pain.

Then the Stone Boy said, "Tell me or I will flatten your other hand," and *Iya* said, "I will tell you. You must skin the bear and the coyote and stretch their skins over poles so as to make a tight tipi. Then you must gather all the pieces of the broken living stone. You must make a fire of the wood of the snake tree and heat these stones over this fire. Then place the stones in the tipi. Then get one of the flattened people off the poles of my tipi and place it in the tipi you have built. Then place the hot stones in the tipi and pour water over the stones. When the steam rises onto the flattened persons, they will be as they were before the bear enticed them."

Then the Stone Boy did as he was told but the skins of the bear and the coyote would not make a full-sized tipi so he made it low and round on top. And when he made fire of the snake tree the branches were so fat that one could heat all the stones red hot. So he had plenty of fuel to heat the stones as often as he wished.

So he placed the flattened people in the sweathouse and steamed them and they became men as they were before they were enticed by the bear.

But he did not know who his mother's brothers were, so he took the arrow he had found and called to all and asked them whose arrow it was, and one man said it was his, and he told him to stand to one side, and he took the stone knife he had found and asked them whose it was, and a man said it was his, and he told him to stand on one side. He then took the wooden bowl he had found and asked them whose it was, and a man said it was his, and he told him to stand to one side. He then took the plum seed dice he had found and asked them whose it was, and a man said it was his, and he told him to stand aside.

Then he told the men he had separated to look at each other and they did so and when they had looked at each other they each embraced the others and the Stone Boy knew that they were brothers.

Then the Stone Boy took them by themselves and told them the story of the four men and the birth of his mother and of the four men going away and never coming back. Then the men said, "We are those four men," and the Stone Boy knew that they were his mother's brothers, so he told them the story of his own birth, and they said, "We believe you because we know of the birth of your mother." Then he told them of his preparation to come for them and his coming and his fight with the bear and the coyote and the stone and the snake tree and how he was master of *Iya* and they said, "We believe you because the bear did entice us and the coyote did jump up and down and the snake did bite us and the stone did roll on us and make us flat like skins and the old woman did spread us out on her tipi and we were in torment."

Then the Stone Boy counseled with them as to what he should do with *Iya* and they advised him to make him flat like a skin but the Stone Boy said, "There is no snake tree to bite him."

So he came back to *Iya* and said, "You have been very evil and now I am your master and I shall punish you for all the evil you have done so that you shall always be in torment as you have kept all these people."

Iya was a great coward and he begged the Stone Boy to spare him and not punish him.

But the Stone Boy said. "I shall flatten you like a skin and spread you on poles."

Then *Iya* said, "I am *Iya* the giant and I will grow so big that you cannot flatten me," and he began to grow larger and larger so that he was a great giant. But the Stone Boy began to trample on him beginning at his feet which he had already flattened and he trampled his legs so that *Iya* fell to his knees and he trampled his thighs so that *Iya* fell to his buttocks. And he trampled his hips so that great floods of water ran from him and this water was bitter and salty and it soaked into the earth and where it comes out in springs and lakes, it makes the water very bad and bitter.

Then he trampled his belly and *Iya* vomited great quantities of cherry stones and the Stone Boy said to him, "What are those cherry stones?" and *Iya* said, "They are the people that I have sucked in with my breath when I went about the earth as a giant."

The Stone Boy said, "How can I make these people as they were when you sucked them in with your breath" and *Iya* said, "Make a fire without smoke." So the Stone Boy got very dry cottonwood and made a fire and when it was burned to coals, *Iya* said, "Get some of the hair from the Great Bear's skin," and he got hair from the Great Bear and *Iya* said, "Put this hair on the fire," and he put it on the fire.

Then there arose a great white smoke and it was like the smoke from wild sage branches and leaves.

Then *Iya* said, "Blow this smoke on the cherry stones," and the Stone boy did so and *Iya* said, "This drives away all my power to do these people any harm."

Iya said, "Get the hair of many women," so the Stone Boy took the hair ornaments from his [jacket] and *Iya* said, "This gives you power over these people to do what you wish to them."

So the Stone Boy said to the people, "Be as you were before *Iya* sucked you in with his breath," and every cherry stone arose and was alive, some as men and some as women and children so that there were a great many people there.

These people were all very hungry and the Stone Boy said to *Iya*, "What shall I give these people to eat?" and *Iya* said, "Give them the meat of the Great Bear," so he cut off a piece of meat of the Great Bear and gave it to a woman and it grew to be a large piece and this woman cut it in two and gave half to another woman and immediately each of these pieces grew to large pieces and each one of these women cut their pieces in two and gave half to other women, so that every time a piece was given away, it grew to be a larger piece.

The women built fires and cooked the meat and all feasted and were happy and sang songs. . . .

But the people spoke many languages and they could not understand each other but the Stone Boy could speak to each one in his own language and he came to some and said to them in their own tongue, "Where is your place?" And they said, "Over the mountains." And he said to them,

"Go to your people." He said this to everyone and when he said this, he gave to the oldest woman of each people a piece of the meat from the Great Bear so that they had plenty of meat to eat while traveling.

Then the Stone Boy said to his mother's brothers, "Now we will go back to your sister, to my mother, but before we go, I will destroy *Iya* so that he may do no more mischief or hurt the people."

So he trod on *Iya's* chest and *Iya's* breath rushed out of his mouth and nostrils like a mighty wind and it whirled and twisted, breaking down trees and tearing up the grass and throwing the water from the lake and even pulling the rocks and earth over the carcasses of the coyote and snake tree so that the Thunderbird came rushing through the air to know what all this tumult was about, and with his cloud shield he rushed into this great whirlwind and roared and flashed the lightning from his eyes and fought the whirlwind and carried it away into the sky.

Then the Stone Boy said to *Iya*, "I will now tread your head and your arms out flat like a dried skin and you shall remain forever here in this evil valley where there is no tree or grass, nor water and where no living thing will ever come near you. The sun shall burn you and the cold shall freeze you and you shall feel and think and be hungry and thirsty but no one shall come near you."

When *Iya* was growing, he grew so large that he lay almost all across the valley, and his hands were up on the hill where the Stone Boy first showed himself and when the Stone Boy told him his fate, his hands grasped for something and he felt the Stone Boy's robe. This he quickly threw over himself and immediately he became invisible. But the Stone Boy saw what he was doing and jumped quickly to trample on his head before he got the robe over himself. When the Stone Boy trampled the breath out of *Iya*, his mouth gaped wide open and he got the robe over his head before the Stone Boy could get his feet on him and when the Stone Boy did trample [him], he stepped into *Iya's* mouth, and he closed his jaws like a trap and caught both of the Stone Boy's feet between his teeth.

Iya could not hurt the Stone Boy but he held the feet very tightly between his teeth and when the Stone Boy drew out one foot, he closed still on the other, so that when that one was dragged out, the moccasin was left in *Iya's* mouth and was invisible and could not be found.

—Told by Bad Wound,
in Walker (1983, 140–53)

The Sacred Arrow (Dakota Sioux)

Four young men lived together. And they all went on a journey, leaving the very youngest of all, their little brother, at home. As he sat inside the tipi, he chanced to look out in time to see a beautiful bird, scarlet all over, as it perched on a tree nearby. So he thought, "*Huhuhe*! How beautiful! As scarlet as nothing scarlet ever was before! I must shoot it for my elder brothers." And because the bird's skin would so add to the beauty of his brothers' quivers, he tried repeatedly to shoot it, but missed every time.

After he had shot off all his arrows in vain, he took down his eldest brother's sacred arrow which he had left at home, and with it, he hit the bird. Unfortunately, the bird flew away, carrying off the sacred arrow still piercing its body. Hakela (Last-born) was scared; how he ought to act was not plain. He knew he should get a severe scolding, if his brothers were to return now. "It is a terrible thing I have done!" he thought, as he hurriedly put on his turtle moccasins and started out in the direction the bird had taken.

After a long distance, he reached a tribal encampment. Behind the circle of tipis, there was a young girl being courted. So he stepped up to her and, "I guess nothing has gone by here," he said. And she, "No. Boy-Beloved did go by, with a sacred arrow piercing him." So he asked how far his tribal camp was, and the girl told him "You keep right on, and you will come to a camp; the second one. And that will be it."

So he continued till he came to a camp; but as that was not the right place, he continued on until he reached the second camp; but before he arrived, he met an old man with a bundle on his back, cutting across the meadow. "Grandfather, where are you going?" he asked; and the reply was, "Why, grandson, I am going to treat a Boy-Beloved who returned home with a sacred arrow in his side."—"Where does he live?" The old man said, "See that big tipi across the camp-circle? That is his home. When I near it, I sing out, 'To doctor have I come! *Kiki*, Rattle-in-the-Horn!' That is the signal for all the people to shut their doors so that I may approach the Boy's tipi unseen, and do my work."—"Grandfather, which medicine do you use?" he asked; so the old man showed it to him. At once Hakela killed the old man and continued on his way, carrying the bundle on his back.

"To doctor, I have come! *Kiki*, Rattle-in-the-Horn!" he sang. And the people said, "There's the medicine-man coming again!" and in haste they all closed their doorways. So he went into Boy-Beloved's tipi where they greeted him with deference. All but Iktomi, the trickster. Sitting in the doorway, he kept saying, "This is not the doctor," until the others rebuked him sharply and told him to go off somewhere, lest he anger the doctor and make him refuse to treat the patient.

When Hakela, disguised as the old man, had finished treating the Boy-Beloved, he said to him, "Grandson, I would stop here for the night. I am old now, and I do get very tired. Tomorrow I shall go back home." So the Boy ordered a sleeping-place to be made for him. When everyone was certain to be asleep, Hakela quietly put on his magic moccasins and then took down the sacred arrow from its hanging-place; and stepping on to the middle of the Boy-Beloved's abdomen, and then scratching Ikto with his foot (for Ikto must have returned in the night; he was now asleep by the doorway), he left the encampment.

So Ikto sprang up, and "Ah, didn't I say this wasn't the doctor!" he said, running hither and yon, waking everybody. They began to chase Hakela. But of course he wore his turtle moccasins. Nothing could catch him, that was plain from the outset. Only a black horse almost caught up with him, but was obliged to give up.

When Hakela reached the last encampment, the people pursued him with zeal, and because he was now fatigued, it looked hopeless for him. Yet again they fell back one at a time, until only a bay was flying after him. Almost upon him, as one might exclaim, "*wis, wi!*" he suddenly fell back and Hakela went on in safety.

Thus did he barely save himself and with effort did he reach home ahead of his brothers. He had rescued the sacred arrow, and once more it was hanging on its accustomed pole. His brothers returned, all ignorant of what had taken place, and everything went smoothly. From that time on, Hakela began to reverence the sacred arrow. That is all.

—Ella Deloria (1978, 61–62)

Seal and Her Younger Brother Lived There (Clackamas Chinook)

This text is the result of Dell Hymes's ethnopoetic retranslation of a text originally presented in a prose translation by Melville Jacobs of a story he recorded from the Clackamas storyteller Victoria Howard. In Hymes's

*re-presentation, the story emerges as a kind of very intense, oblique poetic
drama, whose focus is the conflict between the young girl, who acutely
observes that there is something sinister about her uncle's new "wife," and
her mother's complacent shushing of her in order to maintain social pro-
prieties. See Hymes's masterful account of how his translation and understanding of the story evolved in* "In Vain I Tried to Tell You": Essays in
Native American Ethnopoetics *(1981, 310 ff.).*

[I. THE "WIFE" COMES]
They lived there, Seal, her daughter, her younger brother.
After some time, now a woman got to Seal's younger brother.
They lived there.
          They would "go out" in the evening.
The girl would say,
          she would tell her mother:
          "Mother! Something is different about my uncle's wife.
          It sounds just like a man when she 'goes out.'"
"Shush! Your uncle's wife!"
A long time they lived there like that.
          In the evening they would each "go out."
Now she would tell her,
          "Mother! Something is different about my uncle's wife.
          When she 'goes out' it sounds just like a man."
"Shush!"

[II. THE UNCLE DIES]
Her uncle, his wife, would "lie down" up above on the bed.
Pretty soon the other two would lie down close to the fire,
          they would lie down beside each other.
Some time during the night, something comes on her face.
She shook her mother,
          she told her:
          "Mother! Something comes onto my face."
          "Mmmmmm. Shush. Your uncle, they are 'going.'"
Pretty soon now again, she heard something escaping.
She told her:
          "Mother! Something is going *t'uq t'uq.*

I hear something."
"Shush. Your uncle, they are 'going.'"
The girl got up.
She fixed the fire,
she lit pitch,
she looked where the two were:
Ah! Ah! Blood!
She raised her light to it, thus:
her uncle is on his bed,
his neck is cut,
he is dead.
She screamed.

[III. THE WOMEN LAMENT]
She told her mother:
"I told you,
'Something is dripping.'
You told me,
'Shush, they are "going."'
I had told you,
'Something is different about my uncle's wife.
She would "go out"
with a sound just like a man she would urinate.'
You would tell me,
'Shush!'"
She wept.
Seal said:
"Younger brother! My younger brother!
They are valuable standing there [house posts].
My younger brother!"
She kept saying that.
As for that girl, she wept.
She said,
"In vain I tried to tell you,
'Not like a woman,
with a sound just like a man she would urinate,
my uncle's wife!'
You told me,

'Shush!'
Oh oh my uncle!
Oh, my uncle!"
She wept, that girl.

Now I remember only that far.

—Told by Victoria Howard,
in Jacobs (1959); retranslated
according to ethnopoetic principles
by Dell Hymes (1981, 310–12)

The Revenge against the Sky People (Coos)

It is noteworthy that this story, a Native American "thriller," contains within its plot a version of "Seal and Her Younger Brother"; only here the observant little girl in the Clackamas story is an equally acute and outspoken boy living in the house of the Sky People, and the hero of the Coos story is, as an intruder in disguise, in a position analogous to the mysterious "wife" in "Seal and Her Younger Brother"!

A man lived in kiwe'et. He had an elder brother, who was always building canoes. Once he was working on a canoe (when) a man came there to him. "What do you do with your canoes after you finish them?"—"I always sell my canoes." He kept on working, with his head bent down, while the man was talking to him. Alongside the man who was building lay his dog. All of a sudden he [the stranger] hit the neck of the man who was building, and cut off his head. He took his head home.

The man who was building did not come home, and they went out looking for him. He lay in the canoe, without a head. The little dog was barking alongside the canoe. The dog would look upwards every time it barked. Straight up it would bark. So they began to think, "(Someone) from above must have killed him!" Then the next day the man's younger brother looked for him. The young man shot an arrow upwards, and then would shoot another one. He was shooting the arrows upwards. Every time he shot, his arrow would join (to the other); and as he kept on shooting this way, the arrows reached [down] to him.

Then he climbed up there. He went up on the arrows. He saw people when he had gotten up, and he asked, "From where do you come?" They were taking home a man's head. "We are [going to dance] for it," they said. They were taking home his elder brother's head. They said to the young man, "At a little place [nearby] the wife of the killer is digging fern-roots. Every forenoon she digs fern-roots there." So he went. He did not go very far. Suddenly, indeed, [he saw] a woman digging fern-roots. There was a big river.

So he asked the woman, "Do you have your own canoe?"—"Not so."—"Who ferries you across the river?"—"My husband ferries me across."—"What do you do when he ferries you across?"—"He does not land the canoe. I usually jump ashore."—"What does he do afterward?"—"He usually turns back. Then, when it is almost evening, I go home. He again comes after me. A little ways off [shore] he stops the canoe. Then I jump in with my pack. I get in there all right."

"What do you do with your fern-roots?"—"I usually dry them."—"What do you do with your fern-roots after they are dry?"—"I usually give some of them to all the people who live here. A little ways off in the next house, there live an old man and an old woman. I never give them any fern-roots."—"What do you usually do?"—"Then I cook the roots in a big pot."—"What do you do (then)?"—"I stir them with my hands."—"Doesn't your hand get burned?"—"Not so."—"Does your pot boil? Don't you ever say 'It hurts my hand!'?"—"No, it doesn't hurt me."—"What does your husband do when you lie down?"—"I lie a little ways off from my husband."—"Does your husband usually fall asleep quickly?"—"Yes, he usually falls asleep quickly."

Now he asked her all [these questions], and then he killed her. He skinned the woman, and put on her hide. Indeed, he looked just like the woman. Then he took her load and packed it. He saw the husband coming. The husband was crossing. A little ways off in the river he stopped the canoe. Thus he [the young man] was thinking, "I wonder whether I shall get there if I jump! I will try it from this distance." He packed the load and jumped. One leg touched the water. He pretty nearly did not get there. Thus spoke the man [husband], "Is that you, my wife?" Thus he spoke: "I am tired, this is the reason why I almost did not get (there). My pack is heavy." He [the husband] did not think about it any more.

Whatever the woman had told him, the young man (did it) that way. He made only one mistake. He gave fern-roots to those old people. He opened their door. The two old people saw him when he entered. They did not take the fern-roots which he held in his hands. Then one [of them] shouted, "Someone from below gives us something!" They did not hear it in the next house.

When the thing he was cooking began to boil, he stirred it with his hand. "Ouch! It burned my hand!" The husband heard it. "What happened to you?"—"My finger was sore, this is the reason why I [yelled]." And he [the young man] was looking at the head that was fastened to the ceiling. It was his elder brother's head. The husband said, "You seem to be crying."—"There is so much smoke, my eyes are sore." He [the husband] no longer paid any attention to it.

Now it got to be evening. The woman was going upstairs. Thus spoke the [husband's little brother], "My sister-in-law (looks) like a man!" His grandmother said to him, "The women where she comes from (look) just like men. You must keep quiet!" Nobody again thought about it. From everywhere people (came) there to the murderer to help him. They were dancing for the head. For it they were dancing. Blood was dropping from the head (that) was hanging (there).

Then it got (to be) evening and they went to bed. [. . .] She [the "woman"] had a big knife under her pillow. The husband went to bed first. The woman was walking outside. She bored holes in all the canoes in the village. Only in the one in which she intended to cross she did not bore a hole. As soon as she was finished, she went inside. Then she went to bed a little ways from her husband. At midnight the husband was fast asleep. She got up on the sly. She cut off the head of the husband, and seized her elder brother's head. Then she ran away, and crossed over alone in the canoe.

He (the husband's) mother was sleeping under their bed. The blood dripped down on her, and the old woman lighted a torch. "Blood! Blood! What have you done? You must have killed your wife!" She heard nothing. So everyone woke up. Then they saw the man lying on his bed, without a head. His wife had disappeared, and the head that was hanging from the ceiling was gone. "The woman must have killed her husband."—"It was not a woman," [said the little boy].

Then they followed her. [They] shoved the canoes (into the water), but they kept filling up with water, and they could not follow him.

Then [the young man] went down on his arrows, on which he had climbed up. Then he returned there (home). He brought back his elder brother's head. He assembled all his folks. Now, it is said, they were going to join his elder brother's head. Now they commenced to work. A small spruce tree was standing there. Against that small spruce tree they were joining his head. They danced for it. His head climbed a little bit on his body, and then fell down. Four times it happened that way. His head would go up a little bit, and then fall down again. The fifth time, however, his head stuck on. . . . Then he [the young man] said to his elder brother, "Now you are all right. [. . .]"

These are the Woodpecker people; this is why their heads are red today. The blood on their necks, that's what makes the head red. [Someone] said to them, "You shall be nothing. You shall be woodpeckers. The last people shall see you."

—Leo J. Frachtenberg (1913, 149–57)
For a detailed study of the artistry of this story
and "Seal and Her Younger Brother Lived There,"
see "The Wife Who Goes Out Like a Man,
Comes Back as a Hero," in Ramsey (1999, 96–114)

High Horse's Courting (Lakota Sioux)

The story of High Horse's romantic escapades, which brings comic relief to Black Elk's heartbreaking story of his life and the collapse of the Lakota Way, is probably in itself a droll parody of the heroic tales told by Plains Indian men around the council fire about their feats in battle, hunting, and so on.

You know, in the old days, it was not so very easy to get a girl when you wanted to be married. Sometimes it was hard work for a young man and he had to stand a great deal. Say I am a young man and I have seen a young girl who looks so beautiful to me that I feel all sick when I think about her. I can not just go and tell her about it and then get married if she is willing. I have to be a very sneaky fellow to talk to her at all, and after I have managed to talk to her, that is only the beginning.

Probably for a long time I have been feeling sick about a certain girl because I love her so much, but she will not even look at me, and her parents keep a good watch over her. But I keep feeling worse and worse all the time; so maybe I sneak up to her tepee in the dark and wait until she comes out. Maybe I just wait there all night and don't get any sleep at all and she does not come out. Then I feel sicker than ever about her.

Maybe I hide in the brush by a spring where she sometimes goes to get water, and when she comes by, if nobody is looking, then I jump out and hold her and just make her listen to me. If she likes me too, I can tell that from the way she acts, for she is very bashful and maybe will not say a word or even look at me the first time. So I let her go, and then I sneak around until I can see her father alone, and I tell him how many horses I can give him for his beautiful girl, and by now I am feeling so sick that maybe I would give him all the horses in the world if I had them.

Well, this young man I am telling about was called High Horse, and there was a girl in the village who looked so beautiful to him that he was just sick all over from thinking about her so much and he was getting sicker all the time. The girl was very shy, and her parents thought a great deal of her because they were not young any more and this was the only child they had. So they watched her all day long, and they fixed it so that she would be safe at night too when they were asleep. They thought so much of her that they had a rawhide bed for her to sleep in, and after they knew that High Horse was sneaking around after her, they took rawhide thongs and tied the girl in bed at night so that nobody could steal her when they were asleep, for they were not sure but that their girl might really want to be stolen.

Well, after High Horse had been sneaking around a good while and hiding and waiting for the girl and getting sicker all the time, he finally caught her alone and made her talk to him. Then he found out that she liked him maybe a little. Of course this didn't make him feel well. It made him sicker than ever, but now he felt as brave as a bison bull, and so he went right to her father and said he loved the girl so much that he would give two good horses for her—one of them young and the other not so very old.

But the old man just waved his hand, meaning for High Horse to go away and quit talking foolishness like that.

High Horse was feeling sicker than ever about it, but there was another young fellow who said he would loan High Horse two ponies and when he got some more horses, why, he could just give them back for the ones he had borrowed.

Then High Horse went back to the old man and said he would give four horses for the girl—two of them young and the other two hardly old at all. But the old man just waved his hand and would not say anything.

So High Horse sneaked around until he could talk to the girl again, and he asked her to run away with him. He told her he thought he would just fall over and die if she did not. But she said she would not do that; she wanted to be bought like a fine woman. You see she thought a great deal of herself too.

That made High Horse feel so very sick that he could not eat a bite, and he went around with his head hanging down as though he might just fall down and die any time.

Red Deer was another young fellow, and he and High Horse were great comrades, always doing things together. Red Deer saw how High Horse was acting, and he said: "Cousin, what is the matter? Are you sick in the belly? You look as though you were going to die."

Then High Horse told Red Deer how it was, and said he thought he could not stay alive much longer if he did not marry the girl pretty quick.

Red Deer thought awhile about it, and then he said, "Cousin, I have a plan, and if you are man enough to do as I tell you, then everything will be all right. She will not run away with you; her old man will not take four horses; and four horses are all you can get. You must steal her and run away with her. Then after a while you can come back and the old man cannot do anything because she will be your woman. Probably she wants you to steal her anyway."

So they planned what High Horse had to do, and he said he loved the girl so much that he was man enough to do anything Red Deer or anybody else could think up.

So this is what they did.

That night late they sneaked up to the girl's tepee and waited until it sounded inside as though the old man and the old woman and the girl were sound asleep. Then High Horse crawled under the tepee with a knife. He had to cut the rawhide thongs first, and then Red Deer, who was pulling up the stakes around that side of the tepee, was going to help drag the girl outside and gag her. After that, High Horse could put her across his pony in front of him and be happy all the rest of his life.

When High Horse had crawled inside, he felt so nervous that he could hear his heart drumming, and it seemed so loud he felt sure it would waken the old folks. But it did not, and after a while he began cutting the thongs. Every time he cut one it made a pop and nearly scared him to death. But he was getting along all right and all the thongs were cut down as far as the girl's thighs, when he became so nervous that his knife slipped and stuck the girl. She gave a big, loud yell. Then the old folks jumped up and yelled, too. By this time High Horse was outside, and he and Red Deer were running away like antelope. The old man and some other people chased the young men but they got away in the dark and nobody knew who it was.

Well, if you ever wanted a beautiful girl you will know how sick High Horse was now. It was very bad the way he felt, and it looked as though he would starve even if he did not drop over dead sometime.

Red Deer kept thinking about this, and after a few days he went to High Horse and said: "Cousin, take courage! I have another plan, and I am sure, if you are man enough, we can steal her this time." And High Horse said, "I am man enough to do anything anybody can think up, if only I can get that girl."

So this is what they did.

They went away from the village alone, and Red Deer made High Horse strip naked. Then he painted High Horse solid white all over, and after that he painted black stripes all over the white and black rings around High Horse's eyes. High Horse looked terrible. He looked so terrible that when Red Deer was through painting and took a good look at what he had done, he said it scared even him a little.

"Now," Red Deer said, "if you get caught again, everybody will be so scared they will think you are a bad spirit and will be afraid to chase you."

So when the night was getting old and everybody was sound asleep, they sneaked back into the girl's tepee. High Horse crawled in with his knife, as before, and Red Deer waited outside, ready to drag the girl out and gag her when High Horse had all the thongs cut.

High Horse crept up by the girl's bed and began cutting at the thongs. But he kept thinking, "If they see me they will shoot me because I look so terrible." The girl was restless and kept squirming around in bed, and when a thong was cut, it popped. So High Horse worked very slowly and carefully.

But he must have made some noise, for suddenly the old woman awoke and said to her old man: "Old Man, wake up! There is somebody in this tepee!" But the old man was sleepy and didn't want to be bothered. He said, "Of course there is somebody in this tepee. Go to sleep and don't bother me." Then he snored some more.

But High Horse was so scared by now that he lay very still and as flat to the ground as he could. Now, you see, he had not been sleeping very well for a long time because he was so sick about the girl. And while he was lying there waiting for the old woman, he just forgot everything, even how beautiful the girl was. Red Deer, who was lying outside ready to do his part, wondered and wondered what had happened in there, but he did not dare call out to High Horse.

After a while the day began to break and Red Deer had to leave with the two ponies he had staked there for his comrade and girl, or somebody would see him.

So he left.

Now when it was getting light in the tepee, the girl awoke and the first thing she saw was a terrible animal, all white with black stripes on it, lying asleep beside her bed. So she screamed, and then the old woman screamed and the old man yelled. High Horse jumped up, almost scared to death, and he nearly knocked the tepee down getting out of there.

People were coming running from all over the village with guns and bows and axes, and everybody was yelling.

By now High Horse was running so fast that he hardly touched the ground at all, and he looked so terrible that the people fled from him and let him run. Some braves wanted to shoot him, but the others said he might be some sacred being and it would bring bad trouble to kill him.

High Horse made for the river that was near, and in among the brush he found a hollow tree and dived into it. After a while some braves came there and he could hear them saying that it was some bad spirit that had come out of the water and gone back in again.

That morning the people were ordered to break camp and move away from there. So they did, while High Horse was hiding in his hollow tree.

Now Red Deer had been watching all this from his own tepee and trying to look as though he were as surprised and scared as all the others. So when the camp moved, he sneaked back to where he had seen his comrade disappear. When he was down there in the brush, he called, and High Horse answered, because he knew his friend's voice. They washed off the paint from High Horse and sat down on the river bank to talk about their troubles.

High Horse said he never would go back to the village as long as he lived and he did not care what happened to him now. He said he was going on the war-path all by himself. Red Deer said: "No, cousin, you are not going on the war-path alone, because I am going with you."

So Red Deer got everything ready, and at night they started out on the war-path all alone. After several days they came to a Crow camp just about sundown, and when it was dark they sneaked up to where the Crow horses were grazing, killed the horse-guard, who was not thinking about enemies because he thought all the Lakotas were far away, and drove off about a hundred horses.

They got a big start because all the Crow horses stampeded and it was probably morning before the Crow warriors could catch any horses to ride. Red Deer and High Horse fled with their herd three days and nights before they reached the village of their people. Then they drove the whole herd right into the village and up in front of the girl's tepee. The old man was there, and High Horse called out to him and asked if he thought maybe that would be enough horses for his girl. The old man did not wave him away that time. It was not the horses that he wanted. What he wanted was a son who was a real man and good for something.

So High Horse got his girl after all, and I think he deserved her.

—John A. Neihardt (1979, 52–58)
Told by Black Elk to Neihardt,
and retold by him

Traditional Indian
Songs and Ceremonies

Like the verbal arts of other cultures, the primary forms of traditional Native literatures—narratives, songs, ceremonies— tend to overlap and refer to one another. In traditional narratives (as already noted), characters often break into song at dramatic moments; likewise, some stories (notably origin myths) seem to exist mainly to account for the existence of tribal rituals; and some major rituals, such as the Navajo Night Chant *and the Iroquoian* Condolence Ritual, *often allude to or even retell traditional narratives.*

This interpenetration of forms is especially striking in the case of songs and ceremonies—hence the double focus of this section, emphasizing the rich interplay of ritual and lyrical impulses in Native verbal art. On the one hand, Indian lyrics sometimes have a ritualistic quality, especially if they are incantatory or prayerful. On the other hand, many Native ceremonial texts tend to be lyrically evocative and highly metaphorical; even a casual reading of the Night Chant, *for example, will reveal its intense lyricality, sustained over many thousand lines. So, although they are distinct forms in the traditional repertories, Indian songs and ceremonies do deserve to be read and studied in each other's company.*

Songs

Traditional Native songs and lyrics are typically brief, elliptical, and yet intense in their evocations of feeling. Their subjects are those of all lyric poetry—joy, grief, love, hatred, scorn, religious devotion, doubt, contentment. . . . *According to Francis La Flesche's Omaha informant, their mutual friend Flying Crow composed his last song because he "knew he was near death . . . and before he died he wanted to say to his friends some words that would not be forgotten the moment he spoke them, so he made the song to hold the words." (Francis La Flesche, "The Song of Flying Crow," pp. 163)*

The case of Flying Crow's song (which La Flesche did not publish, probably out of respect for his friend) reminds us that such compositions were at least initially identified with their makers, even as they passed over into the tribal repertory. Presumably, the words of Flying Crow's song were originally inseparable from their musical setting; for us to be reading *Indian songs silently means that we are not getting their full original imaginative force, any more than we can get the full effect of an anonymous Middle English lyric like "Western Wind" without hearing it with its melody.*

What we can *do, to appreciate translated Native songs fairly, is to insist on English translations that scrupulously avoid imposing Anglo literary conventions such as rhyme, regular meter, or stanza forms on the originals, and that faithfully reproduce features of Indian poetry such as extensive repetition of words and phrases and the use of nonverbal sounds. Ethnopoetic scholars like Dell Hymes and Dennis Tedlock make a point of grounding their renditions in the Indian-language texts when possible, thus attempting to understand and make use of the traditional poetics that shaped the oral compositions of singers like Flying Crow and the unknown Papago artist who created this haunting song:*

> *In the great night my heart will go out.*
> *Toward me the darkness comes rattling.*
> *In the great night my heart will go out. (p. 141)*

COURTING SONG (WINTU)

It is above that you and I shall go.
along the Milky Way you and I shall go;
along the flower trail you and I shall go;
picking flowers on our way you and I shall go.

—Dorothy Demetracopoulou (1935, 485)

COURTING SONG (KLAMATH)

Who has touched you at your secret places,
      no one?
I take you for an innocent girl,
      I, who have not yet lived beside you.
          —Albert Gatschet (1890, 347)

COURTING SONG (APACHE)

O Mescalero maiden, don't be afraid!
They are already gossiping about us,
      but don't be frightened.
      Gossips chew rocks!
      Don't be afraid!
          —Morris Opler (1969, 124)

CHINOOK JARGON SONG (CHINOOK)

I don't care
if you desert me.
Many pretty boys are in the town.
Soon I shall have another one.
For me that's easy!
          —Melville Jacobs (1936, 13)

MOCK-COURTING SONG (KLAMATH)

Girl: Young man, I will not love you,
      for you run around with no blanket on.
      I do not desire such a husband.
Boy: And I do not like a frog-shaped woman with swollen eyes!
          —Albert Gatschet (1890, 349)

LULLABY (KIOWA)

There's a baby coming,
it's swimming in the water,
it's just like a little rabbit,
she's got little rabbit feet
                    —Maurice Boyd (1981a, 19)

LULLABY FOR A LITTLE GIRL (TSIMSHIAN)

She will pick roses, this little girl,
        that is why she was born!
She will dig bitter rice with her fingers, this little girl,
        that is why she was born!
In early spring she will gather sap from young hemlocks, this little girl,
        that is why she was born!
She will pick baskets of blueberries, this little girl,
        that is why she was born!
She will gather soapberries, this little girl,
        that is why she was born!
She will gather elderberries, this little girl,
        that is why she was born!
She will gather wild roses, this little girl,
        that is why she was born!
                    —Marius Barbeau, in Garfield and Wengert (1951, 145)

WORKINGMAN'S SONG FOR HIS
FIRSTBORN SON (KWAKIUTL)

Born to be a hunter,
        when I become a man,
            Father,
                ya ha ha ha
Born to be a harpooner,
        when I become a man,
            Father,
                ya ha ha ha

Born to be a boatwright,
    when I become a man,
      Father,
        ya ha ha ha
Born to be a board-splitter,
    when I become a man,
      Father,
        ya ha ha ha
Born to be a craftsman,
    when I become a man,
      Father,
        ya ha ha ha
That you, you will need nothing
    of all you want,
      Father,
        ya ha ha ha
        —Dell Hymes (1981, 51);
        original translation in Boas (1925)

CRADLE SONG (MODOC)

Early in the morning robin will eat ants,
early, early will it pick at the cedar tree,
early in the morning it chatters, *Tchiwi'p, tchiwi'p, tchitch, tsits, tchitch*
      —Albert Gatschet (1894, 213)

THUNDER SONG FOR BLESSING A CHILD (OMAHA)

(a lock of the child's hair is offered to the Thunder god)

Grandfather! Far above on high,
the hair like a shadow passes before you.
Grandfather! Far above on high,
dark like a shadow the hair sweeps before you
    into the midst of your realm.
Grandfather! There above, on high,
dark like a shadow the hair passes before you.

Grandfather! Dwelling afar on high,
like a dark shadow the hair sweeps before you
      into the midst of your realm.
Grandfather! Far above on high,
the hair like a shadow passes before you.
          —Alice Fletcher and
             Francis La Flesche (1911, 124)

THE THUNDER BADGER (NORTHERN PAIUTE)

Thunder Badger lives up in the sky,
he is striped like any badger.
When the earth dries up it makes him angry,
he wants the earth to be moist.
Then he puts his head down and digs like a badger,
then the clouds come up in a flurry,
then the loud earth-cursing comes, the thunder,
then the rain comes down all over.
          —W. C. Marsden (1923, 47);
           English adaptation by Jarold Ramsey

TWO "FLOOD SONGS" (PIMA)

It will drown us;
Earth everywhere floods.
Just then all the birds forget their flapping,
they feel pitiful, bunched and clinging.
Sun dies,
Sun dies.
Earth everywhere dark.
Just then every bird stops cooing.
Earth doesn't echo.
A mockingbird speaks pitifully,
alone distantly talks.
          —Donald Bahr and Vincent Joseph (1994, 557)

SONGS TO PULL DOWN THE RAIN (PAPAGO)

The little red spiders
and the little grey horned toad
together they make the rain to fall;
they make the rain to fall.
Upon the Children's Land
the waters run and overflow,
upon the Streambed Mountain
the waters run and overflow.
Corn is forming.
Corn is forming.
Beside it, squash is forming,
in the yellow flowers
the flies sing.

At the edge of the world
it is growing light.
The trees stand shining.
I like it.
It is growing light.

—Ruth Underhill (1938, 27)

WOMEN'S PLANTING SONG (OSAGE)

I have made a footprint, a sacred one.
I have made a footprint, through it the blades spring upward.
I have made a footprint, over it the blades float in the wind.
I have made a footprint, over it the ears lean forward to one another.
I have made a footprint, over it I pluck the ears.
I have made a footprint, over it I bend the stalks to pluck the ears.
I have made a footprint, over it the blossoms lie gray.
I have made a footprint, smoke arises from my house.
I have made a footprint, there is cheer in my house.
I have made a footprint, I live in the light of day.

—Francis La Flesche (1923, 194)

CORN SONGS (PAPAGO)

On Tecolote fields
the corn is growing green.
I came there, saw the tassels waving in the breeze,
Blowing in the wind,
singing,
am I crazy corn?
Blowing in the wind,
singing,
am I laughing corn?
                    —Ruth Underhill (1938, 44)

QUAIL SONG (PIMA)

The grey quails bunched tight together.
            Above, Coyote trotted by.
                    He stopped. He looked.
The blue quails ran and huddled together.
            Coyote looked at them
                    sideways.
                    —Frank Russell (1903, 347)

SONG ABOUT BATS (YAQUI)

Night people,
            though nothing is done to them,
                    they go sounding, pitifully,
night, night people.
Night people,
            though nothing is done to them,
                    they go sounding, pitifully.
Night, night people.
Over there, I, in the flower-covered,
            cherished, enchanted night world,
                    I am more human.

Though nothing is done to them,
     somewhere, loudly,
        they go sounding pitifully.
Night, night people.
          —Larry Evers and
            Felipe S. Molina (1987, 109)

ANIMAL SONGS (PAPAGO)

A little gray horned toad medicine man
lost his wife.
All over the earth he ran
sorrowing.
(The owl speaks)
"Just before me
the evening is growing red.
I fly out and four times
I hoot."
          —Ruth Underhill (1938, 48, 52)

BUFFALO SONG (OSAGE)

I rise, I rise,
I, whose tread makes the earth rumble.
     I rise, I rise,
I, in whose thighs there is strength.
     I rise, I rise,
I, who whips his back with his tail when in rage.
     I rise, I rise,
I, in whose humped shoulders there is power.
     I rise, I rise,
I, who shakes his mane when angered.
     I rise, I rise,
I, whose horns are sharp and curved.
          —Francis La Flesche (1925, 209)

SALMON SONG (KWAKIUTL)

Many are coming ashore, they with me,
    the true salmon that were.
For they come ashore to you,
    to the post at the center of the heavens.
Dancing from the far side ashore with me,
    the true salmon that were,
for they come to dance with you,
    at the right side of the face of the heavens.
Overtowering,
    surpassing,
        outshining,
            the true salmon that were.
      —Franz Boas (1970, 709)

CREATION SONG (KLAMATH)

I take the earth up in my arms
    And whirl it around in a dance!
On this earth I stand and sing this song.
        —Albert Gatschet (1890, 192)

VISION SONG (HIDATSA)

My Father says
    "When the wind blows
    I will go with it."
        —Edward Curtis (1970a, 147)

DREAM SONG (OJIBWA)

Sometimes
I go along pitying myself
while I am carried by the wind
across the sky.
        —Frances Densmore (1910, 127)

RUNNING SONG (PAPAGO)

I am on my way running,
I am on my way running,
looking toward me is the edge of the world,
I am trying to reach it,
the edge of the world does not look far away,
to that I am on my way running.
                    —Frances Densmore (1929, 142)

WIND SONG (KIOWA)

(sung by grandmothers to young men going on the warpath)
The land is great.
When a man travels on it
        he will never reach land's end.
But because there is a prize offered
to test a man to go as far as he dares,
he goes because he wants to discover his limits.
                    —Maurice Boyd (1981b, 18)

VISION SONG (PAPAGO)

I did not know
I did not know
and then I knew
                    —Ruth Underhill (1979, 45)

PEYOTE SONG (KIOWA)

Let us see, is it real,
this life I am living, is it real?
You, Sayn-daw-kee, who dwells everywhere,
let us see, is it real, this life I am living?
                    —Maurice Boyd (1981b, 107)

SONG (PAPAGO)

In the great night my heart will go out.
      Toward me the darkness comes rattling.
In the great night my heart will go out.
          —Frances Densmore (1929, 126)

DEATH SONG (OMAHA)

Where can I go
that I might live forever?
The old fathers have gone to the spirit land.
Where can I go
that we might live forever?
          —Dorothy Clark Wilson (1974, 373)

SONG FOR RELEASING THE SPIRIT (OMAHA)

Fly over the Four Hills,
spiralling in the wind.
Fly straight and land on the fourth Hill,
land on the tree tops!
The Buffalo will direct you.
The breath goes on;
the body stays.
Do not be sorry!
          —Reo Fortune (1922, 130)

SONG OF A SPIRIT TRAVELING FROM
HIS HUMAN TO HIS SPIRIT HOME (OJIBWA)

Whenever I pause,
      The noise of the village!
Whenever I pause.
          —Frances Densmore (1913, 278)

JARGON VISION SONG (CHINOOK)

There is a land of light,
far away, always light,
and from there the waters shine
and from there the salmon come.

> —Dell Hymes (1981, 55)
> Source: David French

SONGS FROM THE GHOST DANCE

These songs are representative of thousands of songs performed by Indians throughout middle and western America during the time of the Ghost Dance spiritual revival of the late 1880s and 1890s. The primary tenet of the Ghost Dance was the imminent disappearance of the White Man, or at least of his encroachments on Indian territories, and the return of the buffalo. The great chronicler of the Ghost Dance was the ethnographer James Mooney, whose The Ghost Dance Religion *(1892; repr. 1973) is a classic contact-era ethnography. The following songs are from Mooney.*

Whirlwind Song (Pawnee)
I circle around,
I circle around
The boundaries of the earth,
The boundaries of the earth,
Wearing the long wing feathers as I fly,
Wearing the long wing feathers as I fly.

> —James Mooney (1973, 970)

Prayer (Arapaho)
Father, have pity on me,
Father, have pity on me;
I am crying for thirst,
I am crying for thirst.
All is gone—I have nothing to eat,
All is gone—I have nothing to eat.

> —James Mooney (1973, 997)

Morning Star Prayer (Arapaho)
Father, the Morning Star!
Father, the Morning Star!
Look on us, we have danced until daylight.
Look on us, we have danced until daylight.
Take pity on us—Hi'I'I!
Take pity on us—Hi'I'I !
　　　　—James Mooney (1973, 1011)

Song (Pit River)
The snow lies there—*ro'rani!*
The snow lies there—*ro'rani!*
The snow lies there—*ro'rani!*
The snow lies there—*ro'rani!*
The Milky Way lies there,
the Milky Way lies there.
　　　　—James Mooney (1973, 1052)

Song (Lakota)
The whole world is coming,
a nation is coming, a nation is coming,
the Eagle has brought the message to the tribe.
The father says so, the father says so.

Over the whole earth they are coming.
the buffalo are coming, the buffalo are coming,
the Crow has brought the message to the tribe,
the father says so, the father says so.
　　　　—James Mooney (1973, 1072)

Song (Kiowa)
The father will descend,
the father will descend.
The earth will tremble,
the earth will tremble.
Everyone will arise,
everyone will arise.
Stretch out your hands,
stretch out your hands.
　　　　—James Mooney (1973, 1087)

Poor Song (Kiowa)
Heye'heye'heye'heye' Aho'ho !
Heye'heye'heye'heye' Aho'ho !
Because I am poor,
because I am poor,
I pray for every living creature,
I pray for every living creature.
Ao'nyo ! Ao'nyo !
    —James Mooney (1973, 1084)

Tipi Song (Kiowa)
That wind, that wind,
shakes my tipi, shakes my tipi,
and sings a song for me,
and sings a song for me.
    —James Mooney (1973, 1087)

Prayer (Arapaho)
Yani'tsini'hawa'nai !
Yani'tsini'hawa'nai !
We shall live again,
we shall live again.
—James Mooney (1973, 1047)

Ceremonies

Traditional Indian ceremonies range in length from prayers, incantations, and charms of just a few words and phrases, uttered over and over, to the great Navajo healing and blessingway ceremonies, taking many days and nights and involving not only the spoken (or sung) words of the ritual but also episodes of sandpainting, storytelling, pantomime, ritual smoking, eating, drinking, and so on. But whether brief or long, all such ritual forms share a central purpose—to attract and invoke *spiritual power for a particular end, whether for the good of the entire community, as in the rain-gathering rituals of the Pueblo peoples, or for the benefit of an individual. (Often, according to Indian beliefs, the two purposes are seen as harmonious.) And all such traditional exercises share a reliance on* words, *used in such a way as to attain during the ceremony a magical instrumentality, capable of "making things happen" through the verbal invocation of spirit power.*

CEREMONY FOR PRESENTING
A NEWBORN CHILD (OMAHA)

Ho! Ye sun, moon, stars, all ye that move in the heavens,
    I bid you hear me!
Into your midst has come a new life.
    Consent ye, I implore!
Make its path smooth, that it may reach
    the brow of the first hill.

Ho! Ye winds, clouds, rain, mist, all ye that move in the air,
    I bid you hear me!
Into your midst has come a new life.
    Consent ye, I implore!
Make its path smooth, that it may reach the brow of the second hill!

Ho! Ye hills, valleys, rivers, lakes, trees, grasses, all ye of the earth,
    I bid you hear me!
Into your midst has come a new life.
    Consent ye, I implore!
Make its path smooth, that it may reach the brow of the third hill!

Ho! Ye birds, great and small, that fly in the air,
ho! Ye animals, great and small, that dwell in the forest,
ho! Ye insects that creep along the grasses and burrow in the ground—
    I bid you hear me!
Into your midst has come a new life.
Consent ye, I implore!
Make its path smooth, that it may reach the brow of the fourth hill!

Ho! All ye of the heavens, all ye of the air, all ye of the earth:
    I bid you all to hear me!
Into your midst has come a new life!
    Consent ye, consent ye all, I implore!
Make its path smooth—then shall it travel beyond the four hills!

—Alice Fletcher and
Francis La Flesche (1911, 115–16)

NAMING CEREMONY (WISHRAM)

(A ritual leader speaks for the candidate to the assembly,
     and it responds in unison)
This person will be [Spedis]
     A-xi.
This name used to belong to [Spedis], who died a long time ago.
     A-xi.
We want the mountains, creeks, rivers, bluffs, timber to
     know that this person is now named [Spedis].
     A-xi.
We want to let the fishes, birds, winds, snow, rain, sun, moon,
     stars to know that [Spedis] has the same as become alive again.
     His name will be heard again when this person is called.
     A-xi.

—Leslie Spier and
Edward Sapir (1930, 258–59)

FROM THE IROQUOIAN *CONDOLENCE RITUAL*

From the fifteenth century into the nineteenth, the League of the Iroquois Nations (Seneca, Mohawk, Onondaga, Oneida, and Cayuga, and by adoption, the Tuscaroras) regularly performed the Condolence Ritual whenever the head sachem or chief of one of the nations died. Fusing spiritual and political purposes, the Ritual undertakes to condole and heal the grief of the bereaved family and nation of the dead leader, and at the same time to "requicken" and reconsolidate the unity of the entire League, at a moment of crisis and potential instability. Consistent with the matrilineal orientation of Iroquoian society, the League is metaphorically identified throughout as a grieving woman, a widow; the ministrations to "her" in the fifteen Articles of Requickening are remarkably astute both psychologically and politically.

The story of the founding of the League by Hiawatha and his spiritual helper Deganawideh is retold and alluded to, and the past glories of the Iroquoian people are invoked throughout as guides to the present as well as hints of chaotic times to come if the Great League is allowed to disintegrate. At last, with the ritual work of condolence and political "requickening" accomplished, the ceremony identifies the newly chosen sachem, and his inauguration symbolizes the restoration of the entire League.

For background and commentary on the Condolence Ritual, *see John Bierhorst (1984, 109–83).*

Article Eleven: The Council Fire

Now, another thing: that our grandsires, now
long dead, and in whom our minds rested in trust,
decreed because they did not know its face, the
face, indeed, of that Being that abuses us every
day, every night, that Being of Darkness, lying
hard by the lodges where it is black night, yea,
that Being which here at the very tops of our
heads, goes about menacing with its couched
weapon—with its uplifted hatchet—eagerly
muttering its fell purposes, "I, I will destroy the
Work—the Commonwealth," they decreed, I say,
that therefore they would call it the Great
Destroyer, the Being Without a Face, the Being
malefic in Itself, that is, Death.

More than this it has already done; it has put
forth its lethal power there in thy frail lodge of
bark, this one [indicating], my weanling, my
offspring, thou noble one, and so snatching
therefrom one on whom thou didst depend for
words of wisdom and kindly service.

And so now, at this very moment, there is in that
lodge of bark a vacant mat because of this stroke.

And, in striking this cruel blow, it scattered the
Firebrands, thy Chiefs, widely asunder from the
place where thou art wont to kindle thy Council
Fire, and, now, more than this, the Great
Destroyer has danced exultingly, stamping that
hearth underfoot.

Thou sittest there now with bowed head; thou
no longer dost meditate on anything whatsoever

of thy former affairs—wherein thou wast laboring
for thy niece and for thy nephew, for the men
and the women of thy people; yea, for thy
children, and also for thy grandchildren, who run
about thy sides, and for these also who are still
swathed to cradleboards, and also for those
children who, still unborn, whose faces, still
underground, are coming toward thee; yea, for
these warriors and for these women; that is the
extent, indeed, of the solicitude and vigilant care
which were in the hands of him, thy uncle—thy
mother's brother—who has departed, while he
labored for their daily welfare, and who at this
moment is floating away far homeward.

So, now, do thou know it, this one, thou *yaanehr* [child]
my offspring, thou noble one, that the Three
Brothers have perfected their preparations, and
so let them say it, "Now we gather again the
Scattered Firebrands, thy Chiefs, and now, indeed,
do we rekindle the Council Fire for thee. And
Now, in fact, verily, the smoke shall rise again, and
that smoke will be fine, and it will even pierce the
sky."

So, now again, the eyes of the peoples—alien to
us, perhaps—shall again, also, the full number
of our Council Fires.

Now, again, indeed, we raise thee up to full
stature, erect among thy people. We also cheer
up thy mind. More than this, we again set thee
in order around the place where we have
rekindled the Fire for thee, my offspring. . . .

Article Twelve: Woman and Warrior
Now, there is
another thing to be considered

today. It is that wherein the Perfector of our faculties who dwelleth in the sky did not establish this matter in that He desired that He should have assistants everywhere, even down to the earth, that these latter assistants shall devote their solicitous care to the number of matters which pertain especially to the earth and which I have ordained, He says, one and all.

It is that, in fact, that first among others, He caused the body of our mother—the woman—to be of great worth and honor. He purposed that she shall be endowed and entrusted with the duties pertaining to the birth—the becoming— of men, and that she shall, in the next place, circle around the fire in preparing food—that she shall have the care of all that is planted by which life is sustained and supported, and so the power to breathe is fortified, and moreover that the warriors shall be her assistants.

So that, too, is a great calamity, that it may be the Great Destroyer will make a sudden stroke there in the ranks of our mothers, and that he will thus snatch away one there, so that her body shall fall. The evil of this misfortune is that a long file of expected persons shall fall away, which, indeed, would have come into the manyfold lines of grand-children who would have been born from her in the future.
In that case, moreover, her assistants, the warriors, will then just stand around listlessly, but grieving.

For, now, that one on whom they so much depended is now, very probably, floating away to the homeland, and now the minds of all those who still remain have fallen low in grief.

So now, moreover, the Three Brothers, having
perfected their preparations, do say, "Let us
comfort them now and raise up their minds."
And that, indeed, shall happen—they will now
again devote themselves to their cares and their
duties.

More than this, now, thou *yaanehr*, thou noble
one, my offspring, thou hadst a nephew and
niece, that is to say, the warriors and the
women. They are and shall be thy immediate care.

And that more than this, thou *yaanehr*, thou noble
one, thou shalt and must give a full hearing to
whomsoever will speak to thee for counsel or for
service. That too, let the Three Brothers say,
"Do you heed and obey one another." It is, in fact,
a grievous thing, should it be that thou, noble
one, should cast over thy shoulder whatsoever
word is spoken to thee.

That mood of mind may have place only when
the time is near in which the feet òf thy peoples
will hang over the abyss of the sundered earth.
There is no one dwelling beneath the sky who has
the power to come out therefrom, when that shall
have come to pass. Furthermore, this great
responsibility rests both upon thee and upon thy
niece and nephew—that ye listen to and obey
one another.

Thus, too, let it be done, that for one poor short
day, thou mayst continue to think in contentment,
my offspring, thou noble ruler, whom I have been
wont to hold in my bosom.
In this manner then, perhaps, let them do it, the
three Brothers, so denominated ever since they
were in the prime growth of their affairs.

Now, more than this, do you know it, this one
[indicating], my offspring, thou noble ruler,
whom I have been wont to hold in my bosom,
the Word of thy *adonni* is on its way hence to
thee.

—J. W. B. Hewitt (1944, 65–85)

THE NAVAJO *NIGHT CHANT,* FROM THE NINTH DAY

The Night Chant *specifically focuses on one subject or "patient" suffering from what might be called psychosomatic afflictions, including dizziness, paralysis, disorientation, and depression, and over the course of nine days and nights the ceremony endeavors to restore him or her to full, active well-being. But, like the Iroquoian* Condolence Ritual, *the* Night Chant *also has a sociopolitical agenda: having brought a large assembly of Navajos together on behalf of one of their own, it systematically reaffirms the unity of the Navajo world and its solidarity with the natural and spiritual worlds.*

The concept of hozho, *very roughly translated as health or wholeness of being, is central to the* Night Chant, *and in all of its episodes, in words and in ritual actions, either illness is being taken away from the patient or he or she is being purified, revived, and healed. The concept of the* Night Chant *is vast and inclusive of the essentials of Navajo life; it might well be called a charter of the Navajo Way. Its movement through words and actions is slow, incremental, and majestic, like some process in nature, like the coming on of a desert storm or the ripening of a field of grain. Nowhere is this quality of poetic majesty more apparent than in the great Hymn of the Ninth Day, which eventually reprises all that has come before it and prepares for a final night of singing, after which the patient steps out of the Hogan to greet the dawn.*

A full annotated text is available in Bierhorst (1984); for commentary on the Night Chant *and its relationships with the* Condolence Ritual, *see Ramsey (1999, 47–68).*

In Tsegihi,
in the house made of the dawn,
in the house made of the evening twilight,
in the house made of the dark cloud,

in the house made of the he-rain,
in the house made of the dark mist,
in the house made of the she-rain,
in the house made of pollen,
in the house made of grasshoppers,
where the dark mist curtains the doorway,
the path to which is on the rainbow,
where the zigzag lightning stands high on top,
where the he-rain stands high on top,
oh, male divinity!
With your moccasins of dark cloud, come to us.
With your leggings of dark cloud, come to us.
With your shirt of dark cloud, come to us.
With your headdress of dark cloud, come to us.
With your mind enveloped in dark cloud, come to us.
With the dark thunder above you, come to us soaring.
With the shapen cloud at your feet, come to us soaring.
With the far darkness made of the dark cloud over your head,
        come to us soaring.
With the far darkness made of the he-rain over your head,
        come to us soaring.
With the far darkness made of the dark mist over your head,
        come to us soaring.
With the far darkness made of the she-rain over your head,
        come to us soaring.
With the zigzag lightning flung out on high over your head,
        come to us soaring.
With the rainbow hanging high over your head, come to us soaring.
With the far darkness made of the dark cloud on the ends of your wings,
        come to us soaring.
With the far darkness made of the he-rain on the ends of your wings,
        come to us soaring.
With the far darkness made of the dark mist on the ends of your wings,
        come to us soaring.
With the far darkness made of the she-rain on the ends of your wings,
        come to us soaring.
With the zigzag lightning flung out on high on the ends of your wings,
        come to us soaring.

With the rainbow hanging high on the ends of your wings,
>   come to us soaring.
With the near darkness made of the dark cloud, of the he-rain,
>   of the dark mist, and of the she-rain, come to us.
With the darkness on the earth, come to us.
With these I wish the foam floating on the flowing water over
>   the roots of the great corn.
I have made your sacrifice.
I have prepared a smoke for you.
My feet restore for me.
My limbs restore for me.
My mind restore for me.
My voice restore for me.
Today, take out your spell for me.
Today, take away your spell for me.
Away from me you have taken it.
Far off from me it is taken.
Far off you have done it.
Happily I recover.
Happily my interior becomes cool.
Happily my eyes regain their power.
Happily my head becomes cool.
Happily my limbs regain their power.
Happily I hear again.
Happily for me the spell is taken off.
Happily may I walk.
Impervious to pain, may I walk.
Feeling light within, may I walk.
With lively feelings, may I walk.
Happily abundant dark clouds I desire.
Happily abundant dark mists I desire.
Happily abundant passing showers I desire.
Happily an abundance of vegetation I desire.
Happily an abundance of pollen I desire.
Happily abundant dew I desire.
Happily may fair white corn, to the ends of the earth, come with you.
Happily, may fair yellow corn, to the ends of the earth, come with you.
Happily, may fair blue corn, to the ends of the earth, come with you.

Happily may fair corn of all kinds, to the ends of the earth,
     come with you.
Happily may fair plants of all kinds, to the ends of the earth,
     come with you.
Happily may fair goods of all kinds, to the ends of the earth,
     come with you.
Happily may fair jewels of all kinds, to the ends of the earth,
     come with you.
With these before you, happily may they come with you.
With these behind you, happily may they come with you.
With these below you, happily may they come with you.
With these above you, happily may they come with you.
With these all around you, happily may they come with you.
Thus happily you accomplish your tasks.
Happily the old men will regard you.
Happily the old women will regard you.
Happily the young men will regard you.
Happily the young women will regard you.
Happily the boys will regard you.
Happily the girls will regard you.
Happily the children will regard you.
Happily the chiefs will regard you.
Happily, as they scatter in different directions, they will regard you.
Happily, as they approach their homes, they will regard you.
Happily may their roads home be on the trail of pollen.
Happily may they all get back.
In beauty I walk.
With beauty before me, I walk.
With beauty behind me, I walk.
With beauty below me, I walk.
With beauty above me, I walk.
With beauty all around me, I walk.
It is finished in beauty,
It is finished in beauty,
It is finished in beauty,
It is finished in beauty.

                —Washington Matthews (1902, 143–45)

Transitions

Even before American Indians began to read and write in English, they were imaginatively engaging and appropriating stories from English and French and even African sources, as well as from other Native cultures. This impulse to "try out," absorb, and adapt "foreign" imaginative material is expressive of the dynamics of Native oral literature, and such adaptations are valuable for the way they reveal the stresses of contact with alien cultural realities and indicate how Native cultures have used traditional storytelling as a means of making imaginative sense of such realities.

Sometimes the assimilation is relatively straightforward, as with European folktales like "John the Bear" or stories in the "P'tit Jean" cycle, in which the basic story line is preserved while the setting and narrative details become emphatically "Indianized." Bible stories heard from missionaries (usually through two or three steps of translation) must have been much more challenging, and the adaptations of these are typically more drastic. In stories from the New Testament, Christ's redemptive self-sacrifice on our behalf is usually omitted altogether as a theme, because it doesn't "compute" in terms of Native moral systems. And sometimes—perhaps in a spirit of anti-missionary mischief—Christ's apparent failure as an earthly savior/ transformer is followed by the appearance of an authentic Native transformer like Coyote, who knows how to do the job!

Such texts, although often neglected by early collectors and editors, have much to tell us about contact-era experience, and in their imaginative playing of foreign themes off against traditional Indian forms, they point the way to the beginning of American Indian literary writing.

The Gospels According to the Thompson Indians

The [first] people were much oppressed and preyed upon, and so much evil prevailed in the world, that the Chief sent his son Jesus to set things right. After traveling around the world as a transformer, Jesus was killed by the bad people, who crucified him, and he returned to the sky.

After he had returned, the Chief looked over the world, and saw that things had not changed much for the better. Jesus had only set right a very few things. He had done more talking than anything else. [. . .] Jesus worked only for the people's spiritual benefit. He had tried to induce them to be good, and taught them how to pray to the Chief. He taught them no arts, nor wisdom about how to do things, nor did he help to make life easier for them. Neither did he transform or destroy the evil monsters which killed them, nor did he change or arrange the features of the earth in any way. [. . .]

Now, the Chief said, "If matters are not improved, there will be soon no people." Then he sent Coyote to earth to destroy all the monsters and evil beings, to make life easier and better for the people, and to teach them the best way to do things. [. . .] Coyote did a great deal of good, but he did not finish everything properly. Sometimes he made mistakes, and although he was wise and powerful, he did many foolish things. [. . .]

—James Teit (1912, 80–83)

The Tower of Babel (Thompson)

The biblical reason for God's causing "the confusion of tongues"—to punish the insolence and pride of Nimrod and his followers—becomes, in Indian terms, a concern that people will abandon Earth for Heaven! (Cf. Genesis 11.)

After God had made the flood, he went up to the sky again, but, feeling lonely, he thought he would let some of the people come up and live with him. He gave the chief of the people a dream in which he told him to build a pole ladder on which they could ascend to the sky.

The chief told the people God wanted them up above, so they commenced to build as directed. Each day they added a pole, and at last one night the ladder told them, "Tomorrow by noon we are going to reach the sky."

Now God changed his mind, and said to himself, "If people come up here and see what a beautiful country it is, they will all wish to remain here and the earth will be deserted." Therefore that night, while the people slept, he took a language out of his mouth, and threw it into the mouth of the chief. Then he took another language, and threw it into his brother's mouth, and thus he threw a different language into each man's mouth.

When the people awoke in the morning each spoke a different language, and they could not understand one another. Wives spoke the tongues of their husbands, and children, that of their fathers. The chief spoke Shuswap, and his brothers spoke Okanagan and Thompson respectively.

Thus the people began to speak different languages, such as Yakima, Cree, Kootenai, Lillooet, Chilcotin, and Carrier. As the men could not understand one another, they were unable to add the last pole, which would have taken them up to the sky. The people got angry with one another, and the pole ladder at last rotted away.

—James Teit (1912, 400–401)

Saynday Sends Smallpox Away (Kiowa)

Saynday is the Kiowa trickster: in this latter-day story, with his people's lives changing rapidly, he has begun to feel neglected and unneeded—until "Smallpox" arrives.

Saynday was coming along the edge of the prairie and looking at the world about him. Many things had changed since he had brought the people out of the cottonwood tree. He had brought the Sun and the buffaloes to the people, although the buffaloes were now declining in numbers. Instead of deer running free in the woods, the log cabins of white settlers now sat amidst the trees. Even the streams no longer abounded with fish. Saynday grew sad as he wondered if he could any longer help his people.

As he stood pondering over the result of changing times, Saynday suddenly observed a moving spot far away on the prairie. After a while, he could tell that it was slowly approaching him from the east.

In the past, good things had come to Saynday and his people from the east. The Sun always rose in the east, bringing light and warmth, life and growth. The Kiowas faced their camps eastward in reverence and gratitude as they witnessed the daily renewal of life.

On this particular day, however, Saynday felt an odd dark chill as he saw the black spot slowly coming from the east. Instantly Saynday walked eastward as if a magnet were pulling him toward something evil. As the form grew larger, Saynday recognized that the spot was a man on horseback. After a long time the rider and Saynday drew near each other. The stranger wore a black suit and tall dark hat. His horse was also black. Both the rider and the horse were covered with a powdery red dust.

"Who are you and where do you live?" the stranger asked Saynday.

"My name is Saynday. I live among the Kiowas and they call me Old Man Saynday."

The stranger thought for a moment and replied, "I have never heard of you or the Kiowas. Who are they and where do they live?"

"Oh, they live south of here. They are the greatest hunters and war-riors of the southern plains. Who are you, and from where have you come?"

"I am Smallpox," the man replied. "I have come across the Eastern Sea with the white men. Where they go, I go, into their homes and cabins. I am their gift to you. I bring sickness and sometimes death with my breath. Where are the Kiowas camping now?"

With that statement, Smallpox used his coat sleeve to wipe the red dust from his face, and Saynday saw that the man's face was pitted with ugly scars. A foul odor covered the man. Saynday feared that Smallpox would find the Kiowas and kill or disfigure the beautiful women and happy children.

"The Kiowas are poor and few in number," replied Saynday. "They live far, far to the south. But the Pawnees are many, and they live nearby in great houses, partly underground, where they store their riches. They are fat and numerous, with every camp full of people. They are the ones who killed so many Kiowas that it is not worth your time to find the few Kiowas left. You would like the Pawnees."

"Oh, yes," Smallpox replied. "I do my best work in large groups. I shall visit them first, then call on your Kiowas later. Where do these numerous and wealthy Pawnees live?"

"To the north," pointed Saynday, "over those hills and a little beyond. Keep going in that direction and you will find them."

Smallpox immediately reined his horse and departed to the north.

Saynday watched as the black horse and rider slowly plodded away. Then Saynday smiled and was no longer sad, for once again he had helped his people even though times were changing.

And that is how Saynday sent Smallpox away from the Kiowas to the Pawnees!

—Maurice Boyd (1983b, 297–99)

The Garden of Eden (Northern Paiute)

Almost everything was Coyote's way. The Indians planted the apple. When he planted it, he said for all the Indians to come and eat. When he told them that, all the people came.

The white man was a rattlesnake then, and he was on that tree. The white people have eyes just like the rattlesnake. When the Indians tried to come to eat the apples, that snake tried to bite them. That's why the white people took everything away from the Indians; because they were snakes. If that snake hadn't been on the tree, everything would have belonged to the Indian. Just because they were snakes and came here, the white people took everything away. They asked these Indians where they had come from. That's why they took everything and told the Indians to go way out in the mountains and live.

—Isabel Kelly (1938, 375)
Narrator: Charlie Washo

The True Beginning of this Earth (Northern Paiute)

"One time this was all water but just one little island. That is what we are living on now. Old Man Chocktoot was living on top of this mountain. He was living right on top of this mountain. In all directions the land was lower than this mountain. It was burning under the earth. Numuzo'ho was under there, and he kept on eating people.

"The Star [*pa'tazuba*] was coming. When that Star came up, it went into the sky and stayed there. When that Star went up, he said, 'That is too bad; I pity my people. We left them without anything to eat; they are going to starve.' This Star gave us deer, and antelope, and elk, and all kinds of game.

"They had Sun for a god. When the Sun came up, he told his people, 'Don't worry, come to me; I'll help you. Don't worry; be happy all your life. You will come to me.'

"The Sun and the Stars came with the Water. They had the Water for a home. The Indian doctor saw them coming. He let his people know that they were coming. There were many of them. The little streams of spring water are the places from which silver money comes. It comes from the Sun shining on the water.

"The first white man came to this land and saw that silver, but he lost himself and didn't get to it. Finally white people found this place, and they came this way looking for the silver. Those white men brought cattle, sheep, pigs, and horses. Before they came, there were no horses in this land.

"The Sun told his people, 'Deer belong to you. They are for you to eat.' These white men don't know who put the deer and other animals in this land. I think it is all right for me to kill deer, but the white men say they will arrest me. Whenever I see cattle or sheep, I know they don't belong to me; I wouldn't kill them. I feel like going out and killing deer, but I am afraid. I am getting too old. Maybe white people don't know about the beginning of this earth."

—Isabel Kelly (1938, 437–38)
Narrator: Dr. Sam Wata

John the Bear (Assiniboine)

Compare the French/Provencal folktale by this title; a good text in English is One Hundred Favorite Folktales *(Thompson 1968, 2–8). Such stories were probably introduced to Indian communities in the eighteenth and nineteenth centuries by French and French-Canadian explorers and voyageurs.*

A man was living with his wife. The woman was pregnant. One day, while she was picking berries, a big bear saw and abducted the woman, whom he kept in his cave. Before spring, the woman gave birth to a child begotten by her first husband, but with plenty of hair on his body, wherefore he was called *Icma'* (Plenty-of-Hair).

In the spring the bear came out of his cave. The boy looked outside and told his mother, "We had better run away to where you first came from."

But the bear had stopped up the entrance with a big rock, and the woman said, "We can't get out, the rock is too heavy." The boy tried it, and was able to lift it. They fled before the bear returned. They were already near the Indian camp when they heard the bear coming in pursuit. The woman was exhausted, but the boy packed her on his back and ran to the camp. At first the woman went to a stranger's lodge. Then someone told her husband that his wife was back. The chief then took both her and her son home.

The boy used to play with other boys. Once he quarreled with one of them and killed him with a single blow. This happened again on another occasion. Then *Icma'* said to his father, "I don't like to kill any more boys, I'll go traveling." He started out and met two men, who became his comrades. One of them was called Wood-Twister, the other Timber-Hauler. They got to a good lodge, and decided to stay there together.

On the first day, *Icma'* and Wood-Twister went hunting. They bade Timber-Hauler to stay home and cook. While they were away, an ogre that lived in the lodge came out, threw Timber-Hauler on his back, and killed him. The other two found him dead, but *Icma'* restored him to life. The next day *Icma'* said, "Wood-Twister, you stay home, I'll go hunting with Timber-Hauler." At sunset Wood-Twister began cutting firewood. He saw something coming out of the lodge that looked like a man, but wearing a beard down to its waist and with nails as long as bear-claws. It assaulted Wood-Twister, who was found dying by his friends, but was restored by *Icma'*.

The next day *Icma'* said, "You two go hunting, I will stay home." As he was beginning to chop wood, the monster appeared and challenged him to fight. *Icma'* seized its head, cut it off, and left the body in the lodge. When his comrades returned, *Icma'* asked them, "Why did not you kill him like this?" Then he said, "I don't like this house; let us go traveling."

They started out and got to a large camp. The chief said, "My three daughters have been stolen by an [underground] being. Whoever brings them back, may marry them all." *Icma'* told Timber-Hauler to get wood and ordered Wood-Twister to twist a rope of it. Then he made a hole in the ground and put in a box to lower himself in. He descended to the underground country and pulled the rope to inform his friends of his arrival.

He found the three girls. The first one was guarded by a mountain lion, the second by a big eagle, the third by giant cannibals. *Icma'* killed the lion. The girl said, "You had better turn back, the eagle will kill you." But he slew the eagle. Then the girl said, "The cannibals are bad men, you had better go home." "I'll wait for them." The twelve cannibals approached yelling; they were as big as trees. The girl said, "Run as fast as you can." But *Icma'* remained, and made two slings. With the first he hurled a stone that went clean through six of the men and killed them; and with the other sling he killed the remaining cannibals in the same way.

One of the girls gave him a handkerchief, another one a tie, and the youngest a ring. He took them to his box, and pulled the rope. His two companions hoisted up the oldest one. Both wanted to marry her, but *Icma'* pulled the rope again, and they hauled up the second girl. Then *Icma'* sat down in the box with the youngest, and pulled the rope. As they were hauling them up, Wood-Twister said, "Let us cut the rope." The other man refused, but Wood-Twister cut the rope, and *Icma'* fell down. He stayed there a long time, while his companions took the girls to the chief.

At last *Icma'* begged a large bird to carry him above ground. The bird said he did not have enough to eat for such a trip. Then *Icma'* killed five moose, and having packed the meat on the bird's back, mounted with the third girl. Flying up, *Icma'* fed the bird with moose-meat, and when his supply was exhausted, he cut off his own flesh and gave it to the bird to eat.

Icma' came up on the day when his false friends were going to marry the girls. All the people were gathered there. *Icma'* arrived. "I should like to go into the lodge before they are married." When he came in, Wood-Twister was frightened. "I should like to go out, I'll be back in a short time," he said. But he never returned. Then the chief asked, "Which of you three rescued the girls?" Then *Icma'* showed the handkerchief, the tie, and the ring given him by the girls, and got all the three girls for his wives.

—Robert Lowie (1910, 147 ff.)

A Version of the "Tar Baby" Story (Cherokee)

When such Indian versions of this widespread story were first recorded in the nineteenth century, some folklorists concluded African Americans had learned it from the Indians! But the roots of the Tar Baby in "Uncle Remus" and African American folklore generally lie in Africa. See, for example, "The Rubber Man," a Hausa tale from Nigeria, in Cole (1982, 627–30).

Once upon a time there was such a severe drought that all streams of water and all lakes were dried up. In this emergency the beasts assembled together to devise a means to procure water. It was proposed by one to dig a well. All agreed to do so, except the hare. She refused because it would soil her tiny paws. The rest, however, dug their well and were fortunate enough to find water.

The hare, beginning to suffer and thirst and having no right to the well, was thrown upon her wits to procure water. She determined as the easiest way, to steal from the public well. The rest of the animals, surprised to find that the hare was so well supplied with water, asked her where she got it. She replied that she arose early in the morning and gathered the dewdrops. However the wolf and the fox suspected her of theft and hit on the following plan to detect her:

They made a wolf of tar and placed it near the well. On the following night the hare came as usual after her supply of water. On seeing the tar wolf she demanded who was there. Receiving no answer, she repeated the demand, threatening to kick the wolf if he did not reply. Receiving no reply she kicked the wolf, and thus adhered to the tar and was caught.

When the fox and the wolf got hold of her they consulted what it was best to do with her. One proposed cutting her head off. This the hare protested would be useless, as it had often been tried without hurting her. Other methods were proposed for dispatching her, all of which she said would be useless. At last it was proposed to let her loose to perish in a thicket. Upon this the hare affected great uneasiness and pleaded hard for her life. Her enemies, however, refused to listen and she was accordingly let loose. As soon, however, as she was out of reach of her enemies she gave a whoop, and bounding away she exclaimed, "This is where I live!"

—James Mooney (1900, 272)

Francis La Flesche's "The Song of Flying Crow" (Omaha)

Francis La Flesche (1857–1932) grew up in the last years of traditional Omaha culture and participated in one of the tribe's final buffalo hunts. He then went on to become a clerk and translator in the Office of Indian Affairs in Washington in 1881. La Flesche's work with ethnologists James Dorsey and Alice Fletcher led to his collaboration with Fletcher on the classic ethnographic study of his own people The Omaha Tribe *(Fletcher and La Flesche 1911), and it is fair to say that he became the first professional Native American ethnographer, working for most of his career with the U.S. Bureau of American Ethnology. His two-volume study* The Osage Tribe *(1925) is another classic of its kind, marked by its sensitive interplay of scholarly rigor and sympathetic insights from his own Indian identity. That interplay must not have been easy for La Flesche to maintain in his own life, as his short stories (selected by Parins and Littlefield [1995]) and this autobiographical sketch vividly reveal. (La Flesche's memoir of his life in a reservation boarding school,* The Middle Five *(1900), is probably the best account of its kind.)*

At the risk of being accused of "going back to the tent," as many Indian students returned from eastern schools have been accused of "going back to the blanket," I had erected near my brother's cottage, when at home on my vacation last summer, a real Indian tent for my comfort and pleasure during my stay. The last days of my real tent life came to an end years ago when I with other Indians traveled one whole winter through western Kansas in search of buffalo. At that time my proud possessions were a saddle, a bridle, a lariat, and a gun. In singular contrast to these things, I had with me in my temporary "return to the tent" a number of books, magazines, a leather case, and a graphophone. The great herds that my people and I followed over the plains in the days of my youth have gone the same way that my forefathers have gone, never to return. The songs that expressed the emotions of my people, the songs of war, of peace, and of love that used to ring through the wooded hills of my birth were also passing away, and it was to catch as much as possible the dying echoes that I made my visit home armed with a speech and song catching instrument. The tent was a bit of sentiment, the indulgence of which the civilized people will forgive.

It was late in the afternoon when I took possession of my tent. A gentle rain drummed on the heavy canvas and my thoughts traveled back to the days which my life among the white people has since taught me to look upon as wild. The sound of approaching footsteps brought me back to the present and a familiar voice commenting on the weather warned me of a coming visitor. We exchanged the usual greetings and then began to talk of the various things in which we had a common interest. Then other friends came one by one until the tent was full of people all eager to learn and to teach. My well starched collar and cuffs and polished shoes made not the slightest difference in the intimate friendship that we had enjoyed before I left the reservation years ago to dwell in the city of the Nation's Capitol.

When we had all enjoyed the supper that my brother and I had provided and were feeling very good, we filled a huge pipe which we passed around and smoked. A fire was lighted so that we could see each other's faces, and being in a reminiscent mood we began to tell tales of our own adventures and those of other men in other days. Then when the stories of adventures and misadventures, of pathos and of humor began to flag and someone yawned, I said, "Uncle, start for us a song and we will sing, just as we used to do before I went away," addressing a little old man. "Yes," said a friend who sat near me, "let's sing some of the old songs that used to stir the warlike feelings of the men who lived and died long ago."

In a clear and musical voice the little old man gave the first bar of a song familiar to us all and we took it up and made the hills around echo with the sounds of song. Of the thousands of songs I knew a few, some five or six hundred, so I did my part of the singing and enjoyed the thrill of the rhythm. Many other songs were sung and the story of each repeated just as I had heard it years ago. The little old man complimented my memory for songs, then said, "Let us see if you know this one." He started it and all sang with a precision that denoted thorough knowledge of the song. I knew the class to which it belonged, from the vocables used and the terminating notes, but I could not follow, for the song was new to me. "It must be an old one just recalled by some old man."—"It is a new song," said the little old man, "made and given to us by your friend Flying Crow just before he died not very long ago."

"How did he come to make the song?" I asked. "He knew he was near death," replied the little old man, "and before he died he wanted to say to his friends some words that would not be forgotten the moment he spoke them, so he made the song to hold the words. He lay in his tent one day, all silent, but thinking of the many, many people who came into this life, endured its hardships, and enjoyed its pleasures for a little space of time then passed to the land of mystery, the land of spirits. Then he thought of the countless numbers that are to open their eyes to the light of the sun and pass on in the same way. He thought of the lives of the birds, the animals, and the little creatures that crawl and burrow in the earth, how their time, as well as that of men, was measured out long before they were brought to the earth. He had no fear of death but he thought of these things as being full of mystery. Struck with the realization that the duration of life at the longest was but brief, he desired his friends to strive to make each other happy so that they may enter the next world without fear and with a joyous spirit. Although the words in the song are few they at once bring to our minds all these thoughts—and the memory of our friend."

"Let's sing it again," I said. "I like it and I must learn it."

We sang it again and again and now it is so fixed in my memory that I shall never forget it even if I should live to be a hundred years old.

It was past the hour of midnight when my friends took leave of me to go to their homes among the hills. I could hear their voices in the still night until they gradually died away in the distance, then I took to thinking of the song I had just learned and its maker, Flying Crow. We were boys together and went to the same school that was maintained by the missionaries on our reservation for the education of Indian youth. I remember he used to run away quite often and finally he stayed away altogether. He inherited the beliefs of his fathers who for generations had been the keepers of the sacred rites of the tribe. He learned very little of the instructions given in the schoolroom and much less of those given in the chapel which meant nothing to his untutored mind. Born a pagan he died a pagan, with the song of a pagan upon his lips.

—Jarold Ramsey (1999, 241–43)

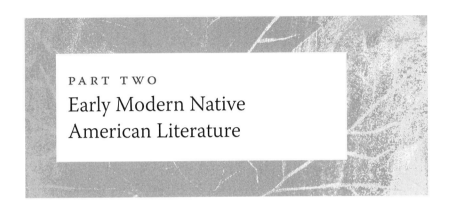

PART TWO

Early Modern Native American Literature

INTRODUCTION

Native American literature courses commonly feature the works of N. Scott Momaday, James Welch, Leslie Marmon Silko, Louise Erdrich, Linda Hogan, Sherman Alexie, and a host of other pivotal contemporary authors. Less commonly taught or referred to are the works of the generations of Native American writers who have preceded them, although increasingly writers like Zitkala-Ša, Pauline Johnson, D'Arcy McNickle, and others are being taught in the classroom and included in anthologies. Indeed, scholarly attention to these writers' works has followed in the wake of the recognition of N. Scott Momaday's Pulitzer Prize–winning novel *House Made of Dawn* and the works of other contemporary Native American authors who have followed him. This anthology has grown out of the desire to emphasize the continuities between oral traditional and late nineteenth- and early twentieth-century Native American writing and modern Native writing. It features the works of Native American writers who are less commonly known but whose works look ahead to and pave the way for contemporary Native writing. It is designed to be used alongside contemporary Native American novels and books of poetry in the classroom. This anthology owes a debt of gratitude to the research of A. Lavonne Ruoff, whose *American Indian Literatures* (1990) was one of the first bibliographic texts to explore the works of early Native American writers, and to Dexter Fisher, Karen Kilcup, and Judith Ranta, who have done pivotal work on early Native women writers.

In Louise Erdrich's *Tracks*, Nanapush, an elder who is about fifty years old in 1912, tells his adopted granddaughter Lulu that in his lifetime, he has seen more change than his people, the Anishinaabeg of North Dakota, have seen in "a hundred upon a hundred [years] before" (Erdrich 1988, 2). Most of the authors featured in this anthology lived through the most turbulent period in Native North American history. They saw the ever-encroaching presence of Anglo-European settlers in their territories; they watched as, in some cases, a third or a half of their tribal communities were lost to epidemics of smallpox and tuberculosis; they witnessed the decline of the buffalo culture of the Plains tribes and the ensuing starvation of the people; many were sent to identity-denying, military-style boarding schools during the years 1879–1934; and many experienced the negative effects of the 1887 Dawes or General Land Allotment Act. In the face of upheaval on a scale that is difficult to imagine, it is not surprising that the history of Native and Anglo-European relations is featured prominently in Native writing from this period and that social critique of Western ethnocentrism, the taking of Native lands, and the impact of the boarding schools and other federal policies on Native children and communities is a major impetus. For example, Zitkala-Ša's "School Days of an Indian Girl" critiques the boarding school experience for the role it plays in "bolstering national identity at the expense of the Native Americans" (Bernadin 1997, 220).

The biographies of the writers featured here are truly astounding both in terms of life experience and accomplishment. For example, D'Arcy McNickle (Cree-Salish) lived from 1904–1977. He published three novels in a forty-year span: *The Surrounded* (1936), *Runner in the Sun: A Story of Indian Maize* (1954), and *Wind from an Enemy Sky* (posthumously in 1978), as well as three historical books and one biography. McNickle spent his life trying to improve the quality of Native American life in the United States in his work for the Bureau of Indian Affairs and as the Director of American Indian Development, Inc. Pauline Johnson (Tehahionwake, Mohawk, 1861–1913) was a poet, short story writer, and stage performer in Canada, and as Bernd C. Peyer notes, during "the 1893–94 season alone, she gave a total of 125 recitals"; she also transcribed traditional Kutenai stories that were narrated to her by Joe Capilano (1989, 15–16).

Many of the writers in this period lived their lives in two worlds: a Native one and a white one. Writers like Francis La Flesche (Omaha, 1857–1932), Charles Eastman (Ohiyesa, Santee Sioux, 1858–1939), Luther Standing Bear (Ota k 'te, Sioux, 1868–1939), and Zitkala-Ša (Sioux, 1876–1938) were raised in their traditional Native communities, knowing their languages and oral storytelling traditions, but they were also part of the first generation of Native writers to be sent to Western boarding schools, to be taught Anglo-European values and literary traditions, and to write in English. They were highly educated in both communities and were even referred to oddly enough as the "Indian Intelligentsia." For example, John Oskison attended Willie Haskell College, Harvard, and Stanford, and he was a novelist and short story writer, an editor, and a correspondent in World War I.

Not surprisingly, then, the question of whether cross-cultural understanding and productive communication is possible is also raised in the works of early modern Native writers like La Flesche, Standing Bear, Zitkala-Ša, Pauline Johnson, John Oskison, and D'Arcy McNickle, and it is explored in a variety of diverse venues from the educational system to religion to marriage. D'Arcy McNickle, in particular, is adept at telling his stories, like his first novel *The Surrounded* (1936), from multiple perspectives; he often adopts sympathetically the perspective of the white outsider, who comes into a Native community with good intentions but brings about disaster for all concerned by ethnocentrically assuming that he or she knows what is best for Native peoples. In conjunction with this, the theme of the mixed-blood figure who is caught between two worlds is prominent in both early modern and contemporary Native American literature. We see it in Mourning Dove's *Cogewea: The Half-Blood*, in Lynn Riggs's *The Cherokee Night*, and in contemporary novels, like Leslie Silko's *Ceremony*, James Welch's *The Death of Jim Loney*, and Gerald Vizenor's *Earth Divers*.

We would also like to say something here about our reasons for including or excluding certain texts, but more importantly, we want to give our readers some sense of the history of the development of the field of Native American literature and of the ways in which these texts relate to one another.

The texts in this segment are arranged chronologically in order of their authors' birth dates. Included are those texts that are important to the development of the field but that also lend themselves well to classroom and literary use; to that end, some writers like Samson Occom (Mohegan, 1723–1792), the first Native American author to publish in English, have been left out. Occom's famous 1772 "Sermon Preached at the Execution of Moses Paul an Indian" is an indictment of the effects of alcohol on Native life, ironically written in the Puritanical tradition of Cotton Mather, but its diction and style render it less accessible for classroom use. For the same reason, we have not included William Apes (Pequot, born in 1798), the author of *Son of the Forest* (1829), a significant author whose works combine a protest style with an affirmation of Christian values and critique Western people's treatment of Native peoples and the effects of alcohol on Native communities; or George Copway (Ojibwa, 1818–1869), whose *The Life History, and Travels of Kah-ge-ga-gah-bowh* (1847) is more of a history and an ethnography. We did, however, include an excerpt from *Life Among the Piutes: Their Ways and Claims* (1883) by Sarah Winnemucca (Thoctmetony, 1844–1891) because although it is both ethnography and personal history, it does illustrate the continuities between the oral tradition and late nineteenth-century experiences and the ways in which Native sacred stories shape the course of her people's history with the whites.

We begin with the work of Betsey Guppy Chamberlain (Algonkian and English, 1797–1886), whose "The Indian Pledge" (published by Judith Ranta) provides a compelling and moralistic account of Native American generosity and hospitality. We also include some early Native American poetry by Jane Johnson Schoolcraft (Ojibwa, 1800–1841); Karen Kilcup's anthology of *Native American Women's Writing 1800–1924* features the works of other Native women poets of this time period and represents a significant contribution to the field. John Rollin Ridge (Chees-quat-a-law-ny or Yellow Bird; Cherokee 1827–1867) was one of the few Native American authors to write fiction and poetry during this time period, and he is credited with being the author of the first novel by a Native American, *The Life and Adventures of Joaquín Murieta, the Celebrated California Bandit*. We have included an excerpt from this novel, which presents the mixed-blood Murieta as a Byronic heroic outlaw whose exploits are retaliation for the greed of white miners. More importantly, we have included some of his never-before anthologized poetry, much of which deals with the beauty of nature in a Romantic vein.

Readers of the early modern works in this anthology may find their literary quality a bit uneven when compared with the often anthologized works of contemporary Native writers. When looking at the works from writers of this time, it is well to remember that criteria for good writing change over time. For example, sentimental writing was popular during the late nineteenth-century, but this is not necessarily the case today. Then too, early modern writers are writing out of a range of impetuses, including social criticism, education, and entertainment; this is true for much writing in general, but it is complicated for Native writers at this time because they are also often writing for the white audience who controlled the publishing industry, and they are sometimes writing out of their own ambivalence toward assimilation. For example, Pauline Johnson's "A Red Girl's Reasoning" (1893) is a passionate and emotional story, true to the Victorian emphasis on sentimentality, as well as an eloquent and powerful critique of European ethnocentrism and the assumption that Christian marriage rites are more valid than Native ones, an attitude that ties into Western culture's historical disregard for Native religious traditions and beliefs. However, at the same time, the language of the story is somewhat stereotypical, perhaps because Johnson was inculcated with these stereotypical views about her people, or perhaps because she knows how her Western readers tend to view Native peoples and is giving them what they expect to hear so that she can critique the larger issue of religious ethnocentrism. So one of the problematic issues with early modern Native American writing is that it sometimes adopts more stereotypical approaches for a variety of possible reasons. For example, Simon Pokagon's (Potawatomi, 1839–1899) *Queen of the Woods* (1899) is one of the few Native American novels written during this period, but there is some controversy over whether Pokagon wrote it (James A. Clifton [1987, 12–17] argues that he did not), and the novel is somewhat stereotypical in its romanticized and nostalgic portrait of Native life; because of this, we choose not to include an excerpt from it. For this same reason, we elected not to include an excerpt from Sylvester Long Clark's (Chief Buffalo Child, Lumbee, 1890–1932) *Long Lance.* Yet we did include an excerpt from Mourning Dove's (Hum-ishu-ma, Colville, 1888–1936) *Cogewea: The Half-Blood*, considered by some to be the first Native American novel written by a woman (others would argue that Laguna Pueblo author Leslie Marmon Silko's *Ceremony* is the first, or Ella Deloria's *Waterlily*, written in the 1940s and published in 1988) because the chapter we excerpted is one that is believed to have been written principally by Mourning Dove and because it deals, albeit rather stereotypically in its language, with the theme of the mixed-blood figure, which is again reflected in Lynn Riggs's play *The Cherokee Night* (1931) and Silko's *Ceremony* (1977).

Humor is also an important feature of Native American oral traditions and writing, both early modern and contemporary. For example, Francis La Flesche's tongue-in-cheek commentary on the naming of Native children with Western names at the boarding school is illustrated with biting humor in "William T. Sherman" from *The Middle Five*. Alexander Posey (Creek, 1873–1908) adopts a dialogic humor through the commentary of Hotgun and other speakers in *The Fus Fixico Letters*. Will Rogers (Cherokee, 1879–1935) was also a well-known political humorist in this period, although we have not used any of his selections here.

Significantly, this anthology of early modern Native American writing ends with two stories by D'Arcy McNickle, whose novels and short fiction truly illustrate the continuities between oral traditional and more contemporary writing. From a literary standpoint, McNickle is one of the best writers in this time period. His first novel *The Surrounded* (1936) is not only a brilliant critique of the impact of Anglo-European settlement of Salish lands in Montana, told from a myriad of different and sympathetic perspectives; it also employs traditional Salish stories as frames for the central themes of the novel. McNickle's writing combines Native oral storytelling techniques and motifs with the multiple-narrative style prominent in the works of Modernist writers like William Faulkner; in this way, his writing also marries different literary traditions. His writing paves the way for the works of contemporary Native writers who followed him and emulated his careful attention to cultural and historical detail. In the wake of attention to Native American writing that followed Momaday's winning of the Pulitzer Prize for *House Made of Dawn* in 1969, D'Arcy McNickle was one of the first writers from the previous generation to be "rediscovered" and written about by critics James Ruppert, John Purdy, and others. Readers of McNickle's works will also be quick to see that contemporary writers like James Welch, Leslie Silko, and Louise Erdrich are inheritors of his legacy.

In James Welch's *Fools Crow*, Feather Woman tells Fools Crow that much will be lost to the Blackfeet, "'But they will know the way it was. The stories will be handed down, they will see that their people were proud and lived in accordance with the Below Ones, the Underwater People—and the Above Ones'" (1986, 360). This affirmation of the importance of stories and the continuation of the oral tradition is also echoed in the works of Leslie Silko and other contemporary Native authors. In view of this affirmation, the works of the early modern Native writers in this anthology are part of the continuum of the oral tradition, as it has changed and adapted, even into the written form, and their stories are important to the ongoing history and development of the field of Native American literature.

Betsey Guppy Chamberlain

*Pen names B.C., Tabitha,
Jemima; Algonkian,
probably Abenaki, 1797–1886*

*Although Betsey Guppy Chamberlain's writings were
popular in her time, it has not been until more recent years that her work
has been rediscovered and publicized in Benita Eisler's 1977 anthology*
The Lowell Offering: Writings by New England Mill Women, 1840–1845
and Judith A. Ranta's 2003 The Life and Writings of Betsey Chamberlain.
*Ranta pieces together what is known about Chamberlain's heritage, life,
and writings and argues that her work is significant for being the earliest
known Native women's writing and for its protest against prejudice and
the injustices perpetrated against Native peoples: "At a time when Native
and mixed-race people were scorned, she found the courage to claim her
heritage proudly and write in defense of Native people" (xii). Chamberlain
is also considered to be an early feminist, New England regionalist, and
humorist writer (3).*

*A writer of mixed Algonkian and English heritage, Betsey Guppy was
born in New Hampshire in 1797. In 1821, she married Josiah Chamberlain;
after his early death in 1823, she moved with their two children to Lowell,
Massachusetts, in 1831 to work in the textile mills (Ranta 2003, xi–xii).
Chamberlain married a total of four times and lived in Illinois for at least
forty years (55), but she is best known for her time and writing in Lowell. In
Lowell, Chamberlain wrote for* The Lowell Offering *(1840–1845) and* The
New England Offering *(1847–1850), two of the first magazines to be published*

entirely by women (xii). All told, Chamberlain published thirty-seven known writings in these journals (xiii). Chamberlain wrote under four pen names: "B.C.," "Betsey," "Tabitha," and "Jemima" (xii). "The Indian Pledge" was first published in The Lowell Offering *in June of 1842, and it draws on Native oral storytelling traditions with its circular structure (91).*

The Indian Pledge

On the door-steps of a cottage in the land of "steady habits," some ninety or an hundred years since, might, on a soft evening in June, have been seen a sturdy young farmer, preparing his scythes for the coming hay-making season. So intent was he upon his work, that he heeded not the approach of a tall Indian, accoutred for a hunting expedition, until "Will you give an unfortunate hunter some supper and lodging for the night?" in a tone of supplication, caught his ear.

The farmer raised his eyes from his work, and darting fury from beneath a pair of shaggy eye-brows, he exclaimed, "Heathen, Indian dog, begone! you shall have nothing here."

"But I am very hungry," said the Indian; "give only a crust of bread and a bone, to strengthen me on my journey."

"Get you gone, you heathen dog!" said the farmer; "I have nothing for you."

"Give me but a cup of cold water," said the Indian, "for I am very faint."

This appeal was not more successful than the others. Reiterated abuse, and to be told to drink when he came to a river, was all he could obtain from one who bore the name of Christian! But the supplicating appeal fell not unheeded on the ear of one of finer mould and more sensibility. The farmer's youthful bride heard the whole, as she sat hushing her infant to rest; and from the open casement she watched the poor Indian, until she saw his dusky form sink, apparently exhausted, on the ground, at no great distance from her dwelling. Ascertaining that her husband was too busied with his work to notice her, she was soon at the Indian's side, with a pitcher of milk, and a napkin filled with bread and cheese. "Will my red brother slake his thirst with some milk?" said this angel of mercy; and as he essayed to comply with her invitation, she untied the napkin, and bade him eat and be refreshed.

"Cantantowwit protect the white dove from the pounces of the eagle," said the Indian; "for *her* sake the unfledged young shall be safe in their nest, and her red brother will not seek to be revenged."

He then drew a bunch of feathers from his bosom, and plucking one of the longest, gave it to her, and said, "When the white dove's mate flies over the Indians' hunting-grounds, bid him wear this on his head."

ᴥ

The summer had passed away. Harvest-time had come and gone, and preparations had been made for a hunting excursion by the neighbors. Our young farmer was to be one of the party; but on the eve of their departure he had strange misgivings relative to his safety. No doubt his imagination was haunted by the form of the Indian, whom, in the preceding summer, he had treated so harshly.

The morning that witnessed the departure of the hunters, was one of surpassing beauty. Not a cloud was to be seen, save one that gathered on the brow of Ichabod, (our young farmer,) as he attempted to tear a feather from his hunting-cap, which was sewed fast to it. His wife arrested his hand, while she whispered in his ear, and a slight quiver agitated his lips as he said, "Well, Mary, if you think this feather will protect me from the arrows of the red-skins, I'll e'en let it remain." Ichabod donned his cap, shouldered his rifle, and the hunters were soon on their way in quest of game.

The day wore away as was usual with people on a like excursion; and at night-fall they took shelter in the den of a bear, whose flesh served for supper, and whose skin spread on bruin's bed of leaves, pillowed their heads through a long November night.

With the first dawn of morning, the hunters left their rude shelter and resumed their chase. Ichabod, by some mishap, soon separated from his companions, and in trying to join them, got bewildered. He wandered all day in the forest, and just as the sun was receding from sight, and he was about sinking down in despair, he espied an Indian hut. With mingled emotions of hope and fear, he bent his steps towards it; and meeting an Indian at the door, he asked him to direct him to the nearest white settlement.

"If the weary hunter will rest till morning, the eagle will show him the way to the nest of his white dove," said the Indian, as he took Ichabod by the hand and led him within his hut. The Indian gave him a supper of parched corn and venison, and spread the skins of animals which he had taken in hunting, for his bed.

The light had hardly begun to streak the east, when the Indian awoke Ichabod, and after a slight repast, the twain started for the settlement of the whites. Late in the afternoon, as they emerged from a thick wood, Ichabod with joy espied his home. A heartfelt ejaculation had scarce escaped his lips, when the Indian stepped before him, and turning around, stared him full in the face, and inquired if he had any recollection of a previous acquaintance with his red brother. Upon being answered in the negative, the Indian said, "Five moons ago when I was faint and weary, you called me an Indian dog, and drove me from your door. I might now be revenged; but Cantantowwit bids me tell you to go home; and hereafter, when you see a red man in need of kindness, do to him as you have been done by. Farewell."

The Indian having said this, turned upon his heel, and was soon out of sight. Ichabod was abashed. He went home purified in heart, having learned a lesson of Christianity from an untutored savage.

Tabitha

—From Judith A. Ranta (2003, 126–28)

Jane Johnson Schoolcraft

Bame-wa-wa-ge-zhik-a-quay,
Woman of the Stars Rushing
Through the Sky; Ojibwa, 1800–1841

Jane Johnson Schoolcraft was born in Sault
St. Marie, Michigan, of mixed Ojibwa and Scotch-Irish heritage. Her
maternal grandfather was the renowned Ojibwa chief, Waub Ojeeg
(White Fisher); growing up, she was educated in Ojibwa language and
traditions and in Western literary conventions (in particular, her work
draws on Romantic traditions). Jane Johnson married ethnographer and
explorer Henry Rowe Schoolcraft, who obtained much of his knowledge
about Ojibwa culture from his wife's family. Henry published The Literary
Voyager or Muzzeniegun, *and Jane wrote traditional Native stories for*
the journal under her Ojibwa name and the pseudonyms of "Leelinau"
and "Rosa"; as a result, she began to be called the "northern Pocahontas"
(Kilcup 2000, 57). Jane's purposes for writing these stories were two-fold:
"to preserve them for future generations and to build bridges of under-
standing between Indian and white cultures" (57). Schoolcraft was not a
prolific writer, but her work was widely known for its contributions to both
Native and Western literary traditions.

"Otagamiad" depicts Schoolcraft's grandfather, Waub Ojeeg, urging
his people to go to war to prevent their enemies from enslaving them, and
"Invocation To My Maternal Grandfather On Hearing His Descent From
Chippewa Ancestors Misrepresented" is a rebuttal to false rumors that
Waub Ojeeg was a child taken from the Sioux, traditional tribal enemies
of the Ojibwa (see also Kilcup 2000, 57–58).

RESIGNATION (1826)

How hard to teach the heart, opprest with grief,
Amid gay, worldly scenes, to find relief;
And the long cherish'd bliss we had in view,
To banish from the mind where first it grew!
But Faith, in time, can sweetly soothe the soul,
And Resignation hold a mild control;
The mind may then resume a proper tone,
And calmly think on hopes forever flown.

Rosa.

—From Henry Rowe Schoolcraft (1962, 26–27)

BY AN OJIBWAY FEMALE PEN
TO SISTERS ON A WALK IN
THE GARDEN, AFTER A SHOWER (1826)

Come, sisters, come! The shower's past,
The garden walks are drying fast,
The Sun's bright beams are seen again,
And nought within, can now detain.
The rain drops tremble on the leaves,
Or drip expiring, from the eaves:
But soon the cool and balmy air,
Shall dry the gems that sparkle there,
With whisp'ring breath shake ev'ry spray,
And scatter every cloud away.

Thus sisters! shall the breeze of hope,
Through sorrows clouds a vista ope;
Thus, shall affliction's surly blast,
By faith's bright calm be still'd at last;
Thus, pain and care,—the tear and sigh,
Be chased from every dewy eye;
And life's mix'd scene itself, but cease,
To show us realms of light and peace.

Rosa.

—From Henry Rowe Schoolcraft (1962, 8)

LINES WRITTEN UNDER
SEVERE PAIN AND SICKNESS (1827)

Ah! why should I at fortune's lot repine,
Or fret myself against the will divine?
All men must go to death's deform'd embrace,
When here below they've run their destin'd race;
Oh! then on Thee, my Savior, I will trust,
For thou art good, as merciful and just,—
In Thee, with my whole heart I will confide,
And hope with Thee, forever to abide.
To Thee, my God, my heart & soul I raise,
And still thy holy, holy name I'll praise!
O! deign to give me wisdom, virtue, grace,
That I thy heavenly will may ever trace;
Teach me each duty always to fulfil,
And grant me resignation to Thy will,
And when Thy goodness wills that I should die,
This dream of life I'll leave without a sigh.

Rosa.

—From Henry Rowe Schoolcraft (1962, 97)

OTAGAMIAD (1827)[1]

In northern climes there liv'd a chief of fame,
LaPointé his dwelling, and Ojeeg his name,
Who oft in war had rais'd the battle cry,
And brav'd the rigors of an Arctic sky;
Nor less in peace those daring talents shone,
That rais'd him to his simple forest throne,
Alike endow'd with skill, such heaven's reward,
To weild [sic] the oaken sceptre, and to guard.
Now round his tent, the willing chieftain's wait,
The gathering council, and the stern debate—
Hunters, & warriors circle round the green,
Age sits sedate, & youth fills up the scene,
While careful hands, with flint & steel prepare,
The sacred fire—the type of public care.

"Warriors and friends"—the chief of chiefs oppress'd,
With rising cares, his burning thoughts express'd.
"Long have our lands been hem'd around by foes,
Whose secret ire, no check or limit knows,
Whose public faith, so often pledg'd in vain,
'Twere base for freemen e'er to trust again.
Watch'd in their cracks our trusting hunters fall,
By ambush'd arrow, or avenging ball;
Our subtil foes lie hid in every pass,
Screen'd in the thicket, shelter'd in the grass,
They pierce our forests, & they cross our lines,
No treaty binds them, & no stream confines
And every spring that clothes the leafy plain,
We mourn our brethren, or our children slain.
Delay but swells our woes, as rivers wild,
Heap on their banks the earth they first despoil'd.
Oh chieftains! listen to my warning voice,
War—war or slavery is our only choice.
No longer sit, with head & arms declin'd,
The charms of ease still ling'ring in the mind;
No longer hope, that justice will be given
If ye neglect the proper means of heaven:
Fear—and fear only, makes our foemen just
Or shun the path of conquest, rage or lust,
Nor think the lands we own, our sons shall share,
If we forget the noble rites of war.
Choose then with wisdom, nor by more delay,
Put off the great—the all important day.
Upon yourselves alone, your fate depends,
'Tis warlike acts that make a nation friends
'Tis warlike acts that prop a falling throne,
And makes peace, glory, empire, all our own.
Oh friends! Think deeply on my counsel—words
I sound no peaceful cry of summer birds!
No whispering dream of bliss without allay
Or idle strain of mute, inglorious joy
Let my bold voice arouse your slumb'ring hearts,

And answer warriors—with uplifted darts,
Thick crowding arrows, bristled o'er the plain,
And joyous warriors rais'd the battle strain."

All but Camudẃa,[2] join'd the shouting throng,
Camudẃa, fam'd for eloquence of tongue
Whose breast resolv'd the coming strife with pain,
And peace still hop'd, by peaceful arts to gain.
"Friends"—he reply'd—"our ruler's words are just,
Fear breeds respect and bridles rage or lust,
But in our haste, by rude and sudden hate,
To prop our own, or crush our neighbors state
Valor itself, should not disdain the skill
By pliant speech, to gain our purpos'd will.
The foe may yet, be reason'd into right.
And if we fail in speech—we still may fight.
At least, one further effort, be our care,
I will myself, the daring message bear,
I give my body, to the mission free,
And if I fall, my country, 'tis for thee!
The wife and child, shall lisp my song of fame,
And all who value peace, repeat my name!"

"'Tis well"—Baimwáwa[3] placidly replied,
"To cast our eyes, with care to either side,
Lest in our pride, to bring a rival low,
Our own fair fields shall fall beneath the foe.
Great is the stake, nor should we lightly yield,
Our ancient league by many a battle seal'd.
The deeds of other days before my eyes,
In all their friendship, love and faith arise,
When hand in hand with him we rov'd the wood,
Swept the long vale, or stem'd the boiling flood.
In the same war path, march'd with ready blade,
And liv'd, and fought, and triumph'd with his aid.
When the same tongue, express'd our joys and pains,
And the same blood ran freely thro' our veins?"

"Not we—not we"—in rage Keewaydin[4] spoke,
"Strong ties have sever'd, or old friendships broke,
Back on themselves the baseless charge must fall,
They sunder'd name, league, language, rites and all.
They, with our firm allies, the Gallic race,
First broke the league, by secret arts and base,
Then play'd the warrior—call'd our bands a clog,
And earn'd their proper title, Fox and Dog.
Next to the false Dacota gave the land,
And leagued in war, our own destruction plan'd.
Do any doubt the words I now advance,
Here is my breast"—he yelled & shook his lance.

"Rage"—interposed the sage Canowakeed,[5]
"Ne'er prompted wit, or bid the council speed
For other aims, be here our highest end,
Such gentle aims as rivet friend to friend.
If harsher fires, in ardent bosoms glow,
At least restrain them, till we meet the foe,
Calm judgment here, demands the care of all,
For if we judge amiss, ourselves shall fall.
Beside, what boasts it, that ye here repeat,
The current tale of ancient scaith or heat,
Love, loss, or bicker, welcome or retort,
Once giv'n in earnest, or return'd sport
Or how, or when, this hapless feud arose,
That made our firmest friends, our firmest foes.
That so it is, by causes new or old,
There are no strangers present, to be told,
Each for himself, both knows & feels & sees,
The growing evils of a heartless peace,
And the sole question, of this high debate,
Is—shall we longer suffer—longer wait,
Or, with heroic will, for strife prepare,
And try the hazard of a gen'ral war!"
                    —From Henry Rowe Schoolcraft (1962, 138–42)

Notes for "Otagamiad"

1. This poem was written by Mrs. Henry Schoolcraft about her grandfather Waub Ojeeg. The original poem, which differs slightly from this one, is published in *The Literary Voyager* and is in the Schoolcraft papers in the Library of Congress.

2. A passing sound [Henry Rowe Schoolcraft's note].

3. The passing thunder [H. R. Schoolcraft's note].

4. The North Wind [H. R. Schoolcraft's note].

5. He Who Takes After the Wind [H. R. Schoolcraft's note].

INVOCATION TO MY MATERNAL GRANDFATHER ON HEARING HIS DESCENT FROM CHIPPEWA ANCESTORS MISREPRESENTED (1827)

Rise bravest chief! of the mark of the noble deer,
   With eagle glance,
   Resume thy lance,
And wield again thy warlike spear!
   The foes of thy line,
   With coward design,
Have dar'd, with black envy, to garble the truth,
And stain, with a falsehood, thy valorous youth.

They say, when a child, thou wert ta'en from the Sioux,
   And with impotent aim,
   To lessen thy fame
Thy warlike lineage basely abuse,
   For they know that our band,
   Tread a far distant land,
And thou noble chieftain! art nerveless and dead,
Thy bow all unstrung, and thy proud spirit fled.

Can the sports of thy youth, or thy deeds ever fade?
   Or those ever forget,
   Who are mortal men yet,
The scenes where so bravely thou'st lifted the blade,
   Who have fought by thy side,
   And remember thy pride,
When rushing to battle, with valor and ire,
Thou saw'st the fell foes of thy nation expire.

Can the warrior forget how sublimely you rose?

Like a star in the west,

When the sun's sunk to rest,

That shines in bright splendor to dazzle our foes;

Thy arm and thy yell,

Once the tale could repel

Which slander invented, and minions detail,

And still shall thy actions refute the false tale.

Rest thou, noblest chief! in thy dark house of clay,

Thy deeds and thy name,

Thy child's child shall proclaim,

And make the dark forests resound with the lay;

Though thy spirit has fled,

To the hills of the dead,

Yet thy name shall be held in my heart's warmest care,

And cherish'd, till valor and love be no more.

Rosa.

—From Henry Rowe Schoolcraft (1962, 142–43)

John Rollin Ridge

Chees-quat-a-law-ny,
Yellow Bird; Cherokee, 1827–1867

John Rollin Ridge is credited with writing the first
novel by a Native American, The Life and Adventures of Joaquín Murieta
(1854). *Murieta, Ridge's Byronic outlaw hero, dedicates his life to getting*
revenge on the avaricious white miners who have driven him off his land
and killed his brother. This story loosely parallels Ridge's own tribal and
family history. Ridge was the half-Cherokee grandson of Major Ridge, who
was a leader of the Cherokee Nation prior to the Indian Removal Act and
Trail of Tears in the 1830s. The Supreme Court ruled that the Cherokees
had the rights to their ancestral homelands east of the Mississippi River,
but then President Andrew Jackson defied the Supreme Court order and
forced the Cherokees and other Native groups, like the Choctaws and
Chickasaws, to leave their ancestral homelands and march west over the
Trail of Tears into Indian Territory (Oklahoma). Ridge was twelve years
old at the time, and his grandfather and father were later killed for their
role in facilitating the sale of Cherokee lands. As a young man, Ridge him-
self shot a man, probably in self-defense, and then fled to the gold mines of
California, where he wrote for several journals, like Hesperian *and* Gold
Era *(Ruoff 1990, 64–65).*

Ridge was one of the few Native writers of his time to write poetry
as well as fiction. His poetry, most of which was written before the age
of twenty, is written in the Romantic tradition of writers like Shelley,
Wordsworth, and Keats—for example, his "Mount Shasta" owes much to
Shelley's "Mt. Blanc." Some of the poetry selections included here from
Ridge's 1868 book Poems *have never before been anthologized.*

MOUNT SHASTA

Behold the dread Mt. Shasta, where it stands
Imperial midst the lesser heights, and, like
Some mighty unimpassioned mind, companionless
And cold. The storms of Heaven may beat in wrath
Against it, but it stands in unpolluted
Grandeur still; and from the rolling mists upheaves
Its tower of pride e'en purer than before.
The wintry showers and white-winged tempests leave
Their frozen tributes on its brow, and it
Doth make of them an everlasting crown.
Thus doth it, day by day and age by age,
Defy each stroke of time: still rising highest
Into Heaven!

Aspiring to the eagle's cloudless height,
No human foot has stained its snowy side;
No human breath has dimmed the icy mirror which
It holds unto the moon and stars and sov'reign sun.
We may not grow familiar with the secrets
Of its hoary top, whereon the Genius
Of that mountain builds his glorious throne!
Far lifted in the boundless blue, he doth
Encircle, with his gaze supreme, the broad
Dominions of the West, which lie beneath
His feet, in pictures of sublime repose
No artist ever drew. He sees the tall
Gigantic hills arise in silentness
And peace, and in the long review of distance
Range themselves in order grand. He sees the
            sunlight
Play upon the golden streams which through the
            valleys
Glide. He hears the music of the great and solemn
            sea,
And overlooks the huge old western wall
To view the birth-place of undying Melody!

Itself all light, save when some loftiest cloud
Doth for a while embrace its cold forbidding
Form, that monarch mountain casts its mighty
Shadow down upon the crownless peaks below,
That, like inferior minds to some great
Spirit, stand in strong contrasted littleness !
All through the long and Summery months of our
Most tranquil year, it points its icy shaft
On high, to catch the dazzling beams that fall
In showers of splendor round that crystal cone,
And roll in floods of far magnificence
Away from that lone, vast Reflector in
The dome of Heaven.
Still watchful of the fertile
Vale and undulating plains below, the grass
Grows greener in its shade, and sweeter bloom
The flowers. Strong purifier! From its snowy
Side the breezes cool are wafted to the "peaceful
Homes of men," who shelter at its feet, and love
To gaze upon its honored form, aye standing
There the guarantee of health and happiness.
Well might it win communities so blest
To loftier feelings and to nobler thoughts
The great material symbol of eternal
Things! And well I ween, in after years, how
In the middle of his furrowed track the plowman
In some sultry hour will pause, and wiping
From his brow the dusty sweat, with reverence
Gaze upon that hoary peak. The herdsman
Oft will rein his charger in the plain, and drink
Into his inmost soul the calm sublimity;
And little children, playing on the green, shall
Cease their sport, and, turning to that mountain
Old, shall of their mother ask: "Who made it?"
And she shall answer,—"GOD!"

And well this Golden State shall thrive, if like
Its own Mt. Shasta, Sovereign Law shall lift
Itself in purer atmosphere—so high
That human feeling, human passion at its base
Shall lie subdued; e'en pity's tears shall on
Its summit freeze; to warm it e'en the sunlight
Of deep sympathy shall fail:
Its pure administration shall be like
The snow immaculate upon that mountain's brow!
           —John Rollin Ridge (1868, 2, 14–16)

HUMBOLDT RIVER[1]

The River of Death, as it rolls
With a sound like the wailing of souls!
And guarding their dust, may be seen
The ghosts of the dead by the green
Billowy heaps on the shore—
Dim shapes, as they crouch by the graves,
And wail with the rush of waves
On seeking the desert before!
Guarding their dust for the morn
Which shall see us, new born
Arise from the womb of the earth—
That through rain or through dearth,
Through calm or through storm,
Through its seasons and times, no part may be lost,
By the ruthless winds tost,
Of the mortal which shall be immortal of form.

No leaf that may bud
By that dark sullen flood;
No flower that may bloom
With its tomb-like perfume,
In that region infectious of gloom;
No subtleized breath
That may ripple that River of Death,

Or, vapory, float in the desolate air,
But is watched with a vigilant, miserly care,
Lest it steal from the dust of the dead that are there;
For the elements aye are in league,
With a patience unknowing fatigue,
To scatter mortality's mould,
And sweep from the graves what they hold!

I would not, I ween, be the wight
To roam by that river at night,
When the souls are abroad in the glooms;
Enough that the day-time is weird
With the mystical sights that are feared
Mid the silence of moonlighted tombs;
Weird shores with their alkaline white—
That loom in the glare of the light;
Weird bones as they bleach in the sun,
Where the beast from his labors is done;
Weird frost-work of poisonous dews
On shrub and on herb, which effuse
The death they have drank to the core;
Weird columns upborne from the floor
Of the white-crested deserts which boil
With the whirlwind's hot, blasting turmoil!
As ghost-like he glides on his way.
Each ghastly, worn pilgrim looks gray
With the dust the envenomed winds flail;
And the beast he bestrides is as pale
As the steed of the vision of John,
With him, the Destroyer, thereon.

Death river, foul river, 'tis well
That into the jaws of thy hell—
The open-mouthed desert[2] should fall
Thy waves that so haunt and appal.
'Tis fit that thou seek the profound
Of all hiding Night underground;

Like the river which nine times around
The realm of grim Erebus wound,
To roll in that region of dread—
A Stygian stream of the dead!
       —John Rollin Ridge (1868, 23–26)

      Notes for "Humbolt River"
  1. For three hundred miles its banks are one continuous burying ground.
    Emigrants to California died on its shores by thousands [Ridge's note].

  2. Sink of the Humboldt [Ridge's note].

TO A STAR SEEN AT TWILIGHT

Hail solitary star!
That shinest from thy far blue height,
And overlookest Earth
And Heaven, companionless in light!
The rays around thy brow
Are an eternal wreath for thee;
Yet thou'rt not proud, like man,
Though thy broad mirror is the sea,
And thy calm home eternity!

Shine on, night-bosomed star!
And through its realms thy soul's eye dart,
And count each age of light,
For their eternal wheel thou art.

Thou dost roll into the past days,
Years, and ages too,
And naught thy giant progress stays.

I love to gaze upon
Thy speaking face, thy calm, fair brow,
And feel my spirit dark
And deep, grow bright and pure as thou.
Like thee it stands alone;
Like thee its native home is night,
But there the likeness ends,—
It beams not with thy steady light.
Its upward path is high,
But not so high as thine—thou'rt far
Above the reach of clouds,
Of storms, of wreck, oh lofty star!
I would all men might look
Upon thy pure sublimity,
And in their bosoms drink
Thy lovliness and light like me;
For who in all the world
Could gaze upon thee thus, and feel
Aught in his nature base,
Or mean, or low, around him steal!

Shine on companionless
As now thou seem'st. Thou art the throne
Of thy own spirit, star!
And mighty things must be alone.
Alone the ocean heaves,
Or calms his bosom into sleep;
Alone each mountain stands
Upon its basis broad and deep;
Alone through heaven the comets sweep,
Those burning worlds which God has thrown
Upon the universe in wrath,
As if he hated them—their path
No stars, no suns may follow, *none*—
'T is great, 't is great to be alone!
                    —John Rollin Ridge (1868, 27–29)

DEDICATION FOR AN ALBUM

These leaves to friendship consecrate
      And pure affection's holy trust,
You ask me now to dedicate
      In form that's due—and so I must.

I would some worthier hand than mine
      The task essayed; for I profane,
With words that shame the sacred Nine,
      The page that else had known no stain.

Yet e'en the rudest terms of speech
      Are hallowed by the truth they breathe;
And so these lines that nothing teach,
      May dare this shrine of love enwreath.

Blest be each spotless page herein,
      Whereon the hand of love shall write,
And worthy of the place they win
      The names that here shall meet the sight.

So that, fair owner of this book,
      When you these leaves shall wander through
In after years, and pause to look
      On name and date no longer new,

A buried past will seem to be
      Within the pages that you turn;
And sweet but mournful memory
      Will linger o'er each hallowed urn.
            —John Rollin Ridge (1868, 45–46)

A NIGHT SCENE

Unbroken silence! save the melody
      That steals on silence unawares, and makes
      It seem scarce more than silence still; that takes
Possession of the senses bodily,
      And claims the slumbering spirit ere it wakes.

Save this low melody of waves, no sound
      Is heard among the circling hills. I sit
      And muse alone—the time and place are fit—
And summon spirits from the blue profound,
      That answer me and through my vision flit.

What beauteous being stands upon yon hill,
      With hair night-hued, and brow and bosom white?
      Around her floats the evening's loving light—
Her feet are lost amid the shadows soft and still,
      But 'gainst the sky her form is pictured to my sight.

How still! how motionless! yet full of life,
      As is of music-tones the sleeping string,
      As is of grace the blue-bird's resting wing!
She pauses there—each limb with beauty rife—
      As if through boundless space her foot might
          spring.

But hark! what tones are filling all the air,
      That drinks them, with the star-light blended now,
      And wavelet-murmurings from below?
Her voice! her harp! swept by the white hand rare
      That moon-like guides the music's tide-like flow.

Strange one! no harp! no voice I've heard like thine,
      No startling beauty like thine own have seen,
      The rounded world and vaulted heaven between.
To gaze on thee 't is madness all divine,
      But o'er the gulf my spirit loves to lean.

Thou art what I may ne'er embrace on earth,
   Thou sweetly moulded one, thou heavenly-eyed!
   But if when we do lay these forms aside,
For us new forms among the stars have birth,
   In some sweet world we'll meet, my spirit bride!

Fair worlds, like ripples o'er the watery deep
   When breezes softly o'er the surface play,
   In circles one by one ye stretch away,
Till, lost to human vision's wildest sweep
   Our souls are left to darkness and dismay.
      —John Rollin Ridge (1868, 62–63)

   "THE 'SINGING SPIRIT'"[1]

Within the forest's depths I wandered once
   And sweetest warbling music heard—
Methought it were the water-sprite at first,
   And then some lonely singing bird!
And still the music in its softness rose
   And fell upon my heart like light,
Which from its dreary realm dispelled
   Pale Sadness, with her robe of night.

The shadows left my sobered, pensive brow,
   My soul uprising freshen'd seemed,
And every thing I gazed upon as now,
   Took hues of which so oft I've dreamed!
I glanced from stem to stem and bough to bough,
   To catch the little warbler's form,
To see what shape embodied thus,
   And made suspense so fine a charm!

I gazed, but could not see. The music thrilled
   Along my being's inmost strings,
Till melody had all my bosom filled,
   And overrun its secret springs.
The tear stood trembling in my eye, and hushed

To feeling's pause was every breath—
The tones became so low, that I
    Half deemed them warning me of death.

And yet there was no dread—I thought, how meet
    'Neath such a dirge to sink and die!
While viewless o'er was heard that harp, how sweet
    To close the dim and fading eye!
Then rose the lifted voice to sudden power,
    And yet not harsh, but rich and deep
As is the feeling of the soul
    When mighty thoughts our natures sweep.

Ah me, 't were vain with language to describe
    The wild sensations of my breast;
Till I some angel's brightest pen can bribe,
    That spirit-thrill must be supprest!
Still floated round those ever changing notes,
    Now with a burst, and now with a moan,
And once I thought in Northern Land
    I'd heard and treasured such a tone!

The music died at last, as sweetest things
    Must die!—and homeward I returned.
But often in my lonely wanderings
    Once more to hear that voice I yearned;
Then grieving that I heard it not, I named
    It in the soul it had enthralled.
And ever after to myself
    The "Singing Spirit" it was called.
        —John Rollin Ridge (1868, 100–102)

Note for "The 'Singing Spirit'"
1. A poem addressed to Miss A. A. B. [Ridge's note].

From *The Life and Adventures of Joaquín Murieta* (1854)

Joaquín with his party, fully bent on the most extensive mischief, entered Calaveras County about the middle of December. This county was then, as it is now, one of the richest in the State of California. Its mountains were veined with gold—the beds of its clear and far-rushing streams concealed the yellow grains in abundance—and the large quartz-leads, like the golden tree of the Hesperides, spread their fruitful branches abroad through the hills. Its fertile valleys bloomed with voluptuous flowers over which you might walk as on a carpet woven of rainbows—or waved with the green and mellow harvests, whose ready music charmed the ear. The busy wheels of the sawmills with their glittering teeth rived the mighty pines, which stood like green and spiral towers, one above another, from base to summit of the majestic peaks. Long tunnels, dimly lighted with swinging lamps or flickering candles, searched far into the bowels of the earth for her hidden secrets. Those which were abandoned served as dens for the cougar and wolf, or, more frequently, the dens of thieves.

Over this attractive field for his enterprizes, Joaquín scattered his party in different directions. He entrusted Reis with the command of twenty men, Luis Vulvia with that of twenty-five, retaining about fifteen for his own use among whom was the terrible Three-Fingered Jack and the no less valuable Valenzuela, and employed the remainder as spies and bearers of news from one point of action to another. Reis went up to the head waters of the Stanislaus River between whose forks the rich valleys, covered with horses, afforded a fine theater for his operations. On all the mountain-fed branches and springs of these forks, the picks and shovels of a thousand miners were busy, and the industrious Chinese had pitched their little, cloth villages in a hundred spots, and each day hurried to and fro like innumerable ants, picking up the small but precious grains. Luis Vulvia—as daring a man as Claudio and as cunning—proceeded to the head waters of the Mokelumne River; and detached portions of these two bands, at intervals, ranged the intermediate space. Joaquín himself had no particular sphere but chose his ground according to circumstances. Keeping Three-Fingered Jack with him most of the time, he yet, once in a while, gave him the charge of a small party with liberty to do as he pleased—a favor which the bloody monster made good use of; so much so that scarcely a man whom he ever met, rich or poor, escaped with his life. The horse which this hideous fellow rode might have rivaled *Bucephalus* in breadth of chest, high spirit, and strength of limb, united with swiftness. No one but a powerful man could have rode him; but Three-Fingered Jack, with a fine Mexican saddle (the best saddles in the world) fastened securely with a broad girth made of horse hair as strong as a band of iron, and curbing him with a huge Spanish bit—with which he might have rent his jaw—managed the royal animal with ease. To see this man, with his large and rugged frame in which the strength of a dozen common men slumbered—his face and forehead scarred with bullets and grooved with the wrinkles of grim thoughts, and his intensely lighted eyes glaring maliciously, like caverned demons, under his shaggy brows—to see such a man mounted upon a raven-black horse whose nostrils drew the air like a gust of wind into his broad chest, whose wrathful hoof pawed the ground as if the spirit of his rider inspired him, and whose wild orbs rolled from side to side in untameable fire—would aptly remind one of old Satan himself, mounted upon a hell-born beast, after he had been "let loose for a thousand years."

Among the many thrilling instances of the daring and recklessness of spirit which belonged to Joaquín, there is one which I do not feel at liberty to omit—especially as it comes naturally and properly in this connection. Shortly after he parted from Reis and Luis Vulvia, he went up into the extreme north of the county. There, at the head of a branch of the South Fork of the Mokelumne River, in a wild and desolate region near the boundary line of Calaveras and El Dorado Counties, were located a company of miners, consisting of twenty-five men. They were at a long distance from any neighbors, having gone there well armed on a prospecting tour which resulted in their finding diggings so rich that they were persuaded to pitch their tents and remain. One morning while they were eating their breakfast on a flat rock—a natural table which stood in front of their tents—armed as usual with their revolvers, a young fellow with very dark hair and eyes rode up and saluted them. He spoke very good English and they could scarcely make out whether he was a Mexican or an American. They requested him to get down and eat with them, but he politely declined. He sat with one leg crossed over his horse's neck very much at his ease, conversing very freely on various subjects, until Jim Boyce, one of the partners who had been to the spring after water, appeared in sight. At the first glance on him, the young horseman flung his reclining leg back over the saddle and spurred his horse. Boyce roared out:

"Boys, that fellow is *Joaquín*; d—n it, shoot him!" At the same instant, he himself fired but without effect.

Joaquín dashed down to the creek below with headlong speed and crossed with the intention, no doubt, to escape over the hills which ran parallel with the stream, but his way was blocked up by perpendicular rocks, and his only practicable path was a narrow digger-trail which led along the side of a huge mountain, directly over a ledge of rocks a hundred yards in length, which hung beatling over the rushing stream beneath in a direct line with the hill upon which the miners had pitched their tents, and not more than forty yards distant. It was a fearful gauntlet for any man to run. Not only was there danger of falling a hundred feet from the rocks, but he must run in a parallel line with his enemies, and in pistol-range, for a hundred yards. In fair view of him stood the whole company with their revolvers drawn. He dashed along that fearful trail as if he had been mounted upon a spirit-steed, shouting as he passed:

"I am Joaquín! kill me if you can!"

Shot after shot came clanging around his head, and bullet after bullet flattened on the wall of slate at his right. In the midst of the first firing, his hat was knocked from his head, and left his long black hair streaming behind him. He had no time to use his own pistol, but, knowing that his only chance lay in the swiftness of his sure-footed animal, he drew his keenly polished bowie-knife in proud defiance of the danger and waved it in scorn as he rode on. It was perfectly sublime to see such super-human daring and recklessness. At each report, which came fast and thick, he kissed the flashing blade and waved it at his foes. He passed the ordeal, as awful and harrowing to a man's nerves as can be conceived, untouched by a ball and otherwise unharmed. In a few moments, a loud whoop rang out in the woods a quarter of a mile distant, and the bold rider was safe!

Joaquín, knowing well the determined character of Jim Boyce, and, deeming it more than probable that he had heard of the different large rewards offered for his capture or death amounting in the aggre-gate to $15,000 or $20,000, he made up his mind speedily that an attack would be made upon him by the whole party of miners if he remained at his encampment, which was some five miles distant from their tents. Concluding that they could not collect their horses together and prepare their arms and ammunition in a proper manner for an attack or pur-suit before night, he conceived a plan, the most brilliant and ingenious that ever entered an outlaw's brain, by which to defeat their purposes and carry out his own original intention of robbing them. Knowing that a trail could very well be made in the night but that it could only be followed in the day-time, he ordered his men, numbering fifteen, to saddle up and make ready for a ride. They obeyed with alacrity and without question, and in a few moments were on their horses and ready to move forward. The chief led the way in silence, proceeding over the pin[e?] ridges in an easterly direction. He rode on vigorously until night over very rough ground, having traversed a distance of twenty miles; but, wishing to place a still greater distance between him and the encampment which he had left, he did not come to final halt until a late hour. Building a huge fire and hitching their animals near by, the wearied bandits hastily threw their blankets down and stretched their limbs upon them for repose. Sentinels alternately sat up until day-light, so that at the first touch of dawn the whole band arose and again started, having lost only four hours in sleep. They journeyed on in the same course as briskly as possible until noon, when, having reached a nice little valley, covered with grass and wild clover, and watered by a beautiful spring which bubbled up from the roots of a clump of evergreen oaks, distant about twenty miles from their last encampment, they stopped for two hours to let their horses graze and to refresh their own rather empty stomachs with the sardines and crackers which they generally carried with them. Here they left strong indications that they had spent the night but established the contrary fact by riding on for the remainder of the day, whose close found them at another distance of twenty miles. Building fires as before and eating a hasty supper, they again mounted, and, having made a circle of five miles in their course, suddenly turned to the westward and encamped about three o'clock, A.M., at a spot distant another common day's journey from the last starting point. Thus traveling and resting, after the lapse of a few days they found themselves in the original trail upon which they had started.

Jim Boyce and company had struck the path of the robbers on the next morning after their departure and had camped each night at the fires which they had left, expecting, as was natural, that they would come to a final stopping-place when they had proceeded as far as they liked. Joaquín smiled with exquisite satisfaction when he perceived that Boyce was certainly ahead of him and, from every indication, unsuspecting in the remotest degree that his arch-enemy was at that moment in his rear.

At night, after a long day's ride over rugged mountains and deep gulches, Jim Boyce and his company, numbering twenty-five men including himself, were seated around one of Joaquín's late fires, which they had rekindled, quietly enjoying their pipes and laughing over the numerous stereotyped jokes, which had descended, like Shak[e]speare, from one gentleman to another, and are too good ever to be worn out. The Heavens were cloudy, and a boundary of solid darkness lay around the lighted ring in which they sat. In the ragged clouds a few stars dimly struggled, and the lonesome scream of the cougar, like the wail of a lost spirit benighted in the infinity of darkness, gave a wild terror to the surrounding woods.

Suddenly and startlingly, the simultaneous reports of fifteen pistols rent the air, the dark outer-wall of the fire-circle blazed, as if a cloud had unbosomed its lightnings, and the astonished survivors of the company bounded up to see fifteen of their number stretched upon the earth and to meet with the deadly repetition of the fifteen revolvers. Panic-stricken and bewildered, the survivors of the second discharge, numbering three men among whom was Jim Boyce, fled head-long into the darkness, and, taking no time to choose their ground, hurried madly and distractedly away from the horrible scene. Joaquín stepped quietly into the circle to see if Jim Boyce was killed, but Three-Fingered Jack leaped in like a demon with his huge knife in his mutilated hand, which had lost none of its strength, but did its three-fingered work far better than many other whole hands could do it, and soon quenched the last spark of beating life in the pale forms around him. Every one must know that death from a bullet flings a sudden and extreme paleness over the countenance, and thus the light from the fire, falling upon the ghastly faces around, displayed a sight so hideous and harrowing that Joaquín exclaimed with a shudder:

"Let's leave here, we will camp tonight, somewhere else."

Searching the bundles upon which the company had been seated, he found in different buckskin purses a sum amounting to not less than thirty thousand dollars. He also added fifteen excellent horses and ten powerful mules to his live-stock.

Jim Boyce and his surviving companions wandered to the distant settlements, which, after many hardships, they reached in safety, and it is pleasant to add that in a short time they raised another company with whom they went back to their rich diggings, and, in spite of their immense loss by Joaquín's robbery, made for themselves ample fortunes, with which they returned to the States. Should Jim Boyce chance to read this humble narrative of mine, I beg him to receive my warmest congratulations.

On one of the head-branches of the Mokelumne River, on the last day of December, a large crowd was gathered in and around a cloth-building in a little mining town, which looked like a half-venture towards civilization in the midst of that wild and savage region. A tall, dark-skinned man sat in the middle of the room, with a huge log-chain around one of his legs. His brow was tall and massive, and his large, gray eyes looked forth with that calm, cold light which unmistakably expresses a deep, calculating intellect, divested of all feeling and independent of all motives which arise from mere impulse or passion—an intellect which is sole in itself, looking at the result merely in all its actions, not considering the question of right or wrong, and working out a scheme of unmitigated villainy as it would a mathematical problem. To the right of this man sat a huge, old fellow with blue eyes, sandy hair, and a severe look, whose scattered law-books and papers on the table near by proclaimed him the justice of the Peace in that district—an office, by the way, as important at that time in California and possessing a jurisdiction as extensive as many of the county courts in other and older States of the Union.

The prisoner was none other than Luis Vulvia, who had been arrested upon a charge of murder and robbery in that town on the day before, under the following circumstances:

A German, living by himself in an isolated tent, was heard to scream "murder!" three times; hearing which horrible cry, five or six men some two hundred yards off ran up to the place and at a glance comprehended the whole scene. The German lay with his throat cut from ear to ear and his pockets turned inside out. Looking hastily around on the outside, they discovered two men, apparently Mexicans, who dodged on the further side of a deserted cabin and disappeared behind some rocks. Going to the rocks and finding no further trace of the fugitives, they went back and alarmed the whole town with a statement of the circumstances. Every eye was vigilant in every quarter, and, just as Luis Vulvia, who had observed the fast increasing excitement, and guessed pretty nearly the character of its cause, was mounting his horse in front of a liquor-shop, he was suddenly knocked down with a bludgeon, disarmed, and securely bound. The people *en masse* securely guarded him during the night which was just at hand, intending to hang him without a trial on the morrow, but were dissuaded by Justice Brown, the tall, severe-looking man above spoken of, who, being a man of influence and a good speaker withal, convinced them that it was better to proceed with him legally, as there was but little doubt of his being found guilty as one of the murderers, in which case he would deliver him over to their just vengeance. Thus the case stood up to the moment in which the subject is introduced.

The witnesses, who ran at the cry of murder to the tent and saw the two Mexicans dodging around the house, could swear no further than that one of them was of about the same size and shape as the prisoner. The barkeeper of the liquor-shop testified, in addition to this, that the prisoner rode up to his door and dismounted just a few moments before his arrest. It was well known, also, that a dozen or more robberies had lately been committed in that neighborhood and that various persons had met upon the roads a gang of suspicious-looking Mexicans armed to the teeth. This constituted all the testimony against Vulvia, whose person was unknown to the community, but whose name was familiar to all by reputation. Had he been recognized as that noted character, no further inquiry would have been made, but he would have been hurried to the first convenient tree and hung *instanter.* He stood on a dangerous brink. Being asked by the justice if he had any proof to offer in his own behalf, he replied that he depended upon some of his acquaintances coming in during the day, who would establish his character as an honest man to the satisfaction of the court. He affirmed his innocence in a calm tone and an unflinching manner, although, could his heart have been read, he relied little upon the possibility of a rescue by his comrades, which was indeed a feeble hope, looking at the immense crowd who stood scowling upon him from every side. A silence of one-half hour rested in the court while the justice was engaged in drawing up a transcript of the case as far as it had proceeded, when a young man superbly dressed and adorned with a splendid gold chain and watch, entered the room with gentlemanly dignity and politely addressed the Justice, to the following effect:

"My name, your Honor, is Samuel Harrington. I am a merchant and packer in the town of San José, and I am just now on my return from the more northern mines, to which I have been packing flour and other provisions. I am encamped within five miles of this place, and having heard from a citizen of your town this morning that a dark-skinned man, with gray eyes, was in custody on a charge of murder and that, although there was no positive proof against him, yet there was so strong a prejudice against Mexicans that there was great danger of his being hung by the infuriated populace, it just struck me that the prisoner might be one of my hired men, a Mexican, whom I sent into town last night, and who, much to my astonishment, did not return. I find that it is indeed the case. Your prisoner is none other than my packer and, consequently, cannot be connected with any robbing or thieving band around here. He has been with me four years, and no man ever sustained a better character. I shall wish, your Honor, to testify in his behalf, but before I take my oath, I would like to prove my identity as Mr. Harrington of San José. Please examine these letters."

He here presented to the Justice, who was already favorably impressed, five or six letters addressed in different hands to "Mr. Samuel Harrington, San José," and bearing the marks of various post offices in the State. The justice showed these letters to several of the crowd, whose countenances immediately relaxed towards the prisoner.

"Mr. Harrington," said Squire Brown, "your evidence will be taken without a moment's scruple."

Harrington accordingly testified to the facts which he had already related, and the prisoner was discharged. Many apologies were made to Mr. H. for detaining his hired man so long, and after many compliments, he and Vulvia departed. As soon as they were clearly out of town, the both indulged in a hearty laugh.

"How came it," said Vulvia to Joaquín, "that you arrived in such good time? I had no expectation but to be hung."

"I happened to reach your camp out here in the mountains last night, having met some of our spies who guided me to it. I had not been there more than two hours before two of your men came in, and reported that they had killed a man in *that little cloth-town*, and inquired for you. Your being absent immediately created apprehension, and having waited for you anxiously till morning, we were at once convinced that you had been captured. Having most fortunately in my possession a package of letters addressed to Samuel Harrington, San José, which I had the good sense, thank God! to preserve at the time I got them into my hands, it immediately flashed on me that in case I found you arrested, I could pass myself off for a respectable merchant and so save your life. It worked to a charm as you see. I make it a practice to preserve documents of this kind, and I find that they come in pretty good play."

"But how did you come by them!" inquired Vulvia.

"Oh, easy enough. I killed a fellow on my way down here the other day and found them in his pockets—and d—d little besides, too!"

"You remind me," said Vulvia, "very much of Padre Jurata, God rest his soul! He saved many of his followers by being present at their trials, or introducing witnesses to prove an *alibi*, or presenting forged pardons on the day of execution, signed in the exact hands of the provincial governors. His knowledge was extensive, and, during his monkish life, the confessional had given him so many important and vital secrets connected with great personages that he could frequently command the services of the wealthiest men and the best-born dames of Mexico. Besides this, he sometimes officiated as one of the Fathers in the remote towns and villages."

Thus conversing, they rode on to Vulvia's camp, some ten miles in the mountains, and were met by a welcome shout from their subordinates. [. . .]

—John Rollin Ridge (1854, 82–96)

Sarah Winnemucca

Thocmetony, Shell Flower;
Paiute, 1844–1891

Sarah Winnemucca's Life Among the Piutes: Their Ways and Claims *(1883) is probably the first autobiography by an American Indian woman. She wrote it in Boston in preparation for an extensive Eastern lecture tour to publicize the plight of her people, the Northern Paiutes of northern Nevada, who had suffered greatly at the hands of whites entering Paiute territory since Sarah's infancy. Her grandfather Truckee, her father, Winnemucca, and her brother, Natchez, were Paiute headmen in succession; hence, she was an eyewitness to crucial episodes in the Paiutes' struggles with miners, ranchers, the U.S. Army, and Indian agents, and her narrative is a vivid and fascinating blend of autobiography, ethnography, and interracial history.*

Life Among the Piutes *begins with a haunting instance of a Native people's mythology's shaping the course of their history with whites. Sarah recalls that when her grandfather Truckee heard rumors that white-skinned people were approaching, he urged his people to welcome them unconditionally as their long-lost brothers according to the Paiute creation myth, in which the First People, some red and some white, were separated because of misconduct but with the hope that eventually they would be reunited. By the time Truckee and his followers came to terms with the bitter invalidity of this mythic interpretation of events, it was already too late to preserve the Paiutes' claim on their homeland. (See "Retroactive Prophecy in Western Indian Narratives," in Ramsey 1999, esp. 199–200.)*

From *Life Among The Piutes:*
Their Ways and Claims (1883)

CHAPTER 1: FIRST MEETING OF PIUTES AND WHITES

I was born somewhere near 1844, but am not sure of the precise time. I was a very small child when the first white people came into our country. They came like a lion, yes, like a roaring lion, and have continued so ever since, and I have never forgotten their first coming. My people were scattered at that time over nearly all the territory now known as Nevada. My grandfather was chief of the entire Piute nation, and was camped near Humboldt Lake, with a small portion of his tribe, when a party travelling eastward from California was seen coming. When the news was brought to my grandfather, he asked what they looked like? When told that they had hair on their faces, and were white, he jumped up and clasped his hands together, and cried aloud,—

"My white brothers,—my long-looked for white brothers have come at last!"

He immediately gathered some of his leading men, and went to the place where the party had gone into camp. Arriving near them, he was commanded to halt in a manner that was readily understood without an interpreter.

Grandpa at once made signs of friendship by throwing down his robe and throwing up his arms to show them he had no weapons; but in vain,—they kept him at a distance. He knew not what to do. He had expected so much pleasure in welcoming his white brothers to the best in the land, that after looking at them sorrowfully for a little while, he came away quite unhappy. But he would not give them up so easily. He took some of his most trustworthy men and followed them day after day, camping near them at night, and travelling in sight of them by day, hoping in this way to gain their confidence. But he was disappointed, poor dear old soul!

I can imagine his feelings, for I have drank [*sic*] deeply from the same cup. When I think of my past life, and the bitter trials I have endured, I can scarcely believe I live, and yet I do; and, with the help of Him who notes the sparrow's fall, I mean to fight for my down-trodden race while life lasts.

Seeing they would not trust him, my grandfather left them, saying,

"Perhaps they will come again next year." Then he summoned his whole people, and told them this tradition:—

"In the beginning of the world there were only four, two girls and two boys. Our forefather and mother were only two, and we are their children. You all know that a great while ago there was a happy family in this world. One girl and one boy were dark and the others were white. For a time they got along together without quarrelling, but soon they disagreed, and there was trouble. They were cross to one another and fought, and our parents were very much grieved. They prayed that their children might learn better, but it did not do any good; and afterwards the whole household was made so unhappy that the father and mother saw that they must separate their children; and then our father took the dark boy and girl, and the white boy and girl, and asked them, 'Why are you so cruel to each other?' They hung down their heads, and would not speak. They were ashamed. He said to them, 'Have I not been kind to you all, and given you everything your hearts wished for? You do not have to hunt and kill your own game to live upon. You see, my dear children, I have power to call whatsoever kind of game we want to eat; and I also have the power to separate my dear children, if they are not good to each other.' So he separated his children by a word. He said, 'Depart from each other, you cruel children;—go across the mighty ocean and do not seek each other's lives.'

"So the light girl and boy disappeared by that one word, and their parents saw them no more, and they were grieved, although they knew their children were happy. And by-and-by the dark children grew into a large nation; and we believe it is the one we belong to, and that the nation that sprung from the white children will some time send some one to meet us and heal all the old trouble. Now, the white people we saw a few days ago must certainly be our white brothers, and I want to welcome them. I want to love them as I love all of you. But they would not let me; they were afraid. But they will come again, and I want you one and all to promise that, should I not live to welcome them myself, you will not hurt a hair on their heads, but welcome them as I tried to do."

How good of him to try and heal the wound, and how vain were his efforts! My people had never seen a white man, and yet they existed, and were a strong race. The people promised as he wished, and they all went back to their work.

The next year came a great emigration, and camped near Humboldt Lake. The name of the man in charge of the trains was Captain Johnson, and they stayed three days to rest their horses, as they had a long journey before them without water. During their stay my grandfather and some of his people called upon them, and they all shook hands, and when our white brothers were going away they gave my grandfather a white tin plate. Oh, what a time they had over that beautiful gift,—it was so bright! They say that after they left, my grandfather called for all his people to come together, and he then showed them the beautiful gift which he had received, from his white brothers. Everybody was so pleased; nothing like it was ever seen in our country before. My grandfather thought so much of it that he bored holes in it and fastened it on his head and wore it as his hat. He held it in as much admiration as my white sisters hold their diamond rings or a sealskin jacket. So that winter they talked of nothing but their white brothers. The following spring there came great news down the Humboldt River, saying that there were some more of the white brothers coming, and there was something among them that was burning all in a blaze. My grandfather asked them what it was like. They told him it looked like a man; it had legs and hands and a head, but the head had quit burning, and it was left quite black. There was the greatest excitement among my people everywhere about the men in a blazing fire. They were excited because they did not know there were any people in the world but the two,—that is, the Indians and the whites; they thought that was all of us in the beginning of the world, and, of course, we did not know where the others had come from, and we don't know yet. Ha! ha! oh, what a laughable thing that was! It was two negroes wearing red shirts!

The third year more emigrants came, and that summer Captain Fremont, who is now General Fremont.

My grandfather met him, and they were soon friends. They met just where the railroad crosses Truckee River, now called Wadsworth, Nevada. Captain Fremont gave my grandfather the name of Captain Truckee, and he also called the river after him. Truckee is an Indian word, it means *all right*, or *very well*. A party of twelve of my people went to California with Captain Fremont. I do not know how long they were gone. . . .

When my grandfather went to California, he helped Captain Fremont fight the Mexicans. When he came back he told the people what a beautiful country California was. Only eleven returned home, one having died on the way back.

They spoke to their people in the English language, which was very strange to them all.

Captain Truckee, my grandfather, was very proud of it, indeed. They all brought guns with them. My grandfather would sit down with us for hours, and would say over and over again, "Goodee gun, goodee, goodee gun, heap shoot." They also brought some of the soldiers' clothes with all their brass buttons, and my people were very much astonished to see the clothes, and all that time they were peaceable toward their white brothers. They had learned to love them, and they hoped more of them would come. Then my people were less barbarous than they are nowadays.

That same fall, after my grandfather came home, he told my father to take charge of his people and hold the tribe, as he was going back to California with as many of his people as he could get to go with him. So my father took his place as Chief of the Piutes, and had it as long as he lived. Then my grandfather started back to California again with about thirty families. That same fall, very late, the emigrants kept coming. It was this time that our white brothers first came amongst us. They could not get over the mountains, so they had to live with us. It was on Carson River, where the great Carson City stands now. You call my people blood-seeking. My people did not seek to kill them, nor did they steal their horses,—no, no, far from it. During the winter my people helped them. They gave them such as they had to eat. They did not hold out their hands and say:—

"You can't have anything to eat unless you pay me." No,—no such word was used by us savages at that time; and the persons I am speaking of are living yet; they could speak for us if they choose to do so.

The following spring, before my grandfather returned home, there was a great excitement among my people on account of fearful news coming from different tribes, that the people whom they called their white brothers were killing everybody that came in their way, and all the Indian tribes had gone into the mountains to save their lives. So my father told all his people to go into the mountains and hunt and lay up food for the coming winter. Then we all went into the mountains. There was a fearful story they told us children. Our mothers told us that the whites were killing everybody and eating them. So we were all afraid of them. Every dust that we could see blowing in the valleys we would say it was the white people. In the late fall my father told his people to go to the rivers and fish, and we all went to Humboldt River, and the women went to work gathering wild seed, which they grind between the rocks. The stones are round, big enough to hold in the hands. The women did this when they got back, and when they had gathered all they could they put it in one place and covered it with grass, and then over the grass mud. After it is covered it looks like an Indian wigwam.

Oh, what a fright we all got one morning to hear some white people were coming. Every one ran as best they could. My poor mother was left with my little sister and me. Oh, I never can forget it. My poor mother was carrying my little sister on her back, and trying to make me run; but I was so frightened I could not move my feet, and while my poor mother was trying to get me along my aunt overtook us, and she said to my mother: "Let us bury our girls, or we shall all be killed and eaten up." So they went to work and buried us, and told us if we heard any noise not to cry out, for if we did they would surely kill us and eat us. So our mothers buried me and my cousin, planted sage bushes over our faces to keep the sun from burning them, and there we were left all day.

Oh, can any one imagine my feelings *buried alive*, thinking every minute that I was to be unburied and eaten up by the people that my grandfather loved so much? With my heart throbbing, and not daring to breathe, we lay there all day. It seemed that the night would never come. Thanks be to God! the night came at last. Oh, how I cried and said: "Oh, father, have you forgotten me? Are you never coming for me?" I cried so I thought my very heartstrings would break.

At last we heard some whispering. We did not dare to whisper to each other, so we lay still. I could hear their footsteps coming nearer and nearer. I thought my heart was coming right out of my mouth. Then I heard my mother say, "'T is right here!" Oh, can any one in this world ever imagine what were my feelings when I was dug up by my poor mother and father? My cousin and I were once more happy in our mothers' and fathers' care, and we were taken to where all the rest were.

I was once buried alive; but my second burial shall be for ever, where no father or mother will come and dig me up. It shall not be with throbbing heart that I shall listen for coming footsteps. I shall be in the sweet rest of peace,—I, the chieftain's weary daughter.

Well, while we were in the mountains hiding, the people that my grandfather called our white brothers came along to where our winter supplies were. They set everything we had left on fire. It was a fearful sight. It was all we had for the winter, and it was all burnt during that night. My father took some of his men during the night to try and save some of it, but they could not; it had burnt down before they got there.

These were the last white men that came along that fall. My people talked fearfully that winter about those they called our white brothers. My people said they had something like awful thunder and lightning, and with that they killed everything that came in their way.

This whole band of white people perished in the mountains, for it was too late to cross them. We could have saved them, only my people were afraid of them. We never knew who they were, or where they came from. So, poor things, they must have suffered fearfully, for they all starved there. The snow was too deep.

Early in the following spring, my father told all his people to go to the mountains, for there would be a great emigration that summer. He told them he had had a wonderful dream, and wanted to tell them all about it.

He said, "Within ten days come together at the sink of Carson, and I will tell you my dream."

The sub-chiefs went everywhere to tell their people what my father had told them to say; and when the time came we all went to the sink of Carson.

Just about noon, while we were on the way, a great many of our men came to meet us, all on their horses. Oh, what a beautiful song they sang for my father as they came near us! We passed them, and they followed us, and as we came near to the encampment, every man, woman, and child were out looking for us. They had a place all ready for us. Oh, how happy everybody was! One could hear laughter everywhere, and songs were sung by happy women and children.

My father stood up and told his people to be merry and happy for five days. It is a rule among our people always to have five days to settle anything. My father told them to dance at night, and that the men should hunt rabbits and fish, and some were to have games of football, or any kind of sport or playthings they wished, and the women could do the same, as they had nothing else to do. My people were so happy during the five days,—the women ran races, and the men ran races on foot and on horses.

My father got up very early one morning, and told his people the time had come,—that we could no longer be happy as of old, as the white people we called our brothers had brought a great trouble and sorrow among us already. He went on and said,—

"These white people must be a great nation, as they have houses that move. It is wonderful to see them move along. I fear we will suffer greatly by their coming to our country; they come for no good to us, although my father said they were our brothers, but they do not seem to think we are like them. What do you all think about it ? Maybe I am wrong. My dear children, there is something telling me that I am not wrong, because I am sure they have minds like us, and think as we do; and I know that they were doing wrong when they set fire to our winter supplies. They surely knew it was our food."

And this was the first wrong done to us by our white brothers.

Now comes the end of our merrymaking.

Then my father told his people his fearful dream, as he called it. He said,—

"I dreamt this same thing three nights,—the very same. I saw the greatest emigration that has yet been through our country. I looked North and South and East and West, and saw nothing but dust, and I heard a great weeping. I saw women crying, and I also saw my men shot down by the white people. They were killing my people with something that made a great noise like thunder and lightning, and I saw the blood streaming from the mouths of my men that lay all around me. I saw it as if it was real. Oh, my dear children! You may all think it is only a dream,— nevertheless, I feel that it will come to pass. And to avoid bloodshed, we must all go to the mountains during the summer, or till my father comes back from California. He will then tell us what to do. Let us keep away from the emigrant roads and stay in the mountains all summer. There are to be a great many pine-nuts this summer, and we can lay up great supplies for the coming winter, and if the emigrants don't come too early, we can take a run down and fish for a month, and lay up dried fish. I know we can dry a great many in a month, and young men can go into the val- leys on hunting excursions, and kill as many rabbits as they can. In that way we can live in the mountains all summer and all winter too."

So ended my father's dream. During that day one could see old women getting together talking over what they had heard my father say. They said,—

"It is true what our great chief has said, for it was shown to him by a higher power. It is not a dream. Oh, it surely will come to pass. We shall no longer be a happy people, as we now are; we shall no longer go here and there as of old; we shall no longer build our big fires as a signal to our friends, for we shall always be afraid of being seen by those bad people."

"Surely they don't eat people?"

"Yes, they do eat people, because they ate each other up in the mountains last winter."

This was the talk among the old women during the day.

"Oh, how grieved we are! Oh, where will it end?"

That evening one of our doctors called for a council, and all the men
gathered together in the council-tent to hear what their medicine man
had to say, for we all believe our doctor is greater than any human being
living. We do not call him a medicine man because he gives medicine
to the sick, as your doctors do. Our medicine man cures the sick by the
laying on of hands, and we have doctresses as well as doctors. We believe
that our doctors can communicate with holy spirits from heaven. We call
heaven the Spirit Land.

Well, when all the men get together, of course there must be smoking the first thing. After the pipe has passed round five times to the right,
it stops, and then he tells them to sing five songs. He is the leader in the
song-singing. He sings heavenly songs, and he says he is singing with the
angels. It is hard to describe these songs. They are all different, and he
says the angels sing them to him.

Our doctors never sing war-songs, except at a war-dance, as they
never go themselves on the war-path. While they were singing the last
song, he said,—

"Now I am going into a trance. While I am in the trance you must
smoke just as you did before; not a word must be spoken while I am in
the trance."

About fifteen minutes after the smoking was over, he began to make a
noise as if he was crying a great way off. The noise came nearer and nearer,
until he breathed, and after he came to, he kept on crying. And then he
prophesied, and told the people that my father's dream was true in one
sense of the word,—that is, "Our people will not all die at the hands of our
white brothers. They will kill a great many with their guns, but they will
bring among us a fearful disease that will cause us to die by hundreds."

We all wept, for we believed this word came from heaven.

So ended our feast, and every family went to its own home in the
pine-nut mountains, and remained there till the pine-nuts were ripe.
They ripen about the last of June.

Late in that fall, there came news that my grandfather was on his way
home. Then my father took a great many of his men and went to meet his
father, and there came back a runner, saying, that all our people must

come together. It was said that my grandfather was bringing bad news. All our people came to receive their chieftain; all the old and young men and their wives went to meet him. One evening there came a man, saying that all the women who had little children should go to a high mountain. They wanted them to go because they brought white men's guns, and they made such a fearful noise, it might even kill some of the little children. My grandfather had lost one of his men while he was away.

So all the women that had little children went. My mother was among the rest; and every time the guns were heard by us, the children would scream. I thought, for one that my heart would surely break. So some of the women went down from the mountain and told them not to shoot any more, or their children would die with fright. When our mothers brought us down to our homes the nearer we came to the camp, the more I cried,—

"Oh, mother, mother, don't take us there!" I fought my mother,—I bit her. Then my father came, and took me in his arms and carried me to the camp. I put my head in his bosom, and would not look up for a long time. I heard my grandfather say,—

"So the young lady is ashamed because her sweetheart has come to see her. Come, dearest, that won't do after I have had such a hard time to come to see my sweetheart, that she should be ashamed to look at me."

Then he called my two brothers to him, and said to them, "Are you glad to see me?" And my brothers both told him that they were glad to see him. Then my grandfather said to them,—

"See that young lady; she does not love her sweetheart any more, does she? Well, I shall not live if she does not come and tell me she loves me. I shall take that gun, and I shall kill myself."

That made me worse than ever, and I screamed and cried so hard that my mother had to take me away. So they kept weeping for the little one three or four days. I did not make up with my grandfather for a long time. He sat day after day, and night after night, telling his people about his white brothers. He told them that the whites were really their brothers, that they were very kind to everybody, especially to children; that they were always ready to give something to children. He told them what beautiful things their white brothers had,—what beautiful clothes they wore, and about the big houses that go on the mighty ocean, and travel faster than any horse in the world. His people asked him how big they were. "Well, as big as that hill you see there, and as high as the mountain over us."

"Oh, that is not possible,—it would sink, surely."

"It is every word truth, and that is nothing to what I am going to tell you. Our white brothers are a mighty nation, and have more wonderful things than that. They have a gun that can shoot a ball bigger than my head, that can go as far off as that mountain you see over there."

The mountain he spoke of at that time was about twenty miles across from where we were. People opened their eyes when my grandfather told of the many battles they had with the Mexicans, and about their killing so many of the Mexicans, and taking their big city away from them, and how mighty they were. These wonderful things were talked about all winter long. The funniest thing was that he would sing some of the soldier's roll-calls, and the air to the Star-spangled Banner, which everybody learned during the winter.

He then showed us a more wonderful thing than all the others that he had brought. It was a paper, which he said could talk to him. He took it out and he would talk to it, and talk with it. He said, "This can talk to all our white brothers, and our white sisters, and their children. Our white brothers are beautiful, and our white sisters are beautiful, and their children are beautiful! He also said the paper can travel like the wind, and it can go and talk with their fathers and brothers and sisters, and come back to tell what they are doing, and whether they are well or sick."

After my grandfather told us this, our doctors and doctresses said,—

"If they can do this wonderful thing, they are not truly human, but pure spirits. None but heavenly spirits can do such wonderful things. We can communicate with the spirits, yet we cannot do wonderful things like them. Oh, our great chieftain, we are afraid your white brothers will yet make your people's hearts bleed. You see if they don't; for we can see it. Their blood is all around us, and the dead are lying all about us, and we cannot escape it. It will come. Then you will say our doctors and doctresses did know. Dance, sing, play, it will do no good; we cannot drive it away. They have already done the mischief, while you were away."

But this did not go far with my grandfather. He kept talking to his people about the good white people, and told them all to get ready to go with him to California the following spring. [. . .]

—Sarah Winnemucca (1994, 5–19)

Francis La Flesche

Omaha, 1857–1932

*Born to a prominent Omaha family (his father, "Iron Eye," was the last principal chief of the Omahas), Francis La Flesche's life spanned buffalo hunting as a boy to becoming the first Native American ethnographer. His long association with the U.S. Bureau of American Ethnography led to major ethnographic works—*The Omaha Tribe *(with Alice Fletcher, 1911),* The Osage Tribe *(1921–1925), and others.*

La Flesche also had literary aspirations, centering on the personal challenges of preserving his Indian identity while living and working in the Anglo academic world. His 1900 memoir The Middle Five, *on his boyhood years at a Nebraska Indian boarding school, is a much-loved classic. His short stories and personal essays, most of them unpublished in his lifetime, are represented in* Ke-Ma-Ha, *edited by James Parins and Daniel Littlefield.*

William T. Sherman
from *The Middle Five* (1900)

He stood on the third board of the fence from the ground, and leaned with his elbows on the top one, now and again kicking with his moccasined foot a loose panel. How long he had been standing there rattling that loose board no one knew, but in time one of the boys noticed him, and suddenly he became an object of the greatest interest among the boys of all sizes at the school. Boys who were playing down by the river, up by the spring, and over by the saw mill came running to see the stranger; and how the word reached them was as much of a mystery as the appearance of the little figure on the fence.

Every one was eager to pelt him with a question, and get as close to him as possible. He answered the questions in monosyllables; but he showed objection to any near approach, by freeing his bare arms from his little buffalo robe and pointing a wooden pop-gun at the eye of the boy who was inclined to be too familiar. We kept at him until we found out that his name was Thiṅ-je-zhin-ga, which, translated into the language of the Missionaries, signified Little Tail.[1]

He had come over from the village to see the school, and was as much interested in us as we were in him. All at once something attracted his attention; his black eyes sparkled, out came one arm from under his robe, and he pointed with a very dirty little finger and said, "Give me one of those!"

The coveted object was a brass button on the jacket of one of the small students. When Little Tail was asked what he wanted to do with it, he said, "Tie it to my scalp-lock." This sounded very funny to us, and we all laughed. The little chap retreated into his robe, covered his head, and looked out at us with one eye.

The bell rang for dinner; and there followed a general scramble to appear promptly at the table, and no thought was given to the queer little visitor. Being the last boy to enter the house, I turned to look back at him, and there he stood perched upon the fence, staring after us as though he wondered why he was so suddenly deserted.

When we came out from dinner, he was still on the fence, but he was busy. He had an ear of roasted corn and was shelling the kernels; when he had nearly a handful he tipped his head back, poured the grains into his mouth, and ate them with relish. After he had stripped half of the cob, he seemed to be satisfied, and the remainder disappeared in the recesses of his robe. As he finished his corn dinner, one of the school-boys said to him, "Little Tail, how would you like to stay and live with us here?"

"I would like it," he promptly replied.

"Will you stay?"

"Yes."

It was soon reported to the superintendent that a new pupil had come. When the afternoon session opened and the pupils were seated, Little Tail was given a seat at one of the desks, but to our delight he slid down and sat on the floor. The teacher rapped the top of his desk with a ruler and cried, "Silence!" and order was restored.

"What is the name of the new boy?" he asked.

"Thin'-je-zhin-ga," answered one of the boys. Gray-beard tried to repeat the name, but only set the whole school laughing. While this was going on, Little Tail reached down to his belt and drew out a roll of milk-weed fibre. It was his ammunition. He tore off enough to make a bullet, chewed it, and, bringing the breach of the pop-gun to his mouth, inserted the ball, twisting the gun with his hands while he pressed the wad in with his teeth, making many motions with his head. By pounding the butt of the rammer on the floor, he drove the ball to the firing point; then raising the gun he began forcing the ball with vigorous thrusts, aiming it at a mischievous boy who sat opposite making faces at him. Bang! went the weapon; the bullet, instead of hitting the object aimed at, struck Gray-beard in the face, and made him throw his head back. We covered our faces to suppress the giggles that bubbled up at this mishap. The wounded man looked sharply at the young artillerist, who, seeing the mischief he had done, very slyly thrust his gun into his robe, and, keeping an eye on his victim, sat perfectly still.

The teacher looked serious, then we became scared. After a moment his face relaxed, and he said in a pleasant tone, "We must have the name of the new boy on the Register, but we cannot have any name that is unpronounceable. We shall have to give him an English name. Will you suggest one?"

A number of hands went up and as many historic names were offered and rejected. Finally it was determined to call him William T. Sherman and that name was entered upon the Register.

After school a few boys were detailed to wash and dress the new arrival; so, with arms full of clothing, towels, and other bathing appliances, the lad was taken up to the boys' dormitory. The first thing to be done was to cut his long hair. A towel was put around his neck, and soon the shears were singing a tune about his ears. He seemed to enjoy it, and laughed at the jokes made by the boys; but when by some chance he caught sight of his scalp-lock lying on the floor like a little black snake, he put his fists into his eyes and fell to sobbing as though his heart would break.

"Pshaw!" said little Isaac, rubbing his closely cropped head, "mine was longer than yours when it was cut off, but I didn't cry!"

"Mine too!" exclaimed Abraham, picking up the braided lock and putting it where his had been; at which the rest of the boys laughed.

When the bath was over, William T. Sherman was dressed. He was delighted with his brand-new clothes, particularly with the long row of brass buttons that adorned the front of the jacket. When it came to the shoes, his grief for the lost scalp-lock was clean forgotten, and he strutted about to show the boys that his shining black shoes sang to his satisfaction.

William T. Sherman was quick to learn, and by the time winter was over he was speaking the peculiar English used by the boys of the school; he said, "fool bird," for quail; "first time," for long ago, and other Indian expressions turned into English. He was fond of arithmetic, and spent much time ciphering on his slate; he would write down the figure 1, 2, or 3, add to it a string of aughts, and then try to read them off. Grammar he abhorred, and in the spelling class, he held a permanent place at the foot. In outdoor sports he excelled; he could beat any boy of his size in leaping and running, and we had yet to learn other things in which he was expert.

One day, during the great June rise, all the boys were at the river watching the huge drift logs floating down the muddy Missouri.

"Say, boys!" exclaimed Ulysses S. Grant, thrusting his hands deep into his pockets; "I bet one hundred dollars that river is strong. I wouldn't like to swim in it; I'm sure the eddies would pull me under."

Gideon, who was always boasting of what his father could do, shouted, "My father could swim clear acrost and back again; he ain't 'fraid of eddies. He—"

"What's that?" cried a number of boys, startled by a heavy splash in the water. We all watched, and two brown feet came to the surface, wiggled, and disappeared. After a moment a round black head slowly arose. "Ha! Ha! I'm not 'fraid eddy!" shouted William T. Sherman, for it was he. A few vigorous strokes brought him to shore again.

"Take off your shirts and pants, boys, let's swim," he said.

We did so, and timidly splashed about the shallow edges of the water. A large tree was drifting down near the middle of the river. William ran up along the bank for quite a distance, and then plunged into the water. It was a beautiful sight to watch him as he threw his arms up and down, moving swiftly toward the tree; he reached it, dived under it, and came up on the other side; then he scrambled on the trunk and shouted for us to come, but none of us dared to go. After a moment he stood up on the tree, flourished an imaginary whip, and cried, "Git up, there!" with a succession of swear words,—genuine swear words. He was imitating the Agency teamster, and did not know what he was saying. He had heard the servant of the Government urge on his horses by such terms, and he was merely repeating them. Those of us who had been at the Mission a long time, and had all the Shorter Catechism in our little heads, and were orthodox by compulsion, if not by conviction, were horrified to hear those dreadful words uttered by a pupil of our school; for we knew some severe punishment awaited the little sinner should there be a traitor among us to make it known to Gray-beard.

Before we had fairly recovered from our shock at hearing this swearing, we were startled by a cry, "Job is drowning!" Not one of us moved, we were so frightened; but, quick as a flash, William T. Sherman sprang from his imaginary wagon, swam swiftly to the boy, caught him by the hair as he was going down for the last time, and brought him to the surface. "Kick! Kick!" he shouted; "make your arms go! Don't stop!" And after a hard struggle the two boys landed.

Job had swallowed considerable water, and become very sick. We didn't know what to do for him; but after we had rubbed and pommelled him, and held him by the heels head downward, he felt better; then we took him to the Mission and put him to bed.

On our way back Sherman spoke very little, but those of us who had been frightened into helplessness had much to say as to what we did or might have done to save Job.

At supper Gray-beard as usual counted the boys, and found one missing, "Where's Job?" he asked.

"He's got the th'tomick ache," said Daniel, his mouth full and his spoon raised half way with a new supply.

School went on the next morning as though nothing had happened. The teachers had not heard of the drowning and the rescue; but the girls had learned all about it and threw admiring glances at Sherman: to them he had become a hero, and each of the different gangs among the boys now wanted this hero as a member.

The recitations for the afternoon session were over, and the bell was tapped as a signal to put away our books and slates, and struck again to call us to order. When all arms were folded, there followed an ominous silence. Graybeard slowly looked around the school-room, as though to read every face turned up to him, then he spoke:

"I have been told that some of the boys in this school are in the habit of swearing; that is one of the things you are forbidden to do. It is wicked to swear, and any boy that I find has been doing so I shall punish very severely. I want you to remember this. After the closing exercises William T. Sherman will come to my room; I have something to say to him."

All eyes on the boys' side turned toward William as we chanted the Lord's prayer; then Gray-beard made his usual supplication, during which the big girls twisted their necks to look at their hero.

The exit from the school-room was quite orderly, but as soon as the groups of boys passed into the hall, they set up a shouting and singing, and made off to their different resorts for play. We, the Middle Five, were the last to go; and, as had been hastily arranged between us, I went to Gray-beard and asked some trivial question in order to give time for Brush to go and advise Sherman as to what answers to make if he was asked as to his being guilty of swearing.

"When he asks you if you been swearing, say, 'No, sir, I don't know what swear is,'" said Brush to Sherman.

"All right."

"Then tell him you been saying what you heard Agency man say to horses; but you don't know what those words mean, maybe they're swear words, you don't know."

Gray-beard went up to his room, followed by William T. Sherman, who for the first time entered that apartment. Boys who committed serious offences were disciplined in that place. I was taken there for fighting Andrew Johnson; Brush took his punishment there when he nearly cut Jonathan's ear off with a wooden sword. Most of us had had peculiar experiences in that room.

William T. Sherman had come to us direct from a tent; our bare school-room and play-room were all that he had seen of the furnishings of a civilized dwelling, so when he was suddenly ushered into Gray-beard's room he was quite dazzled by the bright draperies, pictures, and the polished furniture. He stood with hands in his pockets, mouth and eyes wide-open staring at the things, although twice requested by his host to sit down.

William timidly took the chair assigned him. It rocked backwards, and up went his feet; he clutched wildly at the arms, and the chair rocked forward; he got his footing, then sat perfectly still, fearing the chair would fall over with him.

Gray-beard took a seat facing the boy, and began to question him, "I was told that you had been swearing; is it true?"

Bewilderment at new sights, and the fright of the rocking-chair had put Brush's promptings out of Sherman's head, and in his confusion he answered, "Yes, sir—ma'am."

"It is wicked to swear, and you must be taught to know that it is. Now say what I say," and Gray-beard repeated the third commandment, until Sherman could say it without assistance, and then bade him to keep on until told to stop.

Poor William sat in the treacherous rocking-chair repeating this commandment, while Gray-beard wrote at his desk. William might as well have sat there imitating the cry of some animal or bird, for his mind was not dwelling upon the words he was uttering, but following his eyes as they moved from one strange object to another,—the pictures, the gilt frames, the sea shells, the clock on the mantelpiece, then something hanging near the window absorbed his attention, and his tongue and lips ceased to move as he drew with his finger on his knee the figure 1, adding to it a number of aughts. Gray-beard noted the pause, and said, "Go on, William, don't stop." After some little prompting, the boy resumed, but his finger kept moving, making the figure 1 and a string of aughts after it.

When Gray-beard and William T. Sherman left the school-room, Brush and I and the rest of the Five went toward the spring and sat under the large elm. Brush lay down on the grass and read a book he had borrowed from the superintendent, while the rest of us talked.

"I'd like to see that boy who told on William T. Sherman; I'd give him a licking," said Warren.

"I'd kick him hard," added Edwin.

"I bet it's that tell-tale Edson; he ought to be thumped!" I suggested.

While we were talking, William came and sat down with us. Every now and then a quivering sigh would escape him, although he tried not to show that he had been crying. Little Bob, believing as we did that William had been whipped, and, desiring to express sympathy, said, "Say, did it hurt?" William did not answer; nobody ever answered Bob.

"What did Gray-beard do to you?" I asked, turning to William.

"He made me sit down and say a commandment one hundred times."

"Which one was it? Say it to us."

"I don't want to say it; I said it enough." After a pause he asked, "What is swear?"

"When you call God names, that's swear," said Warren.

"I don't do that. I know God, it's the same Omahas call Wa-kon-da; but I don't know what means lord."

"It's a man just like big chief," explained Lester; "he has plenty of horses and lots of money. When he tells anybody to do anything, he got to do it; that's a lord."

"Is Gray-beard lord?"

"No, Gray-beard isn't lord."

"Say, boys, a one and six aughts is one million, ain't it?"

"Yes," we answered in chorus.

"Gray-beard is lord. He's got one million dollars. I saw it on a book hanging by his window; it had a name, I can't say it, then Bank and Cap'tal, and then a one and six aughts,—that's a million. He's got one million dollars!"

Brush threw his book down, raised himself on his elbow and looked at us with a smile; then he said, "I know that book William T. Sherman saw, it's the book Gray-beard counts the days by, and it's got on it what they call advertisement. That bank wants people to know it has one million dollars capital to go by; I learned that in my arithmetic. Gray-beard isn't a lord; he's a missionary,—the same kind that goes to Africa and Greenland's icy mountains."

—Francis La Flesche (1963, 72–82)

Notes for "William T. Sherman" from The Middle Five

1. He belonged to a band in the Omaha tribe known as Moṅ-thin-ka-ga-hae, people of the underground world; in other words, animals that burrowed and lived in the earth; such had small tails, and the name Little Tail referred to this peculiarity.

The Old Man Who Weeps

"Old Man Who Weeps," that is what the people call me when they think I do not hear. Children pause in their play as I pass by and put their little heads together and whisper: "There is the man who weeps!" What man with a heart of flesh having such memories as I would not weep! It is true that I weep, fifty snows have gone since that fateful morning and in all that time a day has never passed in which I have not shed tears. The hairs of my head are whitened and my body bends under the weight of years but my memory remains as bright as when in the vigor of youth I first saw my little Tah-day-wee.

I stood on the bank of Willow Creek. Along its grassy valley the great camp was being pitched. Men and women hurried toward the stream for wood and water and the children at play noisily chased each other among the tee-pees. Of a sudden I saw coming toward me a young woman. The light footsteps, the swinging of the free arm, and the graceful poise of the head held captive my gaze but as she drew near and I beheld the face with its dimpled cheeks my heart followed my eyes in captivity.

She went by looking neither to the right nor the left, quickly filled the vessel she was carrying with water, turned, and was about to pass me, when I stretched out my hand and gently touched her arm. She paused, dropped her eyes and waited. I whispered to her, she answered me with a smile, and in that moment she was mine, and I, her own. Not long after that we two stood before the people in open acknowledgement of our marriage.

The hunting season was over and the people returned to the permanent village. Soon the gathering of the corn, beans, and squashes began. Although this was a task belonging only to women I went with little Tah-day-wee and her mother to the field and did the heavier part of the work. The women in the adjoining patches shouted with merriment to see a young man toiling in the field but I worked the harder because I loved my little black-eyed bride and she loved me.

In due time all field work was done and the harvest gathered. Winter came with its chilling blasts and passed away, to be succeeded by the gentle spring with its verdant beauty and promise of renewed life. The corn, beans, and squashes were planted and cultivated in due season. Then came the time for the annual buffalo hunt. Throughout the village there was hurry and bustle in the preparation, and one day the whole village was on the march over the prairie making a broad and winding trail toward the buffalo land. How happy I was with little Tah-day-wee for my constant companion. Every morning I saddled her horse and helped her to mount. I knelt on the ground and she put her little moccasined foot upon my shoulder and sprang lightly into the saddle. In crossing a mirey stream I led her horse so that no harm should come to my little Tah-day-wee. Those who noticed these signs of affection smiled and exchanged glances of amusement but we did not care, for we were happy.

After a time we came to Willow Creek and camped in the same bend that we did the year before when I first met my little Tah-day-wee. A year had passed since our courtship and marriage, in all that time not an angry word or look of displeasure had passed between us.

News spread throughout the camp that visitors had arrived from my own people who were camped within a day's journey. Early the next morning I started for the camp of my tribe eager to see my father and mother and relatives whom I had not seen for a long time. In spite of her father's protests little Tah-day-wee went with me; she said she would be so lonely without me! The day was bright as when I first saw her, she was pretty then, but now, she was to me beautiful and good. The flowers in the freshness of their color nodded to the touch of the breezes and sweetened the air with their fragrance. A yellow-throated meadowlark swung to and fro on a gumweed stalk twittering coaxingly to its mate.

A high hill lay across our way, we climbed it to the top when we were startled by the sight of a man who lay there prone on the ground. I quickly drew and strung my bow but there was no occasion for alarm for from the ornamentation of the robe, the cut of the leggings and moccasins I knew the sleeping man to be one of my own tribe. I stooped and touched him lightly on the shoulder, saying "My friend, awake and be on your guard, lest you be surprised by some enemy and slain." With a growl more like a wild beast than a human being he sprang to his feet and drew his knife. His eyes suddenly rested on little Tah-day-wee and he hesitated. For a moment we stood silently facing each other. The beauty of his face and form rather than his menacing attitude, held me transfixed, for in all my life I had never beheld a man so perfect in limb and feature.

He was the first to break the silence, and in a tone and manner as gentle as a woman's he said, "Go, my friend wherever your inclination leads you and leave me to myself. I walk hand in hand with death with a mind fixed upon the destruction of any man who would intrude upon my seclusion. But, speak to me no more. Go, lest I do you harm."

"I offered you no wrong," I replied warmly; "but wakened you to give you friendly warning and possibly to save your father or mother or the woman you love—"

"You will not go!" he broke in angrily. "Then take this!" His arm flew high into the air and the blade of his knife flashed in the bright sunlight. Quickly I seized his wrist in both hands. Then followed a struggle between us that meant death to one or the other. In stature and strength we were evenly matched. Our muscles cracked like the snapping of bow strings as we bent and tossed each other, trampling the flowers and grass into the earth. I did not slacken for an instant my grasp upon the arm that held the deadly weapon. I felt that my hope for life was in the man's exhaustion and to that I strove to preserve my own strength.

But soon I felt in my thighs the oncoming of weakness and then in my arms. I was conscious of panting heavily and could hear the fierce throbbing of my heart. It seemed as though in a moment I must give up, when suddenly I remembered a subtle trick in wrestling I had learned when a lad. I tried it and down we went to the ground with a thud, I on top and still grasping tightly the wrist of the hand that held the knife. "Come quickly!" I called to Tah-day-wee: "take the knife from his hand!" She did not stir. With a dextrous movement I threw my knee heavily on the man's arm and he released his hold on the weapon. I seized it and struck once! twice! thrice! and the man lay motionless in death.

I rose to my feet and stood panting. "Why did you not come and help me when I called you?" I said.

She did not answer, but stood staring at the upturned face of the dead man.

Prompted as by an evil spirit, I asked, "Do you love him?"

"Yes, I love the man," she answered, in slow deliberate tones.

Then as by the rising of a sudden storm, all the love and tenderness I had borne the woman was swept away, and anger and hatred took possession of me with an unrelenting fury, overwhelming all reason and pity. Seizing my bow I fitted an arrow to the string and as I pulled it with all my strength I could hear the grinding of my teeth. The arrow struck; and with a gasp little Tah-day-wee fell forward, her head resting on the shoulder of the prostrate man.

Suddenly I was myself again and stood aghast at the deed I had done. I had committed a wrong against the Giver of Life, against the people whose hospitality I had enjoyed and against myself.

As I stood in bitter self-reproach, I seemed to see the two I had just slain going hand in hand toward the spirit land. "I shall follow!" I cried aloud; "he shall not have her! She is mine!" I picked up the bloody knife and as I turned its deadly point against my breast, the words handed down from the men of old sounded in my ears: "He who purposely kills himself, destroys his soul!" I threw the weapon from my hand and cried, "I must wait 'till death unbidden comes, then shall my spirit follow."

Stripping myself of garments and robe, and bleeding from self-inflicted wounds, I hastened to the people of little Tah-day-wee to tell them of what had happened. The sun was falling to the western hills when I stood in the center of the camp circle. The people gathered hastily and with sobs that I could not suppress, I told my story, omitting nothing. All the tribe heard and many wept in pity for me and little Tah-day-wee, for they knew how happy we were until this fateful day.

I was held blameless and the people welcomed me to their homes as before, but all their kindness could not win me from the desire to follow my little Tah-day-wee. Moved by this desire, I have done many a desperate deed that warriors mistook for an act of valor. In a battle I crashed against a man of might, he thrust his lance through me, but I struck him from his saddle and he lay wrapped in a cloud of dust, his last fight was over, but I lived on. I have been left for dead on the field and when I awoke from my swoon, the faint rays of the new moon were on the shadowy hills and on my companions who were sleeping their last sleep, while I was once more awake here on the earth. Once as I lay helpless and wounded, scarce able to stir, I heard stealthy footsteps approaching and a great grey wolf stood over me. I made a movement to brace myself to meet the jaws of the hungry beast but he cringed and slunk away, and death eluded me once more.

—Francis La Flesche (n.d., Fletcher and
La Flesche Papers, File 4558/48)

Ne-Ma-Ha

"Away! Out of my sight! I wish never to see you again!" exclaimed a tall, fierce-looking man as he violently pushed a boy from him.

The angry voice rose above the rattling of tent poles and the bustle of the people who were busy breaking camp. Startled by this outburst of anger, those nearby paused in their work to see what was the matter, and as they beheld the boy gather up his little robe and bow and walk slowly out of camp with quivering lips and bowed head, they were moved to pity. A murmur of disapproval spread on all sides, but no open protest was made, for the quarrelsome disposition of this man was well known; even the mother, who felt keenly the distress of her child, dared not so much as lift her eyes in reproach.

The lad climbed the nearest hill; reaching the top, he threw himself prone to the ground and wept as though his heart would break. Already the caravan was fording the river below with all the excitement usual in crossing a stream. The mother was the last to move, although she had been among the first in readiness. As she took the trail, leading her horses, she looked back from time to time as though expecting to see her child following.

When he had overcome the first paroxysms of grief, the boy sat up and looked across the river toward the opposite bluffs. There was but one person ascending the rise; all the rest had gone beyond. Although the figure looked small and dim in the distance, the lad recognized his mother, and the thought that she had stopped once more to look for him started afresh the sobs and tears. At last she turned and moved on, and he watched her longingly until she slowly disappeared behind the hills.

An oppressive stillness pervaded the deserted camp over which passed gusts of wind, carrying with them the ashes of dead fires in funnel-shaped clouds. Abandoned now by all the human associates upon which he had unconsciously depended for protection and comfort, the lad cast his eyes about as though seeking for aid from some unknown source. Far off against the green hills he saw groups of buffalo, elk and antelope scattered here and there; above him in the blue sky great birds were soaring in wide circles, and below him the winding river shimmered in the sun. All these objects, which hitherto he had scarcely heeded, now arrested his attention and awakened within him a hope that some of them might take pity on him and bring him help. In the midst of nature's silence the lonely boy remembered the stories told of men, who, when mere lads and bereft of father and mother, had wandered over the prairies where in solitude they cried to Wa-kon-da for help, and their prayers had been heard and answered. Why should not I, he thought, pray to Wa-kon-da; perhaps my cry will be heard and answered.

While this thought was still in his mind, the lad removed his moccasins, leggings, and robe and hid them in a bush close by; then returning to the top of the hill, he put moistened earth upon his face and head, and in a voice tremulous with emotion he cried to Wa-kon-da, using the song and words his mother had taught him.

"Wa-kon-da the-thu wa-pa-thin a-ton-he, Wa-kon-da the-thu wa-pa-thin a-ton-he . . ."

["Wa-kon-da here in need I stand . . ."]

He lifted his little hands to the sky, then brought them down to the earth, then he stretched them to the north, east, south, and west, the paths of the winds, as with tears streaming down his face he chanted his prayer. No suppliant before "the great spirit" was ever more in earnest. Again and again he offered his prayer, but there came no response. The sun steadily took its course, the waters of the river rippled on and the wind sighed as before. At last the boy fell to the ground exhausted and soon he was overcome with sleep.

The day was far spent when the lad was aroused by a mysterious consciousness of the presence near him of some living being. Slowly and cautiously he lifted his head when lo! he beheld standing before him two strange bearded men, leaning on their guns and looking down upon him with pale eyes that gleamed under heavy brows and lashes. To spring up and run was the boy's first impulse but at the same moment there flashed through his mind the thought that this vision might be an answer to his prayer, and he hesitated. The two men, wishing not to frighten the lad, moved toward the river and beckoned him to follow. He rose and silently pointed to the place where he had hidden his clothing and, there being no signs of objection from the men to his getting them, the lad stepped to the bush, dressed himself and followed the strangers.

II.

On the morning following the banishment of the boy, the people again broke camp. Like a great serpent the caravan moved over the rolling prairie, leaving behind a dark, winding trail. Not a cloud broke the deep blue above, and the sun shed a glaring light upon the grassy hills. Toward the middle of the day a dark spot appeared in the western sky, and as though by magic other patches of clouds came to view. No notice was taken of these until a tall man with long hair looked up and exclaimed, "Ah ho! See what is going on above!"

The clouds moved swiftly around and around, then gathered in one surging mass. With lurid glare a bolt shot to the earth, followed by a roar that made the ground tremble and smoke curled upward from the spot where the lightning struck. Straight toward the caravan the cloud swept on with increasing speed; another fiery dart pierced the earth and smoke arose as before. On came the cloud, making a noise like many wings; a third shot fell, and the tall man shouted, "Look out for the fourth!" The cloud was now overhead rolling in angry turmoil. Great drops of rain fell slantwise, sparkling in the sun. The last word was still upon the lips of the tall man when there came a blinding flame with a terrific crash. The people fled in every direction, and a man sank to the ground enveloped in smoke. The cloud rushed on leaving behind the sky calm and blue.

"Ho! They have killed one of us!" cried a voice loud and clear. The word passed swiftly on to the end of the line and the people hurried to the spot where the man lay. No one dared to touch the body, for violent hands had been laid upon it by the thunder gods. One of the chiefs approached and an opening was made for him. He walked to the prostrate form and without touching it, examined it closely. Then turning to the people he said, "Let this be a warning to men who treat their children cruelly. You all know what this man did but yesterday. To all appearances he is dead, but life may yet be lingering. Make haste and bring water, men women, and children, and let there be a continuous flow upon the body."

Back and forth the people ran to a brook nearby and they kept a constant stream of water on the body. After a while there was a slight movement of the arms, then of the legs, and at last the man raised himself to a sitting position. The chief stepped forward and supported him. "I am alive!" gasped the man; "but—I cannot see!" As the people looked at him they saw, burnt around each eye, a black ring.

III.

In the afternoon of a spring day as the shadows were lengthening, Mr. John Merriman, of the firm of Merriman, Prideaux and Company, dealers in furs and general merchandise, sat on the front veranda of his cottage in the residence part of the city of New Orleans. The roses and blossoming vines that twined over the windows and trellises, the garden with its variety of trees, flowers and well-kept walks indicated the thrift of the people who dwelt there. Mrs. Merriman sat near her husband, gently rocking backward and forward as her deft fingers played rapidly over her work. Suddenly she dropped her sewing and shifting her chair so as to face her husband, and said, "Do you think it is best for the boy to go so far away from home? He is young to take all that responsibility; I am afraid it will be too much for him."

"I am sure," replied Mr. Merriman, removing his pipe, "that it will be best not only for him, but for the firm. He is better fitted for the place than any of the men we have, and besides, he will get double the salary he is now paid. Of course we do not know his exact age. It is twenty years since we found him and at that time I think he was about seven. He'll get along all right."

"When did you hear of Krebs' death? How did it happen?"

"The news was brought last week by the steamboat. No details were given, but I don't think it was an accident. My judgment is that someone who was jealous of his success in the management of our business with the Indians killed him."

"Aren't you afraid that Robert might be killed in the same way?"

"There is no danger; the people who are suspected of killing Krebs have left the country and are not likely to return. What's more, Bob is an Indian, and the tribe will protect him."

"Does Robert think that he is going to his own people?"

"Bob doesn't know who his people are, doesn't even know their tribal name. He only remembers his own name and those of his father and mother."

There was a click at the gate and the couple looked up. A tall, swarthy young man strode rapidly up the gravel walk. "Hello Father!" he called; "How is your knee?"

"It's there—so is that infernal rheumatism," answered Mr. Merriman, shifting his leg which rested upon a pillow [on] a chair. "How is my boy?"

"I'm all right," said Robert, for it was he. He stooped to kiss Mrs. Merriman on the brow as was his habit: "Only, I'm sorry I have to go so soon. I wish your knee was well; I don't like to see you suffer."

"Old age, my boy, old age!" replied Mr. Merriman, grasping Robert's hand. "Aches and pains are the companions of old age, if the pain wasn't in my knee it would be in some other part of my body."

"Margaret was here this morning," broke in Mrs. Merriman, as she dusted Robert's shoulders with her handkerchief, "and she feels dreadfully about your going."

"I'll go and see her after supper."

"What time does the steamboat leave?"

"Two o'clock tomorrow afternoon."

IV.

On his arrival at the trading post, Robert Merriman lost no time in examining the books, taking an inventory of the stock, and soon had everything in working order. The men connected with the establishment quickly recognized the ability of the young man and accorded him the respect that they had shown to Krebs, the former manager.

No one really knew who Robert was. The employees who had heard of the principals of the firm, whispered among themselves that he was a son of "old Merriman" by an Osage woman. The Indians took him for a young Spaniard, and they fell to calling him the "little Es-pa-yu-na."

When Robert had every branch of the business well in hand, he gave personal attention to his customers, frequently waiting upon them himself that he might become acquainted with every face and name. It did not satisfy him to deal with the Indians through an interpreter, and he set out to learn the language. The words sounded strangely familiar to him and he repeated them, and the rapidity with which he learned to speak surprised the Indians.

Business thrived, and nothing unusual occurred until one day there came to the store an old woman leading a blind man. Robert waited upon them and from the terms they used when addressing each other he learned that they were husband and wife. There was something familiar in their faces and in the tones of their voices. He was almost certain that he had seen the couple before but was puzzled by the disfigurement of the old man's face. The wife tied her purchases in a bundle, threw it over her back and led her husband out of the store. Robert stood watching them and called out to the interpreter, who happened to be present, "Jack, who is the blind man who just went out with his wife? It seems to me I have seen them somewhere but I can't remember."

"This first time you seen them," replied Jack. "That's Num'-pa-be, he's a pretty bad man."

Robert gave a start as he heard the name. It was that of his father, which he had always remembered. "What was his wife's name?" he hurriedly asked.

"Ne'-da-we."

It was the name of his mother. Suddenly memories of the past long dormant swept through his mind—the scene of his banishment, the strange men who surprised him, and all that happened to him since that event. He strove to recall the features of his mother and father as he saw them as a child, and to trace them in the faces he [had] just looked upon, but the scars on the old man's face perplexed him. At last he asked, "Why do you say the old man is a bad man?"

"Long time ago," answered Jack, "that old man had one boy, his name, 'Ne-ma-ha.'"

"Go on," urged Robert, as he heard his own name.

"I was goin' tell you. I use t' play with that boy when I was little. One time we went buffalo hunt and the old man hit that boy and scare him away, and he never come back again. Next day lightning hit him and pretty near kill him. He's bad man, nobody like him."

Robert now realized that he was among his own people, that his father and mother were living and he had seen them both. In the rush of feeling he could scarcely restrain his desire to run out, overtake and embrace his mother, but the thought that he might be unwelcome to his father made him hesitate.

Leaving the store, he sought a place where he could be alone. His thoughts went back to his home and his adopted parents whom he dearly loved. He put his hand mechanically to a pocket, slowly drew from it a letter received only a few days before this discovery and opened it. His eyes fell upon the closing paragraph, and he read: "I helped your mother fix up your room today. We rearranged all the pictures and the curtains. Your little bow still hangs over the door. Your father and mother and I are all looking anxiously toward the time when we shall see you again. I send you some roses I plucked from your window. Affectionately, Margaret." He returned the letter to its place, thinking that surely it would be right for him to devote the rest of his life to these people who loved and trusted him, yet he felt the promptings of a natural duty toward his real parents so lately discovered.

In the afternoon of the following day, Robert was standing at his desk working over his books, when two Indians entered the store. After an exchange of greetings the men sat down upon a long bench kept for the use of customers and one of them took from his belt his tobacco bag and filled his pipe. As he offered the pipe to his friend to light and to take the first whiffs, he said, "The old man died about the middle of the night, they say, and his wife was all alone with him."

Robert's quick ear caught the words and as he reached to dip his pen, he asked, "Who was that, Uncle?"

"Num'-pa-be, the blind man. Perhaps you know him."

As he heard the name, Robert's pen slipped from his hand and rolled over the neatly written page leaving a trail of dark blotches. Without heeding the accident, he asked, "When will they bury him?"

"They have already buried him. It was a sad ending, they say," continued the man, turning to his friend: "toward the end he kept saying, 'I heard his voice. I heard his voice.'"

Robert stood in silence a few moments, then stole softly out of the building and walked slowly away. Halfway up a hill he came to a solitary tree and sat down leaning against its trunk. The shadows were fast deepening. Dusk came, and then the darkness of night. As he sat, going over the long years of loneliness and suffering through which his father must have passed, there crept into the mind of the young man a fear that he might have been to blame for it all. A feeling of self reproach came over him; then, as though to ease his conscience he welcomed the thought that when he lifted his little hands to the "great spirit" for aid, he was thinking only of his own misery and desolation, and that he did not even for a moment desire the punishment of his father. Suddenly he remembered his mother and hastily made his way toward the village.

The hour of midnight had passed. On a high hill overlooking the Indian lodges a bright fire was burning, by its side stood a woman watching—it was the faithful widow lighting the path for her husband to the land of shadows. Wearily she shaded her face with one hand and looked up at the stars of Wa'-ba-ha (Ursa Major). "It has almost completed its circuit," she murmured; "day will soon come." She stooped to feed the fire once more; a sound caught her ear—and Robert stepped into the light.

Along the horizon a grey streak appeared, gradually, it took on a faint tinge of red, then quickly the whole eastern sky burst into a flame of crimson. With the glow upon his face, Robert said, "Mother, day has come," and taking her tenderly by the hand, he led her slowly down the hill and the two vanished in the rising mist below. (1900–01)

—Francis La Flesche (1900–1901;
Fletcher and La Flesche Papers, File #4558/48)
Also see Parins and Littlefield (1995, 118–29)

Charles Eastman

Ohiyesa; Santee Sioux, 1858–1939

Charles Eastman (Ohiyesa) was born in Minnesota during a time of great hardship for his family and community. He became one of the first Native doctors and autobiographers, and his well-known writing inspired other Native writers, like Luther Standing Bear and Zitkala-Ša, to write their autobiographies. Until age fifteen, Eastman lived the traditional life of a Santee Sioux boy on the reservation, but when his father, Seth Eastman, who had been imprisoned for his role in the 1862 Minnesota Uprising, returned, he sent Ohiyesa to boarding school. Eastman published two accounts of his life: Indian Boyhood *(1902), which spans the years 1858–1873, chronicles his life to the age of fifteen, and depicts his traditional life on the reservation; and* From the Deep Woods to Civilization *(1916), which depicts his life in the white world and critiques Anglo-European ethnocentrism. Eastman also published* Red Hunter and the Animal People *(1904),* Old Indian Days *(1907),* Wigwam Evenings *(1909),* Smoky Day's Wigwam Evenings *(1910, reprint), and* The Soul of the Indian *(1911).*

After he graduated from Dartmouth in 1887 and Boston University Medical School in 1890, Charles Eastman became the agency physician on the Pine Ridge Reservation, just prior to the resurgence of the Ghost Dance and the massacre at Wounded Knee. Eastman married Elaine Goodell, who assisted him with his work, and they eventually moved to Minnesota. Eastman worked in Indian affairs for much of his life.

"An Indian Boy's Training"
from *Indian Boyhood* (1902)

It is commonly supposed that there is no systematic education of their children among the aborigines of this country. Nothing could be farther from the truth. All the customs of this primitive people were held to be divinely instituted, and those in connection with the training of children were scrupulously adhered to and transmitted from one generation to another.

The expectant parents conjointly bent all their efforts to the task of giving the new-comer the best they could gather from a long line of ancestors. A pregnant Indian woman would often choose one of the greatest characters of her family and tribe as a model for her child. This hero was daily called to mind. She would gather from tradition all of his noted deeds and daring exploits, rehearsing them to herself when alone. In order that the impression might be more distinct, she avoided company. She isolated herself as much as possible, and wandered in solitude, not thoughtlessly, but with an eye to the impress given by grand and beautiful scenery.

The Indians believed, also, that certain kinds of animals would confer peculiar gifts upon the unborn, while others would leave so strong an adverse impression that the child might become a monstrosity. A case of hare-lip was commonly attributed to the rabbit. It was said that a rabbit had charmed the mother and given to the babe its own features. Even the meat of certain animals was denied the pregnant woman, because it was supposed to influence the disposition or features of the child.

Scarcely was the embryo warrior ushered into the world, when he was met by lullabies that speak of wonderful exploits in hunting and war. Those ideas which so fully occupied his mother's mind before his birth are now put into words by all about the child, who is as yet quite unresponsive to their appeals to his honor and ambition. He is called the future defender of his people, whose lives may depend upon his courage and skill. If the child is a girl, she is at once addressed as the future mother of a noble race.

In hunting songs, the leading animals are introduced; they come to the boy to offer their bodies for the sustenance of his tribe. The animals are regarded as his friends, and spoken of almost as tribes of people, or as his cousins, grandfathers and grandmothers. The songs of wooing, adapted as lullabies, were equally imaginative, and the suitors were often animals personified, while pretty maidens were represented by the mink and the doe.

Very early, the Indian boy assumed the task of preserving and transmitting the legends of his ancestors and his race. Almost every evening a myth, or a true story of some deed done in the past, was narrated by one of the parents or grandparents, while the boy listened with parted lips and glistening eyes. On the following evening, he was usually required to repeat it. If he was not an apt scholar, he struggled long with his task; but, as a rule, the Indian boy is a good listener and has a good memory, so that the stories were tolerably well mastered. The household became his audience, by which he was alternately criticized and applauded.

This sort of teaching at once enlightens the boy's mind and stimulates his ambition. His conception of his own future career becomes a vivid and irresistible force. Whatever there is for him to learn must be learned; whatever qualifications are necessary to a truly great man he must seek at any expense of danger and hardship. Such was the feeling of the imaginative and brave young Indian. It became apparent to him in early life that he must accustom himself to rove alone and not to fear or dislike the impression of solitude.

It seems to be a popular idea that all the characteristic skill of the Indian is instinctive and hereditary. This is a mistake. All the stoicism and patience of the Indian are acquired traits, and continual practice alone makes him master of the art of wood-craft. Physical training and dieting were not neglected. I remember that I was not allowed to have beef soup or any warm drink. The soup was for the old men. General rules for the young were never to take their food very hot, nor to drink much water.

My uncle, who educated me up to the age of fifteen years, was a strict disciplinarian and a good teacher. When I left the teepee in the morning, he would say: "Hakadah, look closely to everything you see"; and at evening, on my return, he used often to catechize me for an hour or so.

"On which side of the trees is the lighter-colored bark? On which side do they have most regular branches?"

It was his custom to let me name all the new birds that I had seen during the day. I would name them according to the color or the shape of the bill or their song or the appearance and locality of the nest—in fact, anything about the bird that impressed me as characteristic. I made many ridiculous errors, I must admit. He then usually informed me of the correct name. Occasionally I made a hit and this he would warmly commend.

He went much deeper into this science when I was a little older, that is, about the age of eight or nine years. He would say, for instance:

"How do you know that there are fish in yonder lake?"

"Because they jump out of the water for flies at mid-day."

He would smile at my prompt but superficial reply.

"What do you think of the little pebbles grouped together under the shallow water? and what made the pretty curved marks in the sandy bottom and the little sand-banks? Where do you find the fish-eating birds? Have the inlet and the outlet of a lake anything to do with the question?"

He did not expect a correct reply at once to all the voluminous questions that he put to me on these occasions, but he meant to make me observant and a good student of nature.

"Hakadah," he would say to me, "you ought to follow the example of the shunktokecha (wolf). Even when he is surprised and runs for his life, he will pause to take one more look at you before he enters his final retreat. So you must take a second look at everything you see.

"It is better to view animals unobserved. I have been a witness to their courtships and their quarrels and have learned many of their secrets in this way. I was once the unseen spectator of a thrilling battle between a pair of grizzly bears and three buffaloes—a rash act for the bears, for it was in the moon of strawberries, when the buffaloes sharpen and polish their horns for bloody contests among themselves.

"I advise you, my boy, never to approach a grizzly's den from the front, but to steal up behind and throw your blanket or a stone in front of the hole. He does not usually rush for it, but first puts his head out and listens and then comes out very indifferently and sits on his haunches on the mound in front of the hole before he makes any attack. While he is exposing himself in this fashion, aim at his heart. Always be as cool as the animal himself." Thus he armed me against the cunning of savage beasts by teaching me how to outwit them.

"In hunting," he would resume, "you will be guided by the habits of the animal you seek. Remember that a moose stays in swampy or low land or between high mountains near a spring or lake, for thirty to sixty days at a time. Most large game moves about continually, except the doe in the spring; it is then a very easy matter to find her with the fawn. Conceal yourself in a convenient place as soon as you observe any signs of the presence of either, and then call with your birchen doe-caller.

"Whichever one hears you first will soon appear in your neighborhood. But you must be very watchful, or you may be made a fawn of by a large wild-cat. They understand the characteristic call of the doe perfectly well.

"When you have any difficulty with a bear or a wild-cat—that is, if the creature shows signs of attacking you—you must make him fully understand that you have seen him and are aware of his intentions. If you are not well equipped for a pitched battle, the only way to make him retreat is to take a long sharp-pointed pole for a spear and rush toward him. No wild beast will face this unless he is cornered and already wounded. These fierce beasts are generally afraid of the common weapon of the larger animals—the horns, and if these are very long and sharp, they dare not risk an open fight.

"There is one exception to this rule—the grey wolf will attack fiercely when very hungry. But their courage depends upon their numbers; in this they are like white men. One wolf or two will never attack a man. They will stampede a herd of buffaloes in order to get at the calves; they will rush upon a herd of antelopes, for these are helpless; but they are always careful about attacking man."

Of this nature were the instructions of my uncle, who was widely known at that time as among the greatest hunters of his tribe.

All boys were expected to endure hardship without complaint. In savage warfare, a young man must, of course, be an athlete and used to undergoing all sorts of privations. He must be able to go without food and water for two or three days without displaying any weakness, or to run for a day and a night without any rest. He must be able to traverse a pathless and wild country without losing his way either in the day or night time. He cannot refuse to do any of these things if he aspires to be a warrior.

Sometimes my uncle would waken me very early in the morning and challenge me to fast with him all day. I had to accept the challenge. We blackened our faces with charcoal, so that every boy in the village would know that I was fasting for the day. Then the little tempters would make my life a misery until the merciful sun hid behind the western hills.

I can scarcely recall the time when my stern teacher began to give sudden war-whoops over my head in the morning while I was sound asleep. He expected me to leap up with perfect presence of mind, always ready to grasp a weapon of some sort and to give a shrill whoop in reply.

If I was sleepy or startled and hardly knew what I was about, he would ridicule me and say that I need never expect to sell my scalp dear. Often he would vary these tactics by shooting off his gun just outside of the lodge while I was yet asleep, at the same time giving blood-curdling yells. After a time I became used to this.

When Indians went upon the war-path, it was their custom to try the new warriors thoroughly before coming to an engagement. For instance, when they were near a hostile camp, they would select the novices to go after the water and make them do all sorts of things to prove their courage. In accordance with this idea, my uncle used to send me off after water when we camped after dark in a strange place. Perhaps the country was full of wild beasts, and, for aught I knew, there might be scouts from hostile bands of Indians lurking in that very neighborhood.

Yet I never objected, for that would show cowardice. I picked my way through the woods, dipped my pail in the water and hurried back, always careful to make as little noise as a cat. Being only a boy, my heart would leap at every crackling of a dry twig or distant hooting of an owl, until, at last, I reached our teepee. Then my uncle would perhaps say: "Ah, Hakadah, you are a thorough warrior," empty out the precious contents of the pail, and order me to go a second time.

Imagine how I felt! But I wished to be a brave man as much as a white boy desires to be a great lawyer or even President of the United States. Silently I would take the pail and endeavor to retrace my footsteps in the dark.

With all this, our manners and morals were not neglected. I was made to respect the adults and especially the aged. I was not allowed to join in their discussions, nor even to speak in their presence, unless requested to do so. Indian etiquette was very strict, and among the requirements was that of avoiding the direct address. A term of relationship or some title of courtesy was commonly used instead of the personal name by those who wished to show respect. We were taught generosity to the poor and reverence for the "Great Mystery." Religion was the basis of all Indian training.

I recall to the present day some of the kind warnings and reproofs that my good grandmother was wont to give me. "Be strong of heart—be patient!" she used to say. She told me of a young chief who was noted for his uncontrollable temper. While in one of his rages he attempted to kill a woman, for which he was slain by his own band and left unburied as a mark of disgrace—his body was simply covered with green grass. If I ever lost my temper, she would say:

"Hakadah, control yourself, or you will be like that young man I told you of, and lie under a *green blanket!*"

In the old days, no young man was allowed to use tobacco in any form until he had become an acknowledged warrior and had achieved a record. If a youth should seek a wife before he had reached the age of twenty-two or twenty-three, and been recognized as a brave man, he was sneered at and considered an ill-bred Indian. He must also be a skillful hunter. An Indian cannot be a good husband unless he brings home plenty of game.

These precepts were in the line of our training for the wild life.

—Charles A. Eastman (1991, 49–60)

"First Impressions of Civilization"
from *Indian Boyhood* (1902)

I was scarcely old enough to know anything definite about the "Big Knives," as we called the white men, when the terrible Minnesota massacre broke up our home and I was carried into exile. I have already told how I was adopted into the family of my father's younger brother, when my father was betrayed and imprisoned. We all supposed that he had shared the fate of those who were executed at Mankato, Minnesota.

Now the savage philosophers looked upon vengeance in the field of battle as a lofty virtue. To avenge the death of a relative or of a dear friend was considered a great deed. My uncle, accordingly, had spared no pains to instill into my young mind the obligation to avenge the death of my father and my older brothers. Already I looked eagerly forward to the day when I should find an opportunity to carry out his teachings. Meanwhile, he himself went upon the war-path and returned with scalps every summer. So it may be imagined how I felt toward the Big Knives!

On the other hand, I had heard marvelous things of this people. In some things we despised them; in others we regarded them as *wakan* (mysterious), a race whose power bordered upon the supernatural. I learned that they had made a "fireboat." I could not understand how they could unite two elements which cannot exist together. I thought the water would put out the fire, and the fire would consume the boat if it had the shadow of a chance. This was to me a preposterous thing! But when I was told that the Big Knives had created a "fire-boat-walks-on-mountains" (a locomotive) it was too much to believe.

"Why," declared my informant, "those who saw this monster move said that it flew from mountain to mountain when it seemed to be excited. They said also that they believed it carried a thunder-bird, for they frequently heard his usual war-whoop as the creature sped along!"

Several warriors had observed from a distance one of the first trains on the Northern Pacific, and had gained an exaggerated impression of the wonders of the pale-face. They had seen it go over a bridge that spanned a deep ravine and it seemed to them that it jumped from one bank to the other. I confess that the story almost quenched my ardor and bravery.

Two or three young men were talking together about this fearful invention.

"However," said one, "I understand that this fire-boat-walks-on-mountains cannot move except on the track made for it."

Although a boy is not expected to join in the conversation of his elders, I ventured to ask: "Then it cannot chase us into any rough country?"

"No, it cannot do that," was the reply, which I heard with a great deal of relief.

I had seen guns and various other things brought to us by the French Canadians, so that I had already some notion of the supernatural gifts of the white man; but I had never before heard such tales as I listened to that morning. It was said that they had bridged the Missouri and Mississippi rivers, and that they made immense houses of stone and brick, piled on top of one another until they were as high as high hills. My brain was puzzled with these things for many a day. Finally I asked my uncle why the Great Mystery gave such power to the *Washichu* (the rich)—sometimes we called them by this name—and not to us Dakotas.

"For the same reason," he answered, "that he gave to Duta the skill to make fine bows and arrows, and to Wachesne no skill to make anything."

"And why do the Big Knives increase so much more in number than the Dakotas?" I continued.

"It has been said, and I think it must be true, that they have larger families than we do. I went into the house of an *Eashecha* (a German), and I counted no less than nine children. The eldest of them could not have been over fifteen. When my grandfather first visited them, down at the mouth of the Mississippi, they were comparatively few; later my father visited their Great Father at Washington, and they had already spread over the whole country."

"Certainly they are a heartless nation. They have made some of their people servants—yes, slaves! We have never believed in keeping slaves, but it seems that these *Washichu* do! It is our belief that they painted their servants black a long time ago, to tell them from the rest, and now the slaves have children born to them of the same color!

"The greatest object of their lives seems to be to acquire possessions— to be rich. They desire to possess the whole world. For thirty years they were trying to entice us to sell them our land. Finally the outbreak gave them all, and we have been driven away from our beautiful country.

"They are a wonderful people. They have divided the day into hours, like the moons of the year. In fact, they measure everything. Not one of them would let so much as a turnip go from his field unless he received full value for it. I understand that their great men make a feast and invite many, but when the feast is over the guests are required to pay for what they have eaten before leaving the house. I myself saw at White Cliff (the name given to St. Paul, Minnesota) a man who kept a brass drum and a bell to call people to his table; but when he got them in he would make them pay for the food!

"I am also informed," said my uncle, "but this I hardly believe, that their Great Chief (President) compels every man to pay him for the land he lives upon and all his personal goods—even for his own existence— every year!" (This was his idea of taxation.) "I am sure we could not live under such a law.

"When the outbreak occurred, we thought that our opportunity had come, for we had learned that the Big Knives were fighting among themselves, on account of a dispute over their slaves. It was said that the Great Chief had allowed slaves in one part of the country and not in another, so there was jealousy, and they had to fight it out. We don't know how true this was.

"There were some praying-men who came to us some time before the trouble arose. They observed every seventh day as a holy day. On that day they met in a house that they had built for that purpose, to sing, pray, and speak of their Great Mystery. I was never in one of these meetings. I understand that they had a large book from which they read. By all accounts they were very different from all other white men we have known, for these never observed any such day, and we never knew them to pray, neither did they ever tell us of their Great Mystery.

"In war they have leaders and war-chiefs of different grades. The common warriors are driven forward like a herd of antelopes to face the foe. It is on account of this manner of fighting—from compulsion and not from personal bravery—that we count no coup on them. A lone warrior can do much harm to a large army of them in a bad country."

It was this talk with my uncle that gave me my first clear idea of the white man.

I was almost fifteen years old when my uncle presented me with a flint-lock gun. The possession of the "mysterious iron," and the explosive dirt, or "pulverized coal," as it is called, filled me with new thoughts. All the war-songs that I had ever heard from childhood came back to me with their heroes. It seemed as if I were an entirely new being—the boy had become a man!

"I am now old enough," said I to myself, "and I must beg my uncle to take me with him on his next war-path. I shall soon be able to go among the whites whenever I wish, and to avenge the blood of my father and my brothers."

I had already begun to invoke the blessing of the Great Mystery. Scarcely a day passed that I did not offer up some of my game, so that he might not be displeased with me. My people saw very little of me during the day, for in solitude I found the strength I needed. I groped about in the wilderness, and determined to assume my position as a man. My boyish ways were departing, and a sullen dignity and composure was taking their place.

The thought of love did not hinder my ambitions. I had a vague dream of some day courting a pretty maiden, after I had made my reputation, and won the eagle feathers.

One day, when I was away on the daily hunt, two strangers from the United States visited our camp. They had boldly ventured across the northern border. They were Indians, but clad in the white man's garments. It was as well that I was absent with my gun.

My father, accompanied by an Indian guide, after many days' searching had found us at last. He had been imprisoned at Davenport, Iowa, with those who took part in the massacre or in the battles following, and he was taught in prison and converted by the pioneer missionaries, Drs. Williamson and Riggs. He was under sentence of death, but was among the number against whom no direct evidence was found, and who were finally pardoned by President Lincoln.

When he was released, and returned to the new reservation upon the Missouri river, he soon became convinced that life on a government reservation meant physical and moral degradation. Therefore he determined, with several others, to try the white man's way of gaining a livelihood. They accordingly left the agency against the persuasions of the agent, renounced all government assistance, and took land under the United States Homestead law, on the Big Sioux river. After he had made his home there, he desired to seek his lost child. It was then a dangerous undertaking to cross the line, but his Christian love prompted him to do it. He secured a good guide, and found his way in time through the vast wilderness.

As for me, I little dreamed of anything unusual to happen on my return. As I approached our camp with my game on my shoulder, I had not the slightest premonition that I was suddenly to be hurled from my savage life into a life unknown to me hitherto.

When I appeared in sight my father, who had patiently listened to my uncle's long account of my early life and training, became very much excited. He was eager to embrace the child who, as he had just been informed, made it already the object of his life to avenge his father's blood. The loving father could not remain in the teepee and watch the boy coming, so he started to meet him. My uncle arose to go with his brother to insure his safety.

My face burned with the unusual excitement caused by the sight of a man wearing the Big Knives' clothing and coming toward me with my uncle.

"What does this mean, uncle?"

"My boy, this is your father, my brother, whom we mourned as dead. He has come for you."

My father added: "I am glad that my son is strong and brave. Your brothers have adopted the white man's way; I came for you to learn this new way, too; and I want you to grow up a good man."

He had brought me some civilized clothing. At first, I disliked very much to wear garments made by the people I had hated so bitterly. But the thought that, after all, they had not killed my father and brothers, reconciled me, and I put on the clothes.

In a few days we started for the States. I felt as if I were dead and traveling to the Spirit Land; for now all my old ideas were to give place to new ones, and my life was to be entirely different from that of the past.

Still, I was eager to see some of the wonderful inventions of the white people. When we reached Fort Totten, I gazed about me with lively interest and a quick imagination.

My father had forgotten to tell me that the fire-boat-walks-on-mountains had its track at Jamestown, and might appear at any moment. As I was watering the ponies, a peculiar shrilling noise pealed forth from just beyond the hills. The ponies threw back their heads and listened; then they ran snorting over the prairie. Meanwhile, I too had taken alarm. I leaped on the back of one of the ponies, and dashed off at full speed. It was a clear day; I could not imagine what had caused such an unearthly noise. It seemed as if the world were about to burst in two!

I got upon a hill as the train appeared. "O!" I said to myself, "that is the fire-boat-walks-on-mountains that I have heard about!" Then I drove back the ponies.

My father was accustomed every morning to read from his Bible, and sing a stanza of a hymn. I was about very early with my gun for several mornings; but at last he stopped me as I was preparing to go out, and bade me wait.

I listened with much astonishment. The hymn contained the word *Jesus*. I did not comprehend what this meant; and my father then told me that Jesus was the Son of God who came on earth to save sinners, and that it was because of him that he had sought me. This conversation made a deep impression upon my mind.

Late in the fall we reached the citizen settlement at Flandreau, South Dakota, where my father and some others dwelt among the whites. Here my wild life came to an end, and my school days began.

—Charles A. Eastman (1991, 279–89)

E. Pauline Johnson

Tekahionwake; Mohawk,
Canadian, 1861–1913

Pauline Johnson was born on the Six Nations Reserve
near Brantford, Ontario in 1861; she was the daughter of Mohawk leader
George Henry Martin and Emily Susanna Howells (cousin of novelist and
editor William Dean Howells). She chronicles her parents' happy cross-
cultural marriage in "My Mother," in which she also discusses her father's
courageous fight against the trafficking of alcohol on the reservation, for
which he was severely beaten by the whites more than once. Johnson was
one of the first Native women to publish short fiction; she also wrote poetry
and was one of Canada's most popular stage performers from 1892–1907.
Her career was launched by a stirring reading of "A Cry from an Indian
Wife," based on the first mixed-blood rebellion against the Canadian gov-
ernment, led by Louis Riel (1869–1870). As Bernd C. Peyer notes, "during
the 1893–1894 season alone, she gave a total of 125 recitals" (1989, 15–16).
Johnson adopted the name of her paternal great-grandfather, Jacob
Johnson, Tekahionwake or "Double Wampum" (1758–1843) as her stage
and authorial name. She also wrote prose essays on Native and regional
subjects for a number of Canadian magazines. She performed until 1909,
when she settled in Vancouver to write. She died in 1913 from breast cancer.
In 1961, the Canadian government issued a stamp commemorating the
one hundredth anniversary of her birth (Peyer 1989, 16).

Johnson's published works include two collections of poetry: The White
Wampum *(1895) and* Canadian Born *(1903); poems from these texts and*

various periodicals were published in Flint and Feather *(1912). In 1913, she published* Moccasin Maker, *a collection of stories about Canadian women, which includes "My Mother" (1909) and her most popular short story, "A Red Girl's Reasoning," first published in 1893. The* Shagganappi, *a collection of stories for boys was published in 1913.* E. Pauline Johnson, Tekahionwake: Collected Poems and Selected Prose, *edited by Carole Gerson and Veronica Strong-Boag, came out in 2002; in addition to her previously published works, it also includes personal poems, like "Heidleburgh," which have not been previously published. Johnson's writing is known for its sentimentality and powerful social commentary.*

A CRY FROM AN INDIAN WIFE

My Forest Brave, my Red-skin love, farewell;
We may not meet to-morrow; who can tell
What mighty ills befall our little band,
Or what you'll suffer from the white man's hand?
Here is your knife! I thought 'twas sheathed for aye.
No roaming bison calls for it to-day;
No hide of prairie cattle will it maim;
The plains are bare, it seeks a nobler game:
'Twill drink the life-blood of a soldier host.
Go; rise and strike, no matter what the cost.
Yet stay. Revolt not at the Union Jack,
Nor raise thy hand against this stripling pack
Of white-faced warriors, marching West to quell
Our fallen tribe that rises to rebel.
They all are young and beautiful and good;
Curse to the war that drinks their harmless blood.
Curse to the fate that brought them from the East
To be our chiefs—to make our nation least
That breathes the air of this vast continent.
Still their new rule and council is well meant.
They but forget we Indians owned the land
From ocean unto ocean; that they stand
Upon a soil that centuries agone
Was our sole kingdom and our right alone.

They never think how they would feel to-day,
If some great nation came from far away,
Wrestling their country from their hapless braves,
Giving what they gave us—but wars and graves.
Then go and strike for liberty and life,
And bring back honour to your Indian wife.
Your wife? Ah, what of that, who cares for me?
Who pities my poor love and agony?
What white-robed priest prays for your safety here,
As prayer is said for every volunteer
That swells the ranks that Canada sends out?
Who prays for vict'ry for the Indian scout?
Who prays for our poor nation lying low?
None—therefore take your tomahawk and go.
My heart may break and burn into its core,
But I am strong to bid you go to war.
Yet stay, my heart is not the only one
That grieves the loss of husband and of son;
Think of the mothers o'er the inland seas;
Think of the pale-faced maiden on her knees;
One pleads her God to guard some sweet-faced child
That marches on toward the North-West wild.
The other prays to shield her love from harm,
To strengthen his young, proud uplifted arm.
Ah, how her white face quivers thus to think,
Your tomahawk his life's best blood will drink.
She never thinks of my wild aching breast,
Nor prays for your dark face and eagle crest
Endangered by a thousand rifle balls,
My heart the target if my warrior falls.
O! coward self I hesitate no more;
Go forth, and win the glories of the war.
Go forth, nor bend to greed of white men's hands,
By right, by birth we Indians own these lands,
Though starved, crushed, plundered, lies our nation low . . .
Perhaps the white man's God has willed it so.

        —E. Pauline Johnson (2002, 14–15)

AS RED MEN DIE

Captive! Is there a hell to him like this?
A taunt more galling than the Huron's hiss?
He—proud and scornful, he—who laughed at law,
He—scion of the deadly Iroquois,
He—the bloodthirsty, he—the Mohawk chief,
He—who despises pain and sneers at grief,
Here in the hated Huron's vicious clutch,
That even captive he disdains to touch!

Captive! But never conquered; Mohawk brave
Stoops not to be to *any* man a slave;
Least, to the puny tribe his soul abhors,
The tribe whose wigwams sprinkle Simcoe's shores.
With scowling brow he stands and courage high,
Watching with haughty and defiant eye
His captors, as they council o'er his fate,
Or strive his boldness to intimidate.
Then fling they unto him the choice;

   "Wilt thou
Walk o'er the bed of fire that waits thee now—
Walk with uncovered feet upon the coals,
Until thou reach the ghostly Land of Souls,
And, with thy Mohawk death-song please our ear?
Or wilt thou with the women rest thee here?"

His eyes flash like an eagle's, and his hands
Clench at the insult. Like a god he stands.
"Prepare the fire!" he scornfully demands
He knoweth not that this same jeering band
Will bite the dust—will lick the Mohawk's hand;
Will kneel and cower at the Mohawk's feet;
Will shrink when Mohawk war drums wildly beat.

His death will be avenged with hideous hate
By Iroquois, swift to annihilate
His vile detested captors, that now flaunt

Their war clubs in his face with sneer and taunt,
Not thinking, soon that reeking, red, and raw,
Their scalps will deck the belts of Iroquois.

The path of coals outstretches, white with heat,
A forest fir's length—ready for his feet.
Unflinching as a rock he steps along
The burning mass, and sings his wild war song;
Sings, as he sang when once he used to roam
Throughout the forests of his southern home,
Where, down the Genesee, the water roars,
Where gentle Mohawk purls between its shores,
Songs, that of exploit and of prowess tell;
Songs of the Iroquois invincible.

Up the long trail of fire he boasting goes,
Dancing a war dance to defy his foes.
His flesh is scorched, his muscles burn and shrink,
But still he dances to death's awful brink.
The eagle plume that crests his haughty head
Will *never* droop until his heart be dead.
Slower and slower yet his footstep swings,
Wilder and wilder still his death-song rings,
Fiercer and fiercer through the forest bounds
His voice that leaps to Happier Hunting Grounds.
One savage yell—

      Then loyal to his race,
He bends to death—but *never* to disgrace.
      —E. Pauline Johnson (2002, 68–69)

THE SONG MY PADDLE SINGS

West wind, blow from your prairie nest,
Blow from the mountains, blow from the west.
The sail is idle, the sailor too;
O! wind of the west, we wait for you.
Blow, blow!

I have wooed you so,
But never a favour you bestow.
You rock your cradle the hills between,
But scorn to notice my white lateen.

I stow the sail, unship the mast:
I wooed you long but my wooing's past;
My paddle will lull you into rest.
O! drowsy wind of the drowsy west,
Sleep, sleep,
By your mountain steep,
Or down where the prairie grasses sweep!
Now fold in slumber your laggard wings,
For soft is the song my paddle sings.

August is laughing across the sky,
Laughing while paddle, canoe and I,
Drift, drift,
Where the hills uplift
On either side of the current swift.

The river rolls in its rocky bed;
My paddle is plying its way ahead;
Dip, dip,
While the waters flip
In foam as over their breast we slip.

And oh, the river runs swifter now;
The eddies circle about my bow.
Swirl, swirl!
How the ripples curl
In many a dangerous pool awhirl!

And forward far the rapids roar,
Fretting their margin for evermore.
Dash, dash,
With a mighty crash,
They seethe, and boil, and bound, and splash.

Be strong, O paddle! be brave, canoe!
The reckless waves you must plunge into.
Reel, reel,
On your trembling keel,
But never a fear my craft will feel.

We've raced the rapid, we're far ahead!
The river slips through its silent bed.
Sway, sway,
As the bubbles spray
And fall in tinkling tunes away.

And up on the hills against the sky,
A fir tree rocking its lullaby,
Swings, swings,
Its emerald wings,
Swelling the song that my paddle sings.
                —E. Pauline Johnson (2002, 81–83)

PENSEROSO

Soulless is all humanity to me
To-night. My keenest longing is to be
Alone, alone with God's grey earth that seems
Pulse of my pulse and consort of my dreams.

To-night my soul desires no fellowship,
Or fellow-being; crave I but to slip
Through space on space, till flesh no more can bind,
And I may quit for aye my fellow kind.

Let me but feel athwart my cheek the lash
Of whipping wind, but hear the torrent dash
Adown the mountain steep, 'twere more my choice
Than touch of human hand, than human voice.

Let me but wander on the shore night-stilled,

Drinking its darkness till my soul is filled;
The breathing of the salt sea on my hair,
My outstretched hands but grasping empty air.

Let me but feel the pulse of Nature's soul
Athrob on mine, let seas and thunders roll
O'er night and me; sands whirl; winds, waters beat;
For God's grey earth has no cheap counterfeit.
                  —E. Pauline Johnson (2002, 84–85)

OJISTOH

I am Ojistoh, I am she, the wife
Of him whose name breathes bravery and life
And courage to the tribe that calls him chief.
I am Ojistoh, his white star, and he
Is land, and lake, and sky—and soul to me.

Ah! But they hated him, those Huron braves,
Him who had flung their warriors into graves,
Him who had crushed them underneath his heel,
Whose arm was iron, and whose heart was steel
To all—save me, Ojistoh, chosen wife
Of my great Mohawk, white star of his life.

Ah! but they hated him, and councilled long
With subtle witchcraft how to work him wrong;
How to avenge their dead, and strike him where
His pride was highest, and his fame most fair.
Their hearts grew weak as women at his name:
They dared no war-path since my Mohawk came
With ashen bow, and flinten arrow-head
To pierce their craven bodies; but their dead
Must be avenged. Avenged? They dared not walk
In day and meet his deadly tomahawk;
They dared not face his fearless scalping knife;
So—Niyoh![1]—then they thought of me, his wife.

O! evil, evil face of them they sent
With evil Huron speech: "Would I consent
To take of wealth? be queen of all their tribe?
Have wampum, ermine?" Back I flung the bribe
Into their teeth, and said, "While I have life
Know this—Ojistoh is the Mohawk's wife."

Wah! how we struggled! But their arms were strong.
They flung me on their pony's back, with thong
Round ankle, wrist, and shoulder. Then upleapt
The one I hated most: his eye he swept
Over my misery, and sneering said,
"Thus, fair Ojistoh, we avenge our dead."

And we rode, rode as a sea wind-chased,
I, bound with buckskin to his hated waist,
He, sneering, laughing, jeering, while he lashed
The horse to foam, as on and on we dashed.
Plunging through creek and river, bush and trail,
On, on we galloped like a northern gale.
At last, his distant Huron fires aflame
We saw, and nearer, nearer still we came.

I, bound behind him in the captive's place,
Scarcely could see the outline of his face.
I smiled, and laid my cheek against his back:
"Loose thou my hands," I said. "This pace let slack.
Forget we now that thou and I are foes.
I like thee well, and wish to clasp thee close;
I like the courage of thine eye and brow;
I like thee better than my Mohawk now."

He cut the cords; we ceased our maddened haste
I wound my arms about his tawny waist;
My hand crept up the buckskin of his belt;
His knife hilt in my burning palm I felt;
One hand caressed his cheek, the other drew
The weapon softly—"I love you, love you,"

I whispered, "I love you as my life."
And—buried in his back his scalping knife.

Ha! how I rode, rode as a sea wind-chased,
Mad with sudden freedom, mad with haste,
Back to my Mohawk and my home. I lashed
That horse to foam, as on and on I dashed.
Plunging through creek and river, bush and trail,
On, on I galloped like a northern gale.
And then my distant Mohawk's fires aflame
I saw, as nearer, nearer still I came,
My hands all wet, stained with a life's red dye,
But pure my soul, pure as those stars on high—
"My Mohawk's pure white star, Ojistoh, still am I."
                    —E. Pauline Johnson (2002, 114–16)

> *Notes for "Ojistoh"*
> 1. God, in the Mohawk language [Johnson's note].

THE SONGSTER

Music, music with throb and swing,
        Of a plaintive note, and long;
'Tis a note no human throat could sing,
No harp with its dulcet golden string,—
Nor lute, nor lyre with liquid ring,
        Is sweet as the robin's song.

He sings for love of the season
        When the days grow warm and long,
For the beautiful God-sent reason
        That his breast was born for song.

Calling, calling so fresh and clear,
        Through the song-sweet days of May;
Warbling there, and whistling here,
He swells his voice on the drinking ear,

On the great, wide, pulsing atmosphere
    Till his music drowns the day.

He sings for love of the season
    When the days grow warm and long,
For the beautiful God-sent reason
    That his breast was born for song.
        —E. Pauline Johnson (2002, 118–19)

THE CORN HUSKER

Hard by the Indian lodges, where the bush
    Breaks in a clearing, through ill-fashioned fields,
She comes to labour, when the first still hush
    Of autumn follows large and recent yields.

Age in her fingers, hunger in her face,
    Her shoulders stooped with weight of work and years,
But rich in tawny colouring of her race,
    She comes a-field to strip the purple ears.

And all her thoughts are with the days gone by,
    Ere might's injustice banished from their lands
Her people, that to-day unheeded lie,
    Like the dead husks that rustle through her hands.
        —E. Pauline Johnson (2002, 121)

THE QUILL WORKER

Plains, plains, and the prairie land which the sunlight floods and fills,
To the north the open country, southward the Cypress Hills;
Never a bit of woodland, never a rill that flows,
Only a stretch of cactus beds, and the wild, sweet prairie rose;
Never a habitation, save where in the far south-west
A solitary tepee lifts its solitary crest,
Where Neykia in the doorway, crouched in the red sunshine,
Broiders her buckskin mantle with the quills of the porcupine.

Neykia, the Sioux chief's daughter, she with the foot that flies,
She with the hair of midnight and the wondrous midnight eyes,
She with the deft brown fingers, she with the soft, slow smile,
She with the voice of velvet and the thoughts that dream the while—
"Whence come the vague to-morrows? Where do the yesters fly?
What is beyond the border of the prairie and the sky?
Does the maid in the Land of Morning sit in the red sunshine,
Broidering her buckskin mantle with the quills of the porcupine?"

So Neykia, in the westland, wonders and works away,
Far from the fret and folly of the "Land of Waking Day."
And many the pale-faced trader who stops at the tepee door
For a smile from the sweet, shy worker, and a sigh when the hour is o'er.
For they know of a young red hunter who oftentimes has stayed
To rest and smoke with her father, though his eyes were on the maid;
And the moons will not be many ere she in the red sunshine
Will broider his buckskin mantle with the quills of the porcupine.
                    —E. Pauline Johnson (2002, 122–23)

RONDEAU: MORROW-LAND

In Morrow-Land there lies a day
In shadows clad, in garments grey
When sunless hours will come, My Dear,
And skies will lose their lustre clear
Because I shall be leagues away.

Has Fate no other—kindlier way?
No gentler hands on me to lay,
Than I to go—than you stay here
In Morrow-Land?

And O! These days will be so dear—
Throughout the cold and coming year,
This Passion Week of gold and grey
Will haunt my heart and bless my way
In Morrow-Land.
                    —E. Pauline Johnson (2002, 134)

TO C.H.W.

I

In Heidelberg, where you were born
The sunshine must be fine and rare
To leave such warmth within your heart
Such warmth of yellow in your hair,
To touch your thought and soul with that
Which neither suns nor stars impart,
That strange, exquisite gift of God,
That fine and fairy thing called art.
Did Fate decree your art and mine
Should weave into a future skein
When you were born in Heidelberg
And I was born in Vain?

II

In Heidelberg where you were born
The day dawn must wear strange disguise
Now, it has left its wealth of grey
And melting shadows in your eyes
From whose deep sombre beauty all
Your soul God-given speaks the clear
Unblemished strength of all your art
And writes that soul, a soul sincere.
Did Fate decree your promise hour
Meet mine of storm and stress and rain
When you were born in Heidelberg
And I was born in Vain?

   —E. Pauline Johnson (2002, 135)

HEIDLEBURGH

In Heidleburgh, where you were born,
The day dawn must wear strange disguise;
Since it has left is [its] wealth of grey and melting shadows
In your eyes.
Did Fate decree your art and mine
Should weave into a future skein,

When you were born in Heidleburgh
And I was born in vain?

In Heidleburgh, where you were born,
The sunshine must be fine and rare
To leave its wealth of golden sunshine
In your hair.
Did Fate decree your promise hour
Greet mine of storm and stress and rain,
When you were born in Heidleburgh
And I was born in vain?

—E. Pauline Johnson (2002, 135–36)

A Red Girl's Reasoning (1893)

"Be pretty good to her, Charlie, my boy, or she'll balk sure as shooting."

That was what old Jimmy Robinson said to his brand new son-in-law, while they waited for the bride to reappear.

"Oh! you bet, there's no danger of much else. I'll be good to her, help me Heaven," replied Charlie McDonald, brightly.

"Yes, of course you will," answered the old man, "but don't you forget, there's a good big bit of her mother in her, and," closing his left eye significantly, "you don't understand these Indians as I do."

"But I'm just as fond of them, Mr. Robinson," Charlie said assertively, "and I get on with them too, now, don't I?"

"Yes, pretty well for a town boy; but when you have lived forty years among these people, as I have done; when you have had your wife as long as I have had mine—for there's no getting over it, Christine's disposition is as native as her mother's, every bit—and perhaps when you've owned for eighteen years a daughter as dutiful, as loving, as fearless, and, alas! as obstinate as that little piece you are stealing away from me to-day—I tell you, youngster, you'll know more than you know now. It is kindness for kindness, bullet for bullet, blood for blood. Remember, what you are, she will be," and the old Hudson Bay trader scrutinized Charlie McDonald's face like a detective.

It was a happy, fair face, good to look at, with a certain ripple of dimples somewhere about the mouth, and eyes that laughed out the very sunniness of their owner's soul. There was not a severe nor yet a weak line anywhere. He was a well-meaning young fellow, happily dispositioned, and a great favourite with the tribe at Robinson's Post, whither he had gone in the service of the Department of Agriculture, to assist the local agent through the tedium of a long census-taking.

As a boy he had had the Indian relic-hunting craze, as a youth he had studied Indian archaeology and folk-lore, as a man he consummated his predilections for Indianology by loving, winning and marrying the quiet little daughter of the English trader, who himself had married a native woman twenty years ago. The country was all backwoods, and the Post miles and miles from even the semblance of civilization, and the lonely young Englishman's heart had gone out to the girl who, apart from speaking a very few words of English, was utterly uncivilized and uncultured, but had withal that marvellously innate refinement so universally possessed by the higher tribes of North American Indians.

Like all her race, observant, intuitive, having a horror of ridicule, consequently quick at acquirement and teachable in mental and social habits, she had developed from absolute pagan indifference into a sweet, elderly Christian woman, whose broken English, quiet manner, and still handsome copper-coloured face, were the joy of old Robinson's declining years.

He had given their daughter Christine all the advantages of his own learning—which, if truthfully told, was not universal; but the girl had a fair common education, and the native adaptability to progress.

She belonged to neither and still to both types of the cultured Indian. The solemn, silent, almost heavy manner of the one so commingled with the gesticulating Frenchiness and vivacity of the other, that one unfamiliar with native Canadian life would find it difficult to determine her nationality.

She looked very pretty to Charles McDonald's loving eyes, as she reappeared in the doorway, holding her mother's hand and saying some happy words of farewell. Personally she looked much the same as her sisters, all Canada through, who are the offspring of red and white parentage—olive-complexioned, grey-eyed, black-haired, with figure slight and delicate, and the wistful, unfathomable expression in her whole face that turns one so heart-sick as they glance at the young Indians of to-day—it is the forerunner too frequently of "the white man's disease," consumption—but McDonald was pathetically in love, and thought her the most beautiful woman he had ever seen in his life.

There had not been much of a wedding ceremony. The priest had can-tered through the service in Latin, pronounced the benediction in English, and congratulated the "happy couple" in Indian, as a compliment to the assembled tribe in the little amateur structure that did service at the post as a sanctuary.

But the knot was tied as firmly and indissolubly as if all Charlie McDonald's swell city friends had crushed themselves up against the chan-cel to congratulate him, and in his heart he was deeply thankful to escape the flower-pelting, white gloves, rice-throwing, and ponderous stupidity of a breakfast, and indeed all the regulation gimcracks of the usual marriage celebrations, and it was with a hand trembling with absolute happiness that he assisted his little Indian wife into the old muddy buckboard that, hitched to an underbred-looking pony, was to convey them over the first stages of their journey. Then came more adieus, some hand-clasping, old Jimmy Robinson looking very serious just at the last, Mrs. Jimmy, stout, stolid, betraying nothing of visible emotion, and then the pony, roughshod and shaggy, trudged on, while mutual hand-waves were kept up until the old Hudson's Bay Post dropped out of sight, and the buckboard with its light-some load of hearts, deliriously happy, jogged on over the uneven trail.

She was "all the rage" that winter at the provincial capital. The men called her a "deuced fine little woman." The ladies said she was "just the sweetest wildflower." Whereas she was really but an ordinary, pale, dark girl who spoke slowly and with a strong accent, who danced fairly well, sang acceptably, and never stirred outside the door without her husband.

Charlie was proud of her; he was proud that she had "taken" so well among his friends, proud that she bore herself so complacently in the drawing-rooms of the wives of pompous Government officials, but doubly proud of her almost abject devotion to him. If ever human being was worshipped, that being was Charlie McDonald; it could scarcely have been otherwise, for the almost godlike strength of his passion for that little wife of his would have mastered and melted a far more invin-cible citadel than an already affectionate woman's heart.

Favourites socially, McDonald and his wife went everywhere. In fash-ionable circles she was "new"—a potent charm to acquire popularity, and the little velvet-clad figure was always the centre of interest among all the women in the room. She always dressed in velvet. No woman in Canada, has she but the faintest dash of native blood in her veins, but loves velvets and silks. As beef to the Englishman, wine to the Frenchman, fads to the

Yankee, so are velvet and silk to the Indian girl, be she wild as prairie grass, be she on the borders of civilization, or, having stepped within its boundary, mounted the steps of culture even under its superficial heights.

"Such a dolling little appil blossom," said the wife of a local M.P., who brushed up her etiquette and English once a year at Ottawa. "Does she always laugh so sweetly, and gobble you up with those great big grey eyes of hers, when you are togetheah at home, Mr. McDonald? If so, I should think youah pooah brothah would feel himself terribly *de trop.*"

He laughed lightly. "Yes, Mrs. Stuart, there are not two of Christie; she is the same at home and abroad, and as for Joe, he doesn't mind us a bit; he's no end fond of her."

"I'm very glad he is. I always fancied he did not care for her, d'you know."

If ever a blunt woman existed it was Mrs. Stuart. She really meant nothing, but her remark bothered Charlie. He was fond of his brother, and jealous for Christie's popularity. So that night when he and Joe were having a pipe he said: "I've never asked you yet what you thought of her, Joe." A brief pause, then Joe spoke. "I'm glad she loves you."

"Why?"

"Because that girl has but two possibilities regarding humanity— love or hate."

"Humph! Does she love or hate *you*?"

"Ask her."

"You talk bosh. If she hated you, you'd get out. If she loved you I'd *make* you get out."

Joe McDonald whistled a little, then laughed. "Now that we are on the subject, I might as well ask—honestly, old man, wouldn't you and Christie prefer keeping house alone to having me always around?"

"Nonsense, sheer nonsense. Why, thunder, man, Christie's no end fond of you, and as for me—you surely don't want assurances from me?"

"No, but I often think a young couple—"

"Young couple be blowed! After a while when they want you and your old surveying chains, and spindle-legged tripod telescope kickshaws, farther west, I venture to say the little woman will cry her eyes out—won't you, Christie?" This last in a higher tone, as through clouds of tobacco smoke he caught sight of his wife passing the doorway.

She entered. "Oh, no, I would not cry; I never do cry, but I would be heart-sore to lose you, Joe, and apart from that"—a little wickedly—"you may come in handy for an exchange some day, as Charlie does always say when he hoards up duplicate relics."

"Are Charlie and I duplicates?"

"Well—not exactly"—her head a little to one side, and eyeing them both merrily, while she slipped softly on to the arm of her husband's chair—"but, in the event of Charlie's failing me"—everyone laughed then. The "some day" that she spoke of was nearer than they thought. It came about in this wise.

There was a dance at the Lieutenant-Governor's, and the world and his wife were there. The nobs were in great feather that night, particularly the women, who flaunted about in new gowns and much splendour. Christie McDonald had a new gown also, but wore it with the utmost unconcern, and if she heard any of the flattering remarks made about her she at least appeared to disregard them.

"I never dreamed you could wear blue so splendidly," said Captain Logan, as they sat out a dance together.

"Indeed she can, though," interposed Mrs. Stuart, halting in one of her gracious sweeps down the room with her husband's private secretary.

"Don't shout so, captain. I can hear every sentence you uttah—of course Mrs. McDonald can wear blue—she has a morning gown of cadet blue that she is a picture in."

"You are both very kind," said Christie. "I like blue; it is the color of the Hudson's Bay posts, and the factor's residence is always decorated in blue."

"Is it really? How interesting—do tell us some more of your old home, Mrs. McDonald; you so seldom speak of your life at the post, and we fellows so often wish to hear of it all," said Logan eagerly.

"Why do you not ask me of it, then?"

"Well—er, I'm sure I don't know; I'm fully interested in the Ind—in your people—your mother's people, I mean, but it always seems so personal, I suppose; and—a—a—"

"Perhaps you are, like all other white people, afraid to mention my nationality to me."

The captain winced, and Mrs. Stuart laughed uneasily. Joe McDonald was not far off, and he was listening, and chuckling, and saying to himself, "That's you, Christie, lay 'em out; it won't hurt 'em to know how they appear once in a while."

"Well, Captain Logan," she was saying, "what is it you would like to hear—of my people, or my parents, or myself?"

"All, all, my dear," cried Mrs. Stuart clamorously. "I'll speak for him—tell us of yourself and your mother—your father is delightful, I am sure—but then he is only an ordinary Englishman, not half as interesting as a foreigner, or—or, perhaps I should say, a native."

Christie laughed. "Yes," she said, "my father often teases my mother now about how very native she was when he married her; then, how could she have been otherwise? She did not know a word of English, and there was not another English-speaking person besides my father and his two companions within sixty miles."

"Two companions, eh? one a Catholic priest and the other a wine merchant, I suppose, and with your father in the Hudson's Bay, they were good representatives of the pioneers in the New World," remarked Logan, waggishly.

"Oh, no, they were all Hudson's Bay men. There were no rumsellers and no missionaries in that part of the country then."

Mrs. Stuart looked puzzled. "No *missionaries*?" she repeated with an odd intonation.

Christie's insight was quick. There was a peculiar expression of interrogation in the eyes of her listeners, and the girl's blood leapt angrily up into her temples as she said hurriedly, "I know what you mean; I know what you are thinking. You are wondering how my parents were married—"

"Well-er, my dear, it seems peculiar—if there was no priest, and no magistrate, why—a—" Mrs. Stuart paused awkwardly.

"The marriage was performed by Indian rites," said Christie.

"Oh, do tell me about it; is the ceremony very interesting and quaint—are your chieftains anything like Buddhist priests?" It was Logan who spoke.

"Why, no," said the girl in amazement at that gentleman's ignorance. "There is no ceremony at all, save a feast. The two people just agree to live only with and for each other, and the man takes his wife to his home, just as you do. There is no ritual to bind them; they need none; an Indian's word was his law in those days, you know."

Mrs. Stuart stepped backwards. "Ah!" was all she said. Logan removed his eye-glass and stared blankly at Christie. "And did McDonald marry you in this singular fashion?" he questioned.

"Oh, no, we were married by Father O'Leary. Why do you ask?"

"Because if he had, I'd have blown his brains out to-morrow."

Mrs. Stuart's partner, who had hitherto been silent, coughed and began to twirl his cuff stud nervously, but nobody took any notice of him. Christie had risen, slowly, ominously—risen, with the dignity and pride of an empress.

"Captain Logan," she said, "what do you dare to say to me? What do you dare to mean? Do you presume to think it would not have been lawful for Charlie to marry me according to my people's rites? Do you for one instant dare to question that my parents were not as legally—"

"Don't, dear, don't," interrupted Mrs. Stuart hurriedly; "it is bad enough now, goodness knows; don't make—" Then she broke off blindly. Christie's eyes glared at the mumbling woman, at her uneasy partner, at the horrified captain. Then they rested on the McDonald brothers, who stood within earshot, Joe's face scarlet, her husband's white as ashes, with something in his eyes she had never seen before. It was Joe who saved the situation. Stepping quickly across towards his sister-in-law, he offered her his arm, saying, "The next dance is ours, I think, Christie."

Then Logan pulled himself together, and attempted to carry Mrs. Stuart off for the waltz, but for once in her life that lady had lost her head. "It is shocking!" she said, "outrageously shocking! I wonder if they told Mr. McDonald before he married her!" Then looking hurriedly round, she too saw the young husband's face—and knew that they had not.

"Humph! deuced nice kettle of fish—poor old Charlie has always thought so much of honourable birth."

Logan thought he spoke in an undertone, but "poor old Charlie" heard him. He followed his wife and brother across the room. "Joe," he said, "will you see that a trap is called!" Then to Christie, "Joe will see that you get home all right." He wheeled on his heel then and left the ball-room.

Joe *did* see.

He tucked a poor, shivering, pallid little woman into a cab, and wound her bare throat up in the scarlet velvet cloak that was hanging uselessly over her arm. She crouched down beside him, saying, "I am so cold, Joe; I am so cold," but she did not seem to know enough to wrap herself up. Joe felt all through this long drive that nothing this side of Heaven would be so good as to die, and he was glad when the poor little voice at his elbow said, "What is he so angry at, Joe?"

"I don't know exactly, dear," he said gently, "but I think it was what you said about this Indian marriage."

"But why should I not have said it? Is there anything wrong about it?" she asked pitifully.

"Nothing, that I can see—there was no other way; but Charlie is very angry, and you must be brave and forgiving with him, Christie, dear."

"But I did never see him like that before, did you?"

"Once."

"When?"

"Oh, at college, one day, a boy tore his prayer-book in half, and threw it into the grate, just to be mean, you know. Our mother had given it to him at his confirmation."

"And did he look so?"

"About, but it all blew over in a day—Charlie's tempers are short and brisk. Just don't take any notice of him; run off to bed, and he'll have forgotten it by the morning."

They reached home at last. Christie said goodnight quietly, going directly to her room. Joe went to his room also, filled a pipe and smoked for an hour. Across the passage he could hear her slippered feet pacing up and down, up and down the length of her apartment. There was something panther-like in those restless footfalls, a meaning velvetyness that made him shiver, and again he wished he were dead—or elsewhere.

After a time the hall door opened, and someone came upstairs, along the passage, and to the little woman's room. As he entered, she turned and faced him.

"Christie," he said harshly, "do you know what you have done?"

"Yes," taking a step nearer him, her whole soul springing up into her eyes, "I have angered you, Charlie, and—"

"Angered me? You have disgraced me; and, moreover, you have disgraced yourself and both your parents."

"*Disgraced?*"

"Yes, *disgraced*; you have literally declared to the whole city that your father and mother were never married, and that you are the child of—what shall we call it—love? certainly not legality."

Across the hallway sat Joe McDonald, his blood freezing; but it leapt into every vein like fire at the awful anguish in the little voice that cried simply, "Oh! Charlie!"

"How could you do it, how could you do it, Christie, without shame either for yourself or for me, let alone your parents?"

The voice was like an angry demon's—not a trace was there in it of the yellow-haired, blue-eyed, laughing-lipped boy who had driven away so gaily to the dance five hours before.

"Shame? Why should I be ashamed of the rites of my people any more than you should be ashamed of the customs of yours—of a marriage more sacred and holy than half of your white man's mockeries?"

It was the voice of another nature in the girl—the love and the pleading were dead in it.

"Do you mean to tell me, Charlie—you who have studied my race and their laws for years—do you mean to tell me that, because there was no priest and no magistrate, my mother was not married? Do you mean to say that all my forefathers, for hundreds of years back, have been illegally born? If so, you blacken my ancestry beyond—beyond—beyond all reason."

"No, Christie, I would not be so brutal as that; but your father and mother live in more civilized times. Father O'Leary has been at the post for nearly twenty years. Why was not your father straight enough to have the ceremony performed when he *did* get the chance?"

The girl turned upon him with the face of a fury. "Do you suppose," she almost hissed, "that my mother would be married according to your *white* rites after she had been five years a wife, and I had been born in the meantime? *No*, a thousand times I say, *no*. When the priest came with his notions of Christianizing, and talked to them of re-marriage by the Church, my mother arose and said, 'Never—never—I have never had but this one husband; he has had none but me for wife, and to have you re-marry us would be to say as much to the whole world as that we had never been married before.[1] You go away; I do not ask that *your* people be re-married; talk not so to me. I *am* married, and you or the Church cannot do or undo it.'"

"Your father was a fool not to insist upon the law, and so was the priest."

"Law? My people have *no* priest, and my nation cringes not to law. Our priest is purity, and our law is honour. Priest? Was there a *priest* at the most holy marriage known to humanity—that stainless marriage whose offspring is the God you white men told my pagan mother of?"

"Christie, you are *worse* than blasphemous; such a profane remark shows how little you understand the sanctity of the Christian faith—"

"I know what I *do* understand; it is that you are hating me because I told some of the beautiful customs of my people to Mrs. Stuart and those men."

"Pooh! who cares for them? It is not them; the trouble is they won't keep their mouths shut. Logan's a cad and will toss the whole tale about at the club before to-morrow night; and as for the Stuart woman, I'd like to know how I'm going to take you to Ottawa for presentation and the opening, while she is blabbing the whole miserable scandal in every drawing-room, and I'll be pointed out as a romantic fool, and you as worse; I can't understand why your father didn't tell me before we were married; I at least might have warned you to never mention it." Something of recklessness rang up through his voice, just as the panther-likeness crept up from her footsteps and couched herself in hers. She spoke in tones quiet, soft, deadly.

"Before we were married! Oh! Charlie, would it have—made—any—difference?"

"God knows," he said, throwing himself into a chair, his blonde hair rumpled and wet. It was the only boyish thing about him now.

She walked towards him, then halted in the centre of the room. "Charlie McDonald," she said, and it was as if a stone had spoken, "look up." He raised his head, startled by her tone. There was a threat in her eyes that, had his rage been less courageous, his pride less bitterly wounded, would have cowed him.

"There was no such time as that before our marriage, for we *are not married now*. Stop," she said, outstretching her palms against him as he sprang to his feet, "I tell you we are not married. Why should I recognize the rites of your nation when you do not acknowledge the rites of mine? According to your own words, my parents should have gone through your church ceremony as well as through an Indian contract; according to my words, we should go through an Indian contract as well as through a church marriage. If their union is illegal, so is ours. If you think my father is living in dishonour with my mother, my people will think I am living in dishonour with you. How do I know when another nation will come and conquer you as you white men conquered us? And they will have another marriage rite to perform, and they will tell us another truth, that you are not my husband, that you are but disgracing and dishonouring me, that you are keeping me here, not as your wife, but as your—your *squaw*."

The terrible word had never passed her lips before, and the blood stained her face to her very temples. She snatched off her wedding ring and tossed it across the room, saying scornfully, "That thing is as empty to me as the Indian rites to you."

He caught her by the wrists; his small white teeth were locked tightly, his blue eyes blazed into hers.

"Christine, do you dare to doubt my honour towards you? *you*, whom

I should have died for; do you *dare* to think I have kept you here, not as my wife, but—"

"Oh, God! You are hurting me; you are breaking my arm," she gasped.

The door was flung open, and Joe McDonald's sinewy hands clinched like vices on his brother's shoulders.

"Charlie, you're mad, mad as the devil. Let go of her this minute."

The girl staggered backwards as the iron fingers loosed her wrists. "Oh, Joe," she cried, "I am not his wife, and he says I am born—nameless."

"Here," said Joe, shoving his brother towards the door. "Go downstairs till you can collect your senses. If ever a being acted like an infernal fool, you're the man."

The young husband looked from one to the other, dazed by his wife's insult, abandoned to a fit of ridiculously childish temper. Blind as he was with passion, he remembered long afterwards seeing them standing there, his brother's face darkened with a scowl of anger—his wife, clad in the mockery of her ball dress, her scarlet velvet cloak half covering her bare brown neck and arms, her eyes like flames of fire, her face like a piece of sculptured greystone.

Without a word he flung himself furiously from the room, and immediately afterwards they heard the heavy hall door bang behind him.

"Can I do anything for you, Christie?" asked her brother-in-law calmly.

"No, thank you—unless—I think I would like a drink of water, please."

He brought her up a goblet filled with wine; her hand did not even tremble as she took it. As for Joe, a demon arose in his soul as he noticed she kept her wrists covered.

"Do you think he will come back?" she said.

"Oh, yes, of course; he'll be all right in the morning. Now go to bed like a good little girl, and—and, I say, Christie, you can call me if you want anything; I'll be right here, you know."

"Thank you, Joe; you are kind—and good."

He returned then to his apartment. His pipe was out, but he picked up a newspaper instead, threw himself into an armchair, and in a half-hour was in the land of dreams.

When Charlie came home in the morning, after a six-mile walk into the country and back again, his foolish anger was dead and buried. Logan's "Poor old Charlie" did not ring so distinctly in his ears. Mrs. Stuart's horrified expression had faded considerably from his recollection. He thought only of that surprisingly tall, dark girl, whose eyes looked like coals, whose voice pierced him like a flint-tipped arrow. Ah, well, they would never quarrel again like that, he told himself. She loved him so, and would forgive him after he had talked quietly to her, and told her what an ass he was. She was simple-minded and awfully ignorant to pitch those old Indian laws at him in her fury, but he could not blame her. Oh, no, he could not for one moment blame her. He had been terribly severe and unreasonable, and the horrid McDonald temper had got the better of him; and he loved her so. Oh! he loved her so! She would surely feel that, and forgive him, and—He went straight to his wife's room. The blue velvet evening dress lay on the chair into which he had thrown himself when he doomed his life's happiness by those two words, "God knows." A bunch of dead daffodils and her slippers were on the floor, everything—but Christie.

He went to his brother's bedroom door.

"Joe," he called, rapping nervously thereon; "Joe, wake up; where's Christie, d'you know?"

"Good Lord, no," gasped that youth, springing out of his armchair and opening the door. As he did so a note fell from off the handle. Charlie's face blanched to his very hair while Joe read aloud, his voice weakening at every word:

> "DEAR OLD JOE,—I went into your room at daylight to
> get that picture of the Post on your bookshelves. I hope
> you do not mind, but I kissed your hair while you slept;
> it was so curly, and yellow, and soft, just like his.
> Good-bye, Joe.
> CHRISTIE."

And when Joe looked into his brother's face and saw the anguish settle in those laughing blue eyes, the despair that drove the dimples away from that almost girlish mouth; when he realized that this boy was but four-and-twenty years old, and that all his future was perhaps darkened and shadowed for ever, a great, deep sorrow arose in his heart, and he forgot all things, all but the agony that rang up through the voice of the fair, handsome lad as he staggered forward, crying, "Oh! Joe—what shall I do—what shall I do?"

🌿

It was months and months before he found her, but during all that time he had never known a hopeless moment; discouraged he often was, but despondent, never. The sunniness of his ever-boyish heart radiated with a warmth that would have flooded a much deeper gloom than that which settled within his eager young life. Suffer? ah! yes, he suffered, not with locked teeth and stony stoicism, not with the masterful self-command, the reserve, the conquered bitterness of the still-water sort of nature, that is supposed to run to such depths. He tried to be bright, and his sweet old boyish self. He would laugh sometimes in a pitiful, pathetic fashion. He took to petting dogs, looking into their large, solemn eyes with his wistful, questioning blue ones; he would kiss them, as women sometimes do, and call them "dear old fellow," in tones that had tears; and once in the course of his travels, while at a little way-station, he discovered a huge St. Bernard imprisoned by some mischance in an empty freight car; the animal was nearly dead from starvation, and it seemed to salve his own sick heart to rescue back the dog's life. Nobody claimed the big starving creature, the train hands knew nothing of its owner, and gladly handed it over to its deliverer. "Hudson," he called it, and afterwards when Joe McDonald would relate the story of his brother's life he invariably terminated it with, "And I really believe that big lumbering brute saved him." From what, he was never known to say.

But all things end, and he heard of her at last. She had never returned to the Post, as he at first thought she would, but had gone to the little town of B——, in Ontario, where she was making her living at embroidery and plain sewing.

The September sun had set redly when at last he reached the outskirts of the town, opened up the wicket gate, and walked up the weedy, unkept path leading to the cottage where she lodged.

Even through the twilight, he could see her there, leaning on the rail of the verandah—oddly enough she had about her shoulders the scarlet velvet cloak she wore when he had flung himself so madly from the room that night.

The moment the lad saw her his heart swelled with a sudden heat, burning moisture leapt into his eyes, and clogged his long, boyish lashes. He bounded up the steps—"Christie," he said, and the word scorched his lips like audible flame.

She turned to him, and for a second stood magnetized by his passionately wistful face; her peculiar greyish eyes seemed to drink the very life of his unquenchable love, though the tears that suddenly sprang into his seemed to absorb every pulse in his body through those hungry, pleading eyes of his that had, oh! so often, been blinded by her kisses when once her whole world lay in their blue depths.

"You will come back to me, Christie, my wife? My wife, you will let me love you again?"

She gave a singular little gasp, and shook her head. "Don't, oh! don't," he cried piteously. "You will come to me, dear? it is all such a bitter mistake—I did not understand. Oh! Christie, I did not understand, and you'll forgive me, and love me again, won't you—won't you?"

"No," said the girl with quick, indrawn breath.

He dashed the back of his hand across his wet eyelids. His lips were growing numb, and he bungled over the monosyllable "Why?"

"I do not like you," she answered quietly.

"God! Oh! God, what is there left?"

She did not appear to hear the heart-break in his voice; she stood like one wrapped in sombre thought; no blaze, no tear, nothing in her eyes; no hardness, no tenderness about her mouth. The wind was blowing her cloak aside, and the only visible human life in her whole body was once when he spoke the muscles of her brown arm seemed to contract.

"But, darling, you are mine—*mine*—we are husband and wife! Oh, heaven, you *must* love me, you *must* come to me again."

"You cannot *make* me come," said the icy voice, "neither church, nor law, nor even"—and the voice softened—"nor even love can make a slave of a red girl."

"Heaven forbid it," he faltered. "No, Christie, I will never claim you without your love. What reunion would that be? But oh, Christie, you are lying to me, you are lying to yourself, you are lying to heaven."

She did not move. If only he could touch her he felt as sure of her yielding as he felt sure there was a hereafter. The memory of times when he had but to lay his hand on her hair to call a most passionate response from her filled his heart with a torture that choked all words before they reached his lips; at the thought of those days he forgot she was unapproachable, forgot how forbidding were her eyes, how stony her lips. Flinging himself forward, his knee on the chair at her side, his face pressed hardly in the folds of the cloak on her shoulder, he clasped his arms about her with a boyish petulance, saying, "Christie, Christie, my little girl wife, I love you, I love you, and you are killing me."

She quivered from head to foot as his fair, wavy hair brushed her neck, his despairing face sank lower until his cheek, hot as fire, rested on the cool, olive flesh of her arm. A warm moisture oozed up through her skin, and as he felt its glow he looked up. Her teeth, white and cold, were locked over her under lip, and her eyes were as grey stones.

Not murderers alone know the agony of a death sentence.

"Is it all useless? all useless, dear?" he said, with lips starving for hers.

"All useless," she repeated. "I have no love for you now. You forfeited me and my heart months ago, when you said *those two words*."

His arms fell away from her wearily, he arose mechanically, he placed his little grey checked cap on the back of his yellow curls, the old-time laughter was dead in the blue eyes that now looked scared and haunted, the boyishness and the dimples crept away for ever from the lips that quivered like a child's; he turned from her, but she had looked once into his face as the Law Giver must have looked at the land of Canaan outspread at his feet. She watched him go down the long path and through the picket gate, she watched the big yellowish dog that had waited for him lumber up to its feet—stretch—then follow him. She was conscious of but two things, the vengeful lie in her soul, and a little space on her arm that his wet lashes had brushed.

It was hours afterwards when he reached his room. He had said nothing, done nothing—what use were words or deeds? Old Jimmy Robinson was right; she had "balked" sure enough.

What a bare, hotelish room it was! He tossed off his coat and sat for ten minutes looking blankly at the sputtering gas jet. Then his whole life, desolate as a desert, loomed up before him with appalling distinctness. Throwing himself on the floor beside his bed, with clasped hands and arms outstretched on the white counterpane, he sobbed. "Oh! God, dear God, I thought you loved me; I thought you'd let me have her again, but you must be tired of me, tired of loving me, too. I've nothing left now, nothing! it doesn't seem that I even have you to-night."

He lifted his face then, for his dog, big and clumsy and yellow, was licking at his sleeve.

—E. Pauline Johnson (2002, 188–202)

Note for "A Red Girl's Reasoning"
1. Fact [Johnson's note].

Luther Standing Bear

Ota k'te; Sioux, 1868–1939

Luther Standing Bear was part of the first generation of Native children to experience the turbulent and painful transition from the buffalo-hunting culture of the Sioux to reservation life and assimilationist policies like the boarding schools. In 1879, Richard Henry Pratt founded the first boarding school in Carlisle, Pennsylvania. Pratt's model for Native education was a military model. The children's hair was cut, they were dressed in military uniforms, and they were forbidden to speak their Native languages and indoctrinated with Christianity. Pratt's motto for the schools was "Kill the Indian, Save the Man," and his schools left Native children with a legacy of living in two worlds and belonging to neither, of losing their language and their culture, and of learning cultural shame. Luther Standing Bear was in the first class at Carlisle. In 1902, he joined Buffalo Bill's Wild West Show, which toured in the United States and Europe, and following this, in 1912, he sold his land allotment and moved to California, where he became an actor and a supporter of Native causes (Ruoff 1990, 57). In 1928, Standing Bear published My People the Sioux, *his autobiography, with the assistance of E. A. Brininstool. He published a book for children in 1931 called* My Indian Boyhood, *and he wrote about Sioux life and traditions in* Land of the Spotted Eagle *(1933).*

Going East
(from *My People the Sioux*, 1928)

We had spent our summer in playing games, and now it was the fall of the year 1879. My father had his store well stocked, and we were getting along splendidly. It was about the latter part of September, and the days were nice and cool—just the time to play hard and not feel too warm.

A little boy named Waniyetula, or Winter, and I were playing between my father's store, and the agency. He was a distant cousin of mine, but we always called each other "brother." The agency was perhaps a quarter of a mile from our tipi.

Suddenly we observed a great many people gathered around one of the agency buildings, and our curiosity was at once aroused. I said, "Let us go over and see what they are looking at." So we ran as fast as we could. Reaching the building, we looked in through one of the windows and saw that the room was filled with people. Among them were several white men and we noticed one white woman.

When they saw us peeping in at the window, they motioned for us to come inside. But we hesitated. Then they held out some sticks of candy. At this, we ran away some little distance, where we stopped to talk over this strange proceeding. We wondered whether we had better go back again to see what the white people really wanted. They had offered us candy—and that was a big temptation. So we went back and peeped in at the window again. This time the interpreter came to the door and coaxed us inside. He was a half-breed named Charles Tackett. We called him Ikuhansuka, or Long Chin. We came inside very slowly, a step at a time, all the time wondering what it meant.

There we saw two Indian boys dressed in white men's clothes. They had been educated somewhere. They were both Santee Sioux, from the Mud or Missouri River. With their new clothes on they looked like white men.

Then the interpreter told us if we would go East with these white people and learn the ways of the white man, we could be all dressed up, as these Indian boys then were. He told us the white man, whose name was Captain R. H. Pratt, had asked him to tell us this.

However, all this "sweet talk" from the interpreter did not create much impression on me. We had heard this same sort of "sweet talk" many times before, especially when these interpreters were paid by the Government for talking.

My mind was working in an entirely different channel. I was thinking of my father, and how he had many times said to me, "Son, be brave! Die on the battle-field if necessary away from home. It is better to die young than to get old and sick and then die." When I thought of my father, and how he had smoked the pipe of peace, and was not fighting any more, it occurred to me that this chance to go East would prove that I was brave if I were to accept it.

At that time we did not trust the white people very strongly. But the thought of going away with what was to us an enemy, to a place we knew nothing about, just suited me. So I said, "Yes, I will go." Then they said I must bring my father to the agency first, as they wanted to talk the matter over with him.

In the excitement of talking to these white people, we had forgotten all about the promised candy, so we did not get any. I ran home, and when I entered, my people were all eating. My father was sitting between his two wives, and all the five children were there. So I sat down with the others and started telling my father about the white people at the agency. The children listened to what I had to say. There were my sisters, Zintkaziwin and Wanbli Koyakewin, my two brothers, Wopotapi and Nape Sni, and my little sister, Tawahukezanunpawin. As I talked, I ate but little. I was so anxious to get back to the agency again.

After the meal, my father and I went back where the white people were. They were very nice to him, and shook hands. Then they told him, through the interpreter, about the proposed trip East. Father listened to all they had to say, then he turned to me and asked, "Do you want to go, son?" I replied, "Yes."

I do not remember whether I was the first boy to sign up, but they wrote my name in a big book. At that time I was entered as "Ota Kte, or Plenty Kill, son of Standing Bear." After my name was in the book all the white people shook hands with me and said something in the white man's language which I did not understand.

Then my father and I came away together and started for home. He never spoke a word all the way. Perhaps he felt sad. Possibly he thought if I went away with these white people he might never see me again, or else I might forget my own people. It may be he thought I would become educated and betray them; but if he felt any of these fears, he showed no sign of it.

The next day my father invited all the people who lived near by to come to his place. He got all the goods down off the shelves in his store and carried them outside. Then he brought in about seven head of ponies. When all the people were gathered there, he gave away all these things because I was going away East. I was going with the white people, and perhaps might never return; so he was sacrificing all his worldly possessions. Some of the other chiefs also gave away many things.

The day following, the agent told the Indians he had some Government teams ready to take all the children who were going away. My father said he would much rather take me himself as far as possible. Then my sister Zintkaziwin gave herself up to go with me, doing this as an honour.

My father had a light spring wagon, and they loaded this up with a small tipi, some bedding, cooking utensils, and whatever might be needed on the trip. We were to drive to the place where a steamboat was to carry us part of the way. When we were ready to start, I looked over to the spot where my ponies were grazing. How happy they were—and I was leaving them, perhaps never to return! My heart went out to the little animals as I stood there looking at them.

Then I asked my father if I might ride one of the saddle-ponies from Rosebud Agency to Black Pole, a distance of fifty miles, where we were to board the steamboat. He gave me permission, although I knew at the end of the journey my pony and I would have to part for many a long, lonesome day.

About halfway to Black Pole we camped for the night. At this point we met many other Indian boys and girls who were also going East with the white people. Some rode in Government wagons; others came on their ponies as I had done. Many drove their own wagons.

Early the next morning we were all on the road again, my sister riding in the wagon with her mother and father. We were now making the last lap of our journey from the reservation to the steamboat, and it would be only a short time that my pony and I would be together. We did not know where we were going, only that it "was east somewhere."

At last we reached Black Pole. Our tipis were pitched again, as we had to wait the arrival of the boat. However, none of us were in a hurry. Here we had such a good time! We ran, shouted, and played, trying hard to crowd in all the fun possible before we were separated from our people. We waited three days, and then were told that the boat would arrive the following day.

But at this point my sister suddenly experienced a change of heart. She concluded that she did not want any white man's education. However, that really suited me very well, because I figured that she would have been a lot of extra trouble for me. I knew that I could take care of myself all right, but if she were along and anything happened to her, I would be expected, of course, to look out for her, as she was younger than I—and a girl, at that!

Finally the boat arrived. They put a little bridge way out to the shore. It was now just about sundown. Then the Indian boys and girls who were going away were lined up, and as their names were called they went on board the boat. Even at this point some of the children refused to go aboard, and nobody could compel them to. So my sister was not the only one who had "cold feet," as the white people say.

When my name was called, I went right on the boat without any hesitation. By the time all the children were aboard, it was getting quite dark. So they pulled in the little bridge, while the parents of the children stood lined up on the shore and began crying. Then all the children on the boat also started to cry. It was a very sad scene. I did not see my father or stepmother cry, so I did not shed any tears. I just stood over in a corner of the room we were in and watched the others all crying as if their hearts would break. And mind you, some of them were quite young men and women.

Bedtime at length came, but I did not see any nice bed to sleep in that night. We were scattered all over that big room, the boys on one side and the girls on the other. We rolled up in our blankets and tried to go to sleep; but riding in a steamboat with a paddle-wheel at the back which made lots of noise was an experience we were not used to, and it kept us awake.

Along in the night, when we were all supposed to be asleep, I overheard some big boys talking quietly. They were going to get ready to jump off the boat. When I got the drift of their conversation, I jumped up and saw three big boys going down the stairway. The boat appeared not to be moving, so I followed after the three boys to the floor below. There I saw a lot of men bringing cordwood onto the boat. The three boys were standing at the edge of the boat waiting for a chance to jump off and take to the woods.

I remained back at the foot of the stairway watching to see what they would do. Then the larger of the boys said to the others: "Let us not try it this time. I understand they are going to put us off the boat to-morrow anyway, and if they do, we will have a good chance then." So they started back to their blankets on the floor and I got into mine. But I could not get to sleep, because I was wondering where we were going and what was to be done with us after we arrived.

It did not occur to me at that time that I was going away to learn the ways of the white man. My idea was that I was leaving the reservation and going to stay away long enough to do some brave deed, and then come home again alive. If I could just do that, then I knew my father would be so proud of me.

About noon the next day, the interpreter came around and told us we must get ready to leave the boat. Finally it stopped close to the shore and they put out the little bridge and we all got off. We walked quite a distance until we came to a long row of little houses standing on long pieces of iron which stretched away as far as we could see. The little houses were all in line, and the interpreter told us to get inside. So we climbed up a little stairway into one of the houses, and found ourselves in a beautiful room, long but narrow, in which were many cushioned seats.

I took one of these seats, but presently changed to another. I must have changed my seat four or five times before I quieted down. We admired the beautiful room and the soft seats very much. While we were discussing the situation, suddenly the whole house started to move away with us. We boys were in one house and the girls in another. I was glad my sister was not there. We expected every minute that the house would tip over, and that something terrible would happen. We held our blankets between our teeth, because our hands were both busy hanging to the seats, so frightened were we.

We were in our first railway train, but we did not know it. We thought it was a house. I sat next to the window, and observed the poles that were stuck up alongside the iron track. It seemed to me that the poles almost hit the windows, so I changed my seat to the other side.

We rode in this manner for some distance. Finally the interpreter came into the room and told us to get ready to leave it, as we were going to have something to eat. Those who carried bundles were told to leave them in their seats. Some of the older boys began fixing feathers in their hair and putting more paint on their faces.

When the train stopped at the station there was a great crowd of white people there. It was but three years after the killing of Custer by the Sioux, so the white people were anxious to see some Sioux Indians. I suppose many of these people expected to see us coming with scalping-knives between our teeth, bows and arrows in one hand and tomahawk in the other, and to hear a great war-cry as we came off that Iron Horse. The Sioux name for railroad was Maza Canku, or Iron Road. The term "Iron Horse" is merely a white man's name for a moving-picture play.

The place where we stopped was called Sioux City. The white people were yelling at us and making a great noise. When the train stopped, we raised the windows to look out. Soon they started to throw money at us. We little fellows began to gather up the money, but the larger boys told us not to take it, but to throw it back at them. They told us if we took the money the white people would put our names in a big book. We did not have sense enough then to understand that those white people had no way of discovering what our names were. However, we threw the money all back at them. At this, the white people laughed and threw more money at us. Then the big boys told us to close the windows. That stopped the money-throwing.

The interpreter then came in and told us we were to get off here. As we left the little house, we saw that there were lots of what we took to be soldiers lined up on both sides of the street. I expect these were policemen, but as they had on uniforms of some sort, we called them soldiers. They formed up in a line and we marched between them to the eating-place.

Many of the little Indian boys and girls were afraid of the white people. I really did not blame them, because the whites acted so wild at seeing us. They tried to give the war-whoop and mimic the Indian and in other ways got us all wrought up and excited, and we did not like this sort of treatment.

When we got inside the restaurant, there were two long tables with white covers on. There was plenty of fine silverware and all kinds of good food. We all sat down around the table, but we did not try to eat. We just helped ourselves to all the food, scooping it into our blankets, and not missing all the lump sugar. The white people were all crowded up close to the windows on the outside, watching us and laughing their heads off at the way we acted. They were waiting to see how we ate, but we fooled them, for we carried everything back to the iron road, and inside the little houses we sat down in peace and enjoyed our meal.

Then the train started up again, and we traveled all that night. The next day we reached Sotoju Otun Wake, which, translated into Sioux, means "smoky city" or your great city of Chicago. Here we saw so many people and such big houses that we began to open our eyes in astonishment. The big boys said, "The white people are like ants; they are all over—everywhere." We Indians do not call the Caucasian race "white people," but "Wasicun" or "Mila Hanska." This latter means "long knife."

At Chicago we waited a long time. Pretty soon they brought us in all kinds of food. They did not try to feed us at a table again. After the meal was finished, the interpreter told us we were going to have a little dance and enjoy ourselves. We had no tom-tom with us, so they brought a big bass drum from some place. We were in a big room—possibly it was the waiting-room of the station but there were no seats in it. Here the big boys had a good time, and we little fellows looked out the windows and watched the wagons going by. A few white people were allowed to come inside and watch the dance, while there was a great crowd outside.

In the evening we were all loaded on to another iron road, traveling all night, the next day and then another night came. By this time we were all beginning to feel very restless. We had been sitting up all the way from Dakota in those straight seats and were getting very tired. The big boys began to tell us little fellows that the white people were taking us to the place where the sun rises, where they would dump us over the edge of the earth, as we had been taught that the earth was flat, with four corners, and when we came to the edge, we would fall over.

Now the full moon was rising, and we were traveling toward it. The big boys were singing brave songs, expecting to be killed any minute. We all looked at the moon, and it was in front of us, but we felt that we were getting too close to it for comfort. We were very tired, and the little fellows dozed off. Presently the big boys woke everybody. They said they had made a discovery. We were told to look out the window and see what had happened while we were dozing. We did so, and the moon was now behind us! Apparently we had passed the place where the moon rose!

This was quite a mystery. The big boys were now singing brave songs again, while I was wide awake and watchful, waiting to see what was going to happen. But nothing happened.

We afterward learned that at Harrisburg, Pennsylvania, the train turned due west to Carlisle, which placed the moon in our rear. And to think we had expected to be killed because we had passed the moon.

—Luther Standing Bear (1975, 123–32)

Alexander Lawrence Posey

Creek, 1873–1908

Although Alexander Posey's promise as a writer, educator, and spokesman for the Creek Nation of Oklahoma was tragically cut short by his accidental drowning in 1908, he left his distinctive mark as a gifted humorist and satirist. As the owner and editor of a weekly newspaper The Indian Journal *in the first decade of the last century, he wrote a series of incisively funny articles from an Indian perspective on burning issues of the day in "Indian Territory"—on visits to the Creek Nation from U.S. Congressmen, on the Territory's impending attainment of statehood as Oklahoma, and so on. Posey's skill at using Creek/English dialect for humorous effect in these pieces anticipates, and surpasses in subtlety, the later writing of fellow Oklahoman Will Rogers: they have been republished as* The Fus Fixico Letters, *edited by Daniel Littlefield and James Parins (1993). Posey's early poetry is uneven and derivative, but by the time of his death, he was showing signs of real original promise.*

TULLEDEGA

My choice of all choice spots in Indian lands!
Hedged in, shut up by walls of purple hills,
That swell clear cut against our sunset sky.
As though it said, "I have no words for you;
I'm not a part of you; your ways aren't mine."
Hedged in, shut up with low log cabins built—

How snugly!—in the quaint old fashioned way;
With fields of yellow maize, so small that you
Might hide them with your palm while gazing on
Them from the hills around them, high and blue.
Hedged in, shut up with long forgotten ways,
And stories handed down from Sire to son.
Hedged in, shut up with broad Oktaha, like
A flash of glory curled among the hills!
How it sweeps away toward the morning,
Deepened here and there by the beetling
Crag, the music of its dashings mingling
With the screams of eagles whirling over,
With its splendid tribute to the ocean!
—Alexander Lawrence Posey (1910, 1969, 71)

UNTITLED

In that valley country lying east of
'Possum flat, along that clear, cool stream that
Tumbles from the Tulledegan hills, a
Little brook, into the tangled Coon Creek
Woods, and flashes out a river—in that
Land of soft blue springs that murmur all the
Year, and where the breezes, scattering fragrance
Stolen from the pine sprays on the westmost
Mountains, whisper what the mocking bird is
Saying in the sweet June fields, is where I
Picked this story up, one quiet sultry
Summer day, when Bald Hill lay aquiv'ring
'Gainst the far horizon in a dreamy haze.
—Alexander Lawrence Posey (1910, 74)

MY FANCY

Why do trees along the river
        Lean so far out o'er the tide?
Very wise men tell me why, but
        I am never satisfied;
And so I keep my fancy still,
        That trees lean out to save

The drowning from the clutches of
　　　The cold, remorseless wave.
　　　　　　　—Alexander Lawrence Posey (1910, 1969, 85)

　　MOTHER'S SONG
I hear a distant melody,
　　　And years come crowding back to me,
Thro' vistas dim of memory,
　　　As ships to haven from the sea;

Each freighted with the dreams of youth,
　　　And moor them in the restless bay
About my heart a while, and then
　　　Each sails away—so far away!

　　　　　I hear it ever;
　　　　　It ceases never;
　　　　　On land and sea
　　　　　It follows me,

So soft and low and far away,
　　　Like echoes dying in the folded hills.
I hear it there, go where I may,
　　　A cure for all the sad heart's ills.
　　　　　　　—Alexander Lawrence Posey (1910, 103)

　　WHEN LOVE IS DEAD
Who last shall kiss the lips of love, when love is
　　　dead?
Who last shall fold her hands and pillow soft
　　　her head?
Who last shall vigil keep beside her lonely bier?
I ask, and from the dark, cold height without,
　　　I hear
The mystic answer: "I, her mother, Earth,
　　　shall press
Her lips the last, in my infinite tenderness."
　　　　　　　—Alexander Lawrence Posey (1910, 1969, 112)

TO A HUMMINGBIRD

Now here, now there;
E'er poised somewhere
In sensuous air.
I only hear, I cannot see,
The matchless wings that beareth thee.
Art thou some frenzied poet's thought,
That God embodied and forgot?

     —Alexander Lawrence Posey (1910, 1969, 163)

WHEN MOLLY BLOWS THE DINNERHORN

'Tis twelve o'clock in Possum Flat;
The cabbage steams, and bacon's fat;
The bread is made of last year's corn—
When Molly blows the dinner-horn.

The shadows lengthen north and south;
The water wells up in your mouth;
You're neither sober nor forlorn,
When Molly blows the dinner-horn.

A quiet falls, the smoke curls up
Like incense from a censor cup;
It makes you glad that you were born,
When Molly blows the dinner-horn.

The cur, erstwhile stretched in a snore,
Lays stout siege to the kitchen door;
Nor will he raise it, or be gone,
When Molly blows the dinner-horn.

     —Alexander Lawrence Posey (1910, 1969, 138)

ODE TO SEQUOYAH[1]

The names of Waitie and Boudinot—
   The valiant warrior and gifted sage—
And other Cherokees, may be forgot,

But thy name shall descend to every age;
The mysteries enshrouding Cadmus' name
Cannot obscure thy claim to fame.

The people's language cannot perish—nay,
    When from the face of this great continent
Inevitable doom hath swept away
    The last memorial—the last fragment
Of tribes,—some scholar learned shall pore
Upon thy letters, seeking ancient lore.

Some bard shall lift a voice in praise of thee,
    In moving numbers tell the world how men
Scoffed thee, hissed thee, charged with lunacy!
    And who could not give 'nough honor when
At length, in spite of jeers, of want and need,
Thy genius shaped a dream into a deed.
By cloud-capped summits in the boundless west,[2]
    Or mighty river rolling to the sea,
Where'er thy footsteps led thee on that quest,
Unknown, rest thee, illustrious Cherokee!
            —Alexander Lawrence Posey (1910, 1969, 195–96)

Notes on "Ode to Sequoyah"

1. Sequoyah—The Cherokee who invented the Cherokee alphabet.

2. Sequoyah wandered away from his tribe, and died somewhere in the southwest part of the United States or in Mexico.

COYOTE

A few days more, and then
There'll be no secret glen,
Or hollow, deep and dim,
To hide or shelter him.

And on the prairie far,
Beneath the beacon star
On evening's dark'ning shore,
I'll hear him nevermore,

For where the tepee smoke
Curled up of yore, the stroke
Of hammers rings all day,
And grim Doom shouts, "Make way!"

The immemorial hush
Is broken by the rush
Of armed enemies
Unto the utmost seas.

—Alexander Lawrence Posey (1910, 1969, 201)

ON THE CAPTURE AND
IMPRISONMENT OF CRAZY SNAKE[1]

January, 1900

Down with him! chain him! bind him fast!
    Slam to the iron door and turn the key!
The one true Creek, perhaps the last
    To dare declare, "You have wronged me!"
Defiant, stoical, silent,
    Suffers imprisonment!

Such coarse black hair! such eagle eye!
    Such stately mien!—how arrow-straight!
Such will! such courage to defy
    The powerful makers of his fate!
A traitor, outlaw,—what you will,
    He is the noble red man still.

Condemn him and his kind to shame!
    I bow to him, exalt his name!

—Alexander Lawrence Posey (1910, 207)

Note for "On the Capture and Imprisonment of Crazy Snake"
1. Crazy Snake—Chitto Harjo. The leader of a band of Creeks who opposed the abolishment of their tribal rights. Several times Harjo had been imprisoned because of his defying the United States authorities [Posey's note].

From *The Fus Fixico Letters*

LETTER NO. 61

[Undated fragment, perhaps March 1906, typescript in Posey Collection, Thomas Gilcrease Institute of American History and Art]

Posey had interviewed the Creek statesman Yadeka Harjo at his home near Hickory Ground in October 1905 while annotating the tribal rolls for the Dawes Commission. One of the survivors of the removal from Alabama, Yadeka Harjo had served in the Union army during the Civil War and later in Creek tribal government as a delegate to Washington, a district judge, and a member of the House of Warriors. When he died in early 1906, Posey wanted to make his death the subject of a Fus Fixico letter. Among Posey's papers is a fragment, subtitled "Hot Gun on the Death of Yadeka Harjo." The effort, however, is rather sentimental and awkward. Eventually, Posey gave his ideas poetic expression, and he published "Hotgun on the Death of Yadeka Harjo" in January 1908. Both the prose fragment and the poem appear below.

So it was Hot Gun [*sic*] look 'way off, lonesome like, an' smoke slow an' tell Tookpafka Micco an' Wolf Warrior an' Kono Harjo, "Well, so my ol' time frien', Yadeka Harjo, was finished 'is days an' go to be a good Injin. It make me feel sorry to think about it. We been frien's long time. We come together from the Ol' Country, an 'live close neighbor to one 'nuther. He come to my house an' I go to 'is house, an' we set down an' talk till dinner time an', maybe so, stay all night. All time we cultivate big frien'ship an' small sofky patch. We didn't visit one 'nuther 'cause we had business. He didn't had nuthin' I want to get holt of 'cept good will, an' I didn't had nuthin' he like to have 'cept the same thing. So when he see me ridin' up to 'is front gate, he wasn't 'fraid he had to go on my note or vote for me for office. Same way, when I see 'im comin', I wasn't uneasy."

(Tookpafka Micco an' Wolf Warrior an' Kono Harjo pay close 'ten-tion an' think o' the ol' days when Checota was chief[1] an' Injin Territory was a huntin' groun' for the Five Tribes 'stead of a paradise for Illinois politicians.)

"So it was," Hot Gun he go on an' say, "when I was to Yadeka's house las' time, we had long talk. He tell me, 'Well, so my day's gettin' [few][2] an' the way before me's in the shadow. I couldn't see ahead far. Maybe so nex' time you come I be gone. So I want to leave some words for you to han' down.'

"I pay close 'tention an' my ol' time frien', Yadeka Harjo, he go on an' say, 'Well, so I pass through many days; maybe so I was put near hundred years ol'; I couldn't tell.[3] So what I say is ol' man talk. Long time ago He That Looks Over Us give the Injins more lan' than any other people. He put a big ocean on the east side of it an' a big ocean on the west side of it. Then he put summer on the south side an' winter on the north side. He put gold an' silver in the hills an' fishes in the streams an' game in the woods an' on the prairies. He give the Injin the bow an' arrow an' tol' 'im to be happy.'"

HOTGUN ON THE DEATH OF YADEKA HARJO[4]

"Well, so," Hotgun he say,
    "My ol'-time frien', Yadeka Harjo, he
Was died the other day,
    An' they was no ol'-timer left but me.

"Hotulk Emathla he
    Was go to be good Injun long time 'go,
An' Woxie Harjoche
    Been dead ten years or twenty, maybe so.[5]

"All had to die at las';
    I live long time, but now my days was few;
'Fore long, poke weeds and grass
    Be growin' all aroun' my grave house, too."

Wolf Warrior listen close
    An' Kono Harjo pay close 'tention, too,
Tookpafka Micco he almos'
    Let his pipe go out a time or two.
               —From Littlefield and Hunter (1993, 234–37)

Notes for "Letter No. 61"

1. Samuel Checote was chief from 1867 to 1874. See John Bartlett Meserve, "Chief Samuel Checote, with Sketches of Chiefs Locher Harjo and Ward Coachman," *Chronicles of Oklahoma* 16 (December 1938):401–3.

2. A word is missing here. See line ten of the poem. See also Minnie H. Posey, comp., *Poems of Alexander Lawrence Posey*, rev. ed. (Muskogee: OK: Hoffman Printing Co., 1969), 37.

3. A news report said that Yadeka Harjo was past ninety, feeble, blind, and much loved by his neighbors, who planted and harvested crops for him in his late years. The report said, "The old man is telling his friends that he has passed through many days and that his end is near." *Muskogee Times-Democrat*, February 21, 1906.

4. The poem first appeared in *Kansas City Star*, January 19, 1908, and was reprinted in *Indian Journal*, January 24, 1908.

5. Hotulk Emathla was second principal chief in 1895, when Posey was elected to the House of Warriors. Woxie Harjoche has not been identified.

LETTER NO. 62

[*New-State Tribune*, March 8, 1906; *Indian Journal*, March 16, 1906]

Although the Sequoyah statehood petition was introduced in the U.S. Senate, it was obvious by early 1906 that congressional sentiment favored single statehood for Oklahoma and Indian territories. What was not obvious was whether a statehood bill would pass the winter session of 1905–6, although the prospects had looked favorable at first. The Hamilton bill was reintroduced and passed in the House in early February, but bitter political wrangling ensued in the Senate over questions such as whether the admission of the territories of Arizona and New Mexico should be tied to the admission of Oklahoma Territory. By early March, no bill had passed. The tribal governments were due to expire on March 4; with statehood delayed and much tribal business still to conclude, Congress passed a resolution continuing the tribal governments. To conservative Creeks like Hotgun, the delay of statehood, though only temporary, made the future appear even more uncertain.

So it was Hotgun he set by the fire an' smoke slow an' think long time. Then he spit in the ashes an' tell Tookpafka Micco an' Wolf Warrior an' Kono Harjo, "Well, so hist'ry repeats itself, an' they was n't nuthin' new under the sun. The big progress o' modern times was only a var'ation o' ancient civilization. They was n't any difference 'tween nineteen-ought-six, A. D. an' nineteen-ought-six, B. C., only Pharoah rode in a chariot an' Roosevelt busts the bronco; an' 'stead o' the pyramids, we got the Panama canal project; an' 'stead o' Moses an' the Ten Commandments, we got Thomas Lostsome an' the Frenzied Finance; an' 'stead o' tyrants like Nero, we got philanthropists like John D. Rockyfeller; an' 'stead o' Solomon, we got Senator Smoot; an' 'stead o' the Parthenon, we got Tammany Hall; an' 'stead o' the Golden Age o' Pericles, we got the era o' the Big Stick, an' life insurance graft, an' coal strikes, an' railroad rebates, an' machine politics."

Tookpafka Micco an' Wolf Warrior an' Kono Harjo pay close 'tention.

An' Hotgun he go an' say, "Well, so but sometime they was rare exceptions an' hist'ry don't repeat itself. So, that's how come Injin Territory was left standin' after March[4] hunters was n't gettin' num'rous to save the pieces. Congress was take the extinction o' the Injin under advisement an' order Secretary Itscocked to fan the council fire till further notice. So it was the Five Civilized Tribes still had a habitation an' a name, an' Big Chief Porter an' Big Chief Lodges an' Big Chief Brown an' Big Chief Johnson an' Big Chief Makecertain was n't out of a job like Othello."

An' Tookpafka Micco he say, "Well, so then I go to lots o' trouble an' expense for nothin', gettin' ready to take up the white man's burden an' walk off with it. I tell my wife she mus' quit huntin' wild onions in the creek bottom an' gather gossip in the womens' [*sic*] literary club, an' stop poundin' sofky corn an' subscribe for the Ladies' Home Journal, an' hire a creek freedman for a coachman an' go shoppin' in a buggy with red runnin' gears an' a high seat 'stead of on a three hundred pound filly with the colt followin' 'long behin'. Then I was go before the Injin agent an' ask 'im to take off my hobbles so I could sell my land an' buy a pair o' tailor-made breeches with legs like a talkin' machine horn an' a waistcoat that look like the comic supplement o' the Sunday daily. Then I go 'mong the politicians an' help build a machine to swing the full blood vote when the time come."

An' Hotgun he say, "Well, so you better countermand your orders an' stick to your sofky patch an' die a nat'ral death with the rest o' the Injins."

         —From Littlefield and Hunter (1993, 237–40)

Note for "Letter No. 62"
4. A line was apparently omitted here.

   LETTER NO.63

[*New-State Tribune*, March 15, 1906; *Indian Journal*, March 23, 1906.]
As the statehood debate continued in Congress, the rhetoric of men such as Senator Albert J. Beveridge of Indiana heightened fears, long felt by Indian leaders, that the Indians might be left out of the political process. Conventions were held in Oklahoma to urge Congress to act, and

would-be politicians mounted telegram campaigns. Hotgun concludes that Indian Territory and Oklahoma Territory, waiting for statehood, are like Chu-fee, the rabbit, who chose sycamore balls as food and nearly starved to death waiting for them to fall. Although Posey had long ago embraced the idea of progress that would come with the new state, he now believed that prospects for the "common" Indians, as Tookpafka Micco called them, looked dimmer.

"Well, so," Hotgun he say, "if we didn't get statehood this spring, we could had poke greens an' wild onions scrambled with eggs, anyhow."

An' Tookpafka Micco he spit back in the corner o' the fireplace and say, "Well, maybe so, we have greens an' statehood both. The young hoosier statesman from the banks o' the Wabash"[1] was made a big spread-eagle talk in the senate chamber an' created a stir in the galleries an' lobby halls, an' politicans was hurryin' back from the capitol like bees swarmin' an' workin' overtime. So it didn't take a first-class prophet to prophesy 'bout statehood, an' you didn't had to put on your specs to see which way the wind was blowin' the straw."

Wolf Warrior and Kono Harjo grunt like they didn't welcome the news an' shake they heads like they thought the Injin was fall on evil days.

Then Hotgun he say, "Well, so I like to hear what kind o' spiel the young hoosier statesman from the banks o' the Wabash was give' em, anyhow."

An' Tookpafka Micco he go on an' say, "Well, so he tell 'em Oklahoma an' Injin Territory make a fine lookin' couple an' ought to had they picture taken together, so congress could have it enlarged an' hang it up on the map o' our common country. Then he go on an' warm up to the occasion an' pay a glowin' tribute to the pioneers. He say they was overcome the coyote an' exterminate the beaver an' chase all the deer out o' the country with hounds. They was replace the wild animals with domestic ones, like the thrifty razorback; they was chop down saplin's an' buil' huts; they was dig in the sod an' throw up rude abodes; they was laid the foundation o' a new state, an' give civilization a home in the backwoods. An' the women folks was had a hand in it an' did most o' the work, the Lord bless 'em! They was nurse the tow-headed kid with one arm an' made butter with the other one; they was brought in the wood an' cooked; they was make the garden an' slopped the pigs an' put something to eat on the table; they was picked the cotton an' pulled the corn an' made the childrens' [sic] clothes an' patched the old man's overalls; they was 'tended church on Sunday while the old man went to swap horses or, maybe so, set on the damp groun' in the bush playin' poker an' caught 'is death o' cold instead o' the winnin' hand. Then he go on an' tell 'em that was the kind o' people that make the new country fit to live in. He say they was all typical Americans an' Arkansawers [*sic*], an' they was 'bout a million o' 'em ready for civilization.' He say they all go to the new country with nothin' but a big start o' children. Some o' them was squatters an' boomers an' sooners an' intruders with a past,' but they was want forgiveness now an' a chance to get back in the Union."

Then Hotgun he spit over the backlog an' say, "Well, so the young hoosier statesman from the banks o' the Wabash wasn't up on facts an' ancient hist'ry. He was jus' puttin' words together to see how many he had. The Injin was the only bona fide pioneer in this country, an' the Injin squaw was the woman that furnish the magic an' help overcome the wild animals an' carry civilization into the waste places with her sofky pestle an' mortar."

An' Tookpafka Micco he smoke slow and study long time an' say, "Well, so the Lord helps 'em that help 'emselves—except the Injin."

—From Littlefield and Hunter (1993, 240–43)

Note for "Letter No. 63"
1. Senator Albert Jeremiah Beveridge (1862–1927) of Indiana.

John Milton Oskison

Cherokee, 1874–1947

John Oskison was born in 1874 in Indian Territory; he grew up in Oklahoma, attended Willie Haskell College, graduated from Stanford, and did some graduate work at Harvard. Oskison was a popular novelist and short story writer, an editor and feature writer for the New York Evening Post *and* Collier's Weekly, *a freelance writer of essays on Indian affairs, and an army lieutenant and correspondent in World War I. His publications include three novels:* Wild Harvest *(1925);* Black Jack Davy *(1926), which deals with western themes;* Brothers Three *(1935), which deals with farm life during the Great Depression; and a biography of Sam Houston called* A Texas Titan. *One of the major themes in "The Problem of Old Harjo," which was first published in 1907, is the gap in understanding between Native and white cultures; in this poignant story, Oskison critiques the whites' ideas of what it means to be "Christian" through Harjo's dilemma and Miss Evans's growing understanding of it. The reader is also made to see some of the stereotypes that Mrs. Rowell and, by extension, the white culture have about the Native community through a contrast between what Mrs. Rowell says about Harjo and the narrator's description of him.*

The Problem of Old Harjo (1907)

The Spirit of the Lord had descended upon old Harjo. From the new missionary, just out from New York, he had learned that he was a sinner. The fire in the new missionary's eyes and her gracious appeal had convinced old Harjo that this was the time to repent and be saved. He was very much in earnest, and he assured Miss Evans that he wanted to be baptized and received into the church at once. Miss Evans was enthusiastic and went to Mrs. Rowell with the news. It was Mrs. Rowell who had said that it was no use to try to convert the older Indians, and she, after fifteen years of work in Indian Territory missions, should have known. Miss Evans was pardonably proud of her conquest.

"Old Harjo converted!" exclaimed Mrs. Rowell. "Dear Miss Evans, do you know that old Harjo has two wives?" To the older woman it was as if someone had said to her "Madame, the Sultan of Turkey wishes to teach one of your mission Sabbath school classes."

"But," protested the younger woman, "he is really sincere, and—"

"Then ask him," Mrs. Rowell interrupted a bit sternly, "if he will put away one of his wives. Ask him, before he comes into the presence of the Lord, if he is willing to conform to the laws of the country in which he lives, the country that guarantees his idle existence. Miss Evans, your work is not even begun." No one who knew Mrs. Rowell would say that she lacked sincerity and patriotism. Her own cousin was an earnest crusader against Mormonism, and had gathered a goodly share of that wagonload of protests that the Senate had been asked to read when it was considering whether a certain statesman of Utah should be allowed to represent his state at Washington.

In her practical, tactful way, Mrs. Rowell had kept clear of such embarrassments. At first, she had written letters of indignant protest to the Indian Office against the toleration of bigamy amongst the tribes. A wise inspector had been sent to the mission, and this man had pointed out that it was better to ignore certain things, "deplorable, to be sure," than to attempt to make over the habits of the old men. Of course, the young Indians would not be permitted to take more than one wife each.

So Mrs. Rowell had discreetly limited her missionary efforts to the young, and had exercised toward the old and bigamous only that strict charity which even a hopeless sinner might claim.

Miss Evans, it was to be regretted, had only the vaguest notions about "expediency"; so weak on matters of doctrine was she that the news that Harjo was living with two wives didn't startle her. She was young and possessed of but one enthusiasm—that for saving souls.

"I suppose," she ventured, "that old Harjo *must* put away one wife before he can join the church?"

"There can be no question about it, Miss Evans."

"Then I shall have to ask him to do it." Miss Evans regretted the necessity for forcing this sacrifice, but had no doubt that the Indian would make it in order to accept the gift of salvation which she was commissioned to bear to him.

Harjo lived in a "double" log cabin three miles from the mission. His ten acres of corn had been gathered into its fence-rail crib; four hogs that were to furnish his winter's bacon had been brought in from the woods and penned conveniently near to the crib; out in a corner of the garden, a fat mound of dirt rose where the crop of turnips and potatoes had been buried against the corrupting frost; and in the hayloft of his log stable were stored many pumpkins, dried corn, onions (suspended in bunches from the rafters) and the varied forage that Mrs. Harjo number one and Mrs. Harjo number two had thriftily provided. Three cows, three young heifers, two colts, and two patient, capable mares bore the Harjo brand, a fantastic "H" that the old man had designed. Materially, Harjo was solvent, and if the Government had ever come to his aid he could not recall the date.

This attempt to rehabilitate old Harjo morally, Miss Evans felt, was not one to be made at the mission; it should be undertaken in the Creek's own home, where the evidences of his sin should confront him as she explained.

When Miss Evans rode up to the block in front of Harjo's cabin, the old Indian came out, slowly and with a broadening smile of welcome on his face. A clean gray flannel shirt had taken the place of the white collarless garment, with crackling stiff bosom, that he had worn to the mission meetings. Comfortable, well-patched moccasins had been substituted for creaking boots, and brown corduroys, belted in at the waist, for tight black trousers. His abundant gray hair fell down on his shoulders. In his eyes, clear and large and black, glowed the light of true hospitality. Miss Evans thought of the patriarchs as she saw him lead her horse out to the stable; thus Abraham might have looked and lived.

"Harjo," began Miss Evans before following the old man to the covered passageway between the disconnected cabins, "is it true that you have two wives?" Her tone was neither stern nor accusatory. The Creek had heard that question before, from scandalized missionaries and perplexed registry clerks when he went to Muscogee to enroll himself and his family in one of the many "final" records ordered to be made by the

Government preparatory to dividing the Creek lands among the individual citizens.

For answer, Harjo called, first into the cabin that was used as a kitchen and then, in a loud, clear voice, toward the small field, where Miss Evans saw a flock of half-grown turkeys running about in the corn stubble. From the kitchen emerged a tall, thin Indian woman of fifty-five, with a red handkerchief bound severely over her head. She spoke to Miss Evans and sat down in the passageway. Presently, a clear, sweet voice was heard in the field; a stout, handsome woman, about the same age as the other, climbed the rail fence and came up to the house. She, also, greeted Miss Evans briefly. Then she carried a tin basin to the well nearby, where she filled it to the brim. Setting it down on the horse block, she rolled back her sleeves, tucked in the collar of her gray blouse, and plunged her face in the water. In a minute she came out of the kitchen freshened and smiling. 'Liza Harjo had been pulling dried bean stalks at one end of the field, and it was dirty work. At last old Harjo turned to Miss Evans and said, "These two my wife—this one 'Liza, this one Jennie."

It was done with simple dignity. Miss Evans bowed and stammered. Three pairs of eyes were turned upon her in patient, courteous inquiry.

It was hard to state the case. The old man was so evidently proud of his women, and so flattered by Miss Evans' interest in them, that he would find it hard to understand. Still, it had to be done, and Miss Evans took the plunge.

"Harjo, you want to come into our church?" The old man's face lighted.

"Oh, yes, I would come to Jesus, please, my friend."

"Do you know, Harjo, that the Lord commanded that one man should mate with but one woman?" The question was stated again in simpler terms, and the Indian replied, "Me know that now, my friend. Long time ago"—Harjo plainly meant the whole period previous to his conversion—"me did not know. The Lord Jesus did not speak to me in that time and so I was blind. I do what blind man do."

"Harjo, you must have only one wife when you come into our church. Can't you give up one of these women?" Miss Evans glanced at the two, sitting by with smiles of polite interest on their faces, understanding nothing. They had not shared Harjo's enthusiasm either for the white man's God or his language.

"Give up my wife?" A shy smile stole over his face. He leaned closer to Miss Evans. "You tell me, my friend, which one I give up." He glanced from 'Liza to Jennie as if to weigh their attractions, and the two rewarded him with their pleasantest smiles. "You tell me which one," he urged.

"Why, Harjo, how can I tell you!" Miss Evans had little sense of humor; she had taken the old man seriously.

"Then," Harjo sighed, continuing the comedy, for surely the missionary was jesting with him, "'Liza and Jennie must say." He talked to the Indian women for a time, and they laughed heartily. 'Liza, pointing to the other, shook her head. At length Harjo explained, "My friend, they cannot say. Jennie, she would run a race to see which one stay, but 'Liza, she say no, she is fat and cannot run."

Miss Evans comprehended at last. She flushed angrily, and protested, "Harjo, you are making a mock of a sacred subject; I cannot allow you to talk like this."

"But did you not speak in fun, my friend?" Harjo queried, sobering. "Surely you have just said what your friend, the white woman at the mission (he meant Mrs. Rowell) would say, and you do not mean what you say."

"Yes, Harjo, I mean it. It is true that Mrs. Rowell raised the point first, but I agree with her. The church cannot be defiled by receiving a bigamist into its membership." Harjo saw that the young woman was serious, distressingly serious. He was silent for a long time, but at last he raised his head and spoke quietly, "It is not good to talk like that if it is not in fun."

He rose and went to the stable. As he led Miss Evans' horse up to the block it was champing a mouthful of corn, the last of a generous portion that Harjo had put before it. The Indian held the bridle and waited for Miss Evans to mount. She was embarrassed, humiliated, angry. It was absurd to be dismissed in this way by—"by an ignorant old bigamist!" Then the humor of it burst upon her, and its human aspect. In her anxiety concerning the spiritual welfare of the sinner Harjo, she had insulted the man Harjo. She began to understand why Mrs. Rowell had said that the old Indians were hopeless.

"Harjo," she begged, coming out of the passageway, "please forgive me. I do not want you to give up one of your wives. Just tell me why you took them."

"I will tell you that, my friend." The old Creek looped the reins over his arm and sat down on the block. "For thirty years Jennie has lived with me as my wife. She is of the Bear people, and she came to me when I was thirty-five and she was twenty-five. She could not come before, for her mother was old, very old, and Jennie, she stay with her and feed her.

"So, when I was thirty years old I took 'Liza for my woman. She is of the Crow people. She help me make this little farm here when there was no farm for many miles around.

"Well, five years 'Liza and me, we live here and work hard. But there was no child. Then the old mother of Jennie she died, and Jennie got no family left in this part of the country. So 'Liza say to me, 'Why don't you take Jennie in here?' I say, 'You don't care?' and she say, 'No, maybe we have children here then.' But we have no children—never have children. We do not like that, but God He would not let it be. So, we have lived here thirty years very happy. Only just now you make me sad."

"Harjo," cried Miss Evans, "forget what I said. Forget that you wanted to join the church." For a young mission worker with a single purpose always before her, Miss Evans was saying a strange thing. Yet she couldn't help saying it; all of her zeal seemed to have been dissipated by a simple statement of the old man.

"I cannot forget to love Jesus, and I want to be saved." Old Harjo spoke with solemn earnestness. This situation was distracting. On one side stood a convert eager for the protection of the church, asking only that he be allowed to fulfill the obligations of humanity and on the other stood the church, represented by Mrs. Rowell, that set an impossible condition on receiving old Harjo to itself. Miss Evans wanted to cry; prayer, she felt, would be entirely inadequate as a means of expression.

"Oh! Harjo," she cried out, "I don't know what to do. I must think it over and talk with Mrs. Rowell again."

But Mrs. Rowell could suggest no way out; Miss Evans' talk with her only gave the older woman another opportunity to preach the folly of wasting time on the old and "unreasonable" Indians. Certainly the church could not listen even to a hint of a compromise in this case. If Harjo wanted to be saved, there was one way and only one—unless—

"Is either of the two women old? I mean, so old that she is—an—"

"Not at all," answered Miss Evans. "They're both strong and yes, happy. I think they will outlive Harjo."

"Can't you appeal to one of the women to go away? I dare say we could provide for her." Miss Evans, incongruously, remembered Jennie's jesting proposal to race for the right to stay with Harjo.

What could the mission provide as a substitute for the little home that 'Liza had helped to create there in the edge of the woods? What other home would satisfy Jennie?

"Mrs. Rowell, are you sure that we ought to try to take one of Harjo's women from him? I'm not sure that it would in the least advance morality amongst the tribe, but I'm certain that it would make three gentle people unhappy for the rest of their lives."

"You may be right, Miss Evans." Mrs. Rowell was not seeking to create unhappiness, for enough of it inevitably came to be pictured in the little mission building. "You may be right," she repeated, "but it is a grievous misfortune that old Harjo should wish to unite with the church."

No one was more regular in his attendance at the mission meetings than old Harjo. Sitting well forward, he was always in plain view of Miss Evans at the organ. Before the service began, and after it was over, the old man greeted the young woman. There was never a spoken question, but in the Creek's eyes was always a mute inquiry.

Once Miss Evans ventured to write to her old pastor in New York, and explain her trouble. This was what he wrote in reply: "I am surprised that you are troubled, for I should have expected you to rejoice, as I do, over this new and wonderful evidence of the Lord's reforming power. Though the church cannot receive the old man so long as he is confessedly a bigamist and violator of his country's just laws, you should be greatly strengthened in your work through bringing him to desire salvation."

"Oh! it's easy to talk when you're free from responsibility!" cried out Miss Evans. "But I woke him up to a desire for this water of salvation that he cannot take. I have seen Harjo's home, and I know how cruel and useless it would be to urge him to give up what he loves—for he does love those two women who have spent half their lives and more with him. What, what can be done?"

Month after month, as old Harjo continued to occupy his seat in the mission meetings, with that mute appeal in his eyes and a persistent light of hope on his face, Miss Evans repeated the question, "What can be done?" If she was sometimes tempted to say to the old man, "Stop worrying about your soul; you'll get to Heaven as surely as any of us," there was always Mrs. Rowell to remind her that she was not a Mormon missionary. She could not run away from her perplexity. If she should secure a transfer to another station, she felt that Harjo would give up coming to the meetings, and in his despair become a positive influence for evil amongst his people. Mrs. Rowell would not waste her energy on an obstinate old man. No, Harjo was her creation, her impossible convert, and throughout the years, until death—the great solvent which is not always a solvent—came to one of them, would continue to haunt her.

And meanwhile, what?

—John Oskison (1989, 125–35)
First published in *Southern Workman.* April 1907, 235–41

Zitkala-Ša

Gertrude Simmons Bonnin;
Yankton Sioux, 1876–1938

Zitkala-Ša (a name she gave herself, meaning Red Bird) was born in 1876 on the Pine Ridge Sioux Reservation; she was from the Yankton Sioux band. At age eight, she persuaded her mother, based on the influence of missionaries who told her that she would be going to a land full of delicious red apples, to allow her to go to boarding school at White's Manual Institute in Wabash, Indiana. White's was run by the Quakers, who called themselves friends of the Indian, but like most boarding schools, it followed Bureau of Indian Affairs policies. When Zitkala-Ša returned home after three years at the boarding school, it was to the realization that she no longer belonged there. Historically, this was a common experience for children who attended the schools, and it stands in stark contrast to the assimilationist rhetoric of the times. Realizing that her educational experiences made returning to life as she had known it impossible, Zitkala-Ša went on to study at Earlham College from 1896–1897, where, as Dexter Fisher notes in the introduction to American Indian Stories *(1979, xi), she became a distinguished orator and poet, winning second place in the Indiana State Oratorical Contest of 1896. From 1898–1899, she taught at the Carlisle boarding school. Most of Zitkala-Ša's works were published from 1900–1902. These include three installments of her autobiography, "Impressions of an Indian Childhood," "School Days of an Indian Girl," and "An Indian Teacher Among Indians," which were published in 1900 in* The Atlantic Monthly. Harper's Magazine *and*

305

Everybody's Magazine *featured three of her short stories, and in 1901, she published* Old Indian Legends. *Zitkala-Ša's memoirs and short stories are included in the 1921 edition of* American Indian Stories *edited by Dexter Fisher. In collaboration with William Hanson, Zitkala-Ša also wrote an opera called* The Sun Dance Opera, *which premiered in 1913 and is included in* Dreams and Thunder, *edited by P. Jane Hafen. Zitkala-Ša's poetry is also included in Karen Kilcup's anthology of* Native American Women's Writing 1800–1924.

Zitkala-Ša was active in the Pan-Indian Movement, and she and her husband Raymond Bonnin worked for the Bureau of Indian Affairs in Utah. In 1916, she was elected Secretary of the Society of the American Indian. Zitkala-Ša also wrote a treatise on the problems faced by oil-rich tribes, like the Osage in Okalahoma. Throughout her life and in essays like "Why I Am a Pagan," Zitkala-Ša worked to better the quality of Native American life and to try to change assimilationist policies. She at once recognized the importance of getting a Western education and what this cost her in terms of personal isolation and loss of closeness to her mother. Indeed, as critics Susan Bernadin (1997, 212–38) and Martha Cutter (1994, 31–44) point out, the theme of longing for the absent mother runs throughout this narrative and illustrates the ways in which the boarding schools tried to create a national, melting-pot Western identity at the expense of the Native American family structure.

The School Days of an Indian Girl

I.

THE LAND OF RED APPLES.

There were eight in our party of bronzed children who were going East with the missionaries. Among us were three young braves, two tall girls, and we three little ones, Judéwin, Thowin, and I. We had been very impatient to start on our journey to the Red Apple Country, which, we were told, lay a little beyond the great circular horizon of the Western prairie. Under a sky of rosy apples we dreamt of roaming as freely and happily as we had chased the cloud shadows on the Dakota plains. We had anticipated much pleasure from a ride on the iron horse, but the throngs of staring palefaces disturbed and troubled us.

On the train, fair women, with tottering babies on each arm, stopped their haste and scrutinized the children of absent mothers. Large men, with heavy bundles in their hands, halted near by, and riveted their glassy blue eyes upon us.

I sank deep into the corner of my seat, for I resented being watched. Directly in front of me, children who were no larger than I hung themselves upon the backs of their seats, with their bold white faces toward me. Sometimes they took their forefingers out of their mouths and pointed at my moccasined feet. Their mothers, instead of reproving such rude curiosity, looked closely at me, and attracted their children's further notice to my blanket. This embarrassed me, and kept me constantly on the verge of tears.

I sat perfectly still, with my eyes downcast, daring only now and then to shoot long glances around me. Chancing to turn to the window at my side, I was quite breathless upon seeing one familiar object. It was the telegraph pole which strode by at short paces. Very near my mother's dwelling, along the edge of a road thickly bordered with wild sunflowers, some poles like these had been planted by white men. Often I had stopped, on my way down the road, to hold my ear against the pole, and, hearing its low moaning, I used to wonder what the paleface had done to hurt it. Now I sat watching for each pole that glided by to be the last one.

In this way I had forgotten my uncomfortable surroundings, when I heard one of my comrades call out my name. I saw the missionary standing very near, tossing candies and gums into our midst. This aroused us all, and we tried to see who could catch the most of the sweetmeats.

Though we rode several days inside of the iron horse, I do not recall a single thing about our luncheons.

It was night when we reached the school grounds. The lights from the windows of the large buildings fell upon some of the icicled trees that stood beneath them. We were led toward an open door, where the brightness of the lights within flooded out over the heads of the excited palefaces who blocked our way. My body trembled more from fear than from the snow I trod upon.

Entering the house, I stood close against the wall. The strong glaring light in the large whitewashed room dazzled my eyes. The noisy hurrying of hard shoes upon a bare wooden floor increased the whirring in my ears. My only safety seemed to be in keeping next to the wall. As I was wondering in which direction to escape from all this confusion, two warm hands grasped me firmly, and in the same moment I was tossed high in midair. A rosy-checked paleface woman caught me in her arms. I was both frightened and insulted by such trifling. I stared into her eyes, wishing her to let me stand on my own feet, but she jumped me up and down with increasing enthusiasm. My mother had never made a play-thing of her wee daughter. Remembering this I began to cry aloud.

They misunderstood the cause of my tears, and placed me at a white table loaded with food. There our party were united again. As I did not hush my crying, one of the older ones whispered to me, "Wait until you are alone in the night."

It was very little I could swallow besides my sobs, that evening.

"Oh, I want my mother and my brother Dawée! I want to go to my aunt!" I pleaded; but the ears of the palefaces could not hear me. From the table we were taken along an upward incline of wooden boxes, which I learned afterward to call a stairway. At the top was a quiet hall, dimly lighted. Many narrow beds were in one straight line down the entire length of the wall. In them lay sleeping brown faces, which peeped just out of the coverings. I was tucked into bed with one of the tall girls, because she talked to me in my mother tongue and seemed to soothe me.

I had arrived in the wonderful land of rosy skies, but I was not happy, as I had thought I should be. My long travel and the bewildering sights had exhausted me. I fell asleep, heaving deep, tired sobs. My tears were left to dry themselves in streaks, because neither my aunt nor my mother was near to wipe them away.

II.

THE CUTTING OF MY LONG HAIR.

The first day in the land of apples was a bitter-cold one; for the snow still covered the ground, and the trees were bare. A large bell rang for break-fast, its loud metallic voice crashing through the belfry overhead and into our sensitive ears. The annoying clatter of shoes on bare floors gave us no peace. The constant clash of harsh noises, with an undercurrent of many voices murmuring an unknown tongue, made a bedlam within which I was securely tied. And though my spirit tore itself in struggling for its lost freedom, all was useless.

A paleface woman, with white hair, came up after us. We were placed in a line of girls who were marching into the dining room. These were Indian girls, in stiff shoes and closely clinging dresses. The small girls wore sleeved aprons and shingled hair. As I walked noiselessly in my soft moccasins, I felt like sinking to the floor, for my blanket had been stripped from my shoulders. I looked hard at the Indian girls, who seemed not to care that they were even more immodestly dressed than I, in their tightly fitting clothes. While we marched in, the boys entered at an opposite door. I watched for the three young braves who came in our party. I spied them in the rear ranks, looking as uncomfortable as I felt.

A small bell was tapped, and each of the pupils drew a chair from under the table. Supposing this act meant they were to be seated, I pulled out mine and at once slipped into it from one side. But when I turned my head, I saw that I was the only one seated, and all the rest at our table remained standing. Just as I began to rise, looking shyly around to see how chairs were to be used, a second bell was sounded. All were seated at last, and I had to crawl back into my chair again. I heard a man's voice at one end of the hall, and I looked around to see him. But all the others hung their heads over their plates. As I glanced at the long chain of tables, I caught the eyes of a paleface woman upon me. Immediately I dropped my eyes, wondering why I was so keenly watched by the strange woman. The man ceased his mutterings, and then a third bell was tapped. Every one picked up his knife and fork and began eating. I began crying instead, for by this time I was afraid to venture anything more.

But this eating by formula was not the hardest trial in that first day. Late in the morning, my friend Judéwin gave me a terrible warning. Judéwin knew a few words of English; and she had overheard the paleface woman talk about cutting our long, heavy hair. Our mothers had taught us that only unskilled warriors who were captured had their hair shingled by the enemy. Among our people, short hair was worn by mourners, and shingled-hair by cowards!

We discussed our fate some moments, and when Judéwin said, "We have to submit, because they are strong," I rebelled.

"No, I will not submit! I will struggle first!" I answered.

I watched my chance, and when no one noticed I disappeared. I crept up the stairs as quietly as I could in my squeaking shoes,—my moccasins had been exchanged for shoes. Along the hall I passed, without knowing whither I was going. Turning aside to an open door, I found a large room with three white beds in it. The windows were covered with dark green curtains, which made the room very dim. Thankful that no one was there, I directed my steps toward the corner farthest from the door.

On my hands and knees I crawled under the bed, and cuddled myself in the dark corner.

From my hiding place I peered out, shuddering with fear whenever I heard footsteps near by. Though in the hall loud voices were calling my name, and I knew that even Judéwin was searching for me, I did not open my mouth to answer. Then the steps were quickened and the voices became excited. The sounds came nearer and nearer. Women and girls entered the room. I held my breath and watched them open closet doors and peep behind large trunks. Some one threw up the curtains, and the room was filled with sudden light. What caused them to stoop and look under the bed I do not know. I remember being dragged out, though I resisted by kicking and scratching wildly. In spite of myself, I was carried downstairs and tied fast in a chair.

I cried aloud, shaking my head all the while until I felt the cold blades of the scissors against my neck, and heard them gnaw off one of my thick braids. Then I lost my spirit. Since the day I was taken from my mother I had suffered extreme indignities. People had stared at me. I had been tossed about in the air like a wooden puppet. And now my long hair was shingled like a coward's! In my anguish I moaned for my mother, but no one came to comfort me. Not a soul reasoned quietly with me, as my own mother used to do; for now I was only one of many little animals driven by a herder.

III.
THE SNOW EPISODE.

A short time after our arrival we three Dakotas were playing in the snow-drift. We were all still deaf to the English language, excepting Judéwin, who always heard such puzzling things. One morning we learned through her ears that we were forbidden to fall lengthwise in the snow, as we had been doing, to see our own impressions. However, before many hours we had forgotten the order, and were having great sport in the snow, when a shrill voice called us. Looking up, we saw an imperative hand beckoning us into the house. We shook the snow off ourselves, and started toward the woman as slowly as we dared.

Judéwin said: "Now the paleface is angry with us. She is going to punish us for falling into the snow. If she looks straight into your eyes and talks loudly, you must wait until she stops. Then, after a tiny pause, say, 'No.'" The rest of the way we practiced upon the little word "no."

As it happened, Thowin was summoned to judgment first. The door shut behind her with a click.

Judéwin and I stood silently listening at the keyhole. The paleface woman talked in very severe tones. Her words fell from her lips like crackling embers, and her inflection ran up like the small end of a switch. I understood her voice better than the things she was saying. I was certain we had made her very impatient with us. Judéwin heard enough of the words to realize all too late that she had taught us the wrong reply.

"Oh, poor Thowin!" she gasped, as she put both hands over her ears.

Just then I heard Thowin's tremulous answer, "No."

With an angry exclamation, the woman gave her a hard spanking. Then she stopped to say something. Judéwin said it was this: "Are you going to obey my word the next time?"

Thowin answered again with the only word at her command, "No."

This time the woman meant her blows to smart, for the poor frightened girl shrieked at the top of her voice. In the midst of the whipping the blows ceased abruptly, and the woman asked another question: "Are you going to fall in the snow again?"

Thowin gave her bad password another trial. We heard her say feebly, "No! No!"

With this the woman hid away her half-worn slipper, and led the child out, stroking her black shorn head. Perhaps it occurred to her that brute force is not the solution for such a problem. She did nothing to Judéwin nor to me. She only returned to us our unhappy comrade, and left us alone in the room.

During the first two or three seasons misunderstandings as ridiculous as this one of the snow episode frequently took place, bringing unjustifiable frights and punishments into our little lives.

Within a year I was able to express myself somewhat in broken English. As soon as I comprehended a part of what was said and done, a mischievous spirit of revenge possessed me. One day I was called in from my play for some misconduct. I had disregarded a rule which seemed to me very needlessly binding. I was sent into the kitchen to mash the turnips for dinner. It was noon, and steaming dishes were hastily carried into the dining-room. I hated turnips, and their odor which came from the brown jar was offensive to me. With fire in my heart, I took the wooden tool that the paleface woman held out to me. I stood upon a step, and, grasping the handle with both hands, I bent in hot rage over the turnips. I worked my vengeance upon them. All were so busily occupied that no one noticed me. I saw that the turnips were in a pulp, and that further beating could not improve them; but the order was, "Mash these turnips," and mash them I would! I renewed my energy; and as I sent the masher into the bottom of the jar, I felt a satisfying sensation that the weight of my body had gone into it.

Just here a paleface woman came up to my table. As she looked into the jar, she shoved my hands roughly aside. I stood fearless and angry. She placed her red hands upon the rim of the jar. Then she gave one lift and stride away from the table. But lo! the pulpy contents fell through the crumbled bottom to the floor! She spared me no scolding phrases that I had earned. I did not heed them. I felt triumphant in my revenge, though deep within me I was a wee bit sorry to have broken the jar.

As I sat eating my dinner, and saw that no turnips were served, I whooped in my heart for having once asserted the rebellion within me.

IV.

THE DEVIL.

Among the legends the old warriors used to tell me were many stories of evil spirits. But I was taught to fear them no more than those who stalked about in material guise. I never knew there was an insolent chieftain among the bad spirits, who dared to array his forces against the Great Spirit, until I heard this white man's legend from a paleface woman.

Out of a large book she showed me a picture of the white man's devil. I looked in horror upon the strong claws that grew out of his fur-covered fingers. His feet were like his hands. Trailing at his heels was a scaly tail tipped with a serpent's open jaws. His face was a patchwork: he had bearded cheeks, like some I had seen palefaces wear; his nose was an eagle's bill, and his sharp-pointed ears were pricked up like those of a sly fox. Above them a pair of cow's horns curved upward. I trembled with awe, and my heart throbbed in my throat, as I looked at the king of evil spirits. Then I heard the paleface woman say that this terrible creature roamed loose in the world, and that little girls who disobeyed school regulations were to be tortured by him.

That night I dreamt about this evil divinity. Once again I seemed to be in my mother's cottage. An Indian woman had come to visit my mother. On opposite sides of the kitchen stove, which stood in the center of the small house, my mother and her guest were seated in straight-backed chairs. I played with a train of empty spools hitched together on a string. It was night, and the wick burned feebly. Suddenly I heard some one turn our door-knob from without.

My mother and the woman hushed their talk, and both looked toward the door. It opened gradually. I waited behind the stove. The hinges squeaked as the door was slowly, very slowly pushed inward.

Then in rushed the devil! He was tall! He looked exactly like the picture I had seen of him in the white man's papers. He did not speak to my mother, because he did not know the Indian language, but his glittering yellow eyes were fastened upon me. He took long strides around the stove, passing behind the woman's chair. I threw down my spools, and ran to my mother. He did not fear her, but followed closely after me. Then I ran round and round the stove, crying aloud for help. But my mother and the woman seemed not to know my danger. They sat still, looking quietly upon the devil's chase after me. At last I grew dizzy. My head revolved as on a hidden pivot. My knees became numb, and doubled under my weight like a pair of knife blades without a spring. Beside my mother's chair I fell in a heap. Just as the devil stooped over me with outstretched claws my mother awoke from her quiet indifference, and lifted me on her lap. Whereupon the devil vanished, and I was awake.

On the following morning I took my revenge upon the devil. Stealing into the room where a wall of shelves was filled with books, I drew forth The Stories of the Bible. With a broken slate pencil I carried in my apron pocket, I began by scratching out his wicked eyes. A few moments later, when I was ready to leave the room, there was a ragged hole in the page where the picture of the devil had once been.

V.

IRON ROUTINE.

A loud-clamoring bell awakened us at half-past six in the cold winter mornings. From happy dreams of Western rolling lands and unlassoed freedom we tumbled out upon chilly bare floors back again into a paleface day. We had short time to jump into our shoes and clothes, and wet our eyes with icy water, before a small hand bell was vigorously rung for roll call.

There were too many drowsy children and too numerous orders for the day to waste a moment in any apology to nature for giving her children such a shock in the early morning. We rushed downstairs, bounding over two high steps at a time, to land in the assembly room.

A paleface woman, with a yellow-covered roll book open on her arm and a gnawed pencil in her hand, appeared at the door. Her small, tired face was coldly lighted with a pair of large gray eyes.

She stood still in a halo of authority, while over the rim of her spectacles her eyes pried nervously about the room. Having glanced at her long list of names and called out the first one, she tossed up her chin and peered through the crystals of her spectacles to make sure of the answer "Here."

Relentlessly her pencil black-marked our daily records if we were not present to respond to our names, and no chum of ours had done it successfully for us. No matter if a dull headache or the painful cough of slow consumption had delayed the absentee, there was only time enough to mark the tardiness. It was next to impossible to leave the iron routine after the civilizing machine had once begun its day's buzzing; and as it was inbred in me to suffer in silence rather than to appeal to the ears of one whose open eyes could not see my pain, I have many times trudged in the day's harness heavy-footed, like a dumb sick brute.

Once I lost a dear classmate. I remember well how she used to mope along at my side, until one morning she could not raise her head from her pillow. At her deathbed I stood weeping, as the paleface woman sat near her moistening the dry lips. Among the folds of the bedclothes I saw the open pages of the white man's Bible. The dying Indian girl talked disconnectedly of Jesus the Christ and the paleface who was cooling her swollen hands and feet.

I grew bitter, and censured the woman for cruel neglect of our physical ills. I despised the pencils that moved automatically, and the one teaspoon which dealt out, from a large bottle, healing to a row of variously ailing Indian children. I blamed the hard-working, well-meaning, ignorant woman who was inculcating in our hearts her superstitious ideas. Though I was sullen in all my little troubles, as soon as I felt better I was ready again to smile upon the cruel woman. Within a week I was again actively testing the chains which tightly bound my individuality like a mummy for burial.

The melancholy of those black days has left so long a shadow that it darkens the path of years that have since gone by. These sad memories rise above those of smoothly grinding school days. Perhaps my Indian nature is the moaning wind which stirs them now for their present record. But, however tempestuous this is within me, it comes out as the low voice of a curiously colored seashell, which is only for those ears that are bent with compassion to hear it.

VI.
FOUR STRANGE SUMMERS.

After my first three years of school, I roamed again in the Western country through four strange summers.

During this time I seemed to hang in the heart of chaos, beyond the touch or voice of human aid. My brother, being almost ten years my senior, did not quite understand my feelings. My mother had never gone inside of a schoolhouse, and so she was not capable of comforting her daughter who could read and write. Even nature seemed to have no place for me. I was neither a wee girl nor a tall one; neither a wild Indian nor a tame one. This deplorable situation was the effect of my brief course in the East, and the unsatisfactory "teenth" in a girl's years.

It was under these trying conditions that, one bright afternoon, as I sat restless and unhappy in my mother's cabin, I caught the sound of the spirited step of my brother's pony on the road which passed by our dwelling. Soon I heard the wheels of a light buckboard, and Dawée's familiar "Ho!" to his pony. He alighted upon the bare ground in front of our house. Tying his pony to one of the projecting corner logs of the low-roofed cottage, he stepped upon the wooden doorstep.

I met him there with a hurried greeting, and, as I passed by, he looked a quiet "What?" into my eyes.

When he began talking with my mother, I slipped the rope from the pony's bridle. Seizing the reins and bracing my feet against the dashboard, I wheeled around in an instant. The pony was ever ready to try his speed. Looking backward, I saw Dawée waving his hand to me. I turned with the curve in the road and disappeared. I followed the winding road which crawled upward between the bases of little hillocks. Deep water-worn ditches ran parallel on either side. A strong wind blew against my cheeks and fluttered my sleeves. The pony reached the top of the highest hill, and began an even race on the level lands. There was nothing moving within that great circular horizon of the Dakota prairies save the tall grasses, over which the wind blew and rolled off in long, shadowy waves.

Within this vast wigwam of blue and green I rode reckless and insignificant. It satisfied my small consciousness to see the white foam fly from the pony's mouth.

Suddenly, out of the earth a coyote came forth at a swinging trot that was taking the cunning thief toward the hills and the village beyond. Upon the moment's impulse, I gave him a long chase and a wholesome fright. As I turned away to go back to the village, the wolf sank down upon his haunches for rest, for it was a hot summer day; and as I drove slowly homeward, I saw his sharp nose still pointed at me, until I vanished below the margin of the hilltops.

In a little while I came in sight of my mother's house. Dawée stood in the yard, laughing at an old warrior who was pointing his forefinger, and again waving his whole hand, toward the hills. With his blanket drawn over one shoulder, he talked and motioned excitedly. Dawée turned the old man by the shoulder and pointed me out to him.

"Oh, han!" (Oh, yes) the warrior muttered, and went his way. He had climbed the top of his favorite barren hill to survey the surrounding prairies, when he spied my chase after the coyote. His keen eyes recognized the pony and driver. At once uneasy for my safety, he had come running to my mother's cabin to give her warning. I did not appreciate his kindly interest, for there was an unrest gnawing at my heart.

As soon as he went away, I asked Dawée about something else.

"No, my baby sister, I cannot take you with me to the party tonight," he replied. Though I was not far from fifteen, and I felt that before long I should enjoy all the privileges of my tall cousin, Dawée persisted in calling me his baby sister.

That moonlight night, I cried in my mother's presence when I heard the jolly young people pass by our cottage. They were no more young braves in blankets and eagle plumes, nor Indian maids with prettily painted cheeks. They had gone three years to school in the East, and had become civilized. The young men wore the white man's coat and trousers, with bright neckties. The girls wore tight muslin dresses, with ribbons at neck and waist. At these gatherings they talked English. I could speak English almost as well as my brother, but I was not properly dressed to be taken along. I had no hat, no ribbons, and no close-fitting gown. Since my return from school I had thrown away my shoes, and wore again the soft moccasins.

While Dawée was busily preparing to go I controlled my tears. But when I heard him bounding away on his pony, I buried my face in my arms and cried hot tears.

My mother was troubled by my unhappiness. Coming to my side, she offered me the only printed matter we had in our home. It was an Indian Bible, given her some years ago by a missionary. She tried to console me. "Here, my child, are the white man's papers. Read a little from them," she said most piously.

I took it from her hand, for her sake; but my enraged spirit felt more like burning the book, which afforded me no help, and was a perfect delusion to my mother. I did not read it, but laid it unopened on the floor, where I sat on my feet. The dim yellow light of the braided muslin burning in a small vessel of oil flickered and sizzled in the awful silent storm which followed my rejection of the Bible.

Now my wrath against the fates consumed my tears before they reached my eyes. I sat stony, with a bowed head. My mother threw a shawl over her head and shoulders, and stepped out into the night.

After an uncertain solitude, I was suddenly aroused by a loud cry piercing the night. It was my mother's voice wailing among the barren hills which held the bones of buried warriors. She called aloud for her brothers' spirits to support her in her helpless misery. My fingers grew icy cold, as I realized that my unrestrained tears had betrayed my suffering to her, and she was grieving for me.

Before she returned, though I knew she was on her way, for she had ceased her weeping, I extinguished the light, and leaned my head on the window sill.

Many schemes of running away from my surroundings hovered about in my mind. A few more moons of such a turmoil drove me away to the eastern school. I rode on the white man's iron steed, thinking it would bring me back to my mother in a few winters, when I should be grown tall, and there would be congenial friends awaiting me.

VII.
INCURRING MY MOTHER'S DISPLEASURE.

In the second journey to the East I had not come without some precautions. I had a secret interview with one of our best medicine men, and when I left his wigwam I carried securely in my sleeve a tiny bunch of magic roots. This possession assured me of friends wherever I should go. So absolutely did I believe in its charms that I wore it through all the school routine for more than a year. Then, before I lost my faith in the dead roots, I lost the little buckskin bag containing all my good luck.

At the close of this second term of three years I was the proud owner of my first diploma. The following autumn I ventured upon a college career against my mother's will.

I had written for her approval, but in her reply I found no encouragement. She called my notice to her neighbors' children, who had completed their education in three years. They had returned to their homes, and were then talking English with the frontier settlers. Her few words hinted that I had better give up my slow attempt to learn the white man's ways, and be content to roam over the prairies and find my living upon wild roots. I silenced her by deliberate disobedience.

Thus, homeless and heavy-hearted, I began anew my life among strangers.

As I hid myself in my little room in the college dormitory, away from the scornful and yet curious eyes of the students, I pined for sympathy. Often I wept in secret, wishing I had gone West, to be nourished by my mother's love, instead of remaining among a cold race whose hearts were frozen hard with prejudice.

During the fall and winter seasons I scarcely had a real friend, though by that time several of my classmates were courteous to me at a safe distance.

My mother had not yet forgiven my rudeness to her, and I had no moment for letter-writing. By daylight and lamplight, I spun with reeds and thistles, until my hands were tired from their weaving, the magic design which promised me the white man's respect.

At length, in the spring term, I entered an oratorical contest among the various classes. As the day of competition approached, it did not seem possible that the event was so near at hand, but it came. In the chapel the classes assembled together, with their invited guests. The high platform was carpeted, and gayly festooned with college colors. A bright white light illumined the room, and outlined clearly the great polished beams that arched the domed ceiling. The assembled crowds filled the air with pulsating murmurs. When the hour for speaking arrived all were hushed. But on the wall the old clock which pointed out the trying moment ticked calmly on.

One after another I saw and heard the orators. Still, I could not realize that they longed for the favorable decision of the judges as much as I did. Each contestant received a loud burst of applause, and some were cheered heartily. Too soon my turn came, and I paused a moment behind the curtains for a deep breath. After my concluding words, I heard the same applause that the others had called out.

Upon my retreating steps, I was astounded to receive from my fellow-students a large bouquet of roses tied with flowing ribbons. With the lovely flowers I fled from the stage. This friendly token was a rebuke to me for the hard feelings I had borne them.

Later, the decision of the judges awarded me the first place. Then there was a mad uproar in the hall, where my classmates sang and shouted my name at the top of their lungs; and the disappointed students howled and brayed in fearfully dissonant tin trumpets. In this excitement, happy students rushed forward to offer their congratulations. And I could not conceal a smile when they wished to escort me in a procession to the students' parlor, where all were going to calm themselves. Thanking them for the kind spirit which prompted them to make such a proposition, I walked alone with the night to my own little room.

A few weeks afterward, I appeared as the college representative in another contest. This time the competition was among orators from different colleges in our State. It was held at the State capital, in one of the largest opera houses.

Here again was a strong prejudice against my people. In the evening, as the great audience filled the house, the student bodies began warring among themselves. Fortunately, I was spared witnessing any of the noisy wrangling before the contest began. The slurs against the Indian that stained the lips of our opponents were already burning like a dry fever within my breast.

But after the orations were delivered a deeper burn awaited me. There, before that vast ocean of eyes, some college rowdies threw out a large white flag, with a drawing of a most forlorn Indian girl on it. Under this they had printed in bold black letters words that ridiculed the college which was represented by a "squaw." Such worse than barbarian rudeness embittered me. While we waited for the verdict of the judges, I gleamed fiercely upon the throngs of palefaces. My teeth were hard set, as I saw the white flag still floating insolently in the air.

Then anxiously we watched the man carry toward the stage the envelope containing the final decision.

There were two prizes given, that night, and one of them was mine!

The evil spirit laughed within me when the white flag dropped out of sight, and the hands which hurled it hung limp in defeat.

Leaving the crowd as quickly as possible, I was soon in my room. The rest of the night I sat in an armchair and gazed into the crackling fire. I laughed no more in triumph when thus alone. The little taste of victory did not satisfy a hunger in my heart. In my mind I saw my mother far away on the Western plains, and she was holding a charge against me.

—Zitkala-Ša (Gertrude Bonnin) (1979, 47–80)
First published in the February 1900
issue of *Atlantic Monthly*

THE RED MAN'S AMERICA

My country! 'tis to thee,
Sweet land of Liberty,
My pleas I bring.
    Land where OUR fathers died,
    Whose offspring are denied,
    The Franchise given wide,
    Hark, while I sing.

My native country, thee,
Thy Red man is not free,
Knows not thy love.
    Political bred ills,
    Peyote in temple hills,
    His heart with sorrow fills,
    Knows not thy love.

Let Lane's Bill swell the breeze,
And ring from all the trees,
Sweet freedom's song.
    Let Gandy's Bill awake
    All people, till they quake,
    Let Congress, silence break,
    The sound prolong.

Great Mystery, to thee,
Life of humanity,
To thee, we cling.

Grant our home-land be bright,
Grant us just human right,
Protect us by Thy might,
Great God, our kind.
            —Zitkala-Ša (1917a, 64)

A SIOUX WOMAN'S LOVE FOR HER GRANDCHILD

Loosely clad in deerskin, dress of flying fringes,
Played a little blackhaired maiden of the prairies;
Plunged amid the rolling green of grasses waving,
Brimming o'er with laughter, round face all aglowing.
Thru the oval teepee doorway, grandma watched her,
Narrowed aged eyes reflecting love most tender.

Seven summers since a new-born babe was left her.
Death had taken from her teepee, her own daughter.
Tireless love bestowed she on the little Bright eyes,—
Eagerly attended her with great devotion.
Seven summers grew affection intertwining.
Bent old age adorned once more with hopes all budding.

Bright Eyes spied some "gaudy-wings" and chased them wildly.
Sipping dew and honey from the flowers, gaily
Flit the pretty butterflies, here now, then yonder.
"These, the green, wee babes," old grandma mused in wonder.
"One time snug in winter slumber, now in season
Leave their silken cradles; fly with gauzy pinion."

Shouting gleefully, the child roamed on fearlessly
Glossy, her long hair, hung in two braids o'er each ear,
Zephyrs whispered to the flowers, at her passing,
Fragrant blossoms gave assent with gracious nodding.
Conscious lay the crystal dew, on bud and leaflet,
Irridescent joys emitting 'till the sun set.

Monster clouds crept in the sky; fell shadows in the prairie.
Grandma, on her cane, leaned breathless, sad and weary.
Listened vainly for the laughter of her darling.

"Where, Oh where, in sudden desert's endless rolling,
Could the wee girl still be playing?" cried she hoarsely,
Shaking as with ague in that silence somber.

Sobbing bitterly, she saw not men approaching.
Over wrought by sorrow, scarcely heard them talking.
Gusts of wind rushed by; cooled her fever;
Loosed her wisps of hair befitting to a mourner.
"In God's infinitude, where, Oh where is grandchild?"
Winds caught up her moaning, shrieked and shook the teepee.

"Dry your tears, old grandma, cease excessive wailing."
(Empty words addressed they to an image standing.)
"Chieftain's word of sympathy and warning, hear you!
Moving dust-cloud of an army is on coming;
Though you've lost your grandchild, tempt no useless danger.
In the twilight, we must flee hence." This the order.

Duty done, they paused with heads bowed sadly.
These strong men were used to meeting battles bravely,
Yet the anguish of the woman smote them helpless.
Setting of the sun made further searching fruitless,
Darkness, rife with evil omens surging tempest
Came, obliterating hope's last ray for rescue.

Fleeing from the soldiers startled Red Man hurried
Riding travois, ponies face the lightnings, lurid
'Gainst the sudden flashing, angry fires, a figure
Stood, propped by a cane. A soul in torture
Sacrificing life than leave behind her lost one
Greater love hath no man; love surpassing reason.[1]

—Zitkala-Ša (1917b, 230–31)

Note for "A Sioux Woman's Love for Her Grandchild"

1. This incident occurred upon the coming of Custer's army, preliminary to the battle known erroneously in history as "Custer's Massacre" [Zitkala-Ša's note].

Mourning Dove

Christine Quintasket;
Colville, 1888–1936

   Mourning Dove was born in Idaho, the daughter
of Joseph Quintasket (from the Upper Okanagan community in British
Columbia) and Lucy Stukin (Scho-yel-pi or Colville). Unlike many of the
other writers of her generation, she did not have much formal education
beyond the third-grade level and a brief course in business school. Mourning
Dove's Cogewea: The Halfblood *(1927) is often cited as the first novel by a*
Native American woman, although some critics also give that distinction to
Leslie Marmon Silko's Ceremony. *As Dexter Fisher notes in her introduc-*
tion to the novel, "the inspiration behind Cogewea *is an Okanagan folk tale*
that has been variously titled 'Little Chipmunk and the Owl Woman' and
'Coyote Kills Owl Woman'" (Mourning Dove, 1981, xi–xii). Mourning Dove
weaves together oral traditional stories and traditional Native ideas about
power and guardian spirits with the theme of the mixed blood, who strug-
gles with identity issues and prejudice. Mourning Dove had already drafted
an early version of Cogewea *when she met Lucullus McWhorter in 1914 (xii).*
McWhorter was heavily involved in the revision of this novel, to the point
that many critics call it a collaboration. McWhorter's influence is evident in
the Latinate, somewhat stilted language of the novel and also in the some of
the stereotypical slang used in the novel. The chapter that we have included
here is believed to be one that was written primarily by Mourning Dove.
Ultimately, Mourning Dove's novel affirms the importance of traditional
Native values.

From *Cogewea: The Half-Blood*: Chapter VII.

THE "LADIES" AND THE "SQUAW" RACES

Where, in the valley fields and fruits,
Now hums the lively street,
We milled a mob of fighting brutes,
Amid the grim mesquite.
            —*Badger Clark*

"Hurry, Sis!" called Jim, as Cogewea joined him where he was holding the Bay Devil. "Race is on in a few minutes and you want Diamond handled a little 'fore startin'. Ride through the crowd to the track and get him used to the yellin' and shootin'-crackers."

He helped the girl to mount, her face showing but slightly, the heart's throb of anticipation. A riding habit of blue corduroy fitted her slender form admirably. Red, white and blue ribbons fastened her hair, which streaming to the racer's back, lent a picturesque wildness to her figure. Securing the stirrups, she requested Jim to tighten her spur-straps, as they seemed a trifle loose, adding:

"We just must win this race from the whites. See! the Webster girls are among the mounted ladies and they have mighty good horses. But if any of them beat me, they will sure have to run for it."

"My 'spirit-power' tells me you're goin' come out first in this here race," replied Jim solemnly, as he gave a final tug at a refractory spur-strap. "Signs all favorable for winnin'."

Cogewea was assigned place abreast the other riders, her number placing her on the outer circle or flank of the field. Verona, the eldest Webster girl, was a noted rider and her jet mount, known as the "Black Snake", had never lost a race. This was the first match between the two famous riders, and as Cogewea fell into line, Verona, who had second place, stared at her contemptuously and spoke in a voice loud enough to be heard by those standing near:

"Why is this *squaw* permitted to ride? This is a *ladies* race!"

Her companions were unanimous that it was a gross outrage and that they should protest. Stung by the biting insult, Cogewea retorted:

"Perhaps I am allowed because no '*ladies*' of the silvery-hue have entered and this race is being tolerated only that the audience may not be wholly disappointed."

Further colloquy was cut short by the stentorian voice of the starter, as he raised pistol in air:

"*A-l-l ready!*" BANG!

The field was off! and it soon became apparent that the actual contest was to be between the two mighty racers. For the first quarter, the Black led the Bay, by a full length. In the next quarter, the Bay crept ahead until they were running neck and neck. The white rider plied the lash and the gallant Black responding retrieved in part, the lost ground. But at a touch of the spur, the Bay Devil forged along side, where, despite the fierce scourging by the white rider, he hung like a Nemesis. Soon he was a half-neck in the lead, when Verona, maddened at the thought of being beaten by a presumptuous "squaw", swung her shot-loaded quirt, evidently designed at disabling Cogewea's bridle arm. But the Indian girl's quick eye enabled her to avoid the heavy swing, and as the next descended, she caught and wrenched the whip from the frenzied rider's hand. Enraged at the brutality of the assault, she struck with all her force, but the blow falling short, landed athwart the Black Snake's head. This slightly checked his speed and the Bay Devil won by nearly a full length.

The "H-B" boys yelled and threw their sombreros in air as the well matched leaders passed over the chalked-line, the balance of the field thundering in the rear. Diamond, the Bay Devil, circled far before his rider could stop him: and when at last she brought him about, he was reeking with perspiration and quivering with exertion and excitement. Jim was there and helped Cogewea to dismount. He blanketed the racer and led him to the stables, the girl walking at his side.

"By gad! Sis," he exclaimed. "I'm some glad you won this here race. I knowed the Bay Devil would come through if only he had a nervy rider like you; my tiny squaw."

Her eyes sparkled at the compliment, for "squaw" had not been intended as epithetical. She was silent and Jim continued:

"You're sure one gritty little Injun, hittin' back at that there high-toned white gal as you did. The 'H-B' boys are all glad! They saw what she done to you first and know who's in fault. But the white fellers a backin' the Webster hoss are breezin' trouble if the judge gives you the prize. They have the dough and that's what talks, but the best rider of the—"

"She struck first and I had a right to defend myself," broke in Cogewea spiritedly. "It made no difference in hitting her horse, for I was ahead anyway. I had my eyes kinda half shut on account of dust and couldn't see very well."

The Westerner understood and laughed. Reaching the stable, he unsaddled the Bay and giving him over to a care-taker, threw the saddle on White Star.

"Now Sis," he spoke earnestly, "if you win this here 'squaw race', I'll buy you a swell present; cause I'm goin' double up on bets. I raked home fifty bucks on the Bay Devil, and it'll be a hundred on the Star. He's sure some hummer when unwindin', and the way to get his best, is not to whip. Just pull on reins 'nough to give him his head, then see the White Star do some meteoric shootin'."

"Leave it to me while you may prepare to deliver that present," was the self-confident reply. "I'm going over to the Kootenais and rent a buck-skin dress. I have no native costume and this garb would be a dead give away; for they may kick on me riding this race." Then mounting, Cogewea cantered to the Kootenai camp, where she had but little difficulty in securing a complete tribal dress. Very soon she came from the tepee in full regalia, her face artistically decorated with varied paints. The Indian children saw and giggled among themselves. Remounting, she doubled the bright shawl over her knees, lapping it securely. When she rode back to the track, the "H-B" boys recognized her only by the horse.

Proceeding to the grandstand, Cogewea paid her entrance fee of two and a half dollars. Supposing that the Indian girl did not understand English, the judge turned to his companion with the remark:

"Some swell looker for a Kootenai squaw, eh? Mighty good pickin' for a young feller like you. Wish I wasn't so badly married! I'd sure keep an eye out for her. But the Missus would raise a hurry-Cain if she knowed that I rather like some of the squaws around here."

The young man's reply was of like sinister import, and then they began conversing in lowered tones. The girl's eyes filled with tears, as she turned away; brooding over the constantly light spoken words of the "higher" race regarding her people of the incessant insults offered the Indian women by the "gentlemen" whites. She regretted with a pang, the passing of an epoch, when there were no "superiors" to "guide" her simple race to a civilization so manifestly dearth of the primitive law of respect for womanhood; substituting in its stead a social standard

permitting the grossest insult and indignity to the weaker, with the most
brazen impunity.

Cogewea brought White Star in line with the seven other cayuses,
with their Kootenai, or Pend d'Oreille women riders. These last were
gaudy with silk handkerchiefs bound about their heads, bright shawls,
and with beaded mocassined feet. Cogewea alone was bare-headed, her
raven hair reaching loosely below the saddle cantle. She was met with
glances of hatred for the despised "breed". Some of the Indian men were
still hanging to the restless racers, as their wives or sisters made secure
their wraps and settled more firmly in the saddles. The audience lined
either side of the track; on the one the whites clamoring vociferously, on
the other the Indians sedately silent.

The eight horses moved prancing to the place of starting. Cogewea
was assigned position near the centre of the group, where White Star
manifested unusual spirit, causing more or less annoyance to the other
riders. One of the Kootenai girls turned to her and spoke sharply in
good English:

"You have no right to be here! You are half-white! This race is for
Indians and not for *breeds!*"

Cogewea made no reply, but she was overwhelmed with the soul-
yearning for sympathy. For her class—the maligned outcast half-blood—
there seemed no welcome on the face of all God's creation. Denied social
standing with either of the parent races, she felt that the world was crying
out against her.

The signal for starting was the accustomed pistol shot, and Cogewea,
perturbed by the aspersions of the Kootenai woman, was caught
unawares. For some distance, the full-bloods running well bunched, led
by a good score yards; but soon she felt the scorching sting of innumerable sand and dust particles, thrown in her face by the hoofs of the flying
seven. Shielding her eyes by half-closing them she bore on the reins with
slightly increased force. The White Star responded by passing first five
and then six of the contestants, and the main dust-cloud was in the rear.
Gradually the distance between the two leaders lessened and at the end
of the third quarter, the Star began to lap the pinto, whose rider was
considered the best on the Flathead. Contrary to the known custom of
the Indian race rider, this woman had, up to this point, refrained from
using the whip. She now brought it into play and for a space was able to
maintain the lead. But not for long was this to be. Soon the steeds were

running squarely abreast, but as they dashed over the line, White Star was leading by half a neck.

As usual in a close race, those of the whites who had backed their favorites most heavily, crowded to the judges' stand disputing, in language more emphatic than elegant. In marked contrast, there was no contention among the Indian track-gamblers. With them, both winnings and losses alike were accepted with stoic indifference. Jim came to Cogewea, in evident contentment, as he spoke:

"You won, Sis! The judge is in your favor. He says you beat fair and on the level and wants you to come to the stand and get your twenty five bucks. He asked me to bring you over there. He is anxious to see you."

Together they rode to the stand and to the surprise of the judge, Cogewea answered his salutation in perfect English. "His Honour" soon found that this breed girl was not the type he had figured, and he cut this conversation short by directing his assistant to pay her the prize money. He had lost all interest in the Kootenai squaw rider of only a few moments before. He was still more surprised when Cogewea addressed him:

"Pardon me! but there is forty-five dollars more coming to me, as winner of the ladies race."

"You don't mean to tell me that *you* are the one who rode in the ladies' race—that you are claiming the first money on both the ladies and squaw races?" he exclaimed with fierce bluster.

"Yes, I rode in both races! Did all that I could to add to their interest."

"And you now have the effrontery to claim both prizes?"

"Why not? I won both of them."

"Which was irregular and will not be allowed. A protest has already been filed against you in this race, in behalf of Miss Webster, to whom the first prize money will be paid. You never would have led coming in had you not quirted her horse over the head. You will get only the prize for the squaw race. Here Sam!" speaking to his assistant for the second time, "pay this squaw the twenty five dollars as I directed. It is the money she won in the squaw race. Pay her that and no more."

Cogewea again demurred, when Jim, who still sat his horse interposed:

"Here! Sis, you take this here money as the judge offers it. The prizes are different and you don't want to get the two mixed."

Cogewea did as directed and the judge turned away to greet some newly arrived friends. The Westerner accosted him:

"This here business should be settled fair. Every one who saw the race know how the quirt fightin' come 'bout. If the money don't belong to the little gal, why then she ain't goin' to ask for it. But if she won it, then it's hers and you ought give it to her. I am willin' you decide, as you're the proper judge."

"I have decided it and she has been given all the money that she will get." was the emphatic reply. "No Injun can come around here and dictate to me in regard to judging these races. Do you savey that?"

"The white man's rulin' is law," rejoined Jim calmly, "but maybe you'll tell the little gal just why she's not to have this here prize she won so fairly in the ladies' race."

"Because," sneered the now irate judge, "she is a *squaw* and had no right to ride in the *ladies'* race. I would advise you," he added in a menacing tone, "to get away from here if you do not want trouble. This thing is settled and settled for keeps!"

"That's right, pardner," exclaimed a heavy-faced man who, with a group of followers edged his way through the crowd of spectators. "When it comes to the pass that a *squaw* can enter a *ladies'* race and be permitted to win over a girl like Verona Webster, and that too, by quirting her horse over the head, then it is time that *white* people step out and let the damned Injuns run the races! For one, I'm not goin' stand for it and all the boys are with me! If any low born *breed* is looking for trouble, he can now find it in sight!"

The last words were directed to Jim, and the speaker's hand rested dangerously near his pistol's grip. But the half-blood, who had been brought up amid the rough elements of the range, displayed no perturbation at this tirade from the new comer, who stood to the right and apart from the disputants. The position was strategic and Jim was at a disadvantage, should there be gun-play. With stoical disregard, he again addressed the judicial dispenser of prizes:

"Only one word more, Judge, and I ain't trailin' for no disagreeableness. You paid the little gal the twenty five dollars 'cause she's a squaw?"

"Yes, and I am *not* going to pay her the forty five dollars for the same reason; that she *is* a squaw! Do you get that?"

"Stay by it, Judge! We're with you to the last cartridge!" vociferated the heavy face and his backers.

"My hearin' ain't no ways defective," came the serene reply without notice to this side clamor, "But I may be locoed as to your meanin'. I take it that the little gal bein' *a squaw*, she can't be a *lady*! Is that it? She's a waitin' to hear you say that. Tell these here people your 'cisin regardin' the character of the little gal."

The judge was astounded. Here, contrary to all precedents, was a tribesman persistently contending against a deal—however unfair—meted out by his, in every way—"superior." Sitting sidewise his saddle and chewing at a scant moustache, he was looking into the eyes of his antagonist with exasperating calmness. The brazen effrontery of the breed was maddening. The judge, a man of tried nerve in more than one gun fight, like a storm-cloud about to pour its wrath upon a waiting world, paused; choking with livid rage. Addressing a stalky individual wearing a police badge of exaggerated dimensions, who had just stepped within the circle, he bruskly ordered:

"Here, Marshal, put the irons on this rider and lock him up as a dangerous character! He is charged with malicious interference with an honest distribution of race awards, by coming here armed and attempting intimidation of the program officials. There will be plenty of witnesses to make the complaint stick, and he can consider himself fortunate in spending a few months behind bars rather than dangling at a rope's end, which would have happened within a very few seconds had you not so opportunely arrived."

"Slide down from that hoss, Injun, while I ornament yo' with the bracelets," blustered the constable, advancing as he produced a pair of burnished handcuffs. "An' don't make a mistake by thinkin' it only a joke, savvy?"

Jim remained immobile, and something in his demeanor caused the minion of the law to hesitate. It was at this moment that Cogewea, with swift dexterity, dashed the wadded bills which she had received, full in the face of the fuming judge, and vehemently broke forth:

"*Take* your tainted money! I do not want to touch any thing polluted by having passed through your slimy hands! And, since you are disbursing *racial* prizes regardless of merit or justice, pass it on to the full-blood Kootenai woman, who, like your white protegee, won second place only. She is as much entitled to it as is Miss Webster to the money which you are so chivalrously withholding from me. I am as much Caucasian, I regret to admit, as American, and measured by your rum-fogged ideals, a mere nobody; with no rights to be respected."

In low tones she then spoke to Jim in their own tongue. The Westerner, slightly hesitating, readjusted himself in his saddle, turned and rode away by her side without so much as a backward glance at his gun-bestudded enemies. The spiked-heel of might had, as ever scored, but at the cost of no inconsiderable amount of self dignity.

Silent Bob, who had unobserved moved to a point of vantage, sighed audibly:

"Mos' glad th' meller-dramy's over. I'd hater get all shot up an' my 'surance 'sessment unpaid; I'd hater miss a chanct of again skinnin' th' Kootenais'."

The Southerner was well aware that he was assuming an extremely unpopular attitude, and one likely to be resented, but aside from scowls and muttered imprecations, his challenge passed unnoticed.

Discomforted by the withering disdain of Cogewea, and the burning contempt for their prowess by her companion, the pugnacity of the "bunch" had suffered a most undignified backset.

—Mourning Dove (1981, 62–71)

Lynn Riggs

Cherokee, 1899–1954

Lynn Riggs grew up on a northeast Oklahoma ranch, and after a period of "knocking about" in movies in New York City and Hollywood, earned a degree at the University of Oklahoma. He began to publish short stories and poetry soon after college, but it was as a playwright that he made his literary mark—notably for Green Grow the Lilacs, *which had a successful run on Broadway in 1931 and later served as the basis for Rodgers and Hammerstein's hit musical* Oklahoma!; *and* Cherokee Night, *his one specifically "Indian" play, which deals with the identity and social issues faced by mixed bloods at this time. His early stint in Hollywood led to a long association with the movies as a film writer; probably his best film script was for* The Plainsman *(1936), starring Gary Cooper as Wild Bill Hickock. Riggs lived mainly in Greenwich Village and in Santa Fe, New Mexico, where he came under the influence of Southwestern Indian culture, as evoked in his poetry.*

SANTO DOMINGO CORN DANCE

The Chorus

"Bring rain,
As we bring now
Our gift of dance and song
To You—who dance not, nor sing—
Bring rain!"

The Dancers

Bodies
Reddened, and gourds,
Rain girdles, ornaments,
The skins of foxes—what should please
You more?

Portent

But look!
Where the line whips
Like rain in corn, like clouds
Wind beaten, or like the frown
Upon His brow!

Song of the Bodies

"I am
Naked before
You, High One—look! Hear me!
As I stamp this ground worn smooth
By feet.

"Not as
A supplicant
I shake the doors of earth—
Let the green corn spring to meet
My tread!"

The Clouds

Just now
Across the line
Of these red men there swept—
Like wings of thunder at the sun—
Shadows!

The Koshari

As if
Their feet were struck
With scorn, their hands with pride—
Koshari glide, halt, grimace, grin,
And turn.

The Child Dancer

"But that
I am a child,
I should not notice the branch
Of spruce tied on his arm
In my eyes."

The Orchard

Beyond
The baking roofs,
A barren mountain points
Still higher, though its feet are white
With bloom.

Rain

One drum—
No more, one voice,
One slant of bodies,
And my tears will fall like rain
Upon this ground.

—Lynn Riggs (1930, 8–10)

MOON

What I had waited for in the silken wind
Came over me at last. Radiant I stood
In silver. Silver the pavement's end.
Chaste every poplar, every cottonwood.

A light in the *portales* of the hill
Opened the earth. A cricket shook the air.
On Monte Sol guitars of gold, too still
For music, said a silver prayer.

—Lynn Riggs (1930, 38)

SHADOW ON SNOW

I, a shadow, thinking as I go,
Feel the need of a mimicry
To say this in music: how the moon is one
With the snow, and the snow warmer than I shall ever
       be—
I, a shadow, moving across the snow.

There shall be no more shadows after mine shall go
Hissing over ice, cracking the black river glass.
There shall be still a moon, but never a sun,
Never an earth again with its triumphing grass—
Only the moon and the snow.
              —Lynn Riggs (1930, 49)

SPRING MORNING—SANTA FE

The first hour was a word the color of dawn.
The second came, and gorgeous poppies stood,
Backs to a wall. The yellow sun rode on.
A mocking bird sang shrilly from a nest of wood.

The water in the acequia came down
At the stroke of nine, and watery clouds were lifting
Their velvet shadows from the little town.
Gold fired the pavement where the leaves were shifting.

At ten, black shawls of women bowed along
The Alameda. Sleepy burros lay
In the heat and lifted up their ears. A song
Wavered upon the wind and died away.

And the great bells rang out a golden tune.
Words grew in the heart and clanged, the color of noon.
              —Lynn Riggs (1930, 6)

THE HOLLOW

It is quiet here. Tree shade
Is a cool place. I will rest
Easily in the shadow. I will lie
On the earth's breast,
And look at what sky I can see
Through leaves, or perhaps look
At dandelions bowing gravely
To themselves in the brook.

Not thinking of this thing or of that thing,
I will lie
And forget the road I have traveled over
To look at the sky.

Perhaps I shall forget the brown bluff
Over the brook I must climb
As high as the trees are high.
Perhaps I shall forget time
And lie here forever, forgetting
How soon it will be
Before I must leave this hollow
Reluctantly.

                    —Lynn Riggs (1930, 18)

FOOTPRINTS

Over the gold-leaf road, the drenched willow
Leans. The flayed track, smooth as stone,
Will be printed with our feet passing over,
And we shall be gone.

You will not find trace of us after the fall rain
Sweeps again. You will not find
Trace of us in the orchard or the pasture
Or in the mind.

Only these prints of feet—and ephemeral!—
In the sand and clay,
And you will forget why it is we have gone
And which way.

>   —Lynn Riggs (1930, 55)

From *The Cherokee Night*

SCENE SEVEN

In the darkness, a drumbeat rises, grows tremendous in volume, as if in a cramped enclosure its resonance filled all available space, thudding at the walls for more room. The tone dies to a steady insistent beat.

> *Claremore Mound rises in a pale clear light under a wintry night sky, with only a few stars in it. Snow is over the slopes, is standing in the depressions and gullies, is thick on the black branches of trees and bushes, edging them with white. A bitter cold wind from the north pours over the Mound, raking the visible downslope. Snow crystals whirl from limb and rock, glistening. Under the sharp sound of the wind the drumbeat goes on, low and regular. A deep male VOICE begins to sing a Cherokee song. The light on the Mound begins to die down, as if an unseen moon had gone behind a cloud.*

> *Then a fire begins, first to glow, then to blaze, from the exact spot of the picnic fire of Scene One. Its wavering tongues of light are thrown down sharply across the smooth dirt floor of a log house. It becomes bright enough in the room to reveal an obtuse-angled corner of the cabin. The fire comes from in front as if from a rock fireplace. In one of the two sides visible are a small window and a heavy oaken door. Extending along one side is a rough straw cot covered with blankets and crazy quilts, in the corner is a water bucket on a box, washpans, a tall shotgun, cooking utensils, etc. Stools and chairs, primitively hacked out, are scattered about. Outside, the snow covered Mound gleams whitely. The year is 1895.*

> *Inside the cabin, at center, and touched by the firelight,* JOHN GRAY-WOLF, *an Indian about fifty-five or sixty, sits on a low stool, beating a drum. He has just finished singing. His face is dark, prominent, his*

mouth firm; his long black hair is tied in a pigtail and drawn back from a brow of singular nobility. He sits quietly; great serenity and grace flow out of him.

His little grandson, a boy about eight, with black, eager eyes, in a grave dark face, sits on the floor at his right watching excitedly. GRAY-WOLF *finishes, lets the drum rest again on the floor. He smiles at the little boy.*

GRAY-WOLF: You like that, hunh?

SONNY: What's it say, Grampaw?

GRAY-WOLF: It's about huntin', Sonny. It says:

> Listen, let me shoot much game!
> Let my appetite never be satisfied.
> Let the mangled game hang thickly from my belt!
> O Ancient White Fire, I offer you the clotted blood
>   of the birds in payment!

SONNY: Couldn't the birds fly away, Grampaw?

GRAY-WOLF: The hunter is in a tree. He shoots them with
     arrows from his blowgun.

SONNY: *(Intensely.)* I'd fly away—clean acrost the river some'eres!

GRAY-WOLF: The birds don't know.

SONNY: I don't like it.

GRAY-WOLF: You go to bed now.

SONNY: *(Shuddering.)* It's cold. They's ice in the water bucket.

GRAY-WOLF: You go to bed. *(He begins to beat the drum softly. He
     stops.)* Sonny—

SONNY: When you tell me about the Cherokee fighter.

GRAY-WOLF: Then you go?

SONNY: Yes, Grampaw.

GRAY-WOLF: The big fighter of the Cherokee Tribe, when he was in
     a battle didn't want to be killed. So he found out how he
     could put his life up in the top of a sycamore tree while his
     body went on fightin' in the front row of the battle. Then his
     enemies would shoot at his body but couldn't hurt him a-tall.
     His life was safe—way up high in the tree out of sight. Once
     his enemies found out about it. At the next battle, they quit
     shootin' at his body, and shot all their arrows up in the top of
     the sycamore. So the warrior fell down dead.

SONNY: Why did he have to die?

GRAY-WOLF: His life was killed.

SONNY: *(Soberly.)* I don't wanta die. I would run away! Fast!

GRAY-WOLF: *(Gravely.)* When Death wants you, it's better to
sit and wait.

SONNY: I would run! I would run!

GRAY-WOLF: Take the Cherokees at Tahlequah. When one of 'em does
sump'n bad, the law says: "You got to die. You're a bad Indian.
We let you go now to your home. Tell your wife good-bye, tell
your children. But on Saturday, come back and be punished."
The Indian goes away home and says to his wife: "Good-bye,
wife." He says to his children: "Be brave, children." Then he
gets on his pony and rides in to Tahlequah. There they put a
rope around his neck and hang him to a tree.

SONNY: I wouldn't go back and get hung.

GRAY-WOLF: He has to go.

SONNY: Why?

GRAY-WOLF: *(Slowly.)* Death—*wants* him.

*Somewhere outside in the night, two pistol shots ring out, the first more
muffled than the second.* GRAY-WOLF *and the* BOY *turn* quickly,
*stare back into the cabin toward the window and door. Another muffled
shot. Then two more shots, in quick and angry succession, can be heard.*
GRAY-WOLF *gets up, goes to the door and pushes down the heavy
oaken bar, looks at* SONNY, *hardly breathing. Then, going rapidly to the
window, he pulls aside the rough curtain and looks out. He comes down
again, sits.*

SONNY: *(In a whisper, rising to his knees.)* What is it, Grampaw?

GRAY-WOLF: *(In an absorbed tone, a dark memory rising in him.)*
Death.

SONNY: (Startled.) What, Grampaw, what? *(He sits back.)*

GRAY-WOLF: *(Unheeding.)* When your pappy was killed it was a cold
night just like this. His family was hungry. He took a side
of beef from the smokehouse on Rucker's Ranch. To him it
wasn't stealin'. To the Indian, food was sump'n to keep you
and your family alive, sump'n you had a right to. Your father

didn't know the word "stealin'." But they caught him and killed him. A cold night, just like this—*(He shakes his head, comes back to the present, looking round.)* It's better not to get mixed up in things when they's shootin' goin' on. Indian Territory is plumb full of men with six-shooters now—cattle rustlers, desperadoes—*(Breaking off.)* The door's barred. You go to bed now, Sonny. *(He reaches for the drum, involuntarily as if in song he found expression for a mood. There is a bang at the door, repeated and repeated, with the sound of a man's VOICE crying out desperately, the words thick and indistinct. GRAY-WOLF gets up quickly, faces the door from right stage.)* Who is it? What'd you want?

SONNY *has gone to him.*

VOICE: *(Muffled and angry.)* For God's sake! (Then pleading.) Hurry! Let me in!
GRAY-WOLF: Who is it? I can't let you in less'n you tell me—!
VOICE: *(Muttering darkly.)* You want me to break your door down!

The unseen figure moves from the door, his heavy boots crunching the snow piled up around the cabin. Suddenly the glass of the window is smashed inward, and a hand, reaching in, rips off half the curtain. Another hand with a pistol is thrust through and pointed at GRAY-WOLF. A MAN's agonized and angry face can be made out dimly beyond the broken pane.

MAN: You goddamned Indian, open that door! Let me in, I say! *(A spasm of pain comes over his face.)* Hurry, let me in! I'm dyin'—Jesus Christ—

He sways weakly collapsing in the window, sinks to his knees out of sight. The pistol clatters to the floor inside, the hand which held it disappearing over the sharp broken glass of the pane. GRAY-WOLF goes swiftly to the door, draws up the bar and rushes out. Seeing his grandfather disappearing, SONNY cries out in fear.

SONNY: Grampaw! Where—! *(He runs to the window, GRAY-WOLF comes back into sight.)* Grampaw!

GRAY-WOLF *comes in, half carrying a* MAN, *middle-aged, with a lean, hard and desperate face. One hand clutches his side frenziedly. His clothes are thick with fresh blood. His head rolls in pain; muffled groans come from his twisted mouth. Slipping out of* GRAY-WOLF'S *supporting arm, the* MAN *half falls onto the cot, right, doubled up in agony.*

MAN: *(Piteously.)* Stop the blood—Stop the blood.

GRAY-WOLF *goes quickly to the water bucket, jabs the dipper into it sharply to break the ice, pours some water in a pan, picks up a cloth and comes back, bending over the* MAN. *He begins to pull away the clotted clothes, trying with the cold water to stanch the wound. He kneels by the cot. The* MAN *groans.*

GRAY-WOLF: Try to be still now. Sonny, put some more wood on the fire. (SONNY *obeys, struggling with a log.)* It's pretty bad. It'll stop bleedin' if you'll just lay still.
MAN: *(Weakly, assenting.)* Umm.

A single shot rings out sharply. The MAN *struggles upward with a cry, feeling for his pistol.*

GRAY-WOLF: *(Standing up.)* No, no, lay still! *(He bends to stop him.)*
MAN: It's them! Where's my pistol?
GRAY-WOLF: Lay down, I said! You'll bleed to death.
MAN: My pistol—! Where is it? God damn you, what've you done with it!
GRAY-WOLF: You dropped it over there—inside the window. Be quiet!
MAN: Get it, damn you!
GRAY-WOLF: You lay down.
MAN: Anh! *(With an animal-like snarl, he begins to crawl off the cot, clutching his side.)*
GRAY-WOLF: *(Stopping him.)* Here! Lay down! You'll start the blood again! *(The* MAN's *head droops down to the pillow weakly.)*

> I'll get your pistol. *(He goes over and brings the pistol, starts to hand it to him.)*

MAN: *(Lifting his head.)* How many bullets I got left?

GRAY-WOLF: *(Looking.)* Two.

(The MAN's *head falls back. His hand lifts.)*

MAN: Give it to me.

The INDIAN *puts it into his hand.*

GRAY-WOLF: Now you lay still. *(He dabs carefully at the wound with the cold water.)*

MAN: *(Muttering feverishly, in pain.)* They won't get me!

GRAY-WOLF: Now, now—!

MAN: I'll get away yet! I dropped my other pistol in the snow some'eres—I got two bullets left!

GRAY-WOLF: There, be quiet—

MAN: *(With terrible quietness, his voice dead.)* I wish I could sleep.

GRAY-WOLF: *(Compassionately.)* You rest. Take it easy.

There is a moment of silence.

MAN: *(Without feeling or intensity.)* I killed the bastard.

GRAY-WOLF: *(softly)* Who?

MAN: Irwin.

GRAY-WOLF: *(Drawing back, staring at him.)* Old man Irwin?

MAN: Shot him twice, the dirty bastard.

GRAY-WOLF *goes to the stool, sits.*

GRAY-WOLF: *(In a hushed voice.)* He was a good old man.

MAN: He's dead.

GRAY-WOLF: *(Turning a little toward him.)* Why?

MAN: *(With difficulty.)* Wanted the money in his store. He wouldn't tell me where it was. Shot through the lean-to door at me. Got me—in the side. I kicked the door down. There he was—on his knees. Begged me. "Don't kill me. For the sake of my little girl—" *(Fiercely.)* I let him have it!

GRAY-WOLF: *(In a strange hollow voice.)* Shot him dead—
MAN: On his knees he was!
GRAY-WOLF: —In cold blood. *(He is absorbed, as in a dream.* SONNY,
    who has stood motionless by the window, runs to him.)
SONNY: Grampaw!

Without being conscious of it, GRAY-WOLF *puts his arm about the
child. Finally he speaks.*

GRAY-WOLF: I know who you are now. You're Spench.
MAN: *(Weakly, but with some pride.)* Edgar Spench.
GRAY-WOLF: That ain't your right name, though.
SPENCH: No.
GRAY-WOLF: It's Breeden, Edgar Breeden.
SPENCH: Know everthing, don't you?

GRAY-WOLF *stands up abruptly.*

GRAY-WOLF: My little boy—he wants to go out.

The MAN *rolls over, his face toward the* INDIAN, *the pistol in his hand.*

SPENCH: Stay here. Don't you move.
GRAY-WOLF: *(Firmly.)* My little boy. *(They eye each other
    a tense second.)*
SPENCH: *(Dangerously.)* I got two bullets—one for you, one for the kid.
GRAY-WOLF: He'll come right back.
SPENCH: *(After a moment.)* Let him go. You stay here.

The INDIAN *takes the boy to the door,* SONNY *looks up at him
questioningly. The* MAN *on the pallet watches.* GRAY-WOLF'S *face is
inexpressive, masklike.*

GRAY-WOLF: *(Softly.)* Hurry back, Sonny.

SONNY *goes out. Closing, but not barring the door,* GRAY-WOLF
turns, sits, faces the MAN. *Their voices become muted, bell-like,*

as if their words had no meaning, or as if meant only for themselves.
SPENCH'S *voice is weak,* GRAY-WOLF'S *filled with a soft vehemence
and a kind of wonder.*

GRAY-WOLF: The wife you left, she's around some'eres.
SPENCH: Course.
GRAY-WOLF: Still talks about you. Thinks you're sump'n fine,
        'stid of a killer.
SPENCH: Marthy.
GRAY-WOLF: Your boy's a year old now. Looks like you.
SPENCH: Named after me.
GRAY-WOLF: Maybe'll *take* after you. Maybe'll kill men in cold
        blood for a little money, a little filthy gold!
SPENCH: Maybe.
GRAY-WOLF: Florey Newcomb's with child, your child.
SPENCH: Yeow.
GRAY-WOLF: Carries it, tells everbody she's carryin' a kid of
        Edgar Breeden's, proud of herself.
SPENCH: Florey.
GRAY-WOLF: Proud to have a kid by a desperado, a man that don't like
        no one's life but his own, a man that ain't got a heart in him
        no place, that was born with a gun by his side, that—!
SPENCH: *(Softly.)* The blood—
GRAY-WOLF: *(Gets up, goes to him.)* What is it?
SPENCH: Stop the blood.

GRAY-WOLF *kneels down by* SPENCH'S *side. Outside, the wind lifts
for a moment, sighing. The warm glow of the firelight flickers over the two
figures.* GRAY-WOLF *puts the pan under the cot.*

SPENCH: *(After a moment.)* I wish I could sleep.
GRAY-WOLF: You rest. You'll be all right.
SPENCH: Never be all right, never be—!
GRAY-WOLF: Here. Put your head on the pillow.
SPENCH: *(Turning to look at him, the wan beginnings of wonder
        in his eyes.)* Why're you good to me?
GRAY-WOLF: *(Standing up.)* 'Taint nuthin'.

SPENCH: Me, Edgar Spench, wanted everwhur, rewards out for me!
I ain't worth it!

GRAY-WOLF: Lay still!

SPENCH: Robbery, arson—I'm guilty. Wife desertion, rape, murder!

GRAY-WOLF: Why'd you do all them things?

SPENCH: *(With almost a sob in his throat.)* I don't know—!

GRAY-WOLF: Nobody knows.

SPENCH: *(Weakly, feverishly, anguished.)* I tried everthing. Tried to
farm. Too restless. Cattle herdin', ridin' fence. Sump'n
always drove me on. The bosses! Burned down their barns,
rustled their cattle, slept with their wives. Shot the bastards
down—! Sump'n inside—no rest, I don't know—Bad blood.
Too much Indian, they tell me.

GRAY-WOLF: *(The revelation growing in him from what* SPENCH *has
said.)* Not enough Indian.

SPENCH: How—!

GRAY-WOLF: *(With troubled compassion.)* I'm full-blood—
Cherokee. I live peaceful. I ain't troubled. I remember
the way my people lived in quiet times. Think of my
ancestors. It keeps me safe. You though—like my boy.
He's dead. He was half white, like you. They killed him,
had to kill him! Not *enough* Indian. The mixture.
(He sits on the stool again.)

SPENCH: *(Softly.)* When I'm dead, will you bury me?

GRAY-WOLF: You're not dead.

SPENCH: By the Verdigree River. It's quiet there. I was born there.
Bury me deep.

GRAY-WOLF: You're alive.

SPENCH: Lost so much blood. Feel my life runnin' out of me, slow.
White blood, Indian—it don't matter. It spills out, runs out
of me like water. Don't try to stop it any more.

GRAY-WOLF: Don't talk.

SPENCH: Listen. I'll be better off dead. Caused trouble for everbody.
Myself, too. I'll be better off.

GRAY-WOLF: You got to fight.

SPENCH: Fight!

GRAY-WOLF: Fight to live!

SPENCH: *(Shakes his head.)* Not any more. *(With utter weariness, his voice flat, final, unemotional.)* No more fightin'. I've had enough.

A hand with a pistol is shoved through the window and aimed at SPENCH'S *head. A* MAN *and the moving bodies of many* MEN *and* WOMEN *can be seen throughout the window. A* VOICE *roars out.*

TINSLEY: Get away, Gray-Wolf! Jump back!

GRAY-WOLF *springs up and back into the corner.* SPENCH *sits up quickly.* TINSLEY'S *pistol is fired twice in quick succession.* SPENCH *falls back without a sound.*

GRAY-WOLF: *(Crying out in horror.)* No, no! You can't do that, can't do it! In cold blood! *(He turns away leaning against the wall, bent over as if the pain were inside him.)*

TINSLEY *and some* MEN *of the posse rush in.* TINSLEY *is tall, fair, righteous. He crosses to* SPENCH, *right.* GRAY-WOLF *edges downstage to left of door.*

TINSLEY: Dead, all right. The dirty bastard!

SONNY *comes running in, clings to his grandfather.*

TINSLEY: *(Briskly turning, facing nearly front.)* Gray-Wolf. My name's Tinsley. Your little grandson come and told the posse, but don't think that gives you a lien on the reward. I finished him, and I get the money, don't forget that. It's time someone killed him. A bad half-breed, that un. One of *your* tribe, Gray-Wolf. Let this be a lesson and a warnin'. Teach your grandson. Tell everbody what it means to oppose the law. You Indians must think you own things out here. This is God's country out here—and God's a white man. Don't forget that.

Several WOMEN *have come in at the door.*

A MAN: *(By the door.)* Get back, you women. Mrs. Breeden, go on now.

MARTHY BREEDEN, *a gaunt dark woman with a year-old baby in her arms, walks deliberately forward.* FLOREY *follows* MARTHY *in and stops by the door.*

MARTHY: I got to see. *(They make way for her.* TINSLEY *crosses up to window. She stands above the dead man, bends over him.)* Edgar. Husband. They got you. We always knowed they would, didn't we? *(Her face is lined and strong. Her voice is unemotional, but full of a rich warm, earthy and compassionate power. The* OTHERS *watch her, compelled.)* What you done was what they call wrong. You couldn't help it, I know that. You tried to do right. It was too much. You was hounded day and night, inside and outside. By day, men. At night, your thoughts. Now it's over. Sleep. Rest now. *(She shifts the child in her arms, looks down at it.)* But here's your son. In him your trouble. It goes on. In him. It ain't finished. *(She turns, calls to a young woman, who is weeping quietly.* FLOREY *comes over to her.)* Florey. Here's Florey Newcomb, bearin' your child. You're at rest. Sleep. Your disgrace, your wickedness, your pain and trouble live on a while longer. In her child, in my child. In all people born now, about to be born. *(Her face becomes luminous, as her mind gropes toward an impersonal truth.)* Someday, the agony will end. Yours has. Ours will. Maybe not in the night of death, the cold dark night, without stars. Maybe in the sun. It's got to! It's what we live for.

FLOREY: *(Sobbing, crying out.)* He's dead! How can you stand there! Edgar's dead!

MARTHY: *(Compassionately, trying to comfort her.)* It's what he wanted. He'll rest now. Let him die.

FLOREY: But it goes on, it goes on!

MARTHY: In our children, yes. In our children's children, maybe no.

TINSLEY: *(Turning forward, to* GRAY-WOLF.*)* We'll take him away.

GRAY-WOLF: Leave us. It's *our* dead.

TINSLEY *goes out. The* MEN *follow him, quiet and troubled.* GRAY-WOLF *turns round to the door, puts the bolt down. Then he crosses over to the bent figure of* FLOREY, *helps her down onto the stool. Now* MARTHY *crosses in front of* GRAY-WOLF, *stops by the door with her back to the audience. It is like a curious and solemn ritual. A drum has begun to beat, low and throbbing and final. Now* GRAY-WOLF *goes over to the cot and pulls a blanket up over the dead man. He stands up. Turns slowly to face* MARTHY, *who turns to face him. A faraway look is in* GRAY-WOLF's *eyes, a quality of magnificent dignity and despair as if he mourned for his own life, for the life of his son, for his grandson, for* SPENCH, *for the* WOMEN, *for a whole race gone down into darkness. The lights fade slowly. The fire flickers. Claremore Mound glitters in the night. A few stars are in the sky.*

CURTAIN.
THE END

—Lynn Riggs (2003, 198–211)

D'Arcy McNickle

Cree-Salish, 1904–1977

wD'Arcy McNickle (Cree-Salish, adopted into the Montana Flathead Reservation) lived from 1904–1977. When McNickle's parents divorced, he and his two siblings were sent to Chemawa Boarding School in Oregon, despite his mother's protests. As a young man, he sold his land allotment as a member of the Flathead tribe to finance his education abroad. He was the author of three novels: The Surrounded *(1936),* Runner in the Sun: A Story of Indian Maize *(1954), and* Wind from an Enemy Sky *(1978). He also wrote three historical books on Native life:* They Came Here First, Indians and Other Americans *(with Harold Fey), and* Indian Tribes of the United States, *and a biography of Oliver LaFarge. McNickle was very active in Native causes; he worked for the Bureau of Indian Affairs under John Collier and was the director of American Indian Development, Inc., which was founded by the NCAI (National Congress of American Indians). His manuscripts and letters are part of the Ayre collection of the Newberry Library in Chicago; after his death, the Newberry's Center for American Indian History was named for him.*

McNickle aims for realism in his stories. Most of his short fiction was written during the years that he lived in New York City, 1927–1935. As Birgit Hans notes, the "basic theme of his short stories concerns the community and the outsider or individual within the community who infringes upon its traditions. In these stories, the community usually manages to maintain its traditions and to survive" (McNickle 1992, xiv). In "Train Time," which originally appeared in a BIA magazine titled Indians at Work,

McNickle deals with a theme that was to become prominent in his novels and in the works of other twentieth-century novelists, that is, the lack of communication and understanding between white and Native cultures. McNickle often adopts and presents sympathetically the perspective of a white outsider, who despite all of his or her good intentions, brings about disaster for all concerned. In "Hard Riding," Big Face is able to maintain the community values by responding in a tricksterish way to Brinder's profit-motivated plans (see also Birgit Hans in McNickle 1992, xv).

Train Time (1936)

On the depot platform everybody stood waiting, listening. The train had just whistled, somebody said. They stood listening and gazing eastward, where railroad tracks and creek emerged together from a tree-chocked canyon.

Twenty-five boys, five girls, Major Miles—all stood waiting and gazing eastward. Was it true that the train had whistled?

"That was no train!" a boy's voice explained.

"It was a steer bellowing."

"It was the train!"

Girls crowded backward against the station building, heads hanging, tears starting; boys pushed forward to the edge of the platform. An older boy with a voice already turning heavy stepped off the weather shredded boardwalk and stood wide-legged in the middle of the track. He was the doubter. He had heard no train.

Major Miles boomed. "You! What's your name? Get back, here! Want to get killed! All of you, stand back!"

The Major strode about, soldier-like, and waved commands. He was exasperated. He was tired. A man driving cattle through timber had it easy, he was thinking. An animal trainer had no idea of trouble. Let anyone try corralling twenty-thirty Indian kids, dragging them out of hiding places, getting them away from relatives and together in one place, then holding them, without tying them, until train time! Even now, at the last moment, when his worries were almost over, they were trying to get themselves killed!

Major Miles was a man of conscience. Whatever he did, he did earnestly. On this hot end-of-summer day he perspired and frowned and wore his soldier bearing. He removed his hat from his wet brow and thoughtfully passed his hand from the hair line backward. Words tumbled about in his mind. Somehow, he realized, he had to vivify the moment. These children were about to go out from the Reservation and get a new start. Life would change. They ought to realize it, somehow—

"Boys—and girls—" there were five girls he remembered. He had got them all lined up against the building, safely away from the edge of the platform. The air was stifling with end-of-summer heat. It was time to say something, never mind the heat. Yes, he would have to make the moment real. He stood soldier-like and thought that.

"Boys and girls—" The train whistled, dully, but unmistakably. Then it repeated more clearly. The rails came to life, something was running through them and making them sing.

Just then the Major's eye fell upon little Eneas and his sure voice faltered. He knew about little Eneas. Most of the boys and girls were mere names; he had seen them around the Agency with their parents or had caught sight of them scurrying behind tepees and barns when he visited their homes. But little Eneas he knew. With him before his eyes, he paused.

He remembered so clearly the winter day, six months ago, when he first saw Eneas. It was the boy's grandfather, Michel Lamartine, he had gone to see. Michel had contracted to cut wood for the Agency but had not started work. The Major had gone to discover why not.

It was the coldest day of the winter, late in February, and the cabin, sheltered as it was among the pine and cottonwood of a creek bottom, was shot through by frosty drafts. There was wood all about them. Lamartine was a woodcutter besides, yet there was no wood in the house. The fire in the flat-topped cast-iron stove burned weakly. The reason was apparent. The Major had but to look at the bed where Lamartine lay, twisted and shrunken by rheumatism. Only his black eyes burned with life. He tried to wave a hand as the Major entered.

"You see how I am!" the gesture indicated. Then a nerve-strung voice faltered. "We have it bad here. My old woman, she's not much good."

Clearly she wasn't, not for wood-chopping. She sat close by the fire, trying with a good natured grin to lift her ponderous body from a low seated rocking chair. The Major had to motion her back to her ease. She breathed with asthmatic roar. Wood-chopping was not within her range. With only a squaw's hatchet to work with, she could scarcely have come within striking distance of a stick of wood. Two blows, if she had struck them, might have put a stop to her laboring heart.

"You see how it is," Lamartine's eyes flashed.

The Major saw clearly. Sitting there in the frosty cabin, he pondered their plight and wondered if he could get away without coming down with pneumonia. A stream of wind seemed to be hitting him in the back of the neck. Of course, there was nothing to do. One saw too many such situations. If one undertook to provide sustenance out of one's own pocket there would be no end to the demands. Government salaries were small, resources were limited. He could do no more than shake his head sadly, offer some vague hope, some small sympathy. He would have to get away at once.

Then a hand fumbled at the door; it opened. After a moment's struggle, little Eneas appeared, staggering under a full armload of pine limbs hacked into short lengths. The boy was no taller than an ax handle, his nose was running, and he had a croupy cough. He dropped the wood into the empty box near the old woman's chair, then straightened himself.

A soft chuckling came from the bed. Lamartine was full of pride. "A good boy, that. He keeps the old folks warm."

Something about the boy made the Major forget his determination to depart. Perhaps it was his wordlessness, his uncomplaining wordlessness. Or possibly it was his loyalty to the old people. Something drew his eyes to the boy and set him to thinking. Eneas was handing sticks of wood to the old woman and she was feeding them into the stove. When the fire box was full a good part of the boy's armload was gone. He would have to cut more, and more, to keep the old people warm.

The Major heard himself saying suddenly: "Sonny, show me your woodpile. Let's cut a lot of wood for the old folks."

It happened just like that, inexplicably. He went even farther. Not only did he cut enough wood to last through several days, but when he had finished he put the boy in the Agency car and drove him to town, five miles there and back. Against his own principles, he bought a week's store of groceries, and excused himself by telling the boy, as they drove homeward, "Your grandfather won't be able to get to town for a few days yet. Tell him to come see me when he gets well."

That was the beginning of the Major's interest in Eneas. He had decided that day that he would help the boy in any way possible, because he was a boy of quality. You would be shirking your duty if you failed to recognize and to help a boy of his sort. The only question was, how to help?

When he saw the boy again, some weeks later, his mind saw the problem clearly. "Eneas," he said, "I'm going to help you. I'll see that the old folks are taken care of, so you won't have to think about them. Maybe the old man won't have rheumatism next year, anyhow. If he does, I'll find a family where he and the old lady can move in and be looked after. Don't worry about them. Just think about yourself and what I'm going to do for you. Eneas, when it comes school time, I'm going to send you away. How do you like that?" The Major smiled at his own happy idea.

There was silence. No shy smiling, no look of gratitude, only silence. Probably he had not understood.

"You understand, Eneas? Your grandparents will be taken care of. You'll go away and learn things. You'll go on a train."

The boy looked here and there and scratched at the ground with his foot. "Why do I have to go away?"

"You don't have to, Eneas. Nobody will make you. I thought you'd like to. I thought—" The Major paused, confused.

"You won't make me go away, will you?" There was fear in the voice, tears threatening.

"Why, no Eneas. If you don't want to go. I thought—"

The Major dropped the subject. He didn't see the boy again through spring and summer, but he thought of him. In fact, he couldn't forget the picture he had of him that first day. He couldn't forget either that he wanted to help him. Whether the boy understood what was good for him or not, he meant to see to it that the right thing was done. And that was why, when he made up a quota of children to be sent to the school in Oregon, the name of Eneas Lamartine was included. The Major did not discuss it with him again but he set the wheels in motion. The boy would go with the others. In time to come, he would understand. Possibly he would be grateful.

Thirty children were included in the quota, and of them all Eneas was the only one the Major had actual knowledge of, the only one in whom he was personally interested. With each of them, it was true, he had had difficulties. None had wanted to go. They said they "liked it at home," or they were "afraid" to go away, or they would "get sick" in a strange country; and the parents were no help. They too were frightened and uneasy. It was a tiresome, hard kind of duty, but the Major knew what was required of him and never hesitated. The difference was, that in the cases of all these others, the problem was routine. He met it, and passed over it. But in the case of Eneas, he was bothered. He wanted to make clear what this moment of going away meant. It was a breaking away from fear and doubt and ignorance. Here began the new. Mark it, remember it.

His eyes lingered on Eneas. There he stood, drooping, his nose running as on that first day, his stockings coming down, his jacket in need of buttons. But under that shabbiness, the Major knew, was a real quality. There was a boy who, with the right help, would blossom and grow strong. It was important that he should not go away hurt and resentful.

The Major called back his straying thoughts and cleared his throat. The moment was important.

"Boys and girls—"

The train was pounding near. Already it had emerged from the canyon and momently the headlong flying locomotive loomed blacker and larger. A white plume flew upward—Whoo-oo, whoo-oo.

The Major realized in sudden remorse that he had waited too long. The vital moment had come, and he had paused, looked for words, and lost it. The roar of rolling steel was upon them.

Lifting his voice in desperate haste, his eyes fastened on Eneas, he bellowed: "Boys and girls—be good—,"

That was all anyone heard.

—D'Arcy McNickle (1992, 47–52)
First published in *Indians at Work* (1936)

Hard Riding

Riding his gray mare a hard gallop in the summer dust, Brinder Mather labored with thought which couldn't quite come into focus.

The horse labored too, its gait growing heavy as loose sand fouled its footing; but at each attempt to break stride into a trot, there was the prick of spur point, a jerk at the reins. It was a habit with the rider.

"Keep going! Earn your feed, you hammerhead!"

Brinder was always saying that his horses didn't earn their feed. Yet he was the hardest rider in the country.

Feeling as he did about horses, he quite naturally had doubts about Indians. And he had to work with Indians. He was their superintendent . . . a nurse to their helplessness, was the way he sometimes thought of it.

It was getting toward sundown. The eastward mirror of the sky reflected orange and crimson flame thwarting the prismatic heavens. It was after supper, after a hard day at the Agency office, and Brinder was anxious to get his task done and be home to rest. The heat of the day had fagged him. His focusing thought came out in words, audibly.

"They've been fooling with the idea for a month, more than a month, and I still can't tell what they'll do. Somehow I've got to put it over. Either put it over or drop it. I'll tell them that. Take it or leave it. . . ."

Ahead, another mile, he saw the white schoolhouse, the windows ablaze with the evening sun. He wondered if those he had called together would be there, if they would all be there. A full turn-out, he reasoned, would indicate that they were interested. He could be encouraged if he saw them all on hand.

As he drew nearer, he observed that a group stood waiting. He tried to estimate the number . . . twelve or fifteen. Others were still coming. There were riders in the distance coming by other roads. The frown relaxed on his heavy, sun-reddened face. For the moment he was satisfied. He had called the entire Tribal Council of twenty, and evidently they would all be on hand. Good!

He let his horse slow to less than a canter for the first time in the three-mile ride from the Agency.

"Hello, boys. Everybody coming tonight? Let's go inside."

He strode, tall and dignified, through the group.

They smiled to his words, saying nothing. One by one they followed him into the schoolroom. He was always for starting things with a rush; they always hung back. It was a familiar pattern. He walked to the teacher's desk and spread out before him a sheaf of paper which he had brought in a heavy envelope.

In five years one got to know something about Indians. Even in one's first job as superintendent of a Reservation, five years was a good schooling.

The important thing, the first thing to learn, was not to let them stall you. They would do it every time if you let them. They would say to a new idea, "Let us talk about that" or "Give us time. We'll think about it." One had to know when to cut short. Put it over or drop it. Take it or leave it.

Not realizing that at the start, he had let these crazy Mountain Indians stall on him a long time before he had begun to get results. He had come to them with a simple idea and only now, after five years, was it beginning to work.

Cattle . . . that was the idea. Beef cattle. Blooded stock. Good bulls.

Fall round-ups. The shipment East. Cash profits. In language as simple as that he had finally got them to see his point. He had a special liking for cattle. It began long before he had ever seen an Indian, back home in New York State. Boyhood reading about hard riding and fast shooting on the cattle trails . . . that was what started it. Then, in his first job in the Indian Service, he had worked under a hard-minded Scotchman whose record as a stockman was unbeatable. He had learned the gospel from him. He learned to talk the lingo.

"Indians don't know, more than that don't give a damn, about dragging their feet behind a plow. Don't say as I blame 'em. But Indians'll always ride horses. They're born to that. And if they're going to ride horses they might as well be riding herd on a bunch of steers. It pays money."

He put it that way, following his Scotch preceptor. He put it to the Indians, to Washington officials, and to anybody he could buttonhole for a few minutes. It was a complete gospel. It was appropriations of money from Congress for cattle purchases. It won flattering remarks from certain visitors who were always around inquiring about Indian welfare. In time, it won over the Indians. It should have won them sooner.

The point was just that, not to let them stall on you. After five years he had learned his lesson. Put it over, or drop it.

He had taken off his broad-brimmed cattleman's hat and laid it on the desk beside his papers. The hat was part of the creed. He surveyed the score of wordless, pensive, buckskin-smelling Indians, some slouched forward, holding their big hats between their knees; others, hats on, silently smoking.

He had to put it across, this thing he wanted them to do. He had to do it now, tonight, or else drop it. That was what he had concluded.

"I think you fellows have learned a lot since I been with you. I appreciate the way you co-operate with me. Sometimes it's kinda hard to make things clear, but once you see what it means to you, you're all for it. I like that." He paused and mopped his brow. The schoolroom was an oven. The meeting should have been held outside—but never mind.

"In our stock association, we run our cattle together on a common range. We share the costs of riding range, rounding up, branding, and buying breeding bulls. Every time you sell a steer you pay a five-dollar fee into the pot, and that's what pays the bills. That's one of the things I had to tell you about. You didn't understand at first, but once you did, you went ahead. Today, it's paying dividends.

"You never had as much cash profit in your life before. Your steers are better beef animals, because the breeding is better. We got the class in bulls. And you get better prices because you can dicker with the buyers. But you know all that. I'm just reminding you."

Someone coughed in the back of the room and Brinder, always on guard, like the cowboys contending with rustlers and sheepmen he used to read about, straightened his back and looked sharply. But it was only a cough, repeated several times—an irritating, ineffective kind of cigarette cough. No one else in the audience made a sound. All were held in the spell of Brinder's words, or at any rate were waiting for him to finish what he had to say.

"We have one bad defect yet. You know what I mean, but I'll mention it just the same. In other words, fellows, we all of us know that every year a certain number of cattle disappear. The wolves don't get them and they don't die of natural causes. They are always strong, fat, two- or three-year-old steers that disappear, the kind that wolves don't monkey with and that don't die naturally. I ain't pointing my finger at anybody, but you know as well's I do that there's a certain element on the Reservation that don't deserve fresh meat, but always has it. They're too lazy or too ornery or they just don't know what it's all about. But they get fresh meat just the same.

"I want you fellows to get this. Let it sink in deep. Every time a fat steer goes to feed some Slick Steve too lazy to earn his keep, some of you are out around seventy-five, eighty dollars. You lose that much. Ponder that, you fellows."

He rustled the papers on the desk, looking for a row of figures: number of beef animals lost in five years (estimated), their money value, in round numbers. He hurled his figures at them, cudgeling.

"Some of you don't mind the loss. Because, it's poor people getting the meat. It keeps someone from starving. That's what you say. What I say is—that ain't a proper way to look at it. First of all, because it's stealing and we can't go to countenancing stealing, putting up with it, I mean. Nobody has to starve, remember that. If you want to do something on your own book for the old people who can't work, you can. You can do what you like with your money. But lazy people, these Slick Steves who wouldn't work on a bet, nobody should give it easy to them, that's what I'm saying."

He waited a moment, letting the words find their way home. "There's a solution, as I told you last month. We want to set up a court, a court of Indian judges, and you will deal with these fellows in your own way. Give a few of them six months in jail to think it over, and times will begin to change around here. . . ."

That was the very point he had reached the last time he talked to the Council, a month before. He had gone no further, then, because they had begun asking questions, and from their questions he had discovered that they hadn't the least idea what he was driving at. Or so they made it appear. "If we have a tribal court," somebody would ask, "do we have to put somebody in jail?" That, obviously, was intentionally naive. It was intended to stall him off. Or some old man would say: "If somebody has to go to jail, let the Superintendent do it. Why should we have to start putting our own people in jail?" Such nonsense as that had been talked.

Finally, the perennial question of money came up. Would the Government pay for the court? A treacherous question, and he had answered without flinching.

"That's another thing," he had said brightly. "We're going to get away from the idea of the Government paying for everything. Having your own business this way, making a profit from it, you can pay for this yourselves. That will make you independent. It will be your own court, not the Government's court, not the Superintendent's court. No. The court will be supported by the fee money you pay when you sell a steer."

That speech broke up the meeting. It was greeted by a confusion of talk in the native tongue which gradually subsided in form of one speaker, one of the ancients, who obviously was a respected leader. Afterwards, a young, English-speaking tribesman translated.

"The old man here, Looking Glass, says the Government don't give us nothing for nothing. The money it spends on us, that's our own money, he says. It belongs to us and they keep it there at Washington, and nobody can say how much it is or how much has been lost. He says, where is all that money that they can't afford to pay for this court? That's what he says."

There was the snare which tripped up most Agency plans, scratch an old Indian, and the reaction was always the same. "Where's the money the Government owes us? Where's our land? Where's our treaty?" They were like a whistle with only one stop, those old fellows. Their tune was invariable, relentless and shrill. That was why one dreaded holding a meeting when the old men were present. Now the young fellows, who understood Agency plans. . . .

Anyhow, here he was trying it again, going over the plan with great care and patience. Much of the misunderstanding had been ironed out in the meantime. So he had been led to believe.

"This court will put an end to all this trouble," he was going on, trying to gauge the effect of his words, watching for a reaction. At last it came. One of the old men was getting to his feet.

He was a small man, emaciated by age and thin living, yet neat looking. His old wife, obviously, took good care of his clothes, sewed buckskin patches on his overalls and kept him in new moccasins. He talked firmly, yet softly, and not for very long. He sat down as soon as he had finished and let the interpreter translate for him.

"The old man here, Big Face, says the court, maybe, is all right. They have talked it over among themselves, and maybe it's all right. Our agent, he says, is a good man. He rides too fast. He talks too fast. But he has a good heart, so maybe the court is all right. That's what Big Face says."

The words were good, and Brinder caught himself smiling, which was bad practice when dealing with the old fellows. They were masters at laying traps for the unwary—that, too, he had learned in five years. Their own expressions never changed, once they got going, and you could never tell what might be in their minds.

Just the same, he felt easier. Big Face, the most argumentative of the lot, had come around to accept this new idea, and that was something gained. The month had not been lost.

He had something more to say. He was getting to his feet again, giving a tug to his belt and looking around, as if to make sure of his following. He had been appointed spokesman. That much was clear.

He made a somewhat longer speech, in which he seemed to express agitation, perhaps uncertainty. One could never be sure of tone values. Sometimes the most excitable sounding passages of this strange tongue were very tame in English. Brinder had stopped smiling and waited for the translation.

"Big Face here says there's only one thing they can't decide about. That's about judges. Nobody wants to be a judge. That's what they don't like. Maybe the court is all right, but nobody wants to be judge."

Brinder was rather stumped by that. He rose to his feet, quickly, giving everyone a sharp glance. Was this the trap?

"Tell the old man I don't understand that. It is an honor, being a judge. People pay money to be a judge in some places. Tell Big Face I don't understand his objection."

The old man was on his feet as soon as the words had been translated for him.

"It's like this. To be a judge, you got to be about perfect. You got to know everything, and you got to live up to it. Otherwise, you got nothing to say to anybody who does wrong. Anybody who puts himself up to be that good, he's just a liar. And people will laugh at him. We are friends among ourselves and nobody interferes in another person's business. That's how it is, and nobody wants to set himself up and be a judge. That's what Big Face says."

There it was—as neatly contrived a little pitfall as he had ever seen. He had to admire it—all the time letting himself get furious. Not that he let them see it. No, in five years, he had learned that much. Keep your head, and when in doubt, talk your head off. He drew a deep breath and plunged into an explanation of all the things he had already explained, reminding them of the money they lost each year, of the worthless fellows who were making an easy living from their efforts, of the proper way to deal with the problem. He repeated all the arguments and threw in as many more as he could think of.

"You have decided all this. You agree the court is a good thing. But how can you have a court without judges? It's the judges that make a court."

He couldn't tell whether he was getting anywhere or not—in all likelihood, not. They were talking all together once more and it didn't look as if they were paying much attention to him. He waited.

"What's it all about?" he finally asked the interpreter, a young mixed-blood, who was usually pretty good about telling Brinder which way the wind of thought blew among the old people.

"I can't make out," the interpreter murmured, drawing closer to Brinder. "They are saying lots of things. But I think they're going to decide on the judges—they've got some kind of plan—watch out for it—now, one of the old men will speak."

It was Big Face raising to his feet once more. Looking smaller, more wizened than ever. The blurring twilight of the room absorbed some of his substance and made Brinder feel that he was losing his grip on the situation. A shadow is a difficult adversary and Big Face was rapidly turning into one.

"The agent wants this court. He thinks it's a good thing. So we have talked some more—and we agree. We will have this court." He paused briefly, allowing Brinder only a moment's bewilderment.

"Only we couldn't decide who would be judge. Some said this one, some said that one. It was hard. . . ."

Brinder coughed. "Have you decided on any one, Big Face?" He no longer knew which way things were drifting but only hoped for the best.

The old fellow's eyes, misted by age, actually twinkled. In the body of councillors somebody laughed and coughed in the same breath. Feet stirred and bodies shifted. Something was in the air. Haltingly, Big Face named the men—the most amazing trio the Reservation had to offer.

"Walks-in-the-Ground—Jacob Gopher—Twisted Horn . . ."

In the silence that followed, Brinder tried hard to believe he had heard the wrong names. A mistake had been made. It was impossible to take it seriously. These three men—no, it was impossible! The first, an aged imbecile dripping saliva—ready to die! The second, stone deaf and blind! The third, an utter fool, a half-witted clown, to whom no one listened.

"You mean this?" Brinder still could not see the full situation, but was afraid that the strategy was deliberate and final.

"Those will be the judges of this court," Big Face replied, smiling in his usual friendly way.

"But these men can't be judges! They are too old, or else too foolish. No one will listen to them . . ." Brinder broke off short. He saw that he had stated the strategy of the old men especially as they had intended it. His friendliness withered away.

Big Face did not hesitate, did not break off smiling. "It is better, we think, that fools should be judges. If people won't listen to them, no one will mind."

Brinder had nothing to say, not just then. He let the front legs of his chair drop to the floor, picked up his hat. His face had paled. After five years—still to let this happen. . . . Using great effort, he turned it off as a joke. "Boys, you should of elected me judge to your kangaroo court. I would have made a crackerjack."

The Indians laughed and didn't know what he meant, not exactly. But maybe he was right.

—D'Arcy McNickle (1992, 3–11, 47–52)
First published by Birgit Hans
in 1986 in her M.A. thesis

Looking Ahead

So, enterprising readers, where to from here?

Our hope as editors is that, having come this far in your reading of traditional works and early Indian writing, you will want to carry on with an exploration of fiction, poetry, and drama by today's Native American writers. Whether in a formal course of study or on your own, we hope you will be able to pursue in your further readings the imaginative pulse that runs, unbroken, through Native stories and songs from earliest times into the twenty-first century.

To highlight that vital pulse, all through this anthology, we have noted episodes and details in the selections that appear to anticipate elements in later Indian writing. But before following up on such connections, it's important to ask, What sort of light *do* they shed on the modern works that seem to be "harking back" to the older traditions?

First and foremost, it's crucial to keep in mind that Native poets and writers today are sophisticated artists who are ultimately writing about the world as it is now, although from a Native perspective. If they introduce traditional materials into their work, or allude to them, they are probably motivated not just by a simple sense of duty to pass on the old stories, but rather by much more complicated, personal reasons—to use tradition to interpret or provide a perspective on something they are writing about, for example, or to convey the sense that something in the present has a timeless dimension in Native terms.

When a poet like Joy Harjo employs an open, repetitive, "oral" style in a poem like "She Had Some Horses," she is presumably not just offering homage to the oral style of her Creek ancestors' songs; she is self-consciously adopting that style because it allows her to come to authentic Native terms with aspects of modern experience, even though she is writing in English. Likewise, the traditional sense of the sacredness of Native homelands is frequently invoked by modern writers (N. Scott Momaday, for instance, in *The Way to Rainy Mountain*) in ways that are simultaneously affirmative of the timeless value of such places (they still exist) and deeply ironic (they are no longer the same).

Certainly *characters* in traditional storytelling persistently reappear in the modern writing—notably Coyote the Trickster, and other trickster-figures like the Ojibwa Nanabush. But such rascally figures seem to play altered roles when they move from oral tradition into the modern world. Here, in our time, it's usually the case that Coyote and his kind serve mainly to satirize, expose, or hold off the encroaching Anglo world, serving as a kind of uniquely Indian subversive/defensive weapon against the Powers That Be.

By the same token, knowing something about the traditional literatures can help to illuminate modern works even when they do *not* include traditional elements. In Kiowa folklore, the trickster Saynday is a conspicuous and much-loved figure: for N. Scott Momaday to exclude him altogether from his retellings of Kiowa stories in *The Way to Rainy Mountain* appears to be a deliberate, significant choice. Perhaps Momaday leaves Saynday out because his antics would be inappropriate for the author's reverent evocations of his Kiowa origins and those of the Kiowas themselves.

Many Indian novelists and story writers actually incorporate versions of traditional narratives in their work, or at least refer to them. In the case of James Welch's historical novel about the Pikuni Blackfeet after the Civil War, *Fools Crow*, one consequence of this retelling is to heighten the realism of Welch's fictional Pikuni world: Fools Crow's people tell and refer to tribal stories casually, organically, as they would have done long ago. But on a deeper level of narrative strategy, Welch has used Blackfoot myth to structure portions of his plot, as when his hero learns and personalizes the significance of his people's origin myth about the acquisition of "Beaver Medicine," and when Fools Crow actually encounters the mythic figure of Feather Woman, who exists in a kind of limbo between mythic and historical realities that seems to prefigure the fate of Fools Crow and his people.

Perhaps the most elaborate use of traditional stories to shape a modern novel appears in Leslie Silko's *Ceremony*. Her central plot, dealing with the post-WWII suffering and eventual spiritual recovery of an Indian soldier named Tayo, is brilliantly prefigured and "underwritten" by Silko's retelling of episodes from the Pueblo/Keresan creation cycle, wherein the first people foolishly lose the favor of a deity, Nau'ts'ity'i, and suffer greatly, until a team of creatures, led by Hummingbird and Fly, patiently regain what has been lost. Silko's point about Tayo's recovery is that it will happen only when he has gotten back in touch imaginatively and spiritually with the old sacred stories of his heritage, like this one. T. S. Eliot once praised James Joyce's *Ulysses* for employing what Eliot called "the mythic method," which gave Joyce "a way of manipulating a continuous parallel between contemporaneity and antiquity" (Eliot 1923, 480–83). This is exactly what Silko does in *Ceremony*, through her retelling of the Pueblo myth in advance of what happens in the main plot to her modern protagonist, Tayo.

These are only a few instances of what Native writers can do by "harking back" to elements in their traditional heritage. (One might fancifully propose that in such instances maybe it's also a matter of Native tradition "harking *forward*"!) That such manipulations of tribal heritage involve more than just ingenious literary "moves" by the writers should be obvious, and many of them have written eloquently about the reverence and gratitude they feel as artists for the literary lore they have inherited. For Leslie Silko, speaking authorially at the beginning of *Ceremony*, it is literally a matter of life and death, of survival, now as it always was: "You don't have anything if you don't have the stories. / They are all we have to fight off / illness and death" (Silko 1977, 2).

For Elizabeth Woody, a Wasco Chinook poet with deep ancestral ties to the Columbia River, it is a dynamic continuity linking past, present, and future, and empowering her as an individual and as an artist:

> Through my awareness of my history, tradition is alive. I can take my place as a responsible link in a dynamic process. My work embodies tradition, not as static dogma, but as a public devotion to the continuation and enrichment of "The People.". . . We listen, absorbed in the story by blood, by association, listening with the part that is both one's self and many selves. In the sound of water, the sheen of river rock—a song—a poem—a story—is faithful to continuance. (Woody 1994, 16)

The *vitality* of modern Native writing is as remarkable as its diversity, despite its roots in the traditional tribal past. The fact that established "elders" like Silko and Momaday are still active and productive writers alongside relative newcomers like Woody (and poets and writers only now emerging) illustrates how the Native literary continuity we have been following through this anthology is truly open-ended, and, in our time, energetically ongoing. The Native American Renaissance shows no signs of stopping!

If we have done our job as editors, you will have been fortified (and, we hope, stimulated) by the contents of *In Beauty I Walk* to take up and seriously explore Native American writers of the last fifty years, extending and consolidating your understanding of established authors, and also looking out for new talents as they appear. Some excellent critical and bibliographic guides to such explorations are available, and we especially recommend the following:

Bruchac, Joseph. *Survival This Way: Interviews of American Indian Poets*. Tucson: University of Arizona Press, 1987.

Geiogamah, Hanay, and Jaye T. Darby, eds. *Stories of Our Way: An Anthology of American Indian Plays*. Los Angeles: UCLA American Indian Studies Center, 1999.

Jaskoski, Helen, ed. *Early Native American Writing: New Critical Essays*. New York: Oxford, 1996.

Lesley, Craig, ed. *Talking Leaves: Contemporary Native American Short Stories*. New York: Dell, 1991.

Lincoln, Kenneth. *Native American Renaissance*. Los Angeles: University of California Press, 1985.

Niatum, Duane, ed. *Harpers Anthology of Twentieth-Century Native American Poetry*. New York: Harper and Row, 1988.

Owens, Louis. *Other Destinies: Understanding the American Indian Novel*. Norman: University of Oklahoma Press, 1992.

Purdy, John, and James Ruppert. *Nothing But the Truth: An Anthology of Native American Literature*. Upper Saddle River, NJ: Prentice Hall, 2001.

Roemer, Kenneth, ed. *Native American Writers of the United States*. Detroit: Garland, 1999.

Ruoff, LaVonne. *American Indian Literatures: An Introduction, Bibliographic Review, and Selected Bibliography.* New York: Modern Language Association, 1990.

Wiget, Andrew. *Native American Literature.* Boston: Twayne, 1985.

———. *Handbook of Native American Literature.* New York: Garland, 1996.

Witalec, Janet, and Joseph Bruchac, eds. *Native North American Literary Companion.* Detroit: Visible Ink Press, 1995, 1998.

The following journals also regularly publish critical essays, reviews, and interviews of Native writers: *Studies in American Indian Literature, American Indian Quarterly, American Indian Culture and Research Journal,* and *MELUS.*

BIBLIOGRAPHY

Adams, David Wallace. 1997. *Education for Extinction: 1875–1928*. Lawrence: University Press of Kansas.

Allen, Paula Gunn. 1992. *The Sacred Hoop: Recovering the Feminine in American Indian Traditions*. Boston: Beacon Press. (Orig. pub. 1986.)

Bahr, Donald, and Vincent Joseph. 1994. "Pima Oracle Songs." In *Coming to Light: Contemporary Traditions of the Native American Literatures of North America*, ed. Brian Swann. New York: Random House.

Barbeau, Marius, 1951. *The Tsimshian: Their Arts and Music*, ed. Viola Garfield and Paul Wengert. New York: American Ethnological Association, no. 18.

Bernadin, Susan. 1997. "The Lessons of a Sentimental Education: Zitkala-Ša's Autobiographical Narratives." *Western American Literature* 32 (3):212–38.

Bierhorst, John, ed. 1984. *Four Masterworks of American Indian Literature*. Tucson: University of Arizona Press.

Boas, Franz. 1916. *Tsimshian Mythology; based on texts recorded by Henry W. Tate*. Reports of the Bureau of American Ethnology 30. Washington, DC: U.S. Bureau of American Ethnology.

———. 1925. "Stylistic Aspects of Primitive Literature." *Journal of American Folklore* 38:334.

———. 1928. *Keresan Texts*. Vol. 8, pts. 1–2. New York: American Ethnological Society.

———. 1970. *The Social Organization and Secret Societies of the Kwakiutl*. New York: Johnson Reprint Co. (Orig. pub. 1898.)

Boyd, Maurice. 1983a. *Kiowa Voices*. Vol. 1. *Ceremonial Dances, Rituals, and Songs*. Fort Worth: Texas Christian University.

———. 1983b. *Kiowa Voices*. Vol. 2. *Myths, Legends, and Folktales*. Fort Worth: Texas Christian University.

Bright, William, ed. 1993. *A Coyote Reader*. Berkeley: University of California Press.

Bruchac, Joseph. 1987. *Survival This Way: Interviews with Native American Poets*. Tucson: University of Arizona Press.

Burlingame, Lori. 1996. "Cultural Survival in *Runner in the Sun*." In *The Legacy of D'Arcy McNickle: Writer, Historian, Activist*, ed. John Lloyd Purdy. Norman: University of Oklahoma Press.

Chamberlain, Betsey Guppy. 2003. *The Life and Writings of Betsey Chamberlain, Native American Mill Worker*. Ed. Judith Ranta. Boston: Northeastern University Press.

Clements, William M. 1996. *Native American Verbal Art: Texts and Contexts*. Tucson: University of Arizona Press.

Clifton, James A. 1987. "Simon Pokagon's Sandbar: Potawatomi Claims to Chicago's Lakefront." *Michigan History* 71 (5) (Sept./Oct.):12–17.

Cole, Joanna, ed. 1982. *Best-loved Folktales of the World*. New York: Doubleday.

Copway, George. 1997. *Life, Letters, and Speeches*. Ed. A LaVonne Ruoff and Donald B. Smith. Lincoln: University of Nebraska Press.

Curtin, Jeremiah. 1909. "Wasco Tales and Myths." In *Wishram Texts*, vol. 2, ed. Edward Sapir. New York: American Ethnological Society.

———, and J. N. B. Hewitt. 1918. *Seneca Myths and Fictions*. Reports of the Bureau of American Ethnology 32. Washington, DC: U.S. Bureau of American Ethnology.

Curtis, Edward. 1970a. *The North American Indian*. Vol. 4. New York: Johnson Reprint Co. (Orig. pub. 1909.)

———. 1970b. *The North American Indian*. Vol. 8. New York: Johnson Reprint Co. (Orig. pub. 1911.)

———. 1970c. *The North American Indian*. Vol. 13. New York: Johnson Reprint Co. (Orig. pub. 1924.)

Cutter, Martha J. 1994. "Zitkala-Šä's Autobiographical Writings: The Problems of a Canonical Search for Language and Identity." *MELUS* 19 (1) (Spring):31–44.

Deloria, Ella. 1978. *Dakota Texts*. Ed. Agnes Picotte and Paul N. Pavich. Vermillion, SD: Dakota Press.

Densmore, Frances. 1910. *Chippewa Music*, Vol. 1. Bulletin of the Bureau of American Ethnology 50. Washington, DC: Government Printing Office.

———. 1913. *Chippewa Music*. Vol. 2. Bulletin of the Bureau of American Ethnology 53. Washington, DC: Smithsonian Institution.

———. 1929. *Papago Music*. Bulletin of the Bureau of American Ethnology 90. Washington, DC: Smithsonian Institution.

Demetracopoulou, Dorothy. 1935. "Wintu Songs." *Anthropos* 30:483–94.

Dixon, Roland. 1911. "Shasta Myths." *Journal of American Folklore* 13:364 ff.

Eastman, Charles A. 1991. *Indian Boyhood*. Lincoln: University of Nebraska Press. (Orig. pub. 1902.)

Eliot, T. S. 1923. "Tradition and the Individual Talent." *The Dial* 75:480–83.

Erdrich, Louise. 1988. *Tracks*. New York: Henry Holt and Co.

Evers, Larry, and Felipe S. Molina, eds. 1987. *Yaqui Deer Songs/Maso Bwikan: A Native American Poetry*. Tucson: University of Arizona Press.

Fletcher, Alice C., and Francis La Flesche. 1911. *The Omaha Tribe*. Twenty-seventh Annual Report of the Bureau of American Ethnology. Washington, DC: Government Printing Office.

Fortune, Reo. 1932. *Omaha Secret Societies*. Columbia University Contributions to Anthropology 14. New York: Columbia University Press.

Frachtenberg, Leo J. 1913. *Coos Texts*. Columbia University Contributions to Anthropology 1. New York: Columbia University Press.

Frey, Rodney, ed. 1995. *Stories That Made the World: Oral Literatures of the Indian People of the Inland Northwest*. Norman: University of Oklahoma Press.

Frost, Robert. 1979. *The Poetry of Robert Frost*. Ed. Edward Connery Lathem. New York: Holt, Rinehart, and Winston.

Gatschet, Albert. 1890. *The Klamath Indians of Southwest Oregon*. Contributions to North American Ethnography 2. Washington DC: Government Printing Office.

———. 1894. "Songs of the Modoc Indians." *American Anthropologist* 7:340–52.

Grinnell, George Bird. 1961. *Pawnee Hero Stories and Folk Tales*. Lincoln: University of Nebraska Press.

———. 1962. *Blackfoot Lodge Tales*. Lincoln: University of Nebraska Press.

Hewitt, J. B. 1944. "The Re-quickening Address of the Iroquois Condolence Council." *Journal of the Washington Academy of Sciences* (March 15): 65–85.

Hobson, Geary, ed. 1979. *The Remembered Earth: An Anthology of Native American Literature*. Albuquerque, NM: Red Earth Press.

Hymes, Dell. 1981. *"In Vain I Tried to Tell You": Essays in Native American Ethnopoetics*. Philadelphia: University of Pennsylvania Press.

———. 2002. *Now I Know Only This Far: Essays in Ethnopoetics*. Lincoln: University of Nebraska Press.

Jacobs, Melville. 1936. *Texts in Chinook Jargon*. University of Washington Publications in Anthropology 7. Seattle: University of Washington Press.

———. 1954. *Clackamas Chinook Texts*. Part 2. Publications of the Indiana Research Center in Anthropology, Folklore, and Linguistics. Bloomington: Indiana University Press.

———, ed. 1959. *Content and Style of an Oral Literature: Clackamas Chinook Myths and Tales*. Viking Fund Publications in Anthropology 26. New York: Wenner-Gren Foundation.

———. 1960. *The People Are Coming Soon: Analyses of Clackamas Chinook Myths and Tales*. Seattle: University of Washington Press.

———, ed. 1990. *Nehalem Tillamook Tales*. Told by Clara Pearson, recorded by Elizabeth Jacobs. Rev. ed., with new introduction by Jarold Ramsey and appendix by Dell Hymes. Corvallis: Oregon State University Press. (Orig. pub. 1959.)

Jaskoski, Helen, ed. 1996. *Early Native American Writing: New Critical Essays*. Norman: University of Oklahoma Press.

Johnson, E. Pauline. 1912. *Flint and Feather: The Complete Poems of Pauline Johnson (Tekahionwake)*. Intro. by Theodore Watts-Dunston. Toronto: Hodder and Stoughton.

———. 1987. *The Moccasin Maker*. Tucson: University of Arizona Press.

Johnson, E. Pauline, Tekahionwake. 2002. *E. Pauline Johnson, Tekahionwake: Collected Poems and Selected Prose*. Ed. Carole Gerson and Veronica Strong-Boag. Toronto: University of Toronto Press.

Jones, Suzi, and Jarold Ramsey, eds. 1994. *The Stories We Tell: An Anthology of Oregon Folk Literature*. Corvallis: Oregon State University Press.

Kelly, Isabel. 1938. "Northern Paiute Tales." *Journal of American Folklore* 51:367–437.

Kilcup, Karen L., ed. 2000. *Native American Women's Writing 1800–1924*. Malden, MA: Blackwell Publishers.

Kroeber, Karl. 1981. "Scarface vs. Scar-face: The Problem of Versions." *Journal of the Folklore Institute* 18:1–3.

———, ed. 1994. *American Indian Persistence and Resurgence*. Durham, NC: Duke University Press.

———. 1998. *Artistry in Native American Myths*. Lincoln: University of Nebraska Press.

———. 1999. *Traditional Literatures of the American Indians: Texts and Interpretations*. Lincoln: University of Nebraska Press. (Orig. pub. 1984.)

La Flesche, Francis. 1923. *The Osage Tribe*. Part 1, Reports of the U.S. Bureau of American Ethnology 36. Washington, DC: Smithsonian Institution.

———. 1925. *The Osage Tribe*. Part 2, *The Rites of Vigil*. Washington, DC: 39th Annual Report of the Bureau of American Ethnology.

———. 1963. *The Middle Five: Indian Schoolboys of the Omaha Tribe*. Lincoln: University of Nebraska Press. (Orig. pub. 1900.)

———. 1995. *Ke-Ma-Ha: The Omaha Stories of Francis La Flesche*. Ed. James W. Parins and Daniel F. Littlefield Jr. Lincoln: University of Nebraska Press.

———. n.d. "Ne-Ma-Ha." Fletcher-La Flesche Papers #4558/48. Smithsonian National Anthropological Archives.

———. n.d. "The Old Man Who Weeps." Fletcher-La Flesche Papers #4558/48. Smithsonian National Anthropological Archives.

———. n.d. "The Song of Flying Crow." Fletcher-La Flesche Papers #4558/48. Smithsonian National Anthropological Archives.

Larson, Charles R. 1978. *American Indian Fiction*. Albuquerque: University of New Mexico Press.

Lincoln, Kenneth. 1985. *Native American Renaissance*. Berkeley: University of California Press.

Lowie, Robert. 1910. *The Assiniboines*. Anthropological Papers of the American Museum of Natural History 4. New York: American Museum of Natural History.

———. 1918. "Myths and Traditions of the Crow Indians." Anthropological Papers of the American Museum of Natural History 25. New York: American Museum of Natural History.

Marriott, Alice, and Carol Raichlin, eds. 1968. *American Indian Mythology*. New York: New American Library.

Marsden, W. C. 1927. "Notes on the Paiute Language." University of California Publications in American Archaeology and Ethnology 20:180–91.

Matthews, Washington. 1902. *The Night Chant: A Navajo Ceremony*. Memoirs of the American Museum of Natural History 6. New York: American Museum of Natural History.

McNickle, D'Arcy. 1992. *The Hawk is Hungry and Other Stories*. Ed. Birgit Hans. Tucson: University of Arizona Press.

Mooney, James. 1900. *Myths of the Cherokees*. Reports of the U.S. Bureau of American Ethnology 19. Washington, DC: Smithsonian Institution.

———. 1973. *The Ghost Dance Religion and Wounded Knee*. New York: Dover. (Orig. pub. 1892.)

Mourning Dove (Christine Quintasket). 1981. *Cogewea: the Half-Blood, a Depiction of the Great Montana Cattle Range*. Intro. Dexter Fisher. Lincoln: University of Nebraska Press. (Orig. pub. 1927.)

Murray, David. 1991. *Forked Tongues: Speech, Writing, and Representation in North American Indian Texts*. Bloomington: Indiana University Press.

Neihardt, John, ed. 1979. *Black Elk Speaks*. Lincoln: University of Nebraska Press.

O'Connell, Barry, ed. 1997. *A Song of the Forest and Other Writings by William Apess, A Pequot*. Amherst: University of Massachusetts Press.

Opler, Morris. 1969. *Apache Life Ways*. Publications in Anthropology, Ethnography Series. Chicago: University of Chicago Press.

Ortiz, Simon, ed. 1998. *Speaking for the Generations: Native American Writers and Writing*. Tucson: University of Arizona Press.

Oskison, John Milton. 1989. "The Problem of Old Harjo." In *The Singing Spirit: Early Short Stories by North American Indians*, ed. Bernd C. Peyer. Tucson: University of Arizona Press.

Owens, Louis. 1992. *Other Destinies: Understanding the American Indian Novel*. Norman: University of Oklahoma Press.

Parins, James, and Daniel Littlefield Jr. 1985. *A Bibliography of American Indian Writers 1772–1924*. Native American Bibliography 2. Metuchen, NJ: Scarecrow Press.

Parsons, Elsie Clews. 1918. "Zuni Tales." *Journal of American Folklore* 223:1–58.

———. 1929. *Kiowa Tales*. Memoirs of the American Folklore Society 22. New York: G. Stechert and Co.

Peyer, Bernd C., ed. 1989. *The Singing Spirit: Early Short Stories by North American Indians*. Tucson: University of Arizona Press.

Phinney, Archie. 1934. *Nez Perce Texts*. Columbia University Contributions to Anthropology 25. New York: Columbia University Press.

Posey, Alexander. 1910. *The Poems of Alexander Lawrence Posey*. Ed. Mrs. Minnie H. Posey, with memoir by William E. Connelly. Topeka, KS: Crane.

Posey, Alexander Lawrence. 1993. *The Fus Fixico Letters*. Ed. Daniel F. Littlefield Jr. and Carol A. Petty Hunter. Foreword by A. LaVonne Brown Ruoff. Lincoln: University of Nebraska Press.

Purdy, John, and James Ruppert, eds. 2001. *Nothing But the Truth: An Anthology of Native American Literature*. Upper Saddle River, NJ: Prentice Hall.

Radin, Paul. 1972. *The Trickster*. New York: Schocken Books.

Ramsey, Jarold. 1977. *Coyote Was Going There: Indian Literature of the Oregon Country*. Seattle: University of Washington Press.

———. 1990. "Thoreau's Last Words and America's First Literatures." In *Re-defining American Literary History*, ed. A. LaVonne Ruoff and Jerry Ward. New York: Modern Language Association.

———. 1993. "Native American Poetry." In *The Princeton Encyclopedia of Poetry and Poetics*, ed. T. V. F. Brogan et al., rev. 7th ed. Princeton, NJ: Princeton University Press.

———. 1999. *Reading the Fire: The Traditional Indian Literatures of America*. Seattle: University of Washington Press.

Ranta, Judith. 2003. *The Life and Writings of Betsey Guppy Chamberlain: Native American Mill Worker*. Boston: Northeastern University Press.

Ridge, John Rollin. 1868. *Poems*. San Francico: Henry Payot and Co.

———. 1977. *The Life and Adventures of Joaquín Murieta, the Celebrated California Bandit*. Intro. Joseph H. Jackson. Norman: University of Oklahoma Press. (Orig. pub. 1854.)

Riggs, Lynn. 1930. *The Iron Dish*. Garden City, NY: Doubleday.

———. 2003. *The Cherokee Night and Other Plays*. Foreword by Jace Weaver. Norman: University of Oklahoma Press.

Ruoff, A. LaVonne. 1990. *American Indian Literatures: An Introduction, Bibliographic Review, and Selected Bibliography*. New York: Modern Language Association.

Russell, Frank. 1908. *The Pima Indians*. Reports of the U.S. Bureau of American Ethnology 26, 1889–90. Washington, DC: Smithsonian Institution.

Schoolcraft, Henry Rowe. 1962. *The Literary Voyager, or Muzzeniegun*. Ed. Phillip P. Mason. East Lansing: Michigan State University Press.

Silko, Leslie. 1977. *Ceremony*. New York: Viking.

———. 1981. *Storyteller*. New York: Arcade.

Soens, A. L. 1999. *I, The Song: Classical Poetry of Native North America*. Salt Lake City: University of Utah Press.

Spier, Leslie, and Edward Sapir. 1930. *Wishram Ethnography*. University of Washington Publications in Anthropology 3, no. 2. Seattle: University of Washington Press.

Standing Bear, Luther. 1975. *My People the Sioux*. Ed. E. A. Brinninstool. Lincoln: University of Nebraska Press. (Orig. pub. 1928.)

Sturtevant, William C., gen. ed. 1978–current. *Handbook of North American Indians*. Washington DC: Smithsonian Institution. (20 vols. in progress.)

Swann, Brian, ed. 1995. *Coming to Light: Contemporary Translations of the Native Literatures of America*. New York: Macmillan.

———, ed. 1987. *Recovering the Word: Essays in Native American Literature*. Berkeley: University of California Press.

———, and Arnold Krupat, eds. 1987. *I Tell You Now: Autobiographical Essays by Native American Writers*. Lincoln: University of Nebraska Press.

Tedlock, Dennis. 1972. *Finding the Center.* New York: Dial Press.

———. 1983. *The Spoken Word and the Work of Interpretation.* Philadelphia: University of Pennsylvania Press.

Teit, James. 1912. *Mythology of the Thompson Indians.* Memoirs of the American Museum of Natural History 12, pt. 1. New York: G. Stechert and Co.

———. 1917. "Okanagan Tales." Memoirs of the American Folklore Society 11. In *Folk-tales of the Salish and Sahaptin Tribes,* ed. Franz Boas. New York: American Folklore Society.

Thompson, Stith, ed. 1966. *Tales of the North American Indians.* Bloomington: Indiana University Press.

———. 1968. *One Hundred Favorite Folktales.* Bloomington: Indiana University Press.

Trout, Lawanna, ed. 1999. *Native American Literature: An Anthology.* Lincolnwood, IL: National Textbook Co.

Toelken, J. Barre, and Tacheeni Scott. 1999. "Poetic Translation and the 'Pretty Languages of Yellowman.'" In *Traditional Literature of the American Indians: Texts and Interpretations,* ed. Karl Kroeber. Lincoln: University of Nebraska Press.

Underhill, Ruth. 1938. *Singing for Power.* Berkeley: University of California Press.

———. 1979. *Papago Woman.* New York: Holt, Rinehart and Winston.

Vecsey, Christopher. 1988. *Imagine Ourselves Richly: Mythic Narratives of North American Indians.* New York: Crossroads.

Walker, James R. 1983. *Lakota Myths.* Ed. Elaine Jahner. Lincoln: University of Nebraska Press.

Welch, James. 1986. *Fools Crow.* New York: Penguin Books.

Wiget, Andrew, ed. 1985. *Native American Literature.* Boston: Twayne.

———. 1994. *Dictionary of Native American Literature.* New York: Garland.

Winnemucca, Sarah. 1994. *Life Among the Piutes: Their Wrongs and Claims.* Ed. Mrs. Horace Mann with a foreword by Catherine S. Fowler. Reno: University of Nevada Press. (Orig. pub. 1883.)

Wilson, Dorothy Clark. 1974. *Bright Eyes: The Story of Susette La Flesche.* New York: McGraw Hill.

Wissler, Clark, and D. C. Duvall. 1995. *Mythology of the Blackfoot Indians.* Lincoln: University of Nebraska Press.

Woody, Elizabeth. 1994. *Seven Hands Seven Hearts.* Portland, OR: Eighth Mountain Press.

Zitkala-Ša (Z. S.). 1917a. "The Red Man's America." *The American Indian Magazine* 5, no. 1 (Jan.–Mar.):64.

———. 1917b. "A Sioux Woman's Love for Her Grandchild." *The American Indian Magazine* 5, no. 4 (Oct.–Dec.):230–31.

———. (Gertrude Simmons Bonnin). 1979. *American Indian Stories*. Ed. and foreword by Dexter Fisher. Lincoln: University of Nebraska Press. (Orig. pub. 1921.)

———. 2001. *Dreaming of Thunder: Stories, Poems, and the Sun Dance Opera*. Ed. P. Jane Hafen. Lincoln: University of Nebraska Press.

Zolbrod, Paul. 1984. *Diné Bahane': The Navajo Creation Story*. Albuquerque: University of New Mexico Press.

———. 1995. *Reading the Voice: Native American Oral Poetry and the Printed Page*. Salt Lake City: University of Utah Press.